I'm getting quite rickety these ... g my teeth ... t a crick in ...?!

—...imoto, 2014

岸本斉史

Author/artist Masashi Kishimoto was born in 1974 in rural Okayama Prefecture, Japan. After spending time in art college, he won the Hop Step Award for new manga artists with his manga **Karakuri** (Mechanism). Kishimoto decided to base his next story on traditional Japanese culture. His first version of **Naruto**, drawn in 1997, was a one-shot story about fox spirits; his final version, which debuted in **Weekly Shonen Jump** in 1999, quickly became the most popular ninja manga in Japan.

NARUTO VOL. 71
SHONEN JUMP Manga Edition

STORY AND ART BY MASASHI KISHIMOTO

Translation/Mari Morimoto
Touch-up Art & Lettering/John Hunt
Design/Sam Elzway
Editor/Alexis Kirsch

Printed in the U.S.A.

Published by VIZ Media, LLC
P.O. Box 77010
San Francisco, CA 94107

10 9 8 7 6 5 4 3 2 1
First printing, August 2015

SHONEN JUMP MANGA EDITION

NARUTO

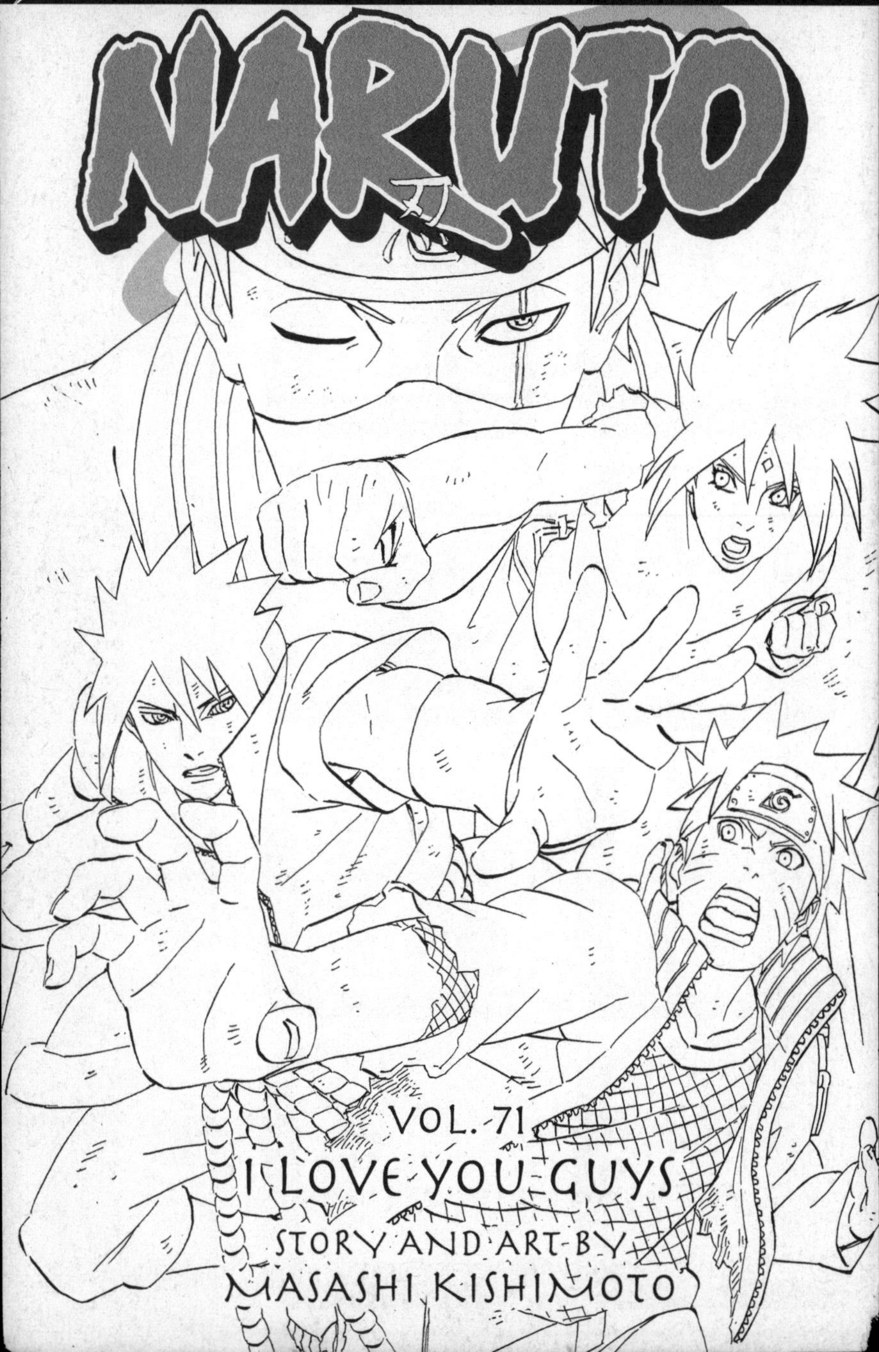

VOL. 71

I LOVE YOU GUYS

STORY AND ART BY

MASASHI KISHIMOTO

CHARACTERS

Naruto うずまきナルト

Sasuke うちはサスケ

Kakashi はたけカカシ

Sakura 春野サクラ

Sage of Six Paths 六道仙人

Kaguya 大筒木カグヤ

Madara うちはマダラ

Obito うちはオビト

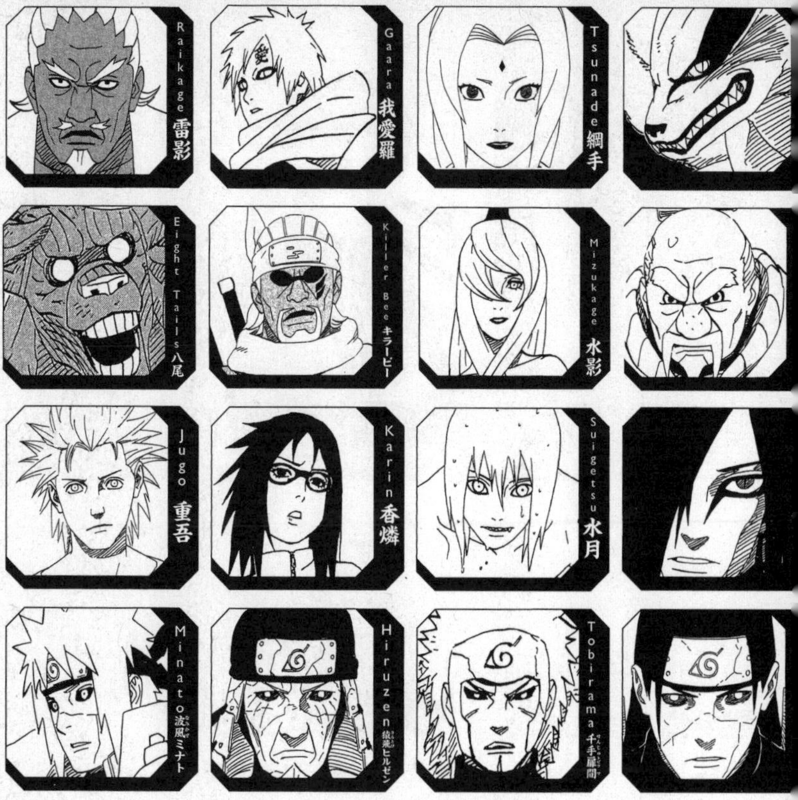
Tsunade 綱手
Gaara 我愛羅
Raikage 雷影
Mizukage 水影
Killer Bee キラービー
Eight Tails 八尾
Suigetsu 水月
Karin 香燐
Jugo 重吾
Tobirama 千手扉間
Hiruzen 猿飛ヒルゼン
Minato 波風ミナト

THE STORY SO FAR...

Naruto, the biggest troublemaker at the Ninja Academy in the Village of Konohagakure, finally becomes a ninja along with his classmates Sasuke and Sakura. They grow and mature through countless trials and battles. However, Sasuke, unable to give up his quest for vengeance, leaves Konohagakure to seek Orochimaru and his power...

Two years pass. Naruto grows up and engages in fierce battles against the Tailed Beast-targeting Akatsuki. And the Fourth Great Ninja War against the Akatsuki finally begins. Having been revived thanks to Rinne Rebirth, Madara then captures all the biju and gains Six Paths power. Naruto and Sasuke counter with powers they received from the Sage of Six Paths but Madara succeeds in activating the Infinite Tsukuyomi and sending everyone else into a world of dreams. And just when things couldn't get worse, Black Zetsu suddenly betrays Madara and revives Kaguya!

CONTENTS

Number 680: Once More

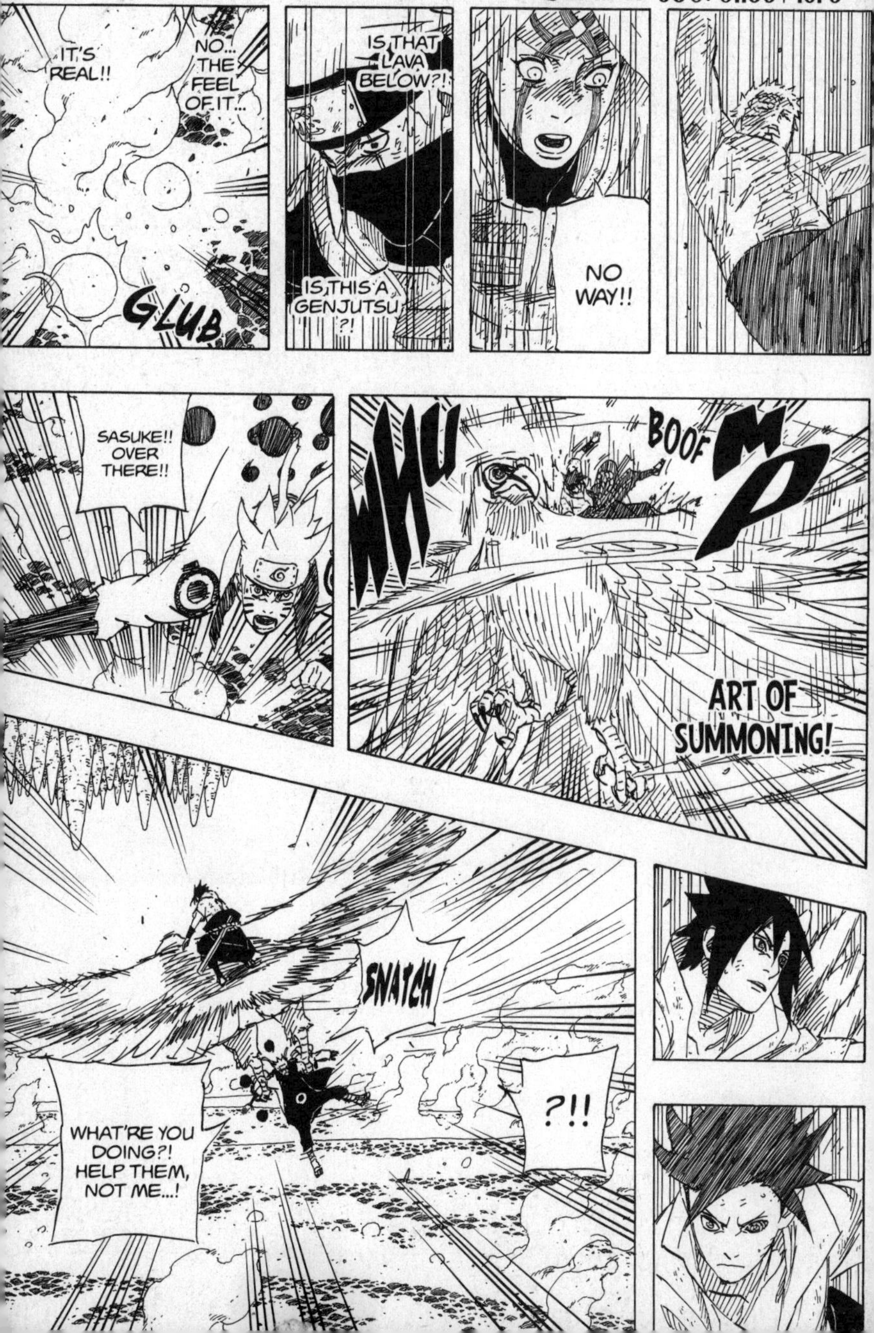
NO WAY!!
IS THAT LAVA BELOW?!
IS THIS A GENJUTSU?!
NO... THE FEEL OF IT...
IT'S REAL!!
GLUB
WHU
BOOF
MP
ART OF SUMMONING!
SASUKE!! OVER THERE!!
SNATCH
?!!
WHAT'RE YOU DOING?! HELP THEM, NOT ME...!

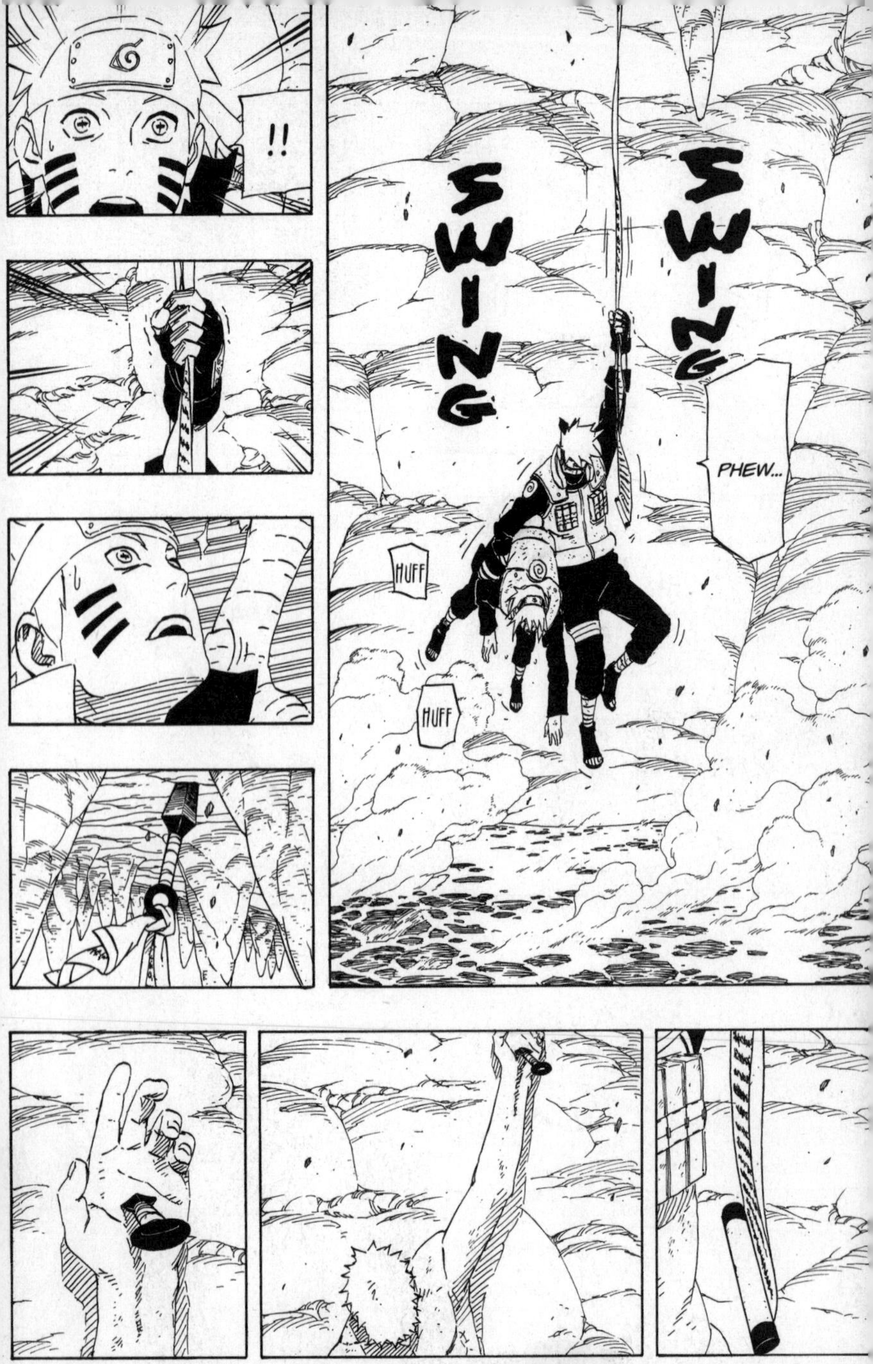
SWING
SWING
PHEW...
HUFF
HUFF
!!

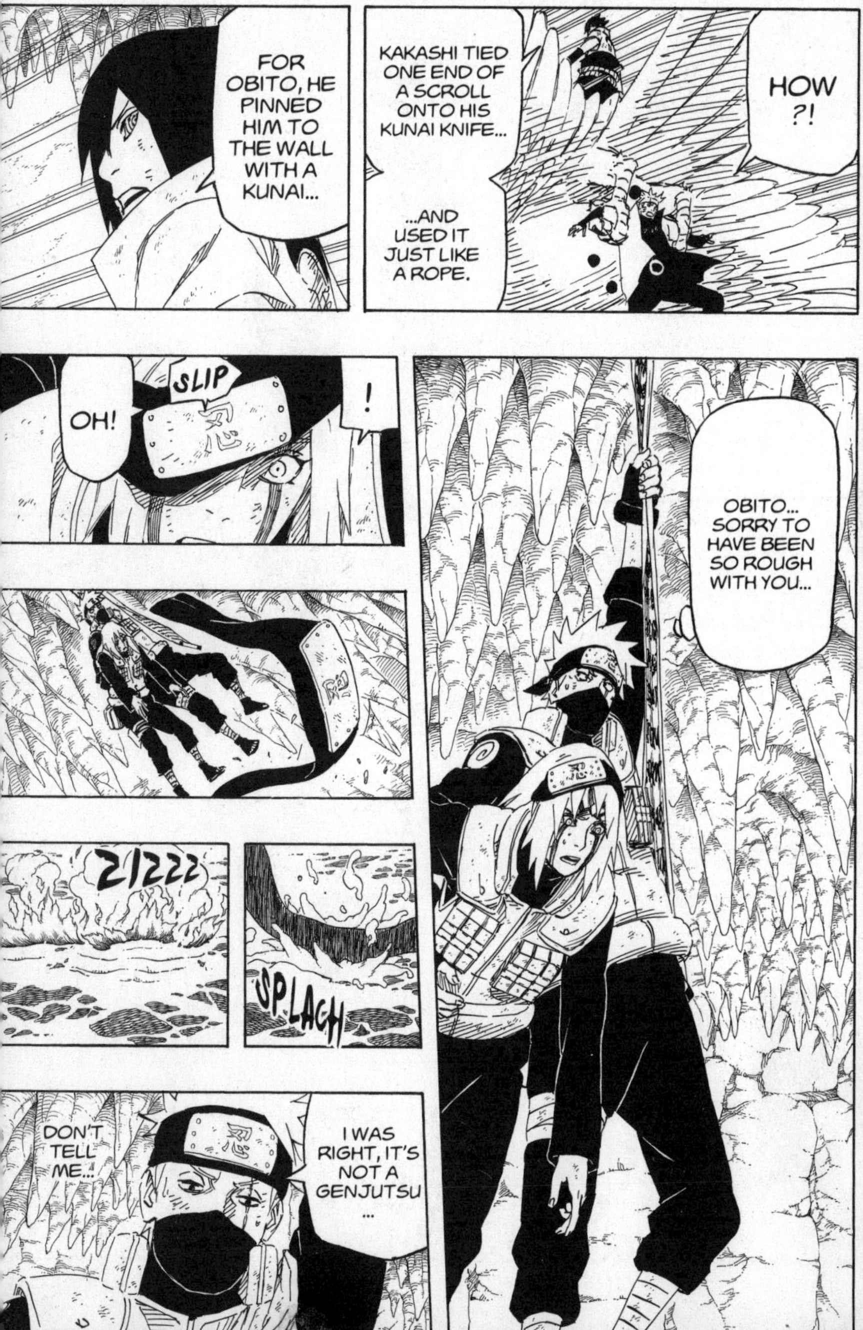
HOW ?!
KAKASHI TIED ONE END OF A SCROLL ONTO HIS KUNAI KNIFE...
...AND USED IT JUST LIKE A ROPE.
FOR OBITO, HE PINNED HIM TO THE WALL WITH A KUNAI...
OBITO... SORRY TO HAVE BEEN SO ROUGH WITH YOU...
!
SLIP
OH!
SPLACH
ZIZZZ
I WAS RIGHT, IT'S NOT A GENJUTSU ...
DON'T TELL ME...

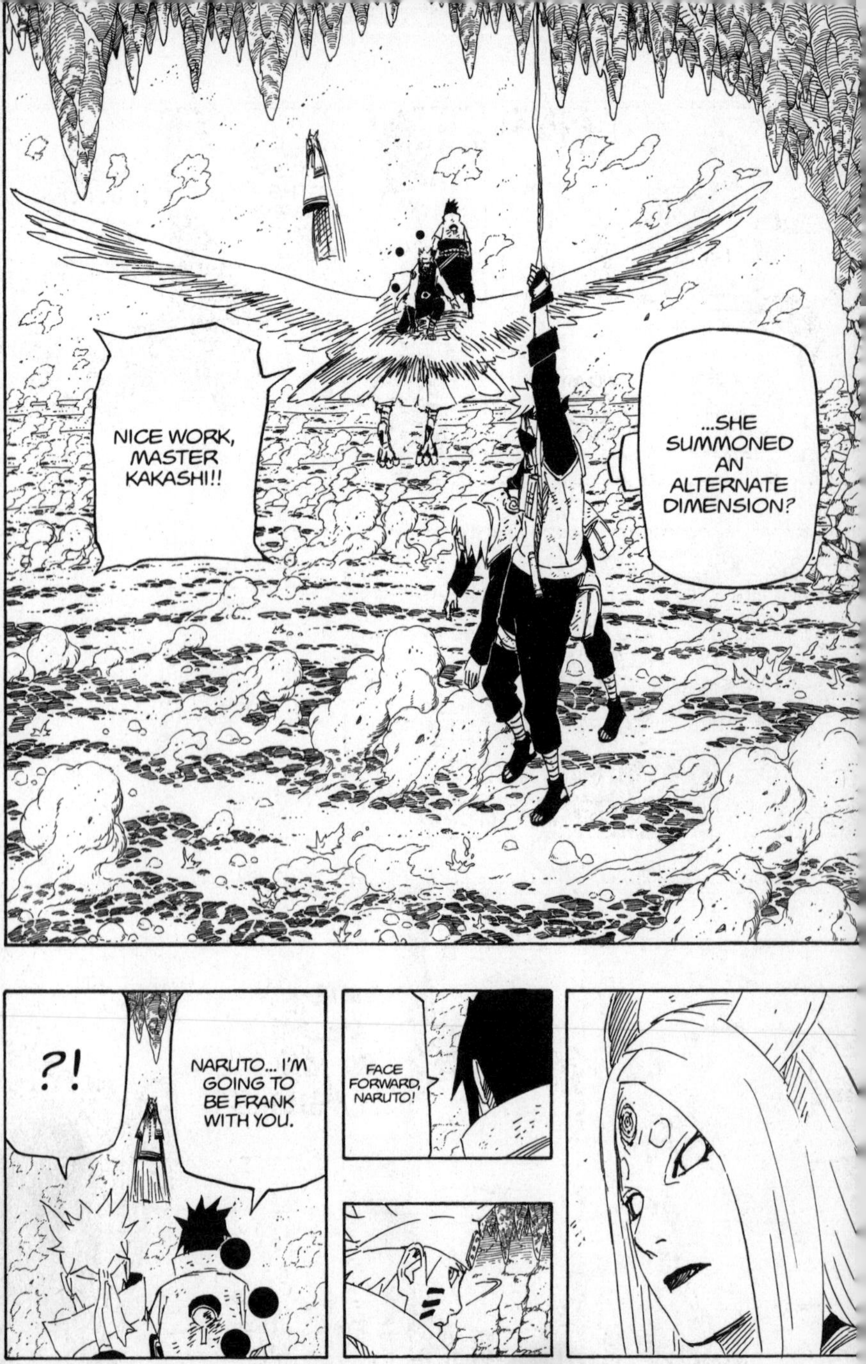
...SHE SUMMONED AN ALTERNATE DIMENSION?
NICE WORK, MASTER KAKASHI!!
FACE FORWARD, NARUTO!
NARUTO... I'M GOING TO BE FRANK WITH YOU.
?!

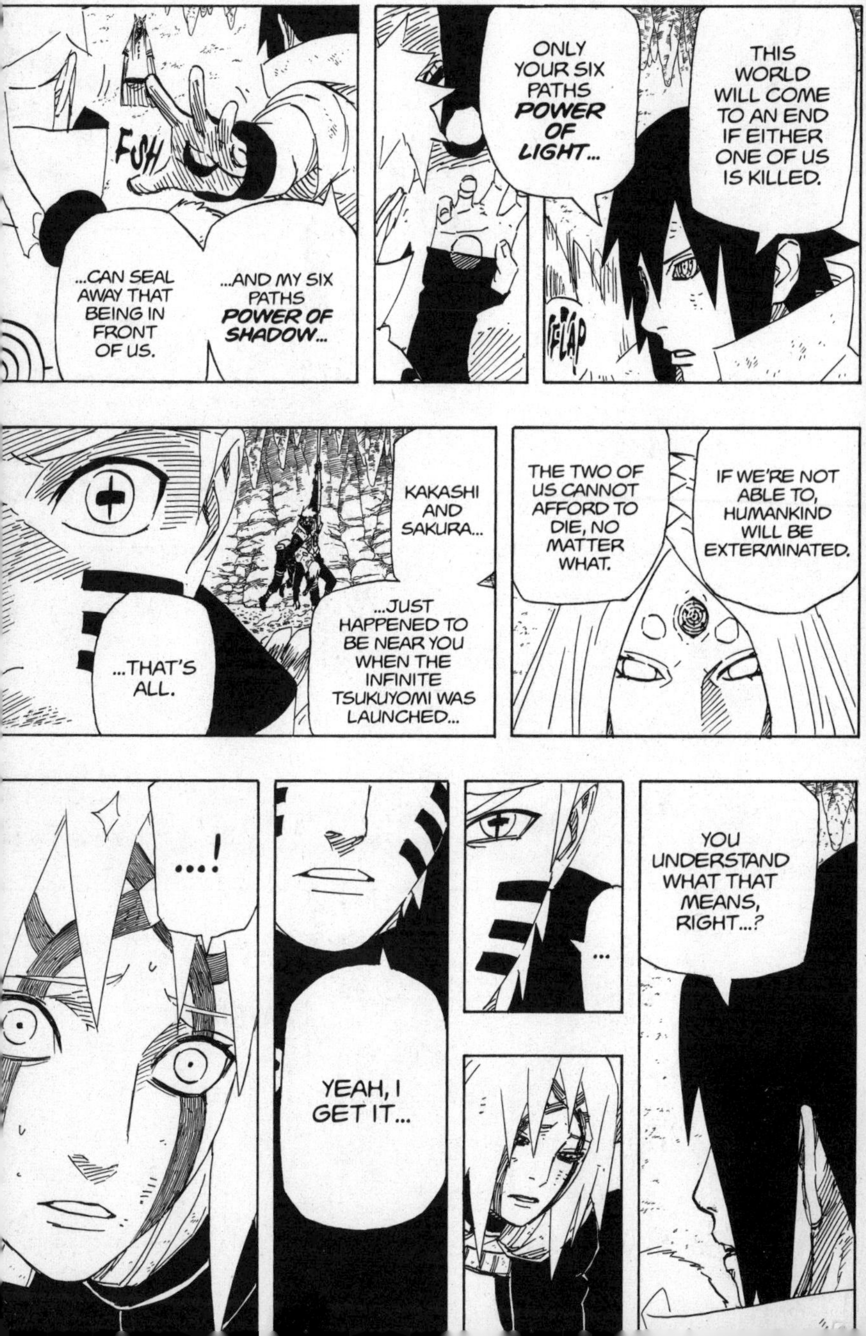
THIS WORLD WILL COME TO AN END IF EITHER ONE OF US IS KILLED.
FLAP
ONLY YOUR SIX PATHS POWER OF LIGHT...
FSH
...AND MY SIX PATHS POWER OF SHADOW...
...CAN SEAL AWAY THAT BEING IN FRONT OF US.
IF WE'RE NOT ABLE TO, HUMANKIND WILL BE EXTERMINATED.
THE TWO OF US CANNOT AFFORD TO DIE, NO MATTER WHAT.
KAKASHI AND SAKURA...
...JUST HAPPENED TO BE NEAR YOU WHEN THE INFINITE TSUKUYOMI WAS LAUNCHED...
...THAT'S ALL.
YOU UNDERSTAND WHAT THAT MEANS, RIGHT...?
...
YEAH, I GET IT...
...!

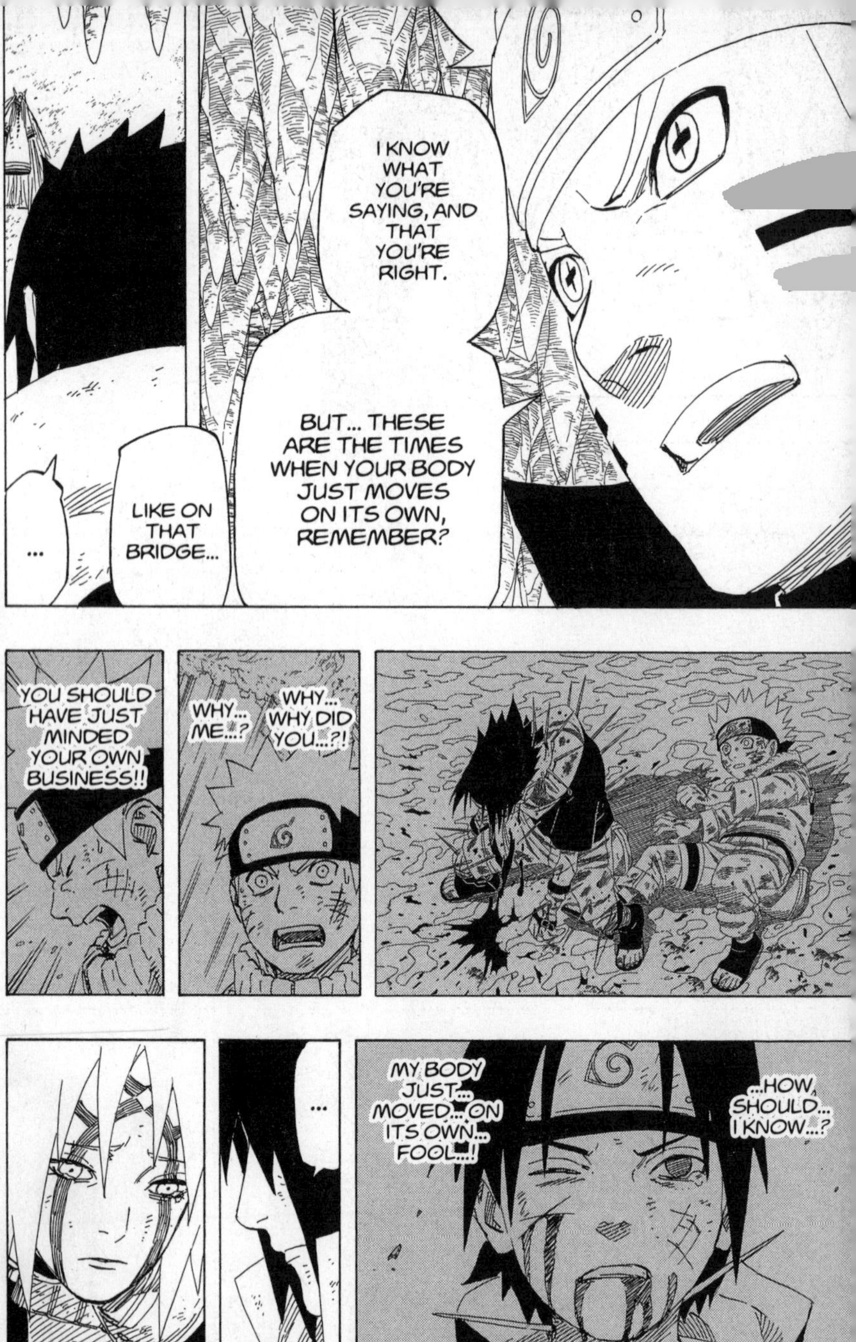
I KNOW WHAT YOU'RE SAYING, AND THAT YOU'RE RIGHT.
BUT... THESE ARE THE TIMES WHEN YOUR BODY JUST MOVES ON ITS OWN, REMEMBER?
LIKE ON THAT BRIDGE...
...
WHY... WHY DID YOU...?!
WHY... ME...?
YOU SHOULD HAVE JUST MINDED YOUR OWN BUSINESS!!
...HOW, SHOULD... I KNOW...?
MY BODY JUST... MOVED... ON ITS OWN... FOOL...!
...

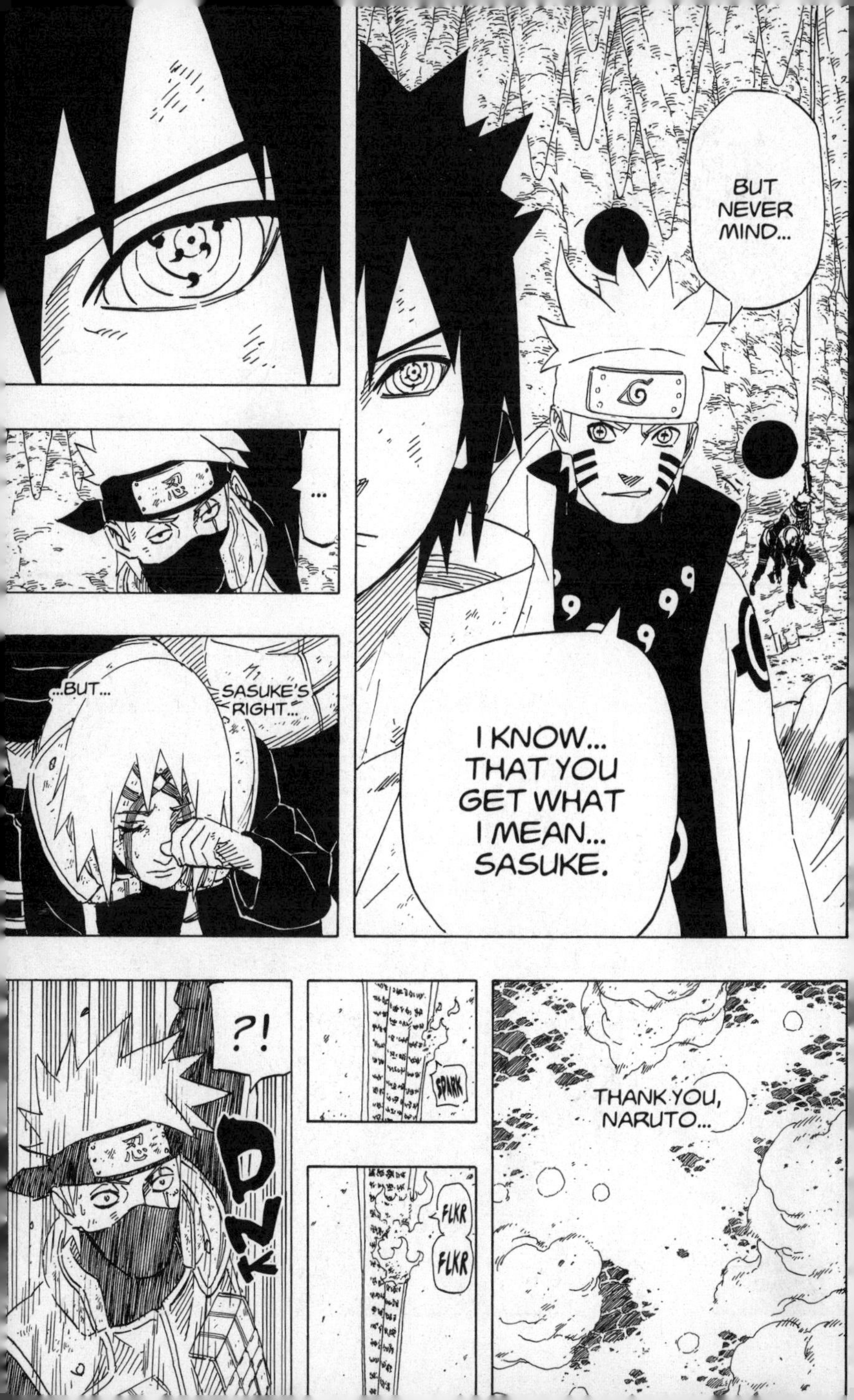
BUT NEVER MIND...
I KNOW... THAT YOU GET WHAT I MEAN... SASUKE.
...
SASUKE'S RIGHT...
...BUT...
THANK YOU, NARUTO...
SPARK
FLKR
FLKR
?!

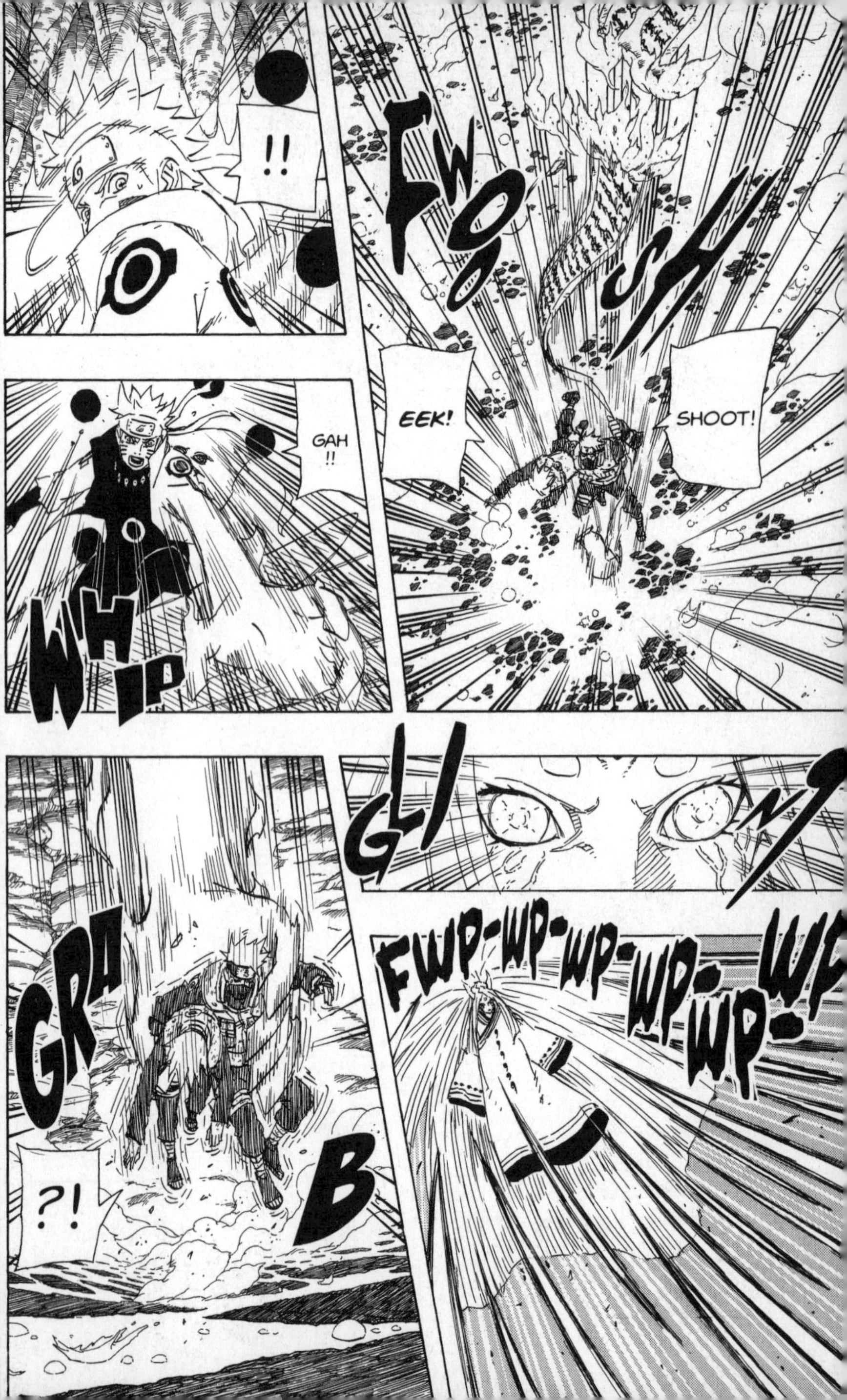
FWOOSH
SHOOT!
EEK!
!!
GAH!!
WHIP
GLINT
FWP-WP-WP-WP-WP-WP-WP
GRAB
?!

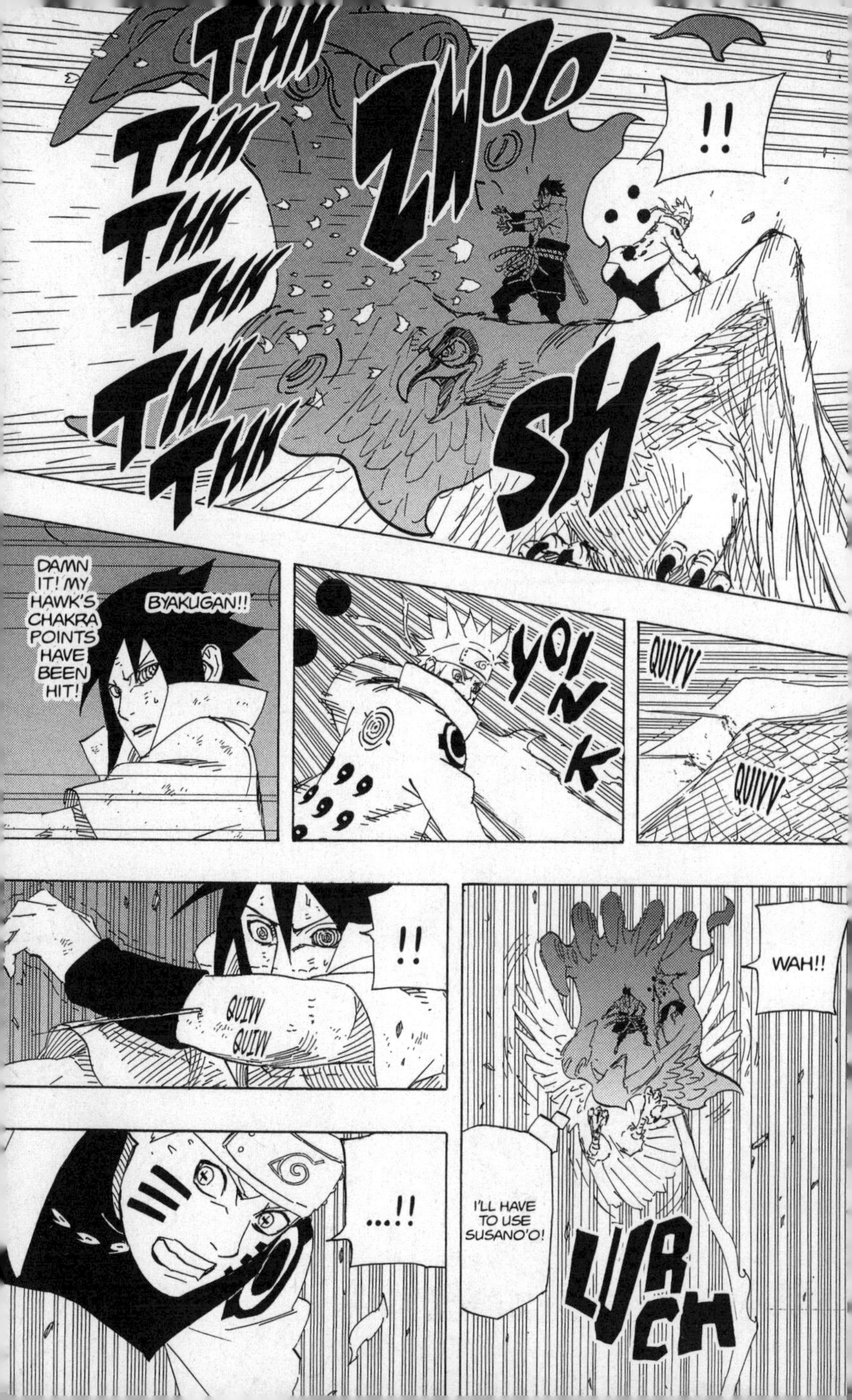
!!
ZWOO
THK THK THK THK THK THK THK
SH
QUIVV
QUIVV
YOINK
BYAKUGAN!!
DAMN IT! MY HAWK'S CHAKRA POINTS HAVE BEEN HIT!
WAH!!
I'LL HAVE TO USE SUSANO'O!
LURCH
!!
QUIVV QUIVV
...!!

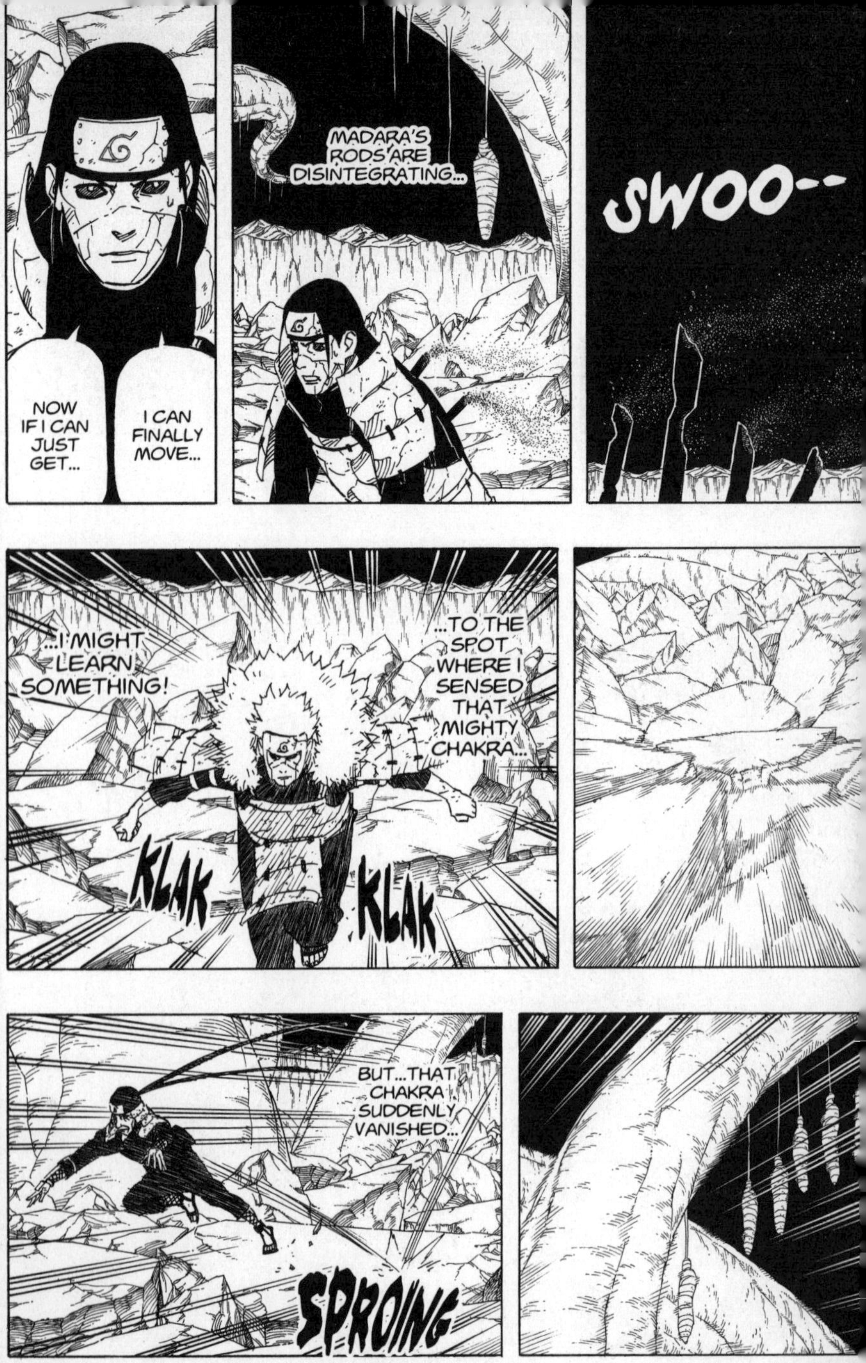
SWOO--
MADARA'S RODS ARE DISINTEGRATING...
I CAN FINALLY MOVE...
NOW IF I CAN JUST GET...
...TO THE SPOT WHERE I SENSED THAT MIGHTY CHAKRA...
...I MIGHT LEARN SOMETHING!
KLAK
KLAK
BUT...THAT CHAKRA SUDDENLY VANISHED...
SPROING

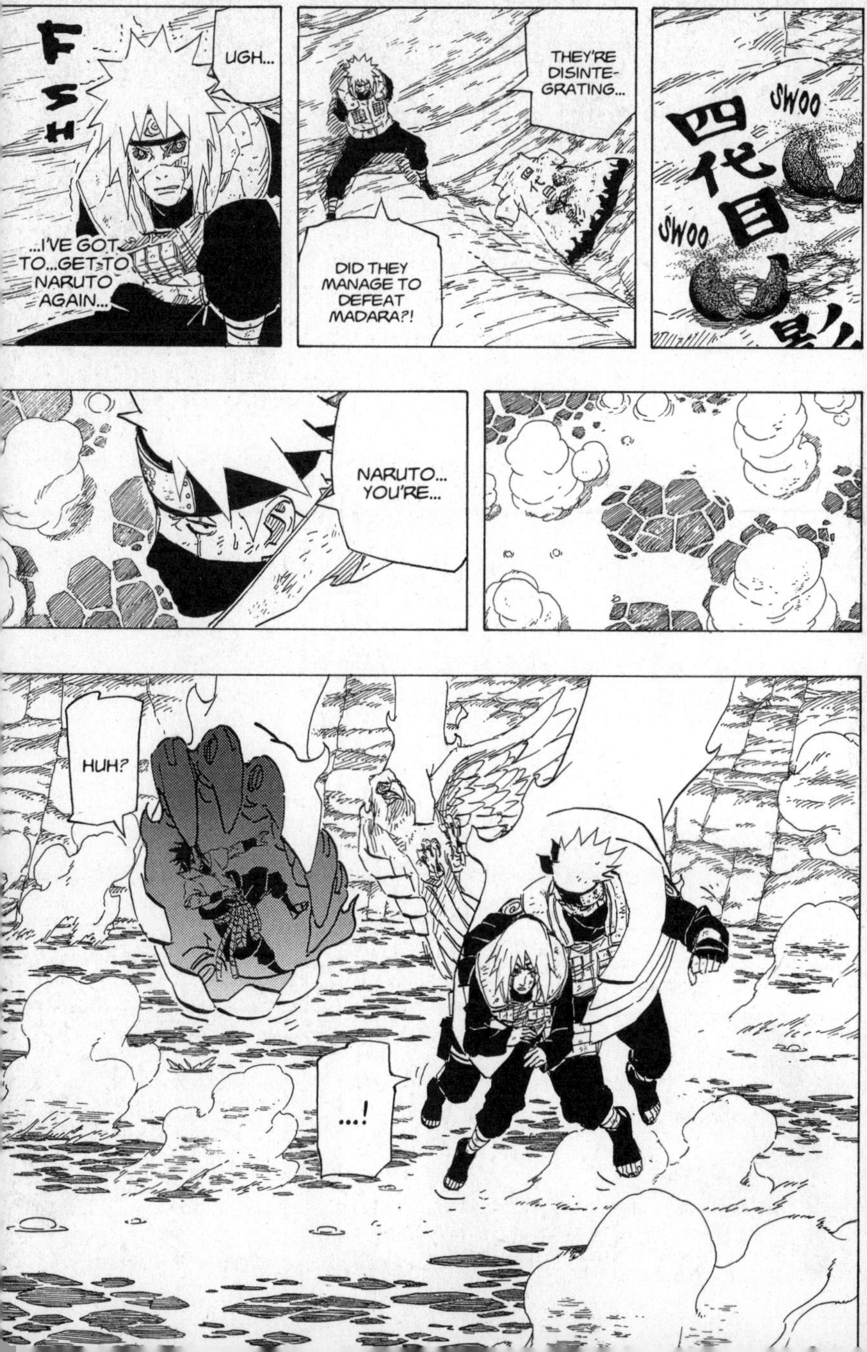
SWOO
四代目
SWOO
THEY'RE DISINTE-GRATING...
DID THEY MANAGE TO DEFEAT MADARA?!
UGH...
FSH
...I'VE GOT TO...GET TO NARUTO AGAIN...
NARUTO... YOU'RE...
HUH?
...!

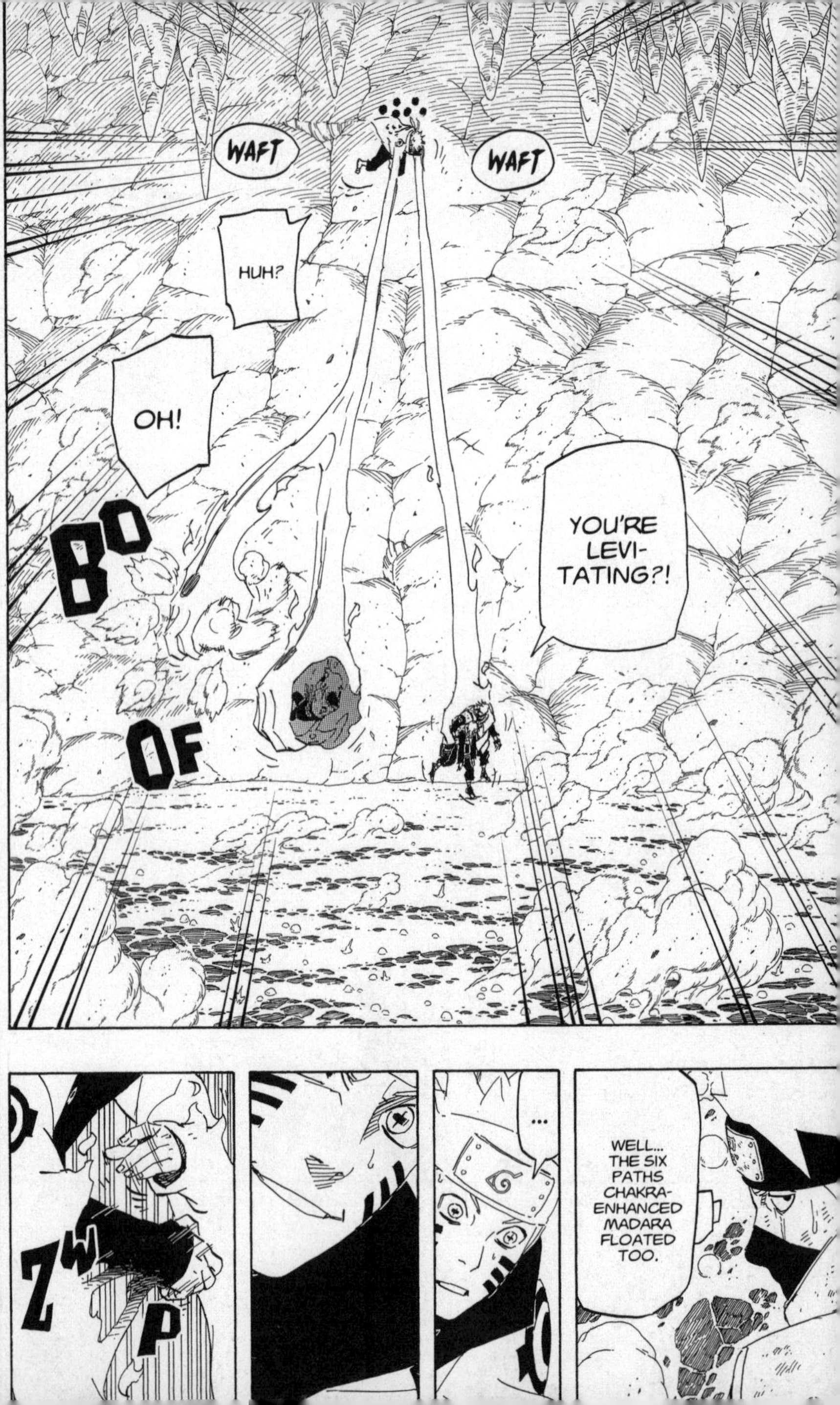
WAFT
WAFT
HUH?
OH!
YOU'RE LEVI-TATING?!
BOOF
WELL... THE SIX PATHS CHAKRA-ENHANCED MADARA FLOATED TOO.
...
ZWP

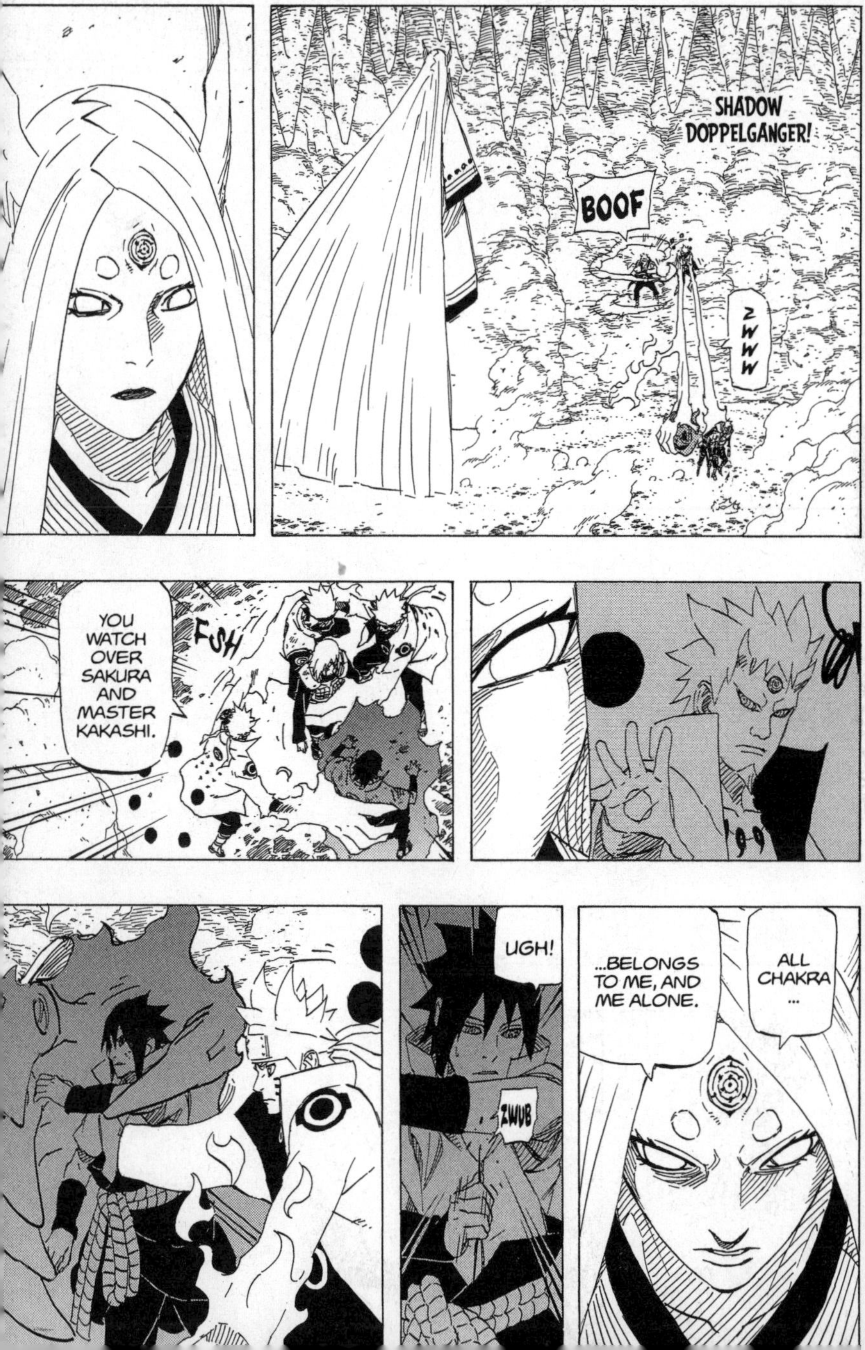
SHADOW DOPPELGANGER!
BOOF
ZWWW
YOU WATCH OVER SAKURA AND MASTER KAKASHI.
FSH
ALL CHAKRA ...
...BELONGS TO ME, AND ME ALONE.
UGH!
ZWUB

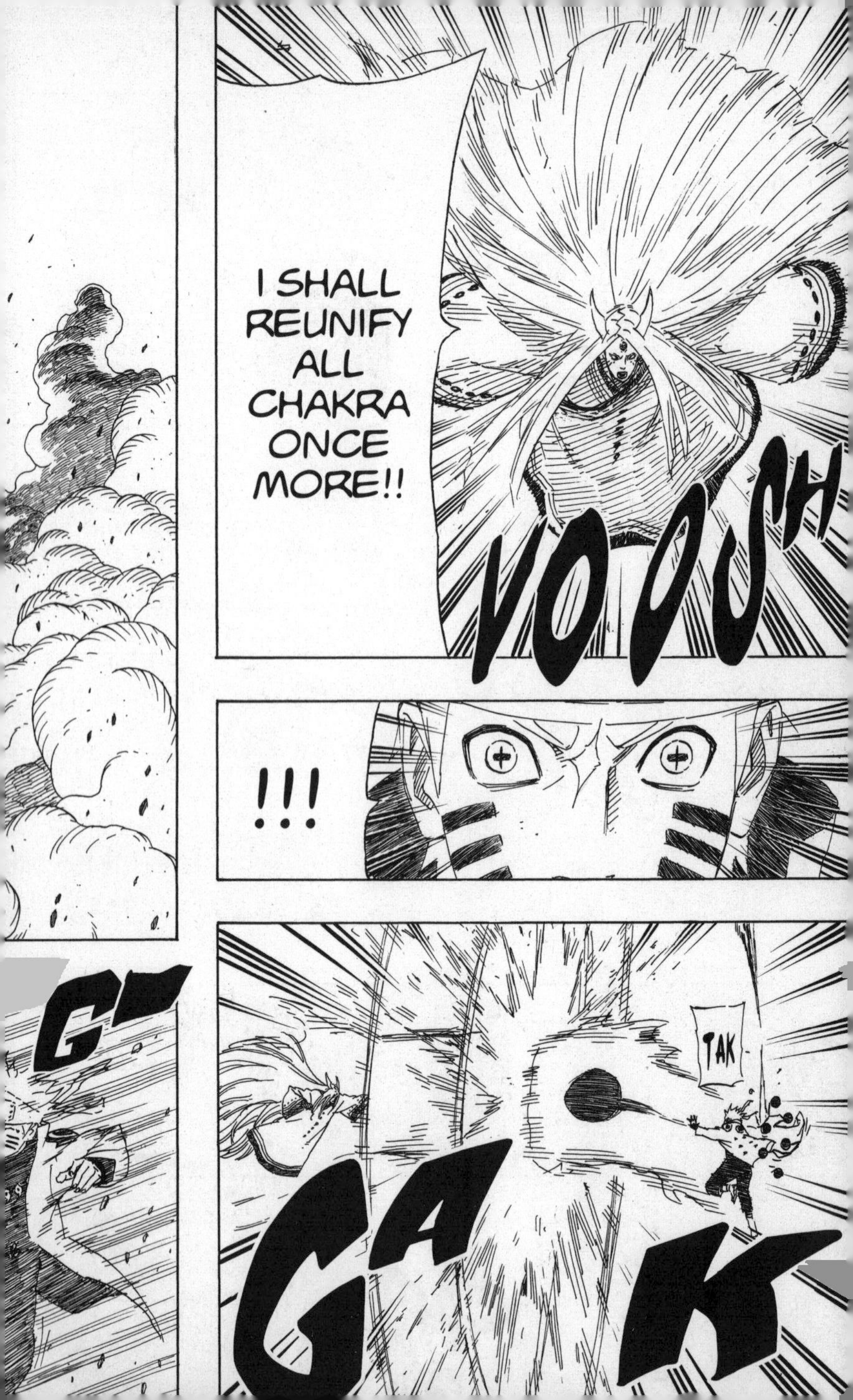
I SHALL REUNIFY ALL CHAKRA ONCE MORE!!
VOOOSH
!!!
TAK
GAK
G

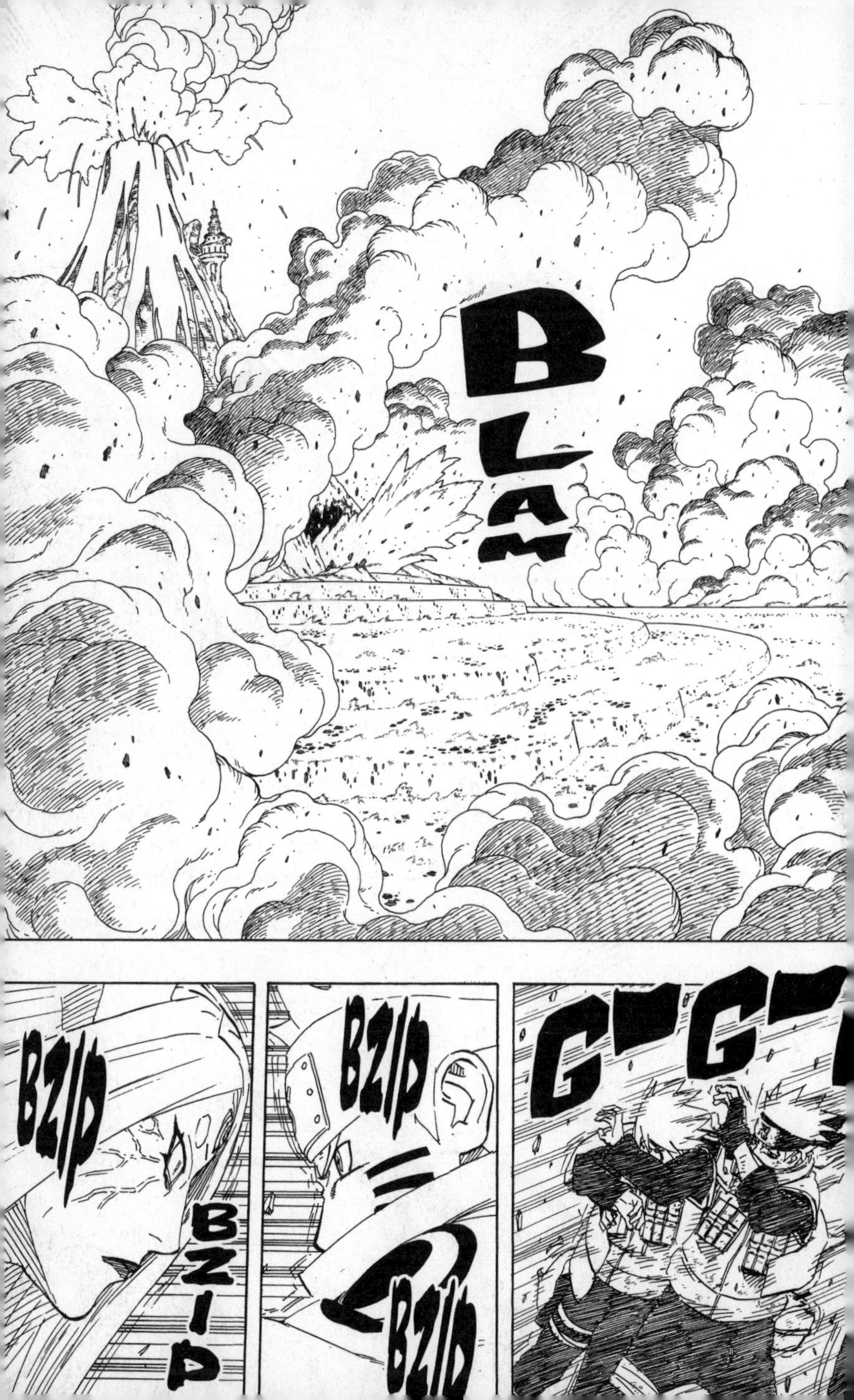
BLAM
BZIP
BZIP
BZIP
BZIP

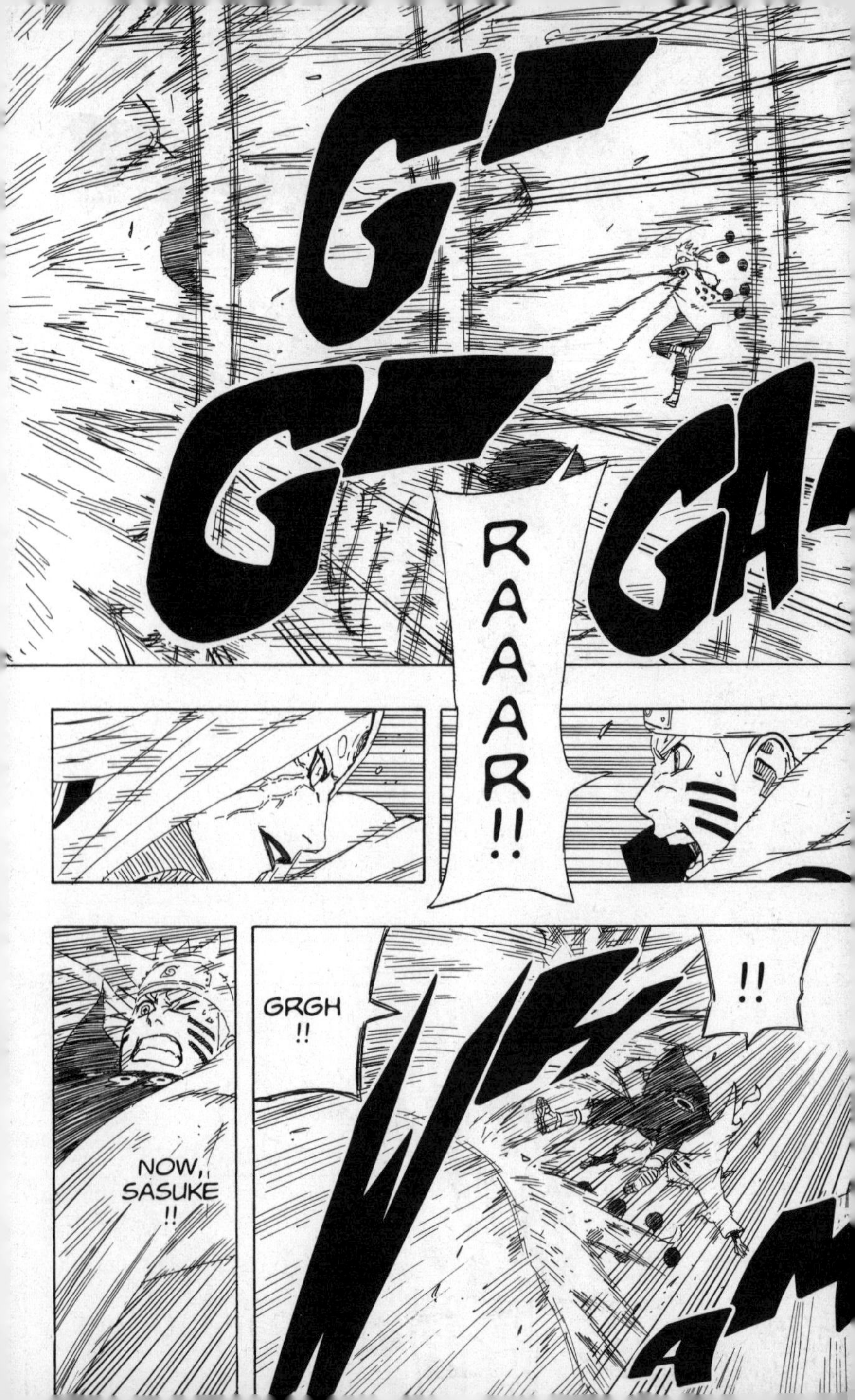
GI GI GA
RAAAR!!
!!
GRGH!!
WHAM
NOW, SASUKE!!

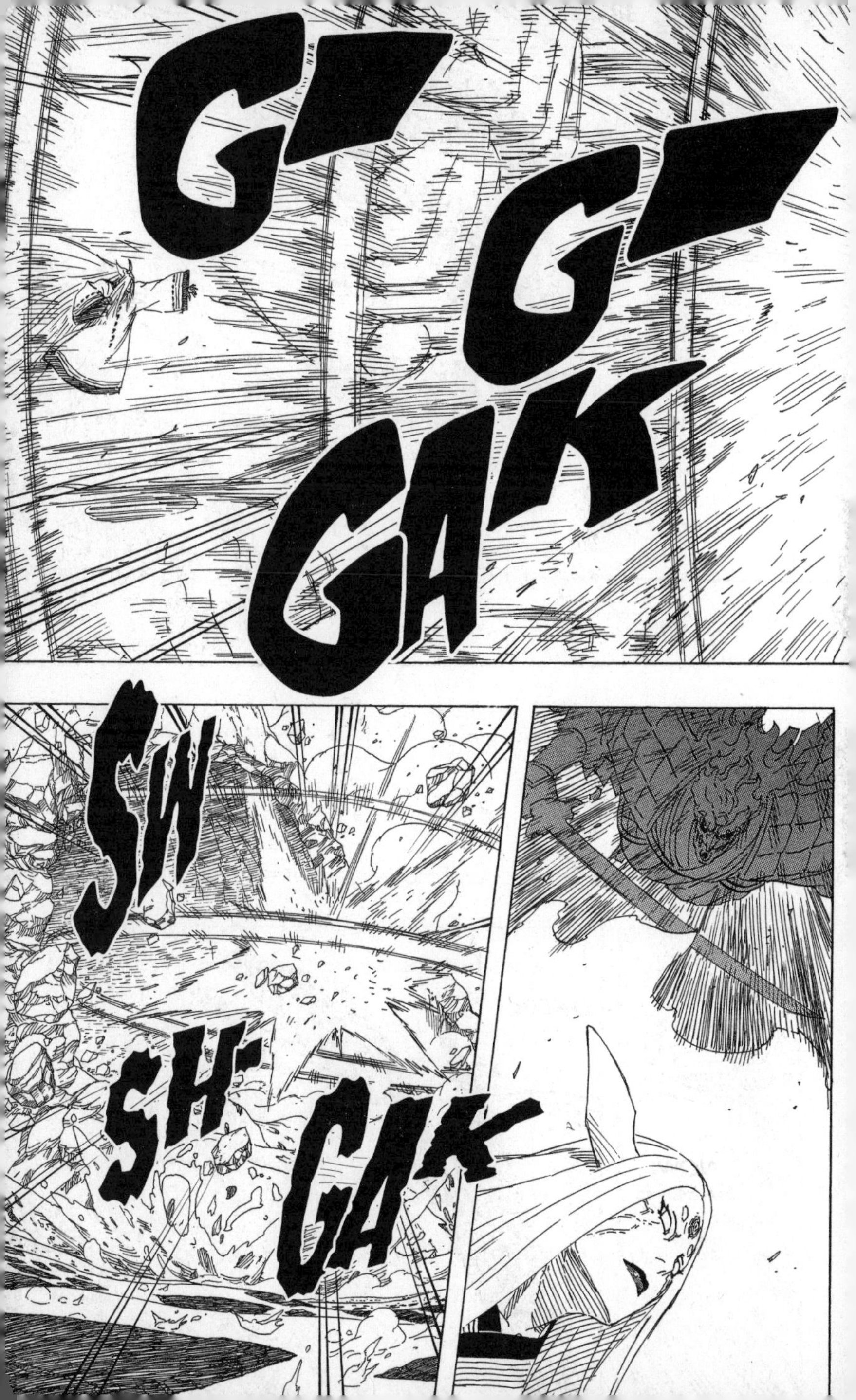
GI-GI-GAK
SW
SH-GAK

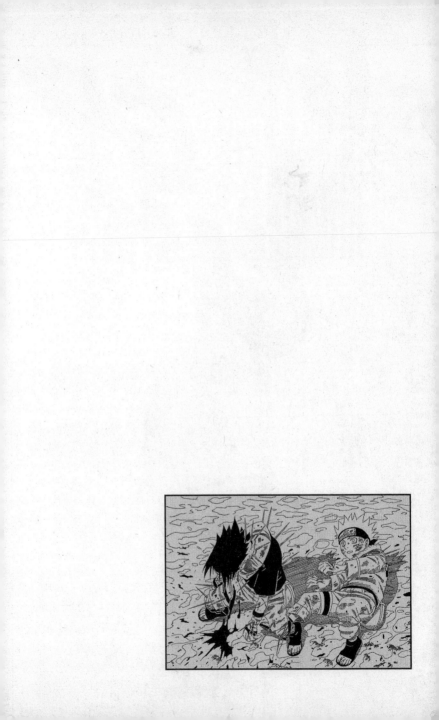

Number 681: Kaguya's Tears

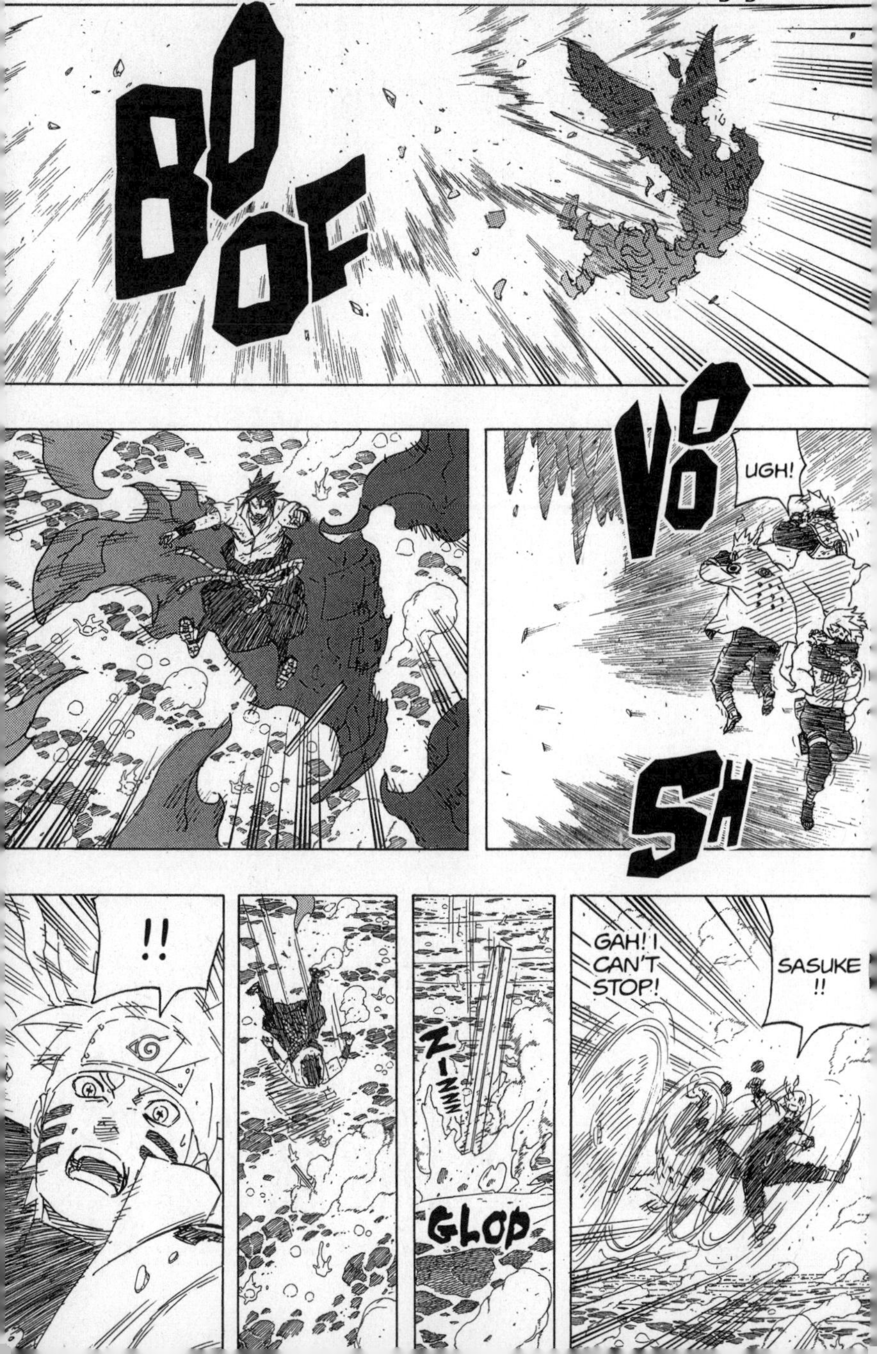
BOOF
VOO
UGH!
SH
SASUKE!!
GAH! I CAN'T STOP!
ZIZZZ
GLOP
!!

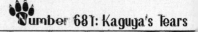

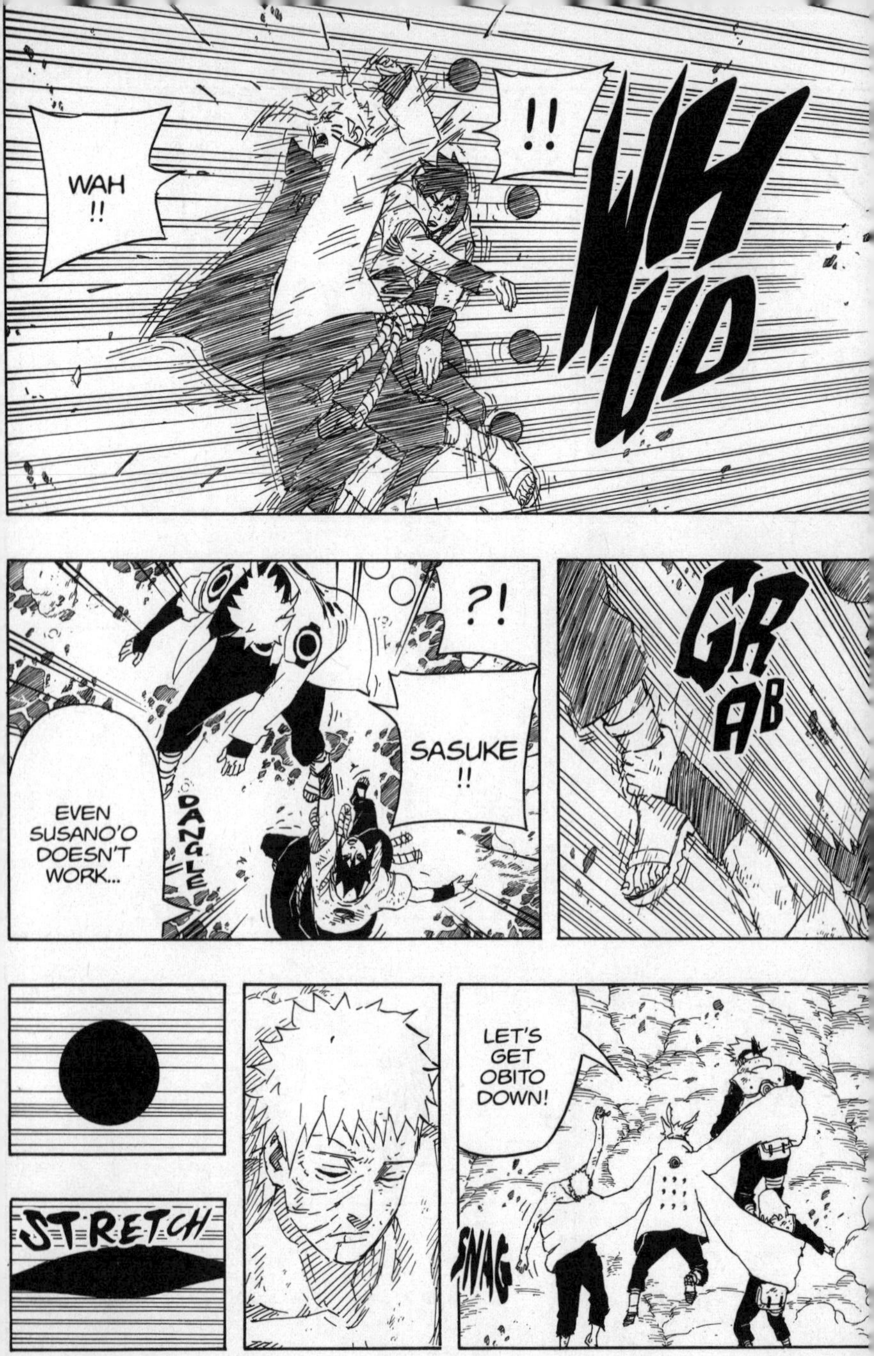
WHUD
!!
WAH !!
GRAB
?!
SASUKE !!
DANGLE
EVEN SUSANO'O DOESN'T WORK...
LET'S GET OBITO DOWN!
SNAG
STRETCH

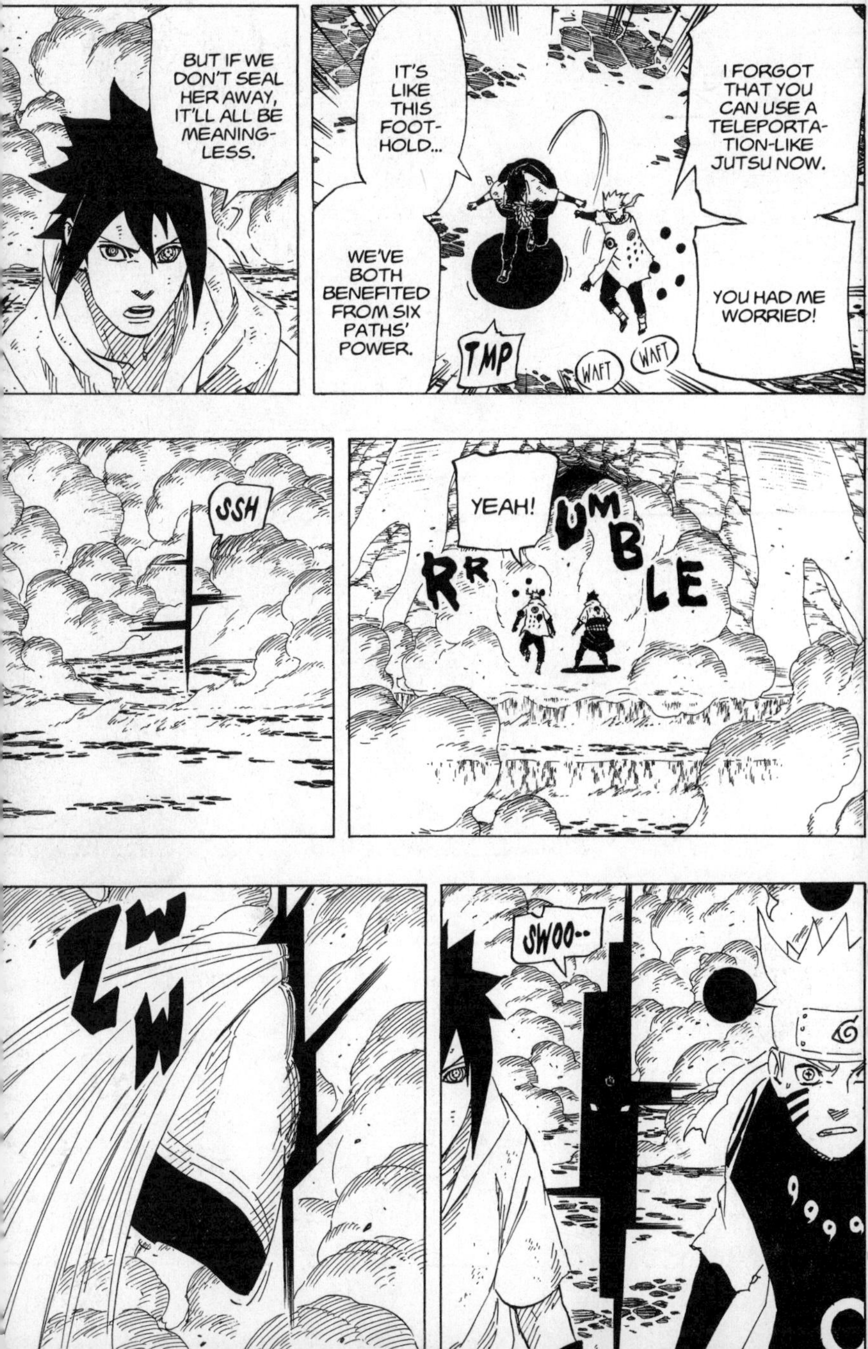
I FORGOT THAT YOU CAN USE A TELEPORTATION-LIKE JUTSU NOW.
YOU HAD ME WORRIED!
IT'S LIKE THIS FOOTHOLD...
WE'VE BOTH BENEFITED FROM SIX PATHS' POWER.
TMP
WAFT
WAFT
BUT IF WE DON'T SEAL HER AWAY, IT'LL ALL BE MEANINGLESS.
YEAH!
RRUMBLE
SSH
SWOO--
ZWW

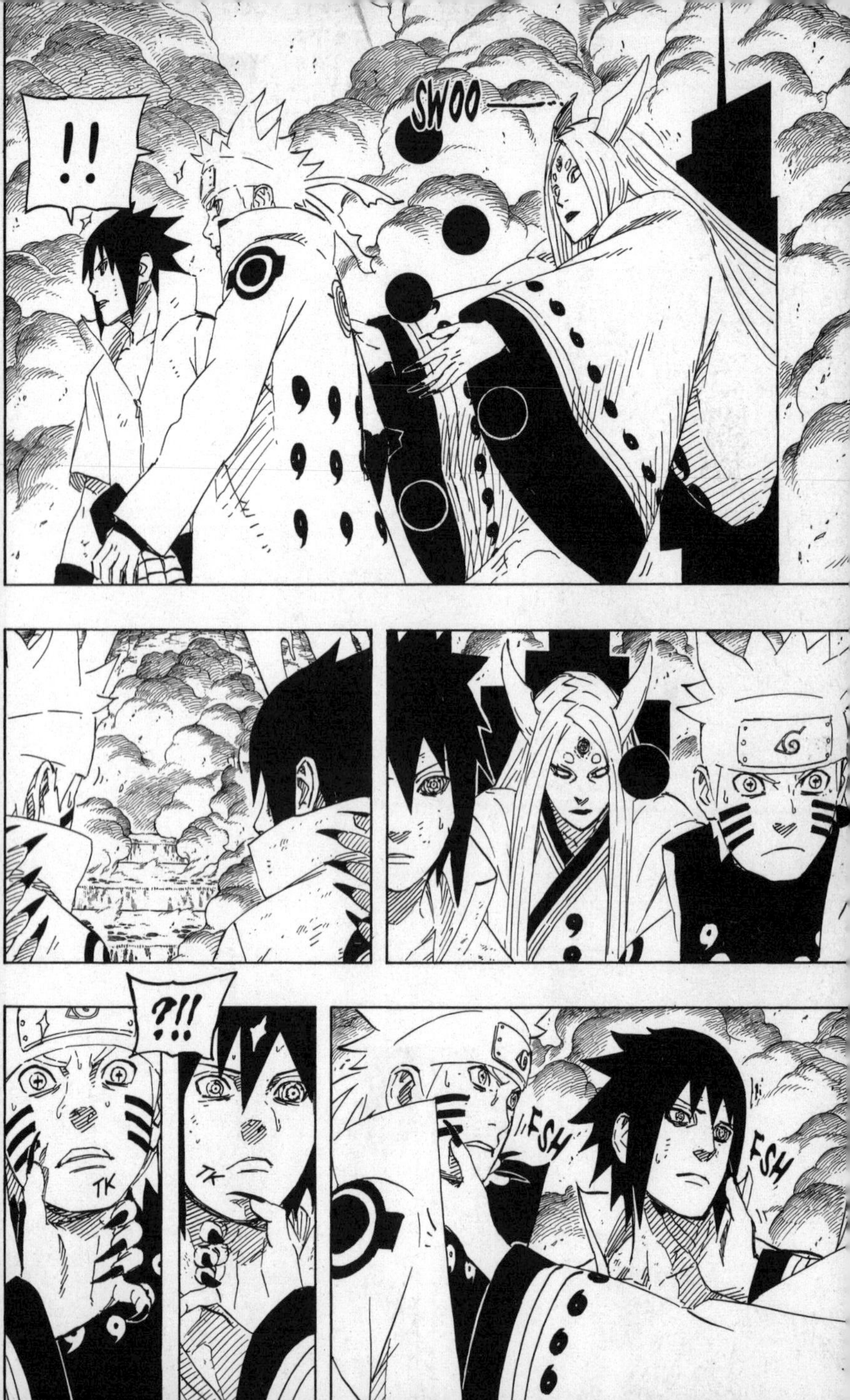
SWOO—
!!
FSH
FSH
?!!
TK
TK

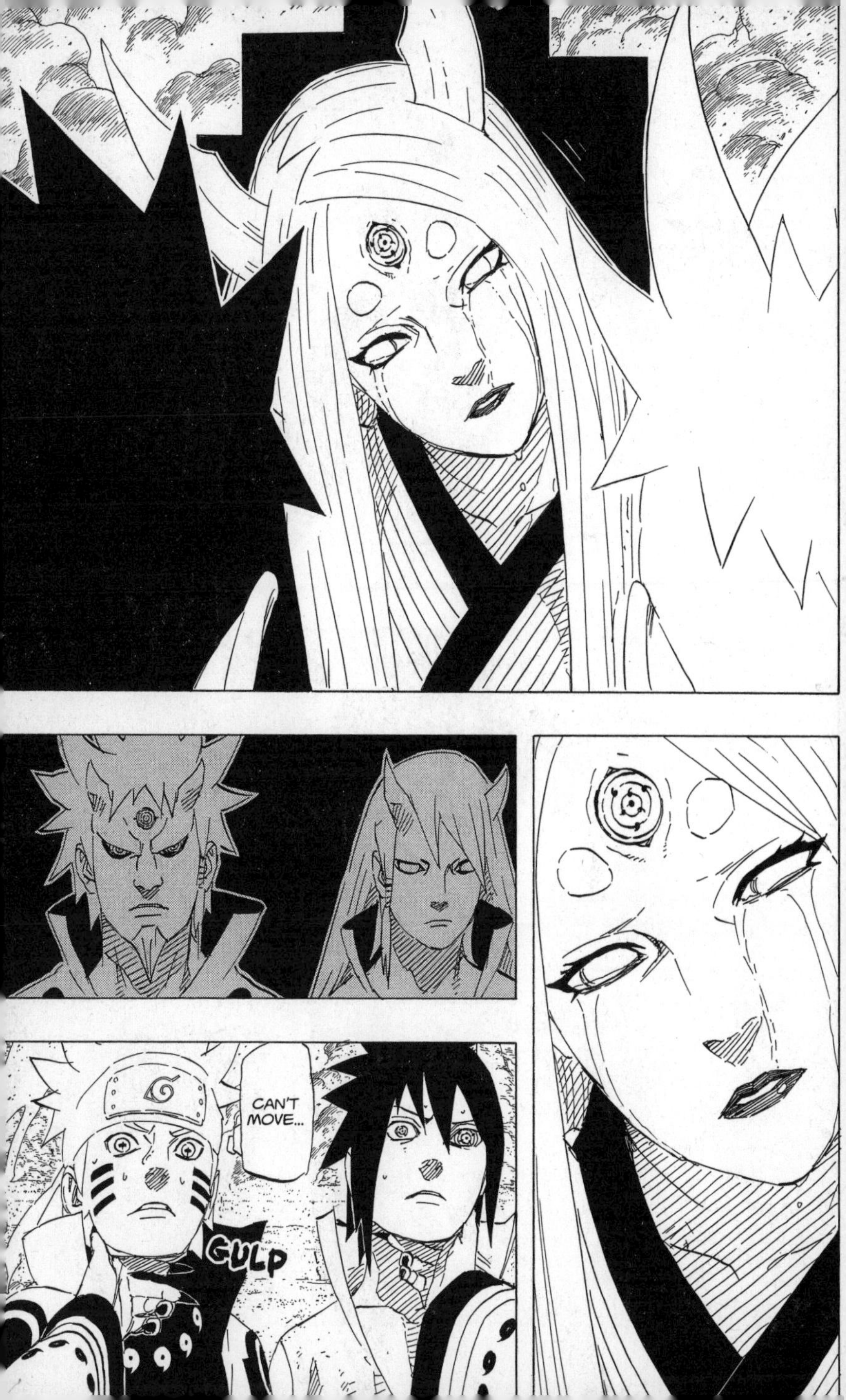
CAN'T MOVE...
GULP

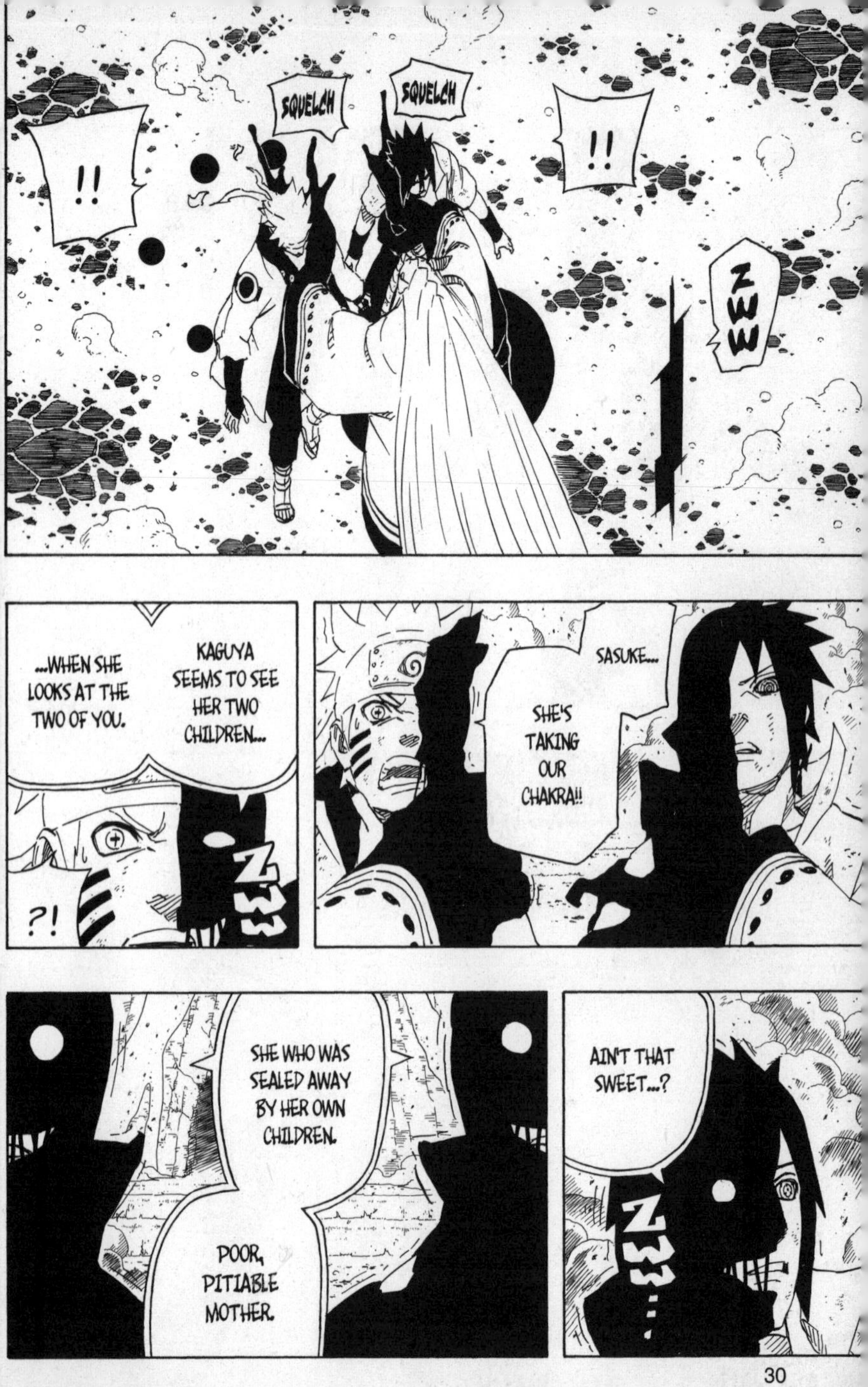
ZWW
!!
SQUELCH
SQUELCH
!!
SASUKE...
SHE'S TAKING OUR CHAKRA!!
KAGUYA SEEMS TO SEE HER TWO CHILDREN...
...WHEN SHE LOOKS AT THE TWO OF YOU.
ZWW
?!
AIN'T THAT SWEET...?
ZWW...
SHE WHO WAS SEALED AWAY BY HER OWN CHILDREN.
POOR, PITIABLE MOTHER.

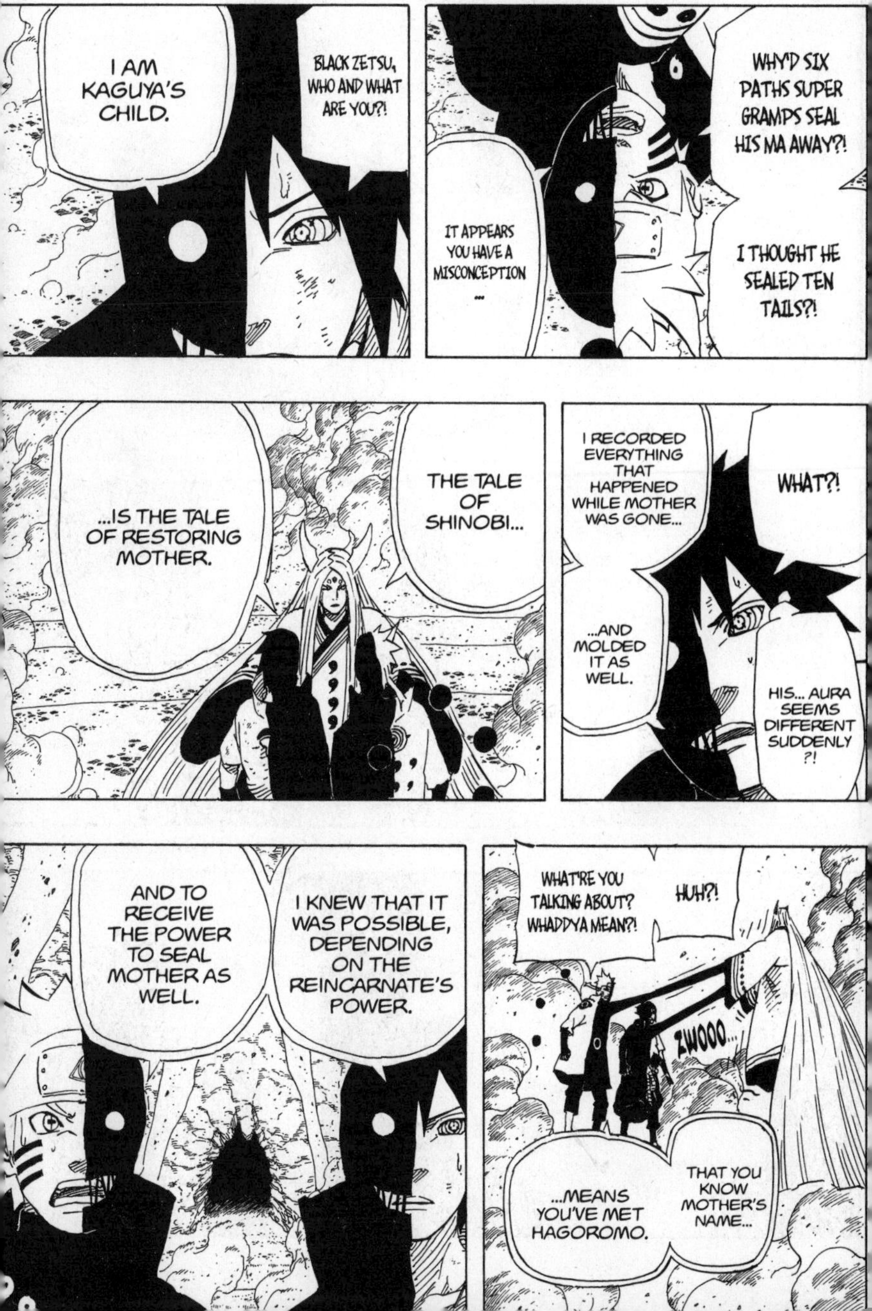
WHY'D SIX PATHS SUPER GRAMPS SEAL HIS MA AWAY?!
I THOUGHT HE SEALED TEN TAILS?!
IT APPEARS YOU HAVE A MISCONCEPTION ...
BLACK ZETSU, WHO AND WHAT ARE YOU?!
I AM KAGUYA'S CHILD.
WHAT?!
HIS... AURA SEEMS DIFFERENT SUDDENLY ?!
I RECORDED EVERYTHING THAT HAPPENED WHILE MOTHER WAS GONE...
...AND MOLDED IT AS WELL.
THE TALE OF SHINOBI...
...IS THE TALE OF RESTORING MOTHER.
HUH?!
WHAT'RE YOU TALKING ABOUT? WHADDYA MEAN?!
ZWOOO...
THAT YOU KNOW MOTHER'S NAME...
...MEANS YOU'VE MET HAGOROMO.
I KNEW THAT IT WAS POSSIBLE, DEPENDING ON THE REINCARNATE'S POWER.
AND TO RECEIVE THE POWER TO SEAL MOTHER AS WELL.

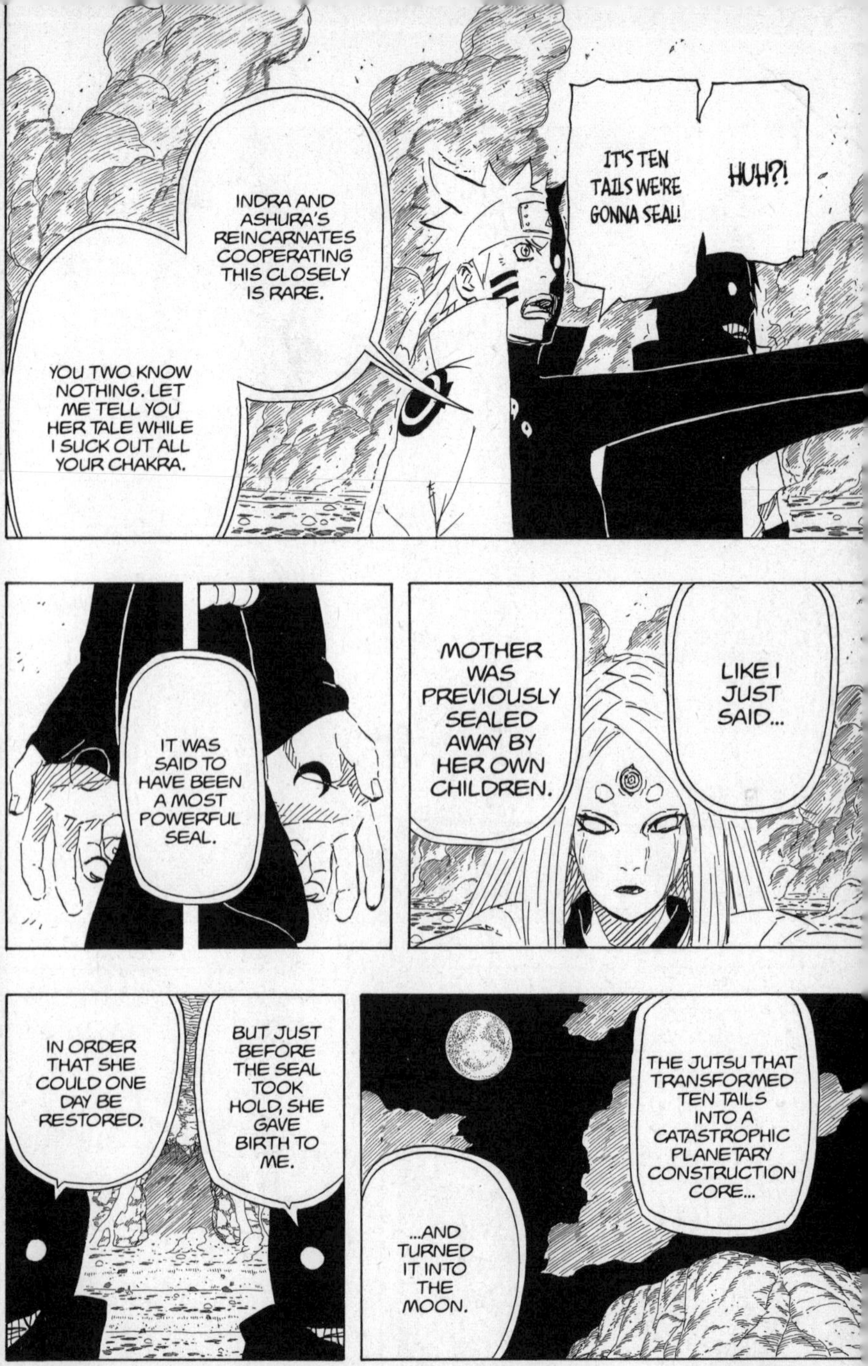
HUH?!
IT'S TEN TAILS WE'RE GONNA SEAL!
INDRA AND ASHURA'S REINCARNATES COOPERATING THIS CLOSELY IS RARE.
YOU TWO KNOW NOTHING. LET ME TELL YOU HER TALE WHILE I SUCK OUT ALL YOUR CHAKRA.
LIKE I JUST SAID...
MOTHER WAS PREVIOUSLY SEALED AWAY BY HER OWN CHILDREN.
IT WAS SAID TO HAVE BEEN A MOST POWERFUL SEAL.
THE JUTSU THAT TRANSFORMED TEN TAILS INTO A CATASTROPHIC PLANETARY CONSTRUCTION CORE...
...AND TURNED IT INTO THE MOON.
BUT JUST BEFORE THE SEAL TOOK HOLD, SHE GAVE BIRTH TO ME.
IN ORDER THAT SHE COULD ONE DAY BE RESTORED.

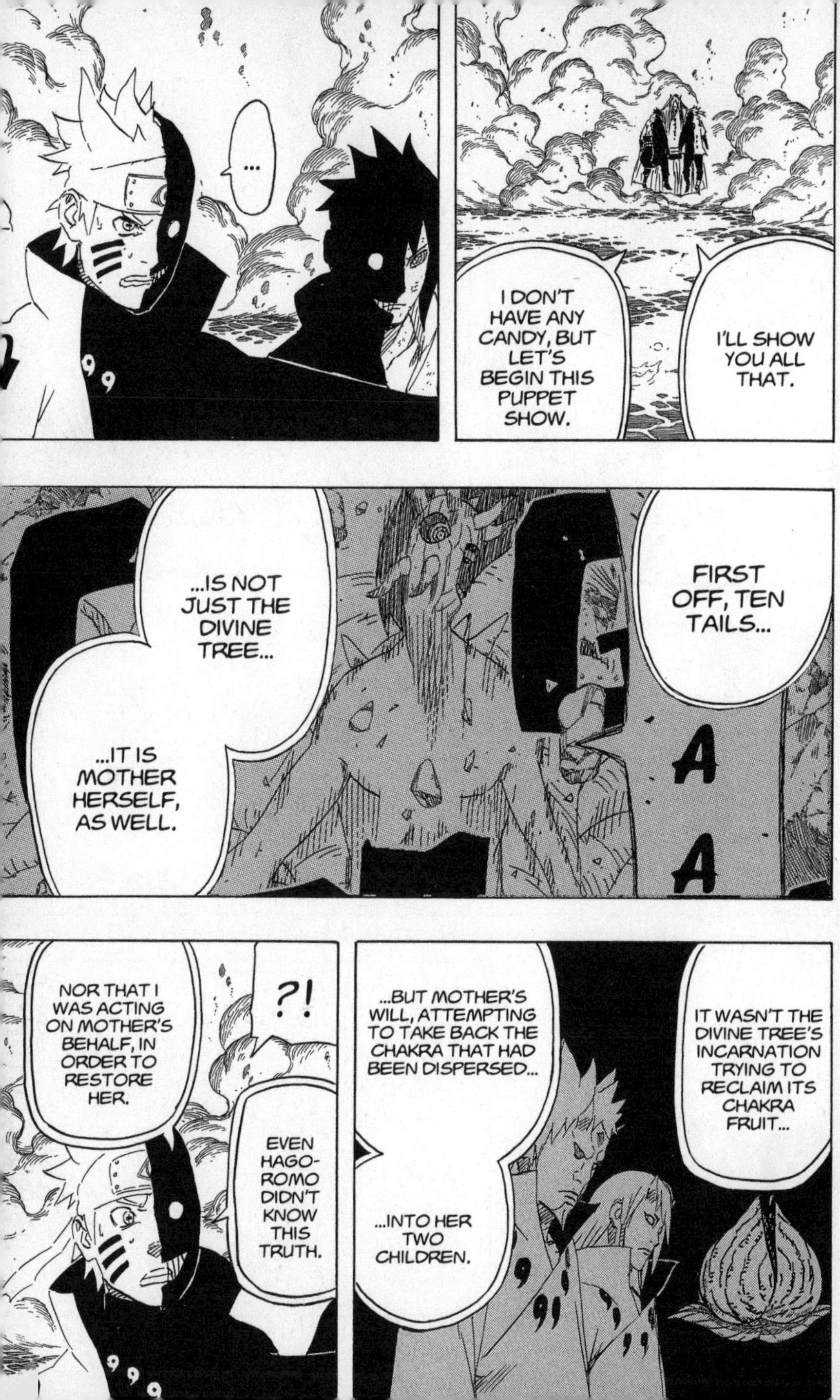

I'LL SHOW YOU ALL THAT.
I DON'T HAVE ANY CANDY, BUT LET'S BEGIN THIS PUPPET SHOW.
...
FIRST OFF, TEN TAILS...
A
A
...IS NOT JUST THE DIVINE TREE...
...IT IS MOTHER HERSELF, AS WELL.
IT WASN'T THE DIVINE TREE'S INCARNATION TRYING TO RECLAIM ITS CHAKRA FRUIT...
...BUT MOTHER'S WILL, ATTEMPTING TO TAKE BACK THE CHAKRA THAT HAD BEEN DISPERSED...
...INTO HER TWO CHILDREN.
?!
EVEN HAGO-ROMO DIDN'T KNOW THIS TRUTH.
NOR THAT I WAS ACTING ON MOTHER'S BEHALF, IN ORDER TO RESTORE HER.

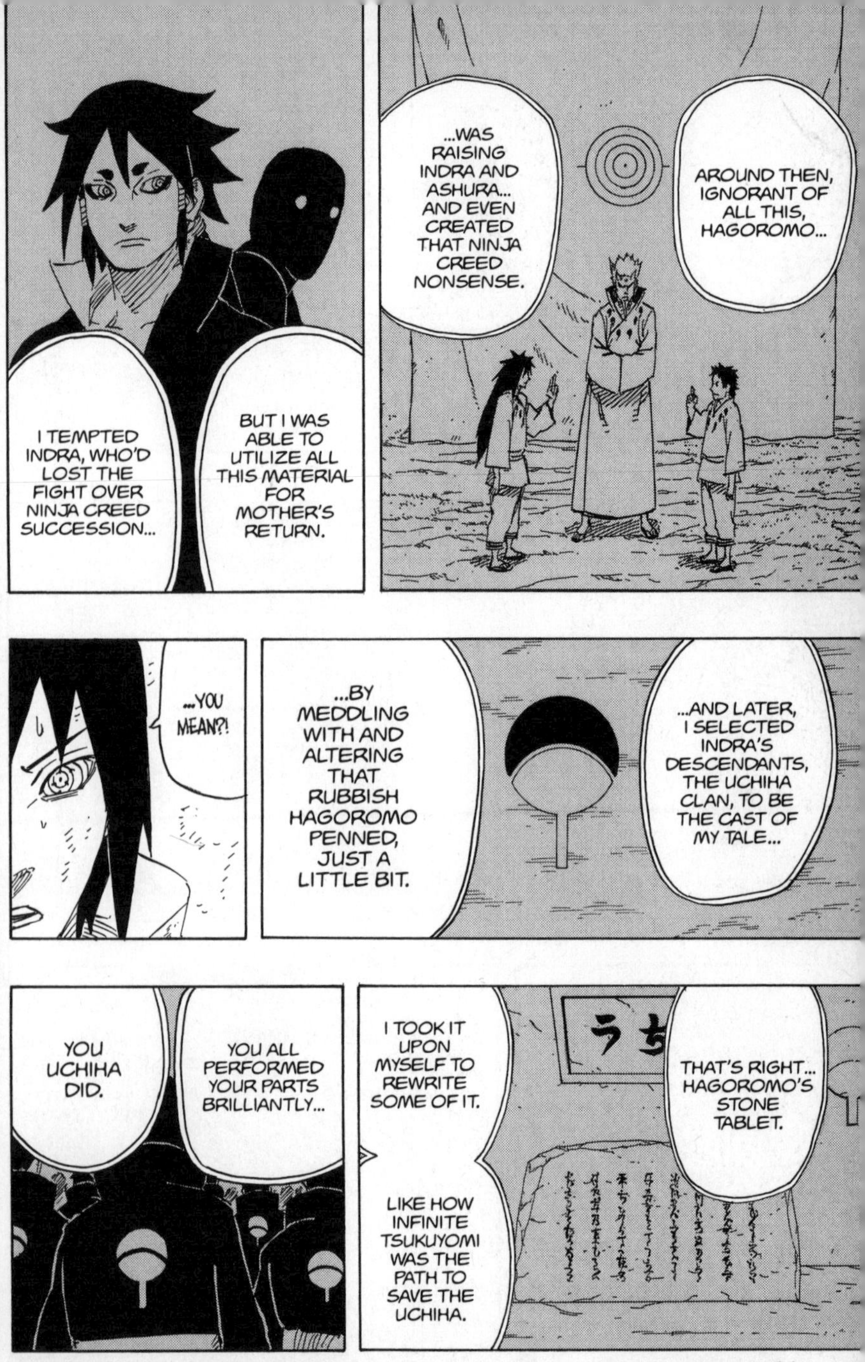
AROUND THEN, IGNORANT OF ALL THIS, HAGOROMO...
...WAS RAISING INDRA AND ASHURA... AND EVEN CREATED THAT NINJA CREED NONSENSE.
BUT I WAS ABLE TO UTILIZE ALL THIS MATERIAL FOR MOTHER'S RETURN.
I TEMPTED INDRA, WHO'D LOST THE FIGHT OVER NINJA CREED SUCCESSION...
...AND LATER, I SELECTED INDRA'S DESCENDANTS, THE UCHIHA CLAN, TO BE THE CAST OF MY TALE...
...BY MEDDLING WITH AND ALTERING THAT RUBBISH HAGOROMO PENNED, JUST A LITTLE BIT.
...YOU MEAN?!
THAT'S RIGHT... HAGOROMO'S STONE TABLET.
I TOOK IT UPON MYSELF TO REWRITE SOME OF IT.
LIKE HOW INFINITE TSUKUYOMI WAS THE PATH TO SAVE THE UCHIHA.
YOU ALL PERFORMED YOUR PARTS BRILLIANTLY...
YOU UCHIHA DID.

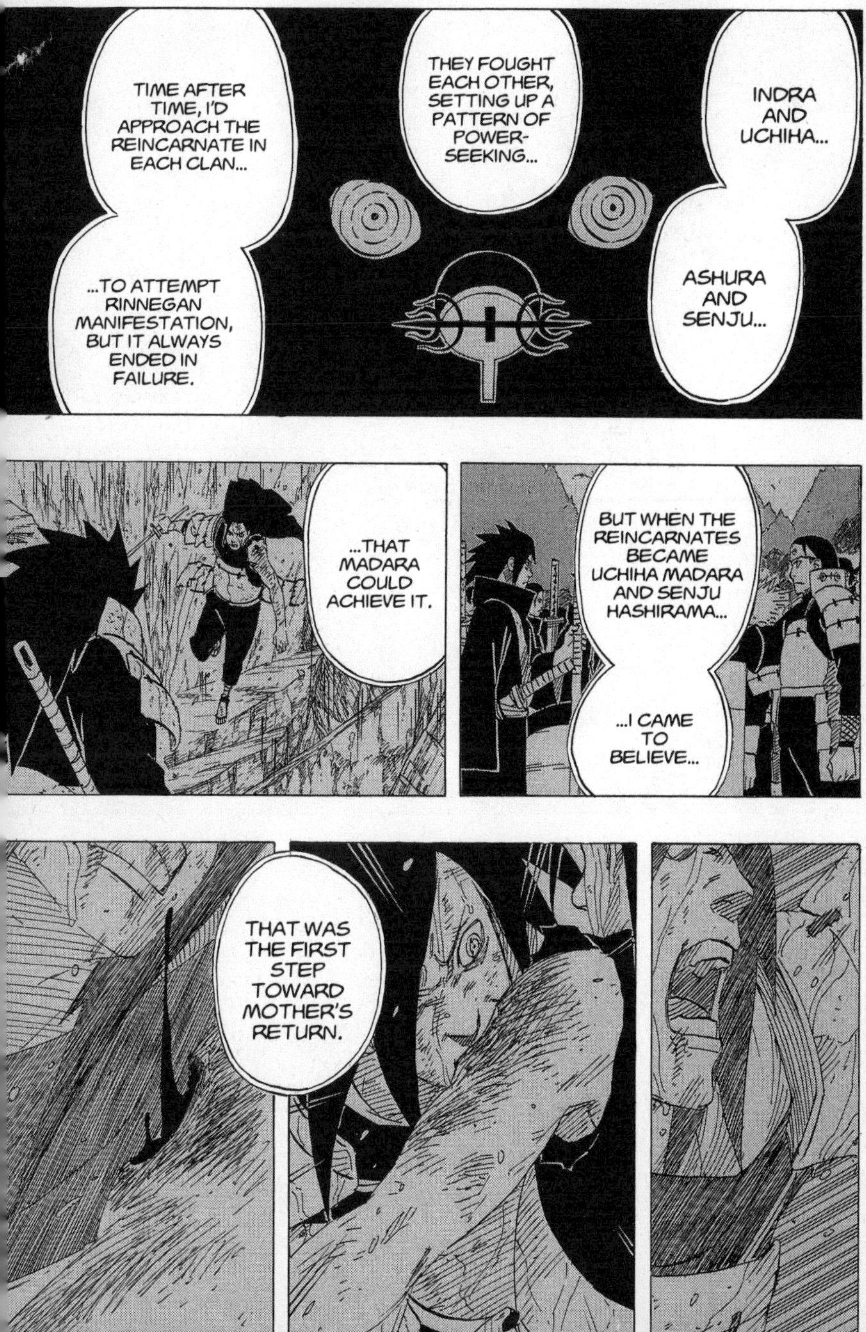
INDRA AND UCHIHA...
ASHURA AND SENJU...
THEY FOUGHT EACH OTHER, SETTING UP A PATTERN OF POWER-SEEKING...
TIME AFTER TIME, I'D APPROACH THE REINCARNATE IN EACH CLAN...
...TO ATTEMPT RINNEGAN MANIFESTATION, BUT IT ALWAYS ENDED IN FAILURE.
BUT WHEN THE REINCARNATES BECAME UCHIHA MADARA AND SENJU HASHIRAMA...
...I CAME TO BELIEVE...
...THAT MADARA COULD ACHIEVE IT.
THAT WAS THE FIRST STEP TOWARD MOTHER'S RETURN.

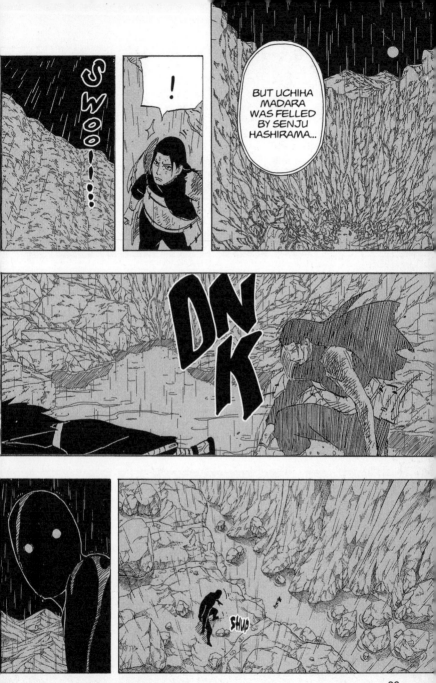

BUT UCHIHA MADARA WAS FELLED BY SENJU HASHIRAMA...

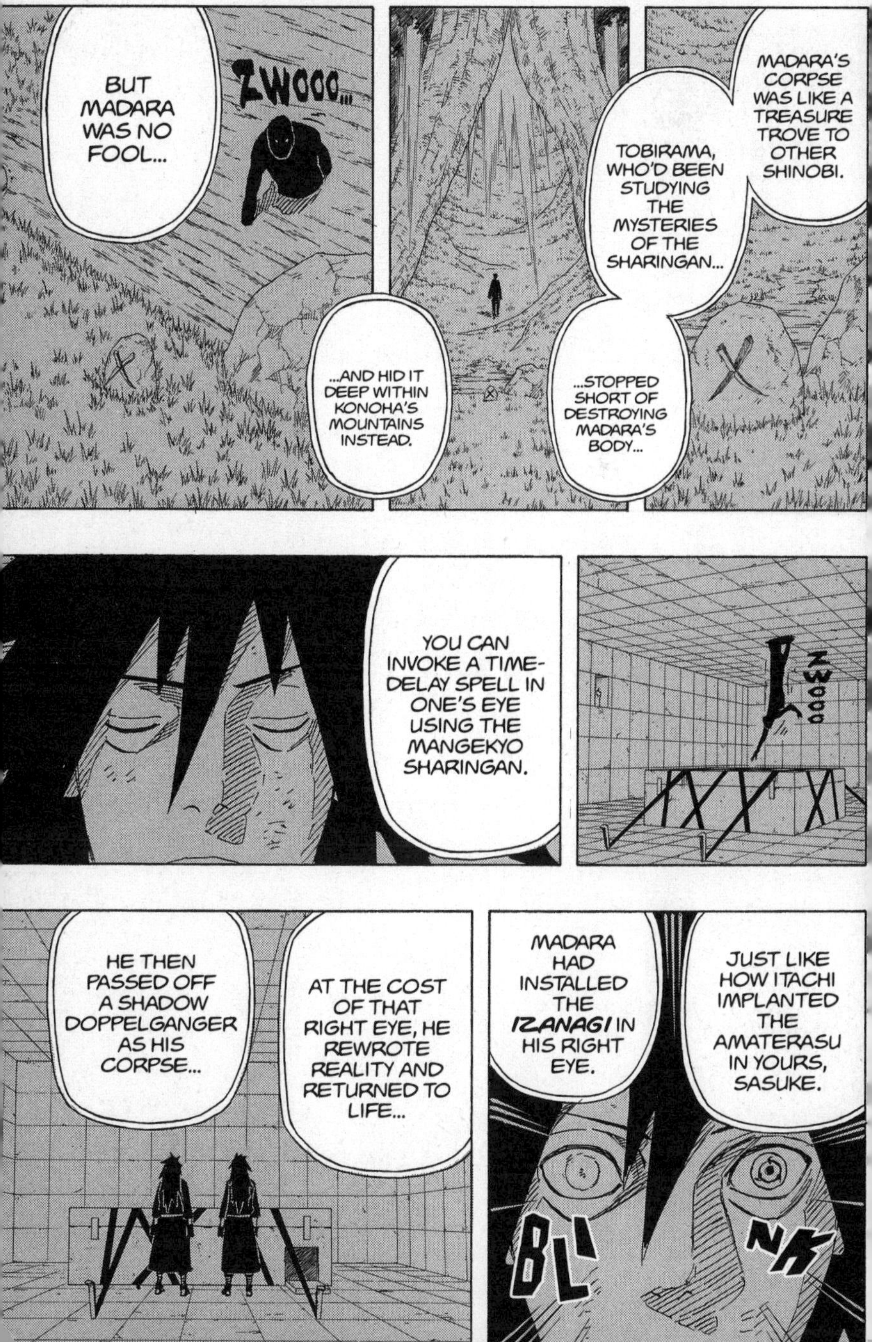
MADARA'S CORPSE WAS LIKE A TREASURE TROVE TO OTHER SHINOBI.
TOBIRAMA, WHO'D BEEN STUDYING THE MYSTERIES OF THE SHARINGAN...
...STOPPED SHORT OF DESTROYING MADARA'S BODY...
...AND HID IT DEEP WITHIN KONOHA'S MOUNTAINS INSTEAD.
BUT MADARA WAS NO FOOL...
ZWOOO...
ZWOOO
YOU CAN INVOKE A TIME-DELAY SPELL IN ONE'S EYE USING THE MANGEKYO SHARINGAN.
JUST LIKE HOW ITACHI IMPLANTED THE AMATERASU IN YOURS, SASUKE.
MADARA HAD INSTALLED THE *IZANAGI* IN HIS RIGHT EYE.
BLINK
AT THE COST OF THAT RIGHT EYE, HE REWROTE REALITY AND RETURNED TO LIFE...
HE THEN PASSED OFF A SHADOW DOPPELGANGER AS HIS CORPSE...

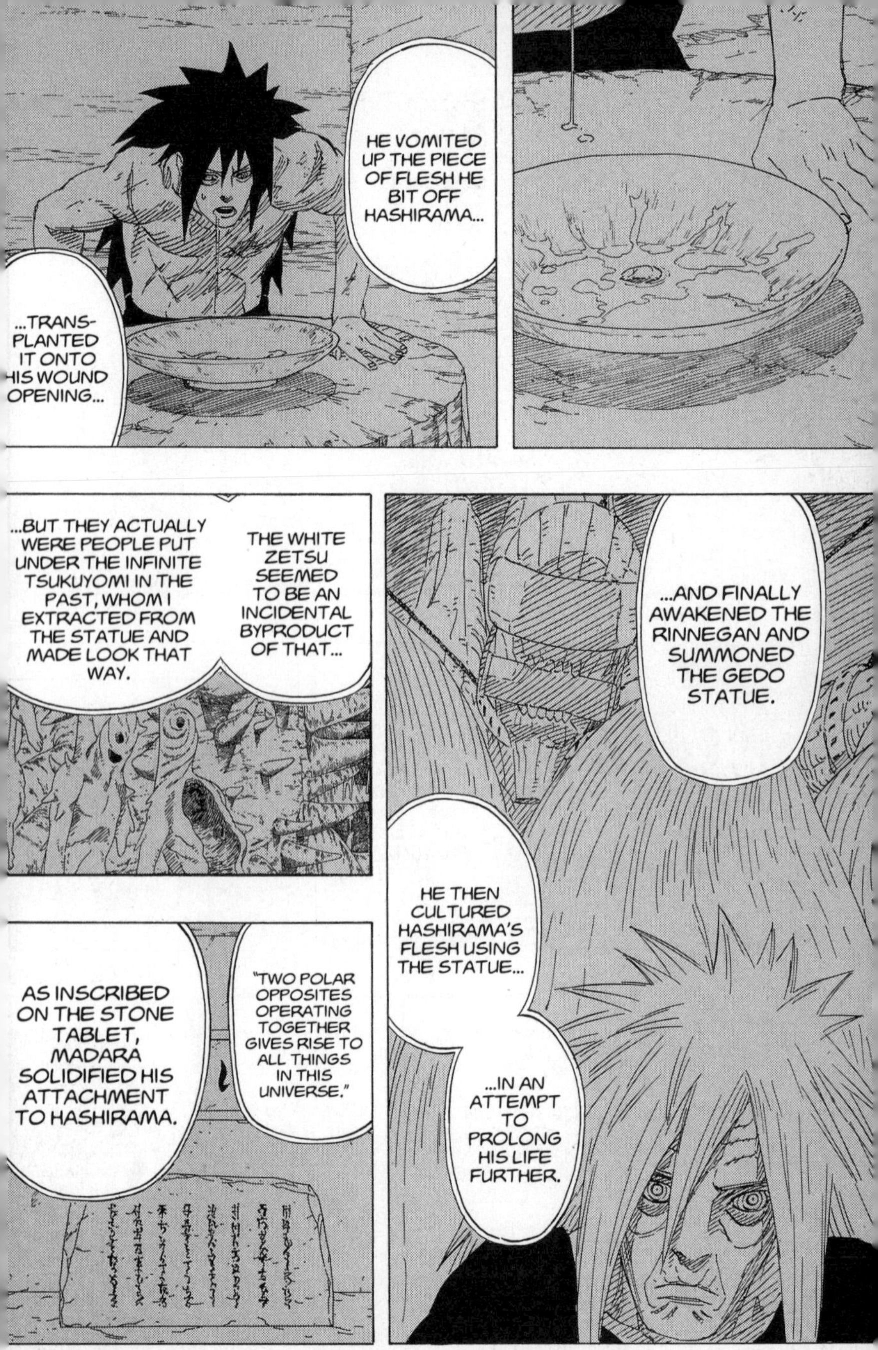
HE VOMITED UP THE PIECE OF FLESH HE BIT OFF HASHIRAMA...
...TRANS-PLANTED IT ONTO HIS WOUND OPENING...
...AND FINALLY AWAKENED THE RINNEGAN AND SUMMONED THE GEDO STATUE.
HE THEN CULTURED HASHIRAMA'S FLESH USING THE STATUE...
...IN AN ATTEMPT TO PROLONG HIS LIFE FURTHER.
THE WHITE ZETSU SEEMED TO BE AN INCIDENTAL BYPRODUCT OF THAT...
...BUT THEY ACTUALLY WERE PEOPLE PUT UNDER THE INFINITE TSUKUYOMI IN THE PAST, WHOM I EXTRACTED FROM THE STATUE AND MADE LOOK THAT WAY.
"TWO POLAR OPPOSITES OPERATING TOGETHER GIVES RISE TO ALL THINGS IN THIS UNIVERSE."
AS INSCRIBED ON THE STONE TABLET, MADARA SOLIDIFIED HIS ATTACHMENT TO HASHIRAMA.

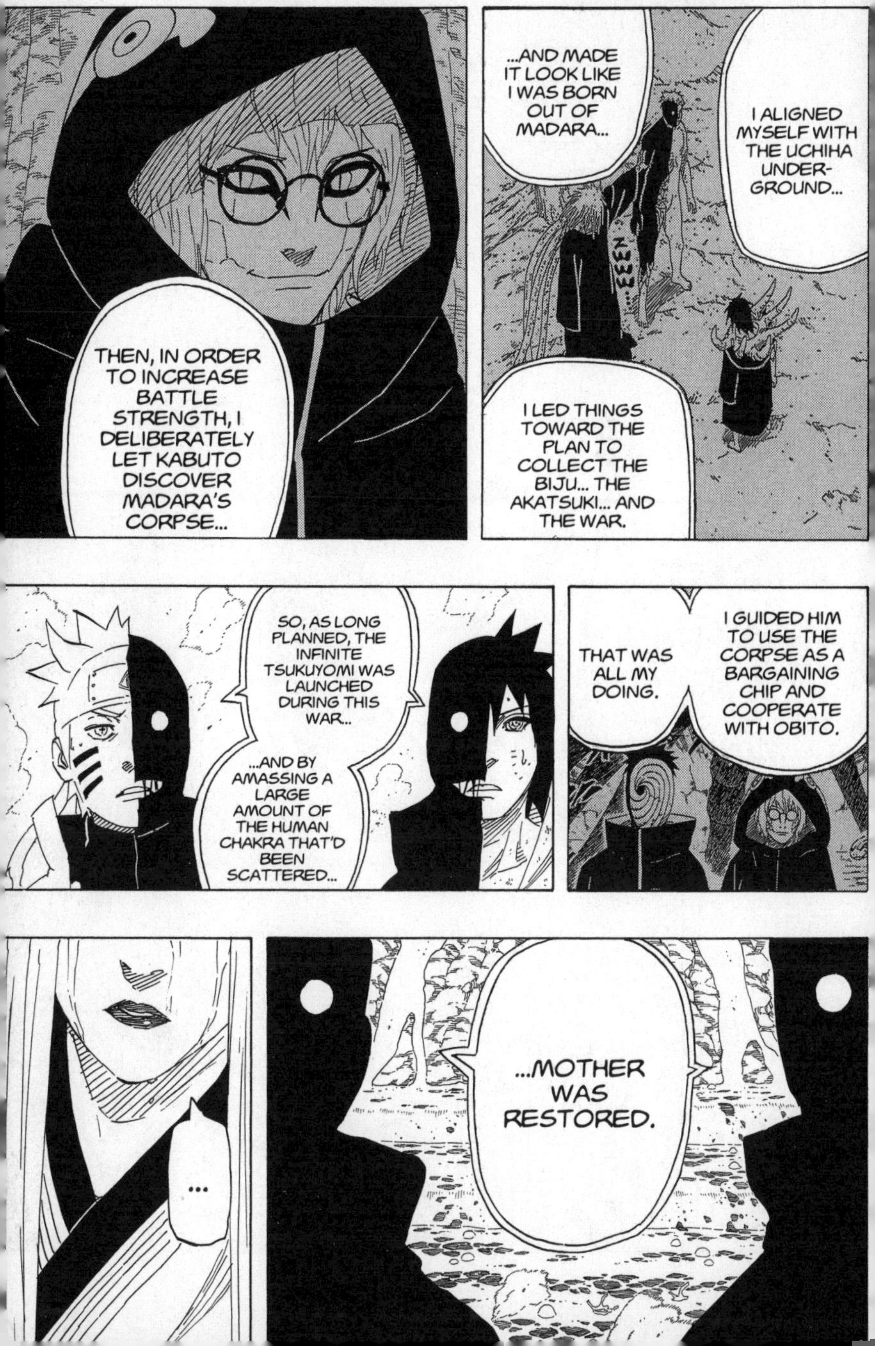
I ALIGNED MYSELF WITH THE UCHIHA UNDER-GROUND...
...AND MADE IT LOOK LIKE I WAS BORN OUT OF MADARA...
I LED THINGS TOWARD THE PLAN TO COLLECT THE BIJU... THE AKATSUKI... AND THE WAR.
THEN, IN ORDER TO INCREASE BATTLE STRENGTH, I DELIBERATELY LET KABUTO DISCOVER MADARA'S CORPSE...
I GUIDED HIM TO USE THE CORPSE AS A BARGAINING CHIP AND COOPERATE WITH OBITO.
THAT WAS ALL MY DOING.
SO, AS LONG PLANNED, THE INFINITE TSUKUYOMI WAS LAUNCHED DURING THIS WAR...
...AND BY AMASSING A LARGE AMOUNT OF THE HUMAN CHAKRA THAT'D BEEN SCATTERED...
...MOTHER WAS RESTORED.
...

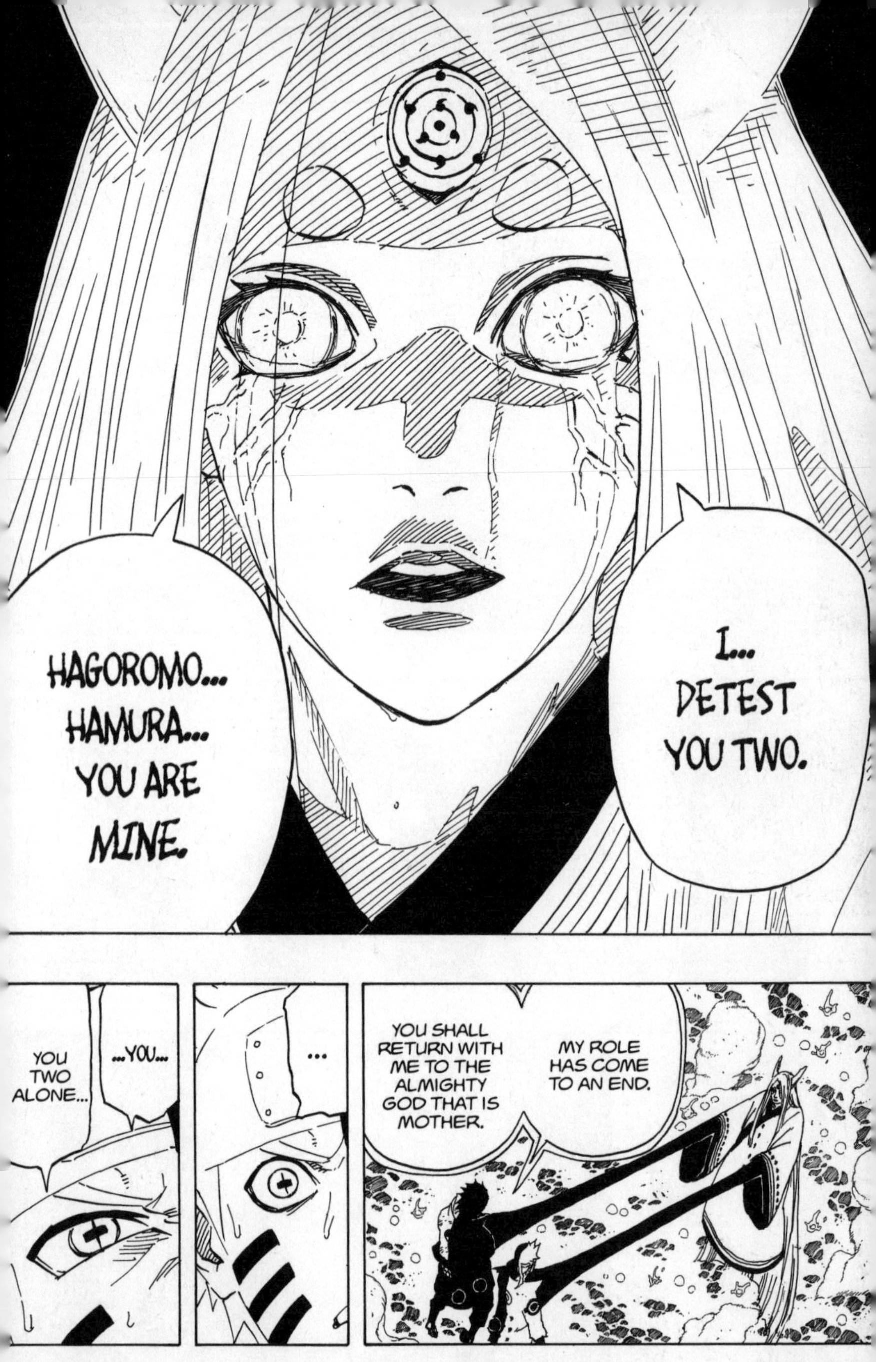
I... DETEST YOU TWO.
HAGOROMO... HAMURA... YOU ARE MINE.
MY ROLE HAS COME TO AN END.
YOU SHALL RETURN WITH ME TO THE ALMIGHTY GOD THAT IS MOTHER.
...
...YOU...
YOU TWO ALONE...

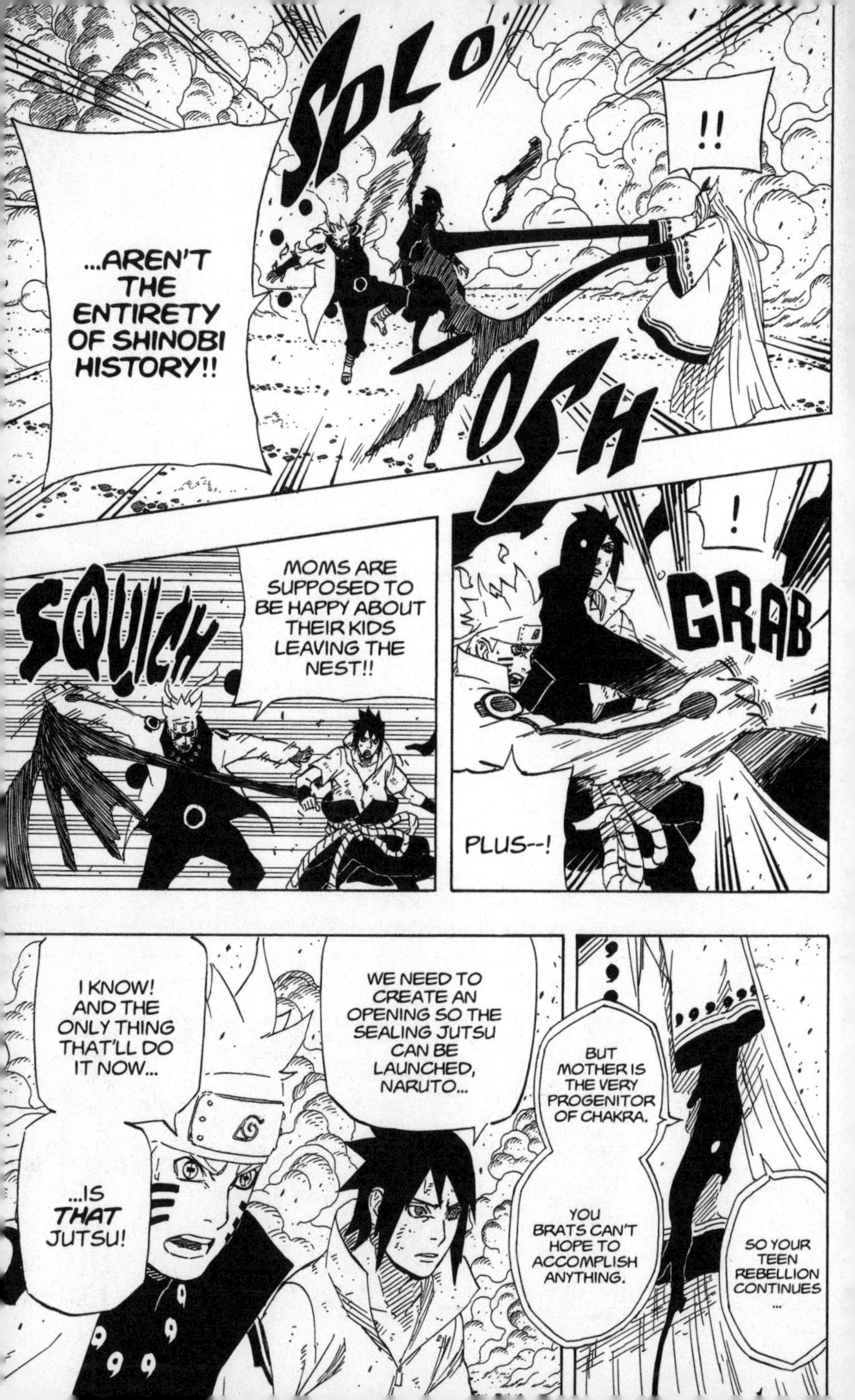
!!
SPLO
OSH
...AREN'T THE ENTIRETY OF SHINOBI HISTORY!!
!
GRAB
PLUS--!
SQUICH
MOMS ARE SUPPOSED TO BE HAPPY ABOUT THEIR KIDS LEAVING THE NEST!!
SO YOUR TEEN REBELLION CONTINUES...
BUT MOTHER IS THE VERY PROGENITOR OF CHAKRA.
YOU BRATS CAN'T HOPE TO ACCOMPLISH ANYTHING.
WE NEED TO CREATE AN OPENING SO THE SEALING JUTSU CAN BE LAUNCHED, NARUTO...
I KNOW! AND THE ONLY THING THAT'LL DO IT NOW...
...IS *THAT* JUTSU!

Number 682: Bet Ya Never Seen This

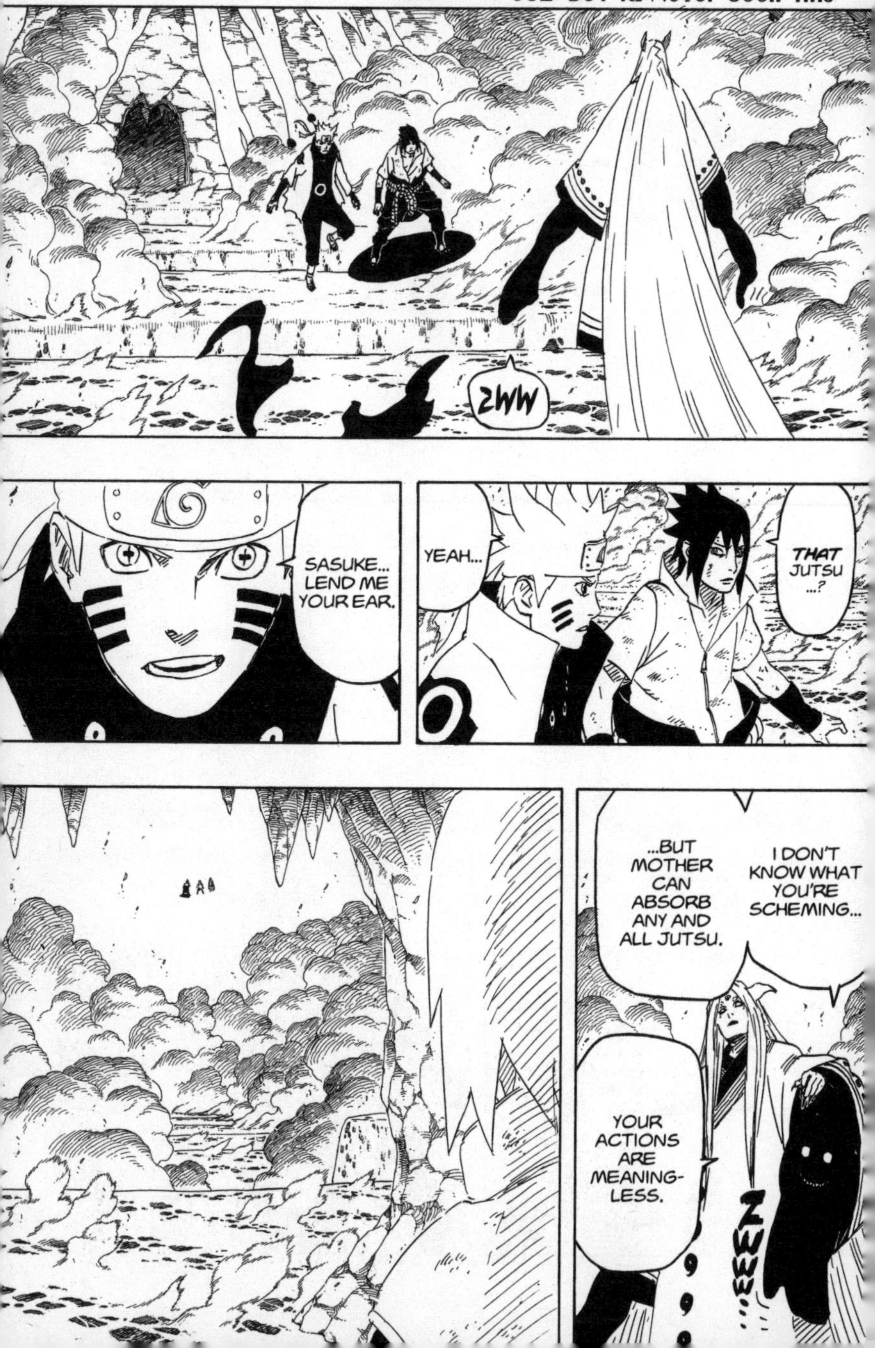
ZWW
THAT JUTSU ...?
YEAH...
SASUKE... LEND ME YOUR EAR.
I DON'T KNOW WHAT YOU'RE SCHEMING...
...BUT MOTHER CAN ABSORB ANY AND ALL JUTSU.
YOUR ACTIONS ARE MEANING-LESS.
ZWWW...

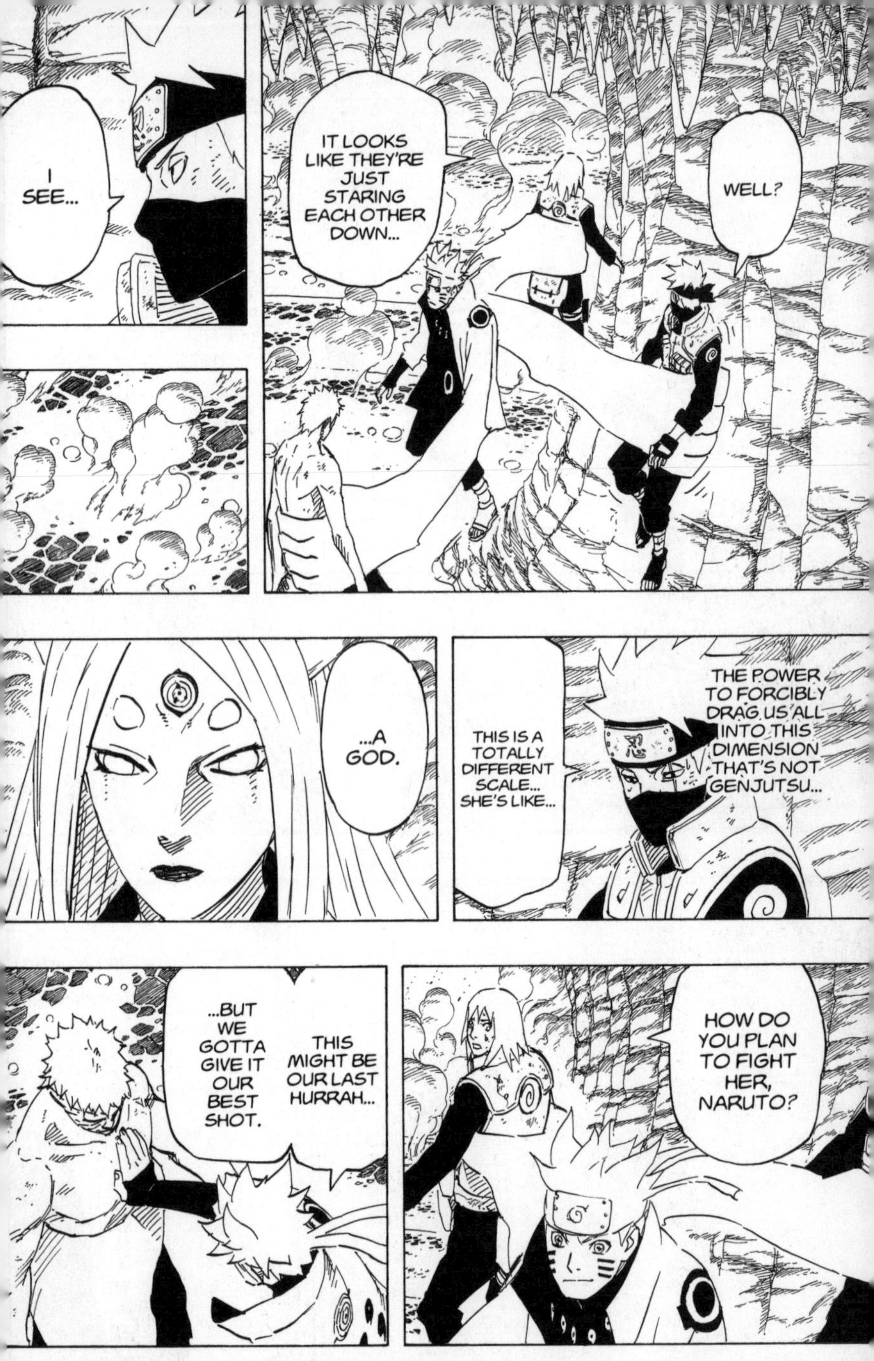
WELL?
IT LOOKS LIKE THEY'RE JUST STARING EACH OTHER DOWN...
I SEE...
THE POWER TO FORCIBLY DRAG US ALL INTO THIS DIMENSION THAT'S NOT GENJUTSU...
THIS IS A TOTALLY DIFFERENT SCALE... SHE'S LIKE...
...A GOD.
HOW DO YOU PLAN TO FIGHT HER, NARUTO?
THIS MIGHT BE OUR LAST HURRAH...
...BUT WE GOTTA GIVE IT OUR BEST SHOT.

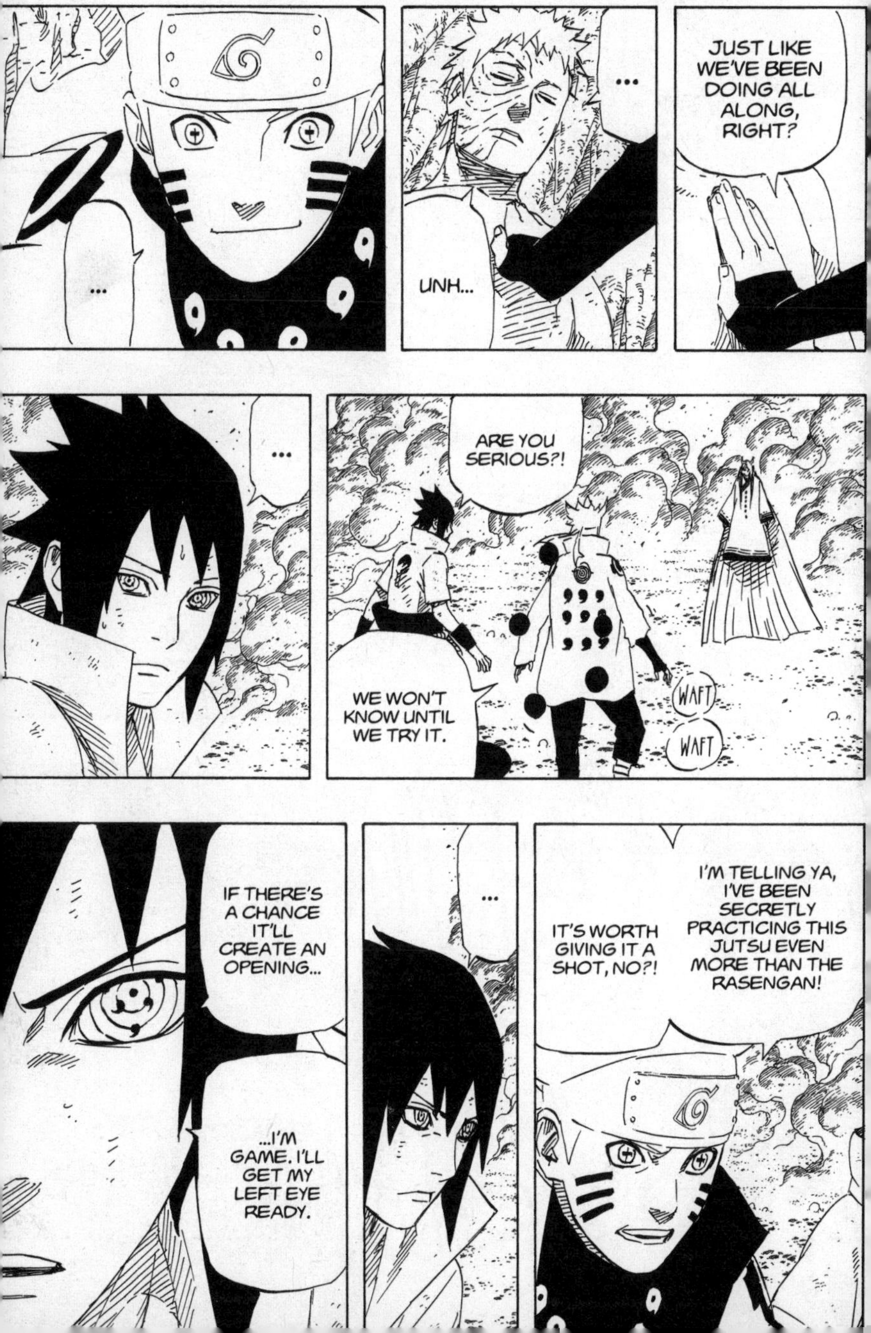
JUST LIKE WE'VE BEEN DOING ALL ALONG, RIGHT?
...
UNH...
...
ARE YOU SERIOUS?!
WE WON'T KNOW UNTIL WE TRY IT.
WAFT
WAFT
...
I'M TELLING YA, I'VE BEEN SECRETLY PRACTICING THIS JUTSU EVEN MORE THAN THE RASENGAN!
IT'S WORTH GIVING IT A SHOT, NO?!
...
IF THERE'S A CHANCE IT'LL CREATE AN OPENING...
...I'M GAME. I'LL GET MY LEFT EYE READY.

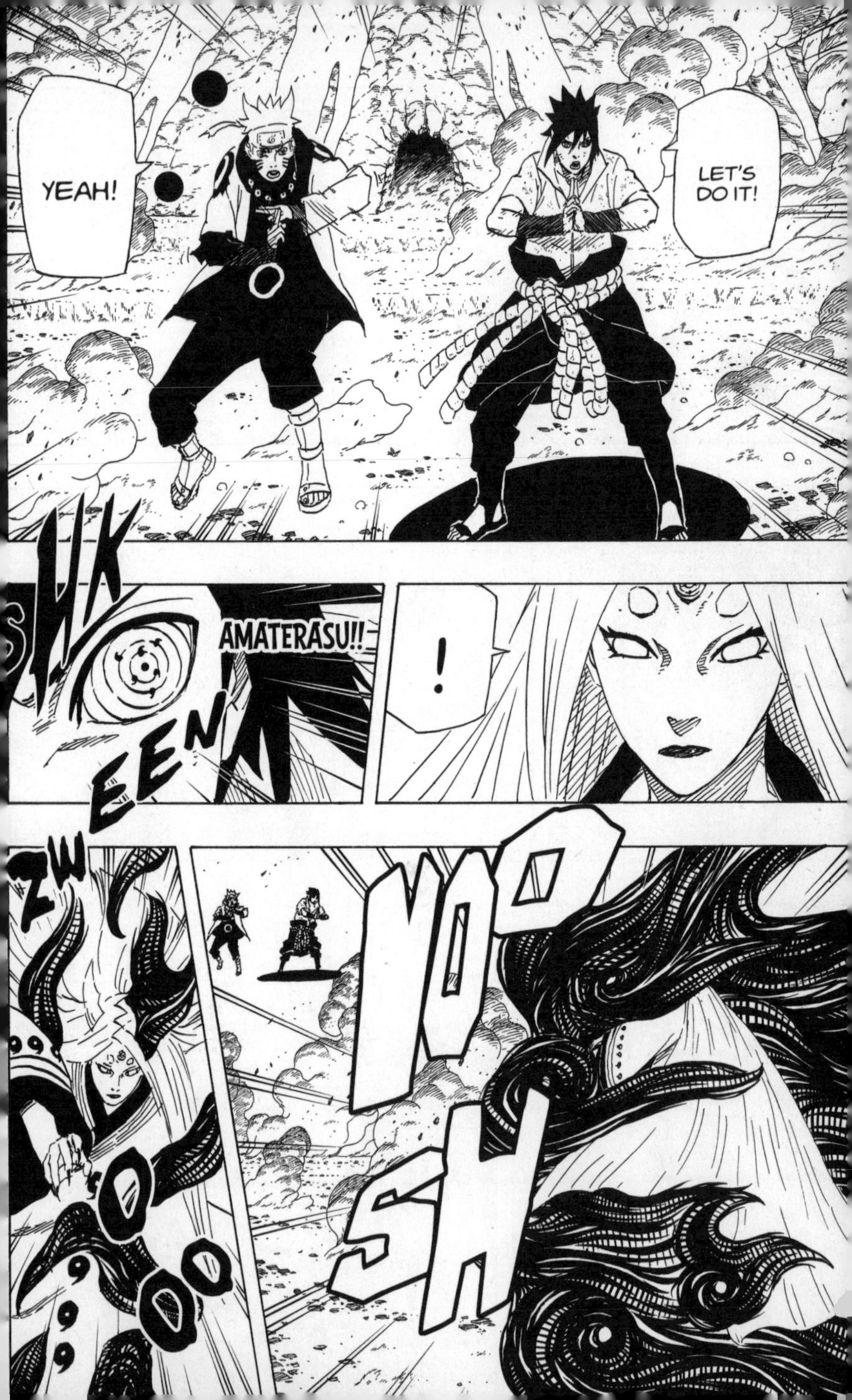
LET'S DO IT!
YEAH!
!
AMATERASU!!

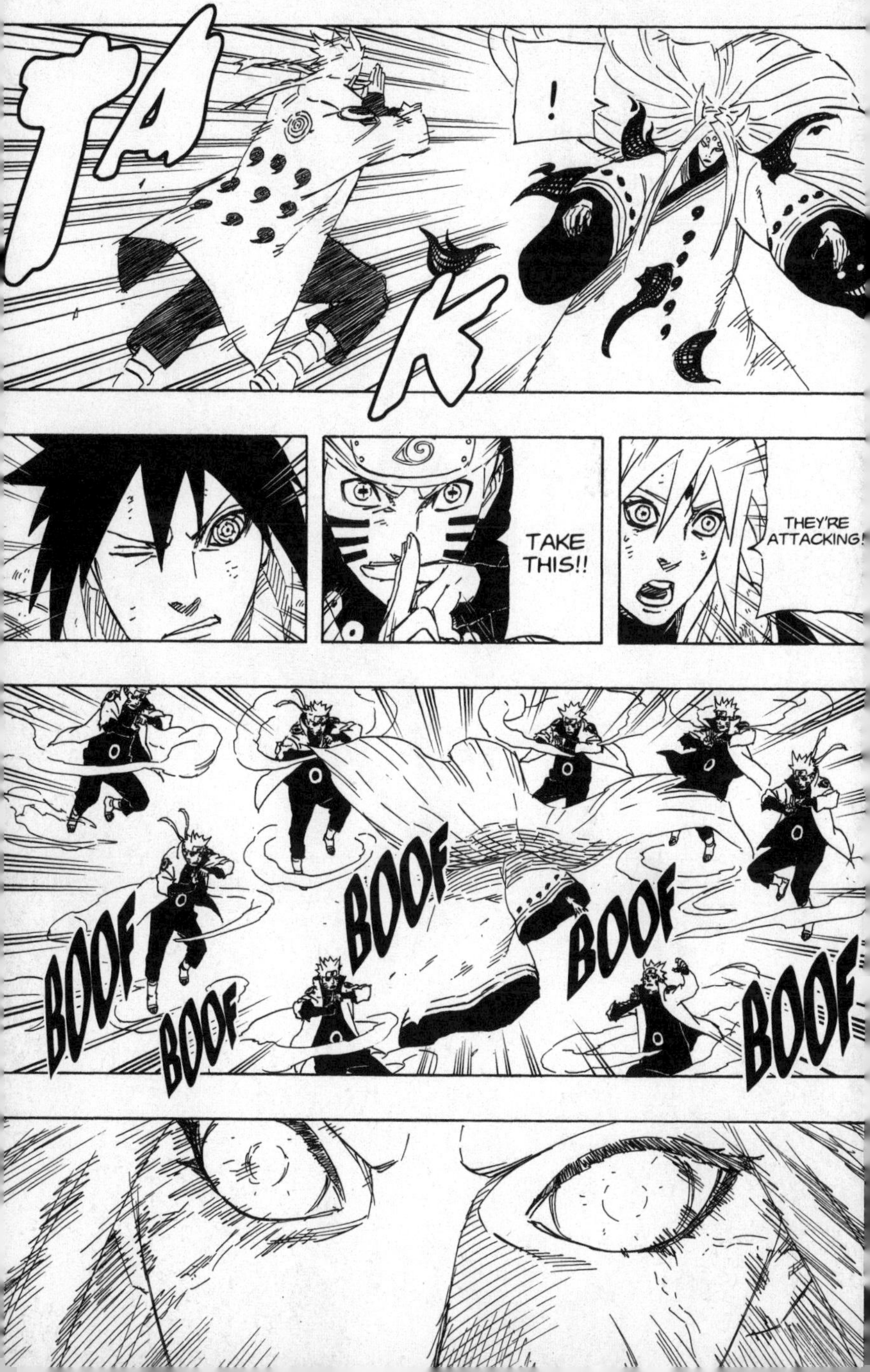
!
TA
K
THEY'RE ATTACKING!
TAKE THIS!!
BOOF
BOOF
BOOF
BOOF
BOOF
BOOF

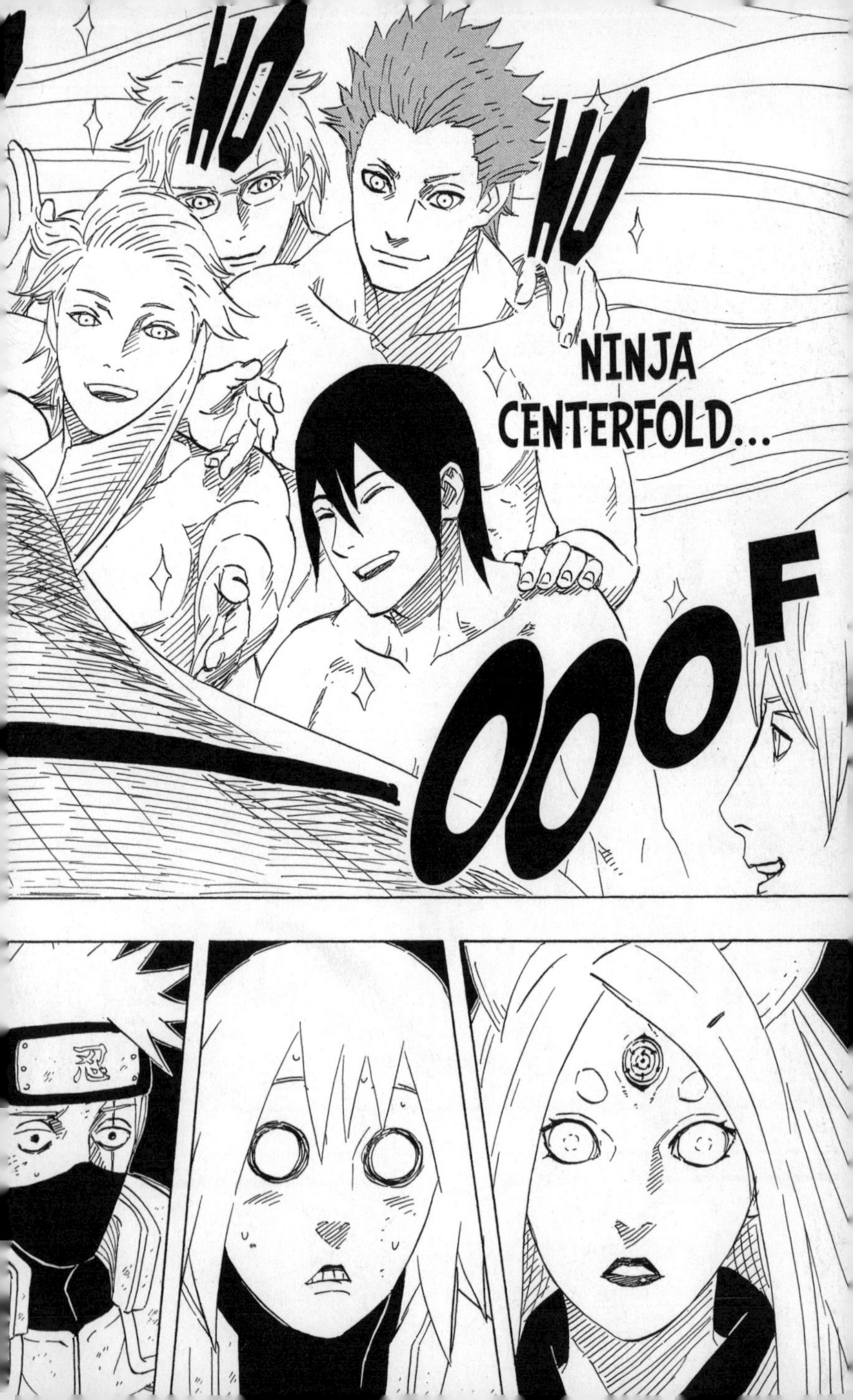
HO
HO
NINJA CENTERFOLD...
OOOF

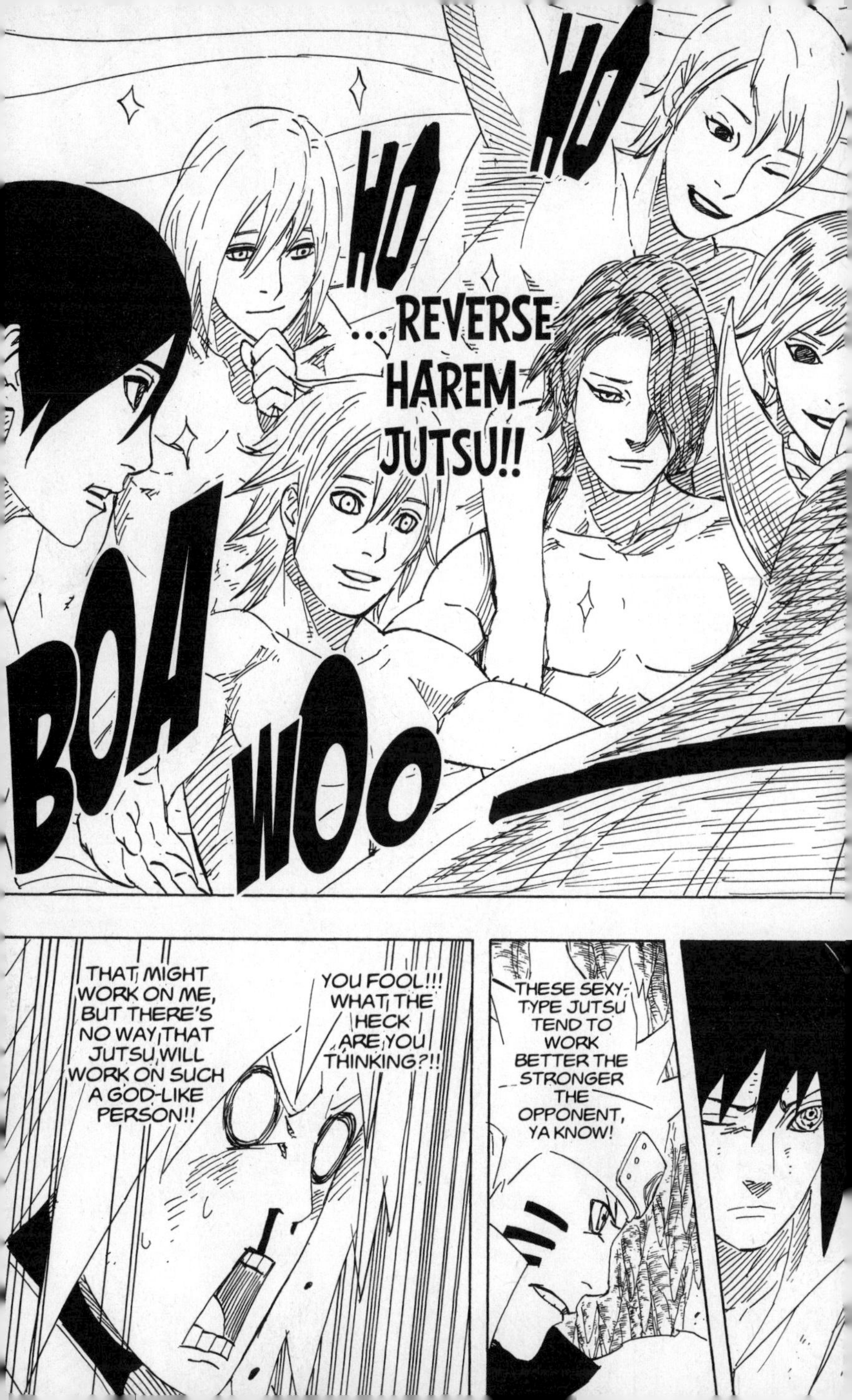
HO
HO
...REVERSE HAREM JUTSU!!
BOA
WOO
THESE SEXY-TYPE JUTSU TEND TO WORK BETTER THE STRONGER THE OPPONENT, YA KNOW!
YOU FOOL!!! WHAT THE HECK ARE YOU THINKING?!!
THAT MIGHT WORK ON ME, BUT THERE'S NO WAY THAT JUTSU WILL WORK ON SUCH A GOD-LIKE PERSON!!

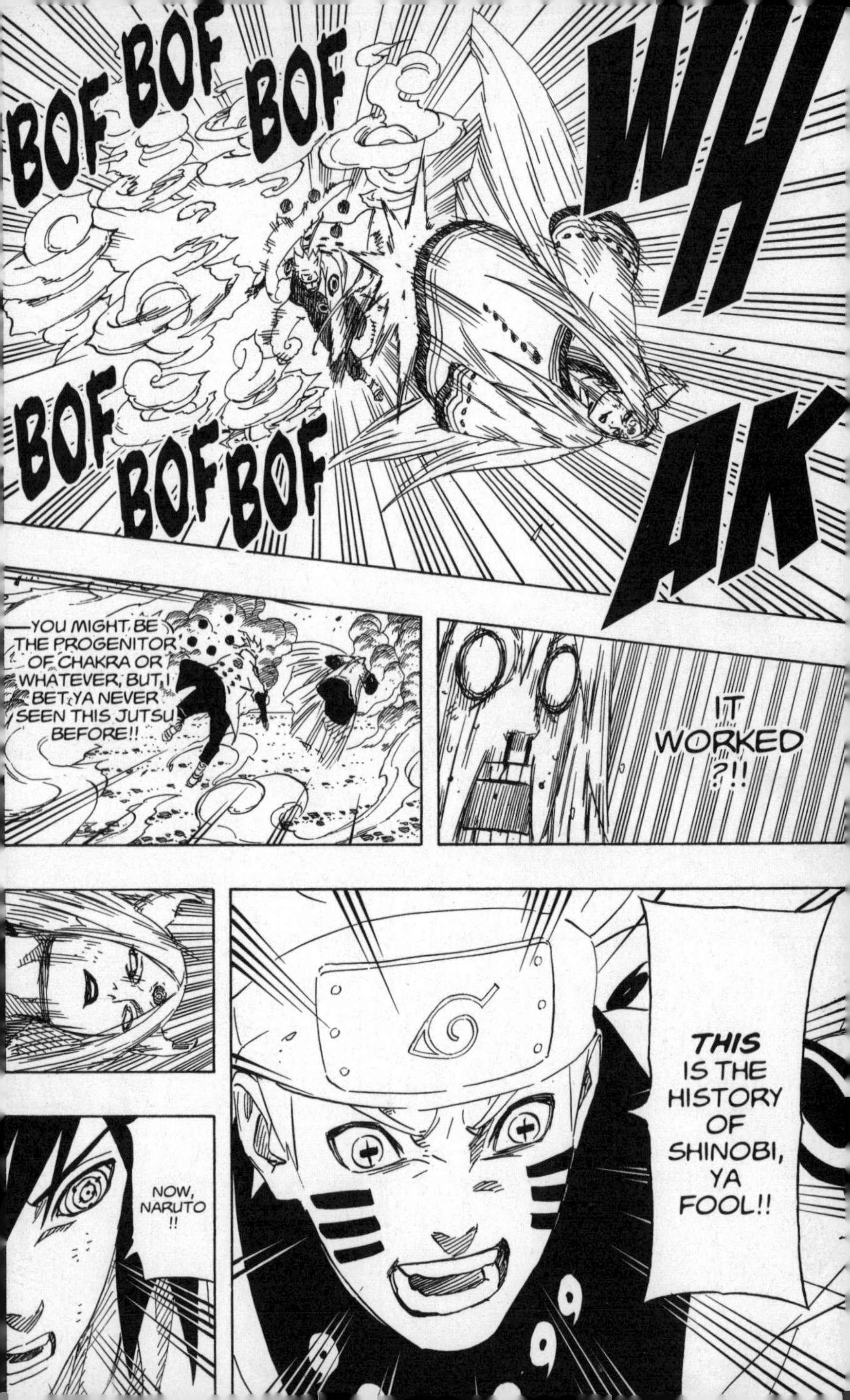
WHAK
BOF BOF BOF
BOF BOF BOF
IT WORKED ?!!
—YOU MIGHT BE THE PROGENITOR OF CHAKRA OR WHATEVER, BUT I BET YA NEVER SEEN THIS JUTSU BEFORE!!
THIS IS THE HISTORY OF SHINOBI, YA FOOL!!
NOW, NARUTO !!

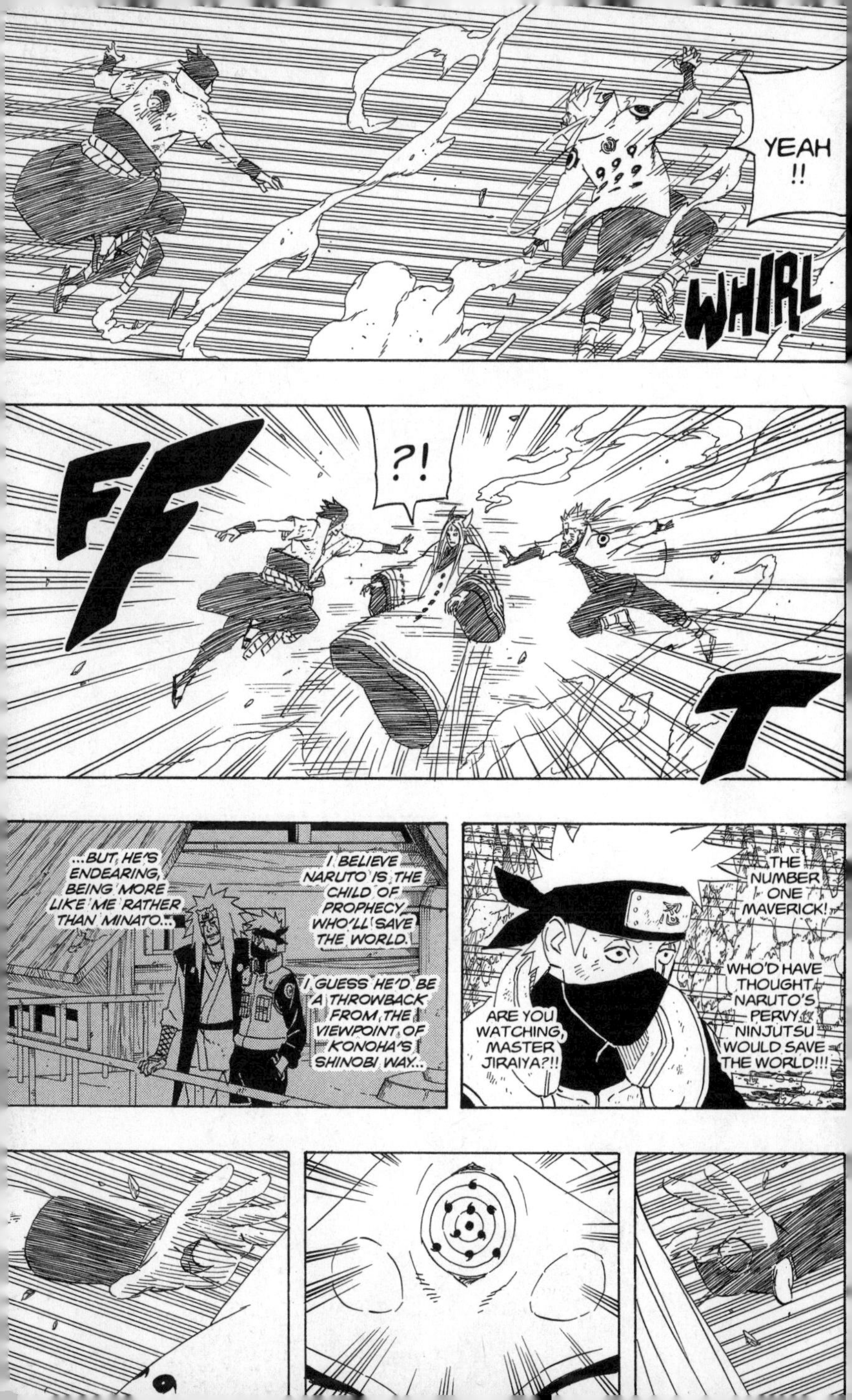

YEAH !!
WHIRL
?!
FF
T
THE NUMBER ONE MAVERICK!
WHO'D HAVE THOUGHT NARUTO'S PERVY NINJUTSU WOULD SAVE THE WORLD!!!
ARE YOU WATCHING, MASTER JIRAIYA?!!
I BELIEVE NARUTO IS THE CHILD OF PROPHECY WHO'LL SAVE THE WORLD.
I GUESS HE'D BE A THROWBACK FROM THE VIEWPOINT OF KONOHA'S SHINOBI WAY...
...BUT, HE'S ENDEARING, BEING MORE LIKE ME RATHER THAN MINATO...

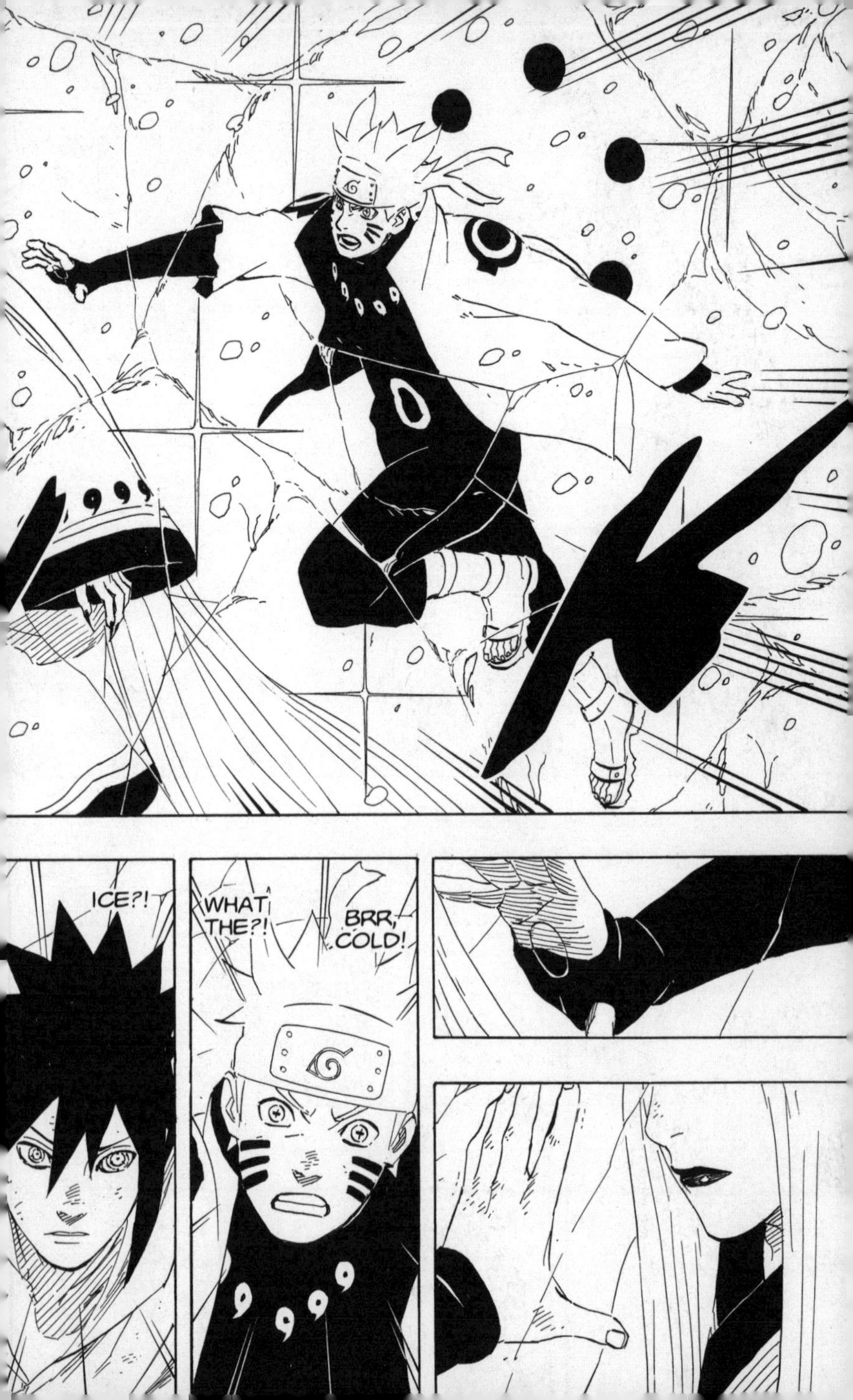
BRR, COLD!
WHAT THE?!
ICE?!

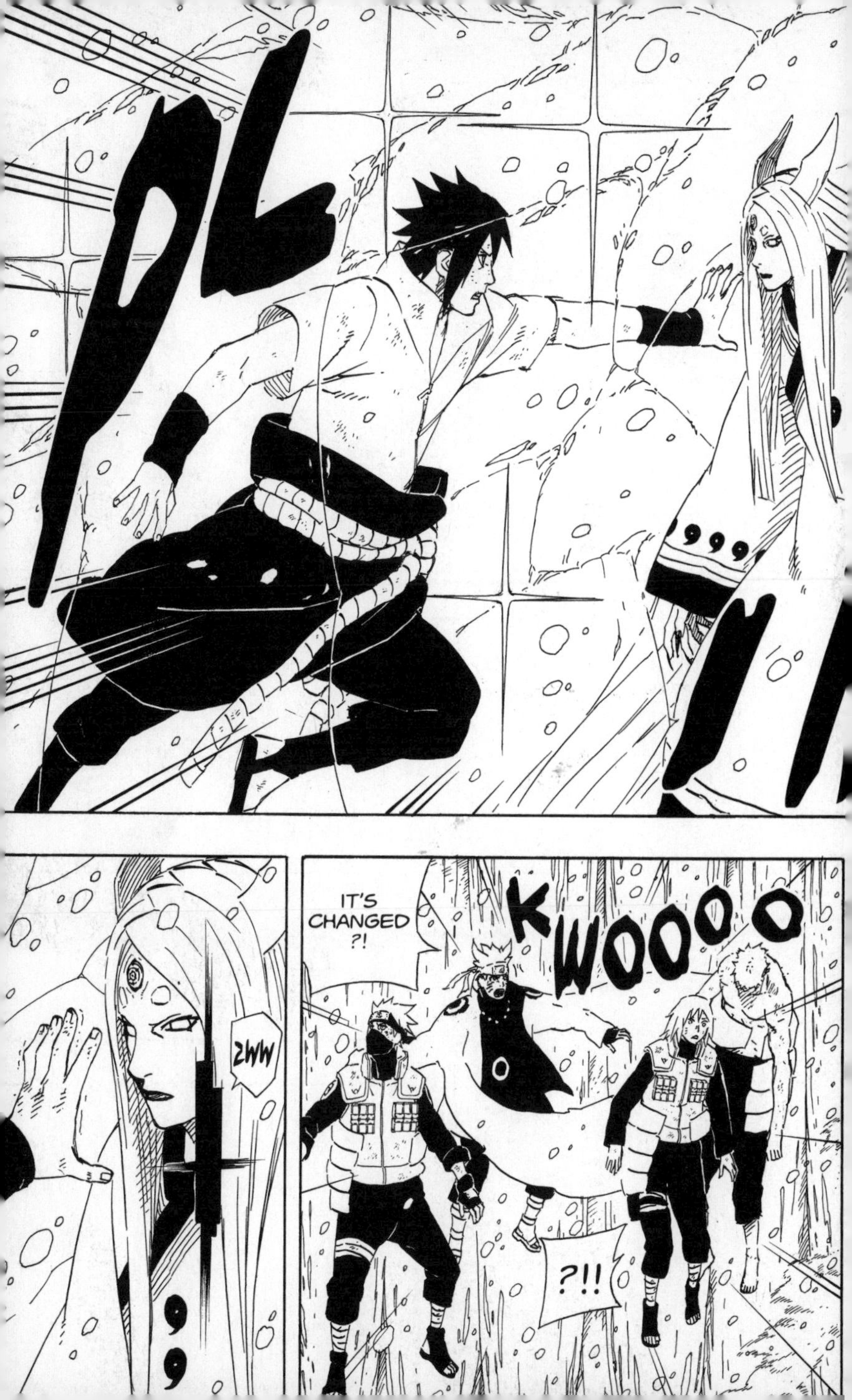

IT'S CHANGED ?!
KWOOOO
?!!

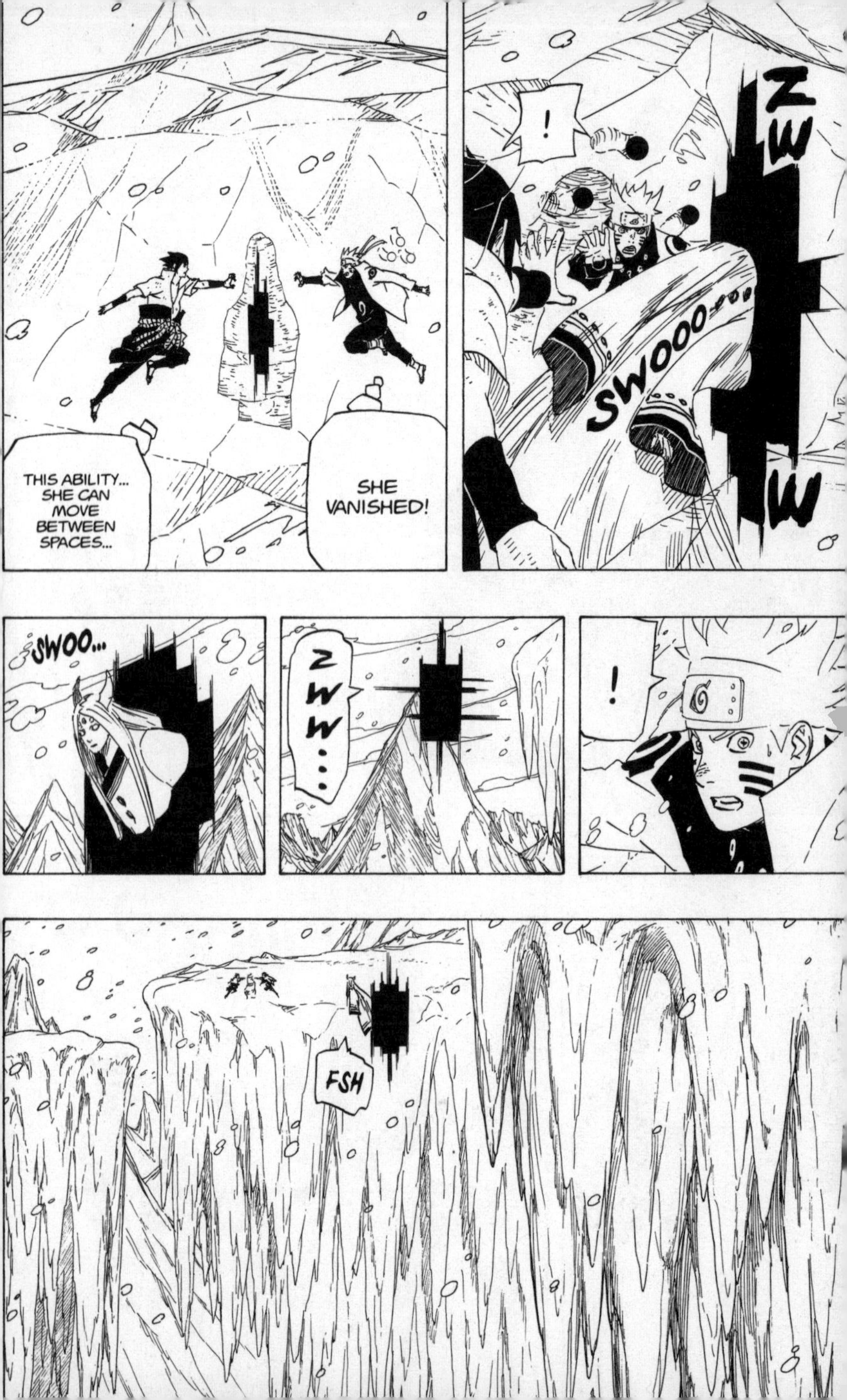
!
ZWW
SWOOO
SHE VANISHED!
THIS ABILITY... SHE CAN MOVE BETWEEN SPACES...
!
ZWW...
SWOO...
FSH

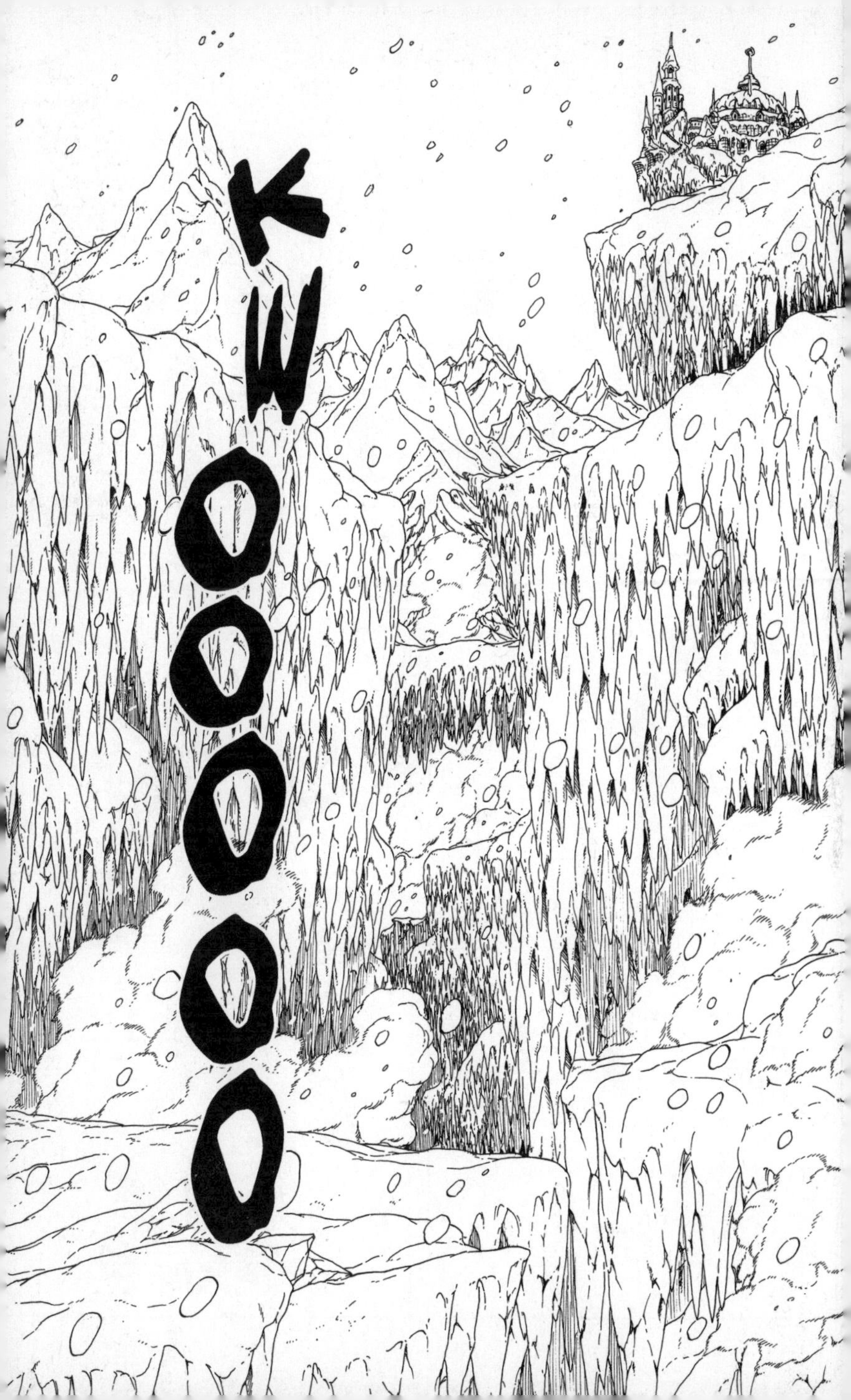
KWOOOOO

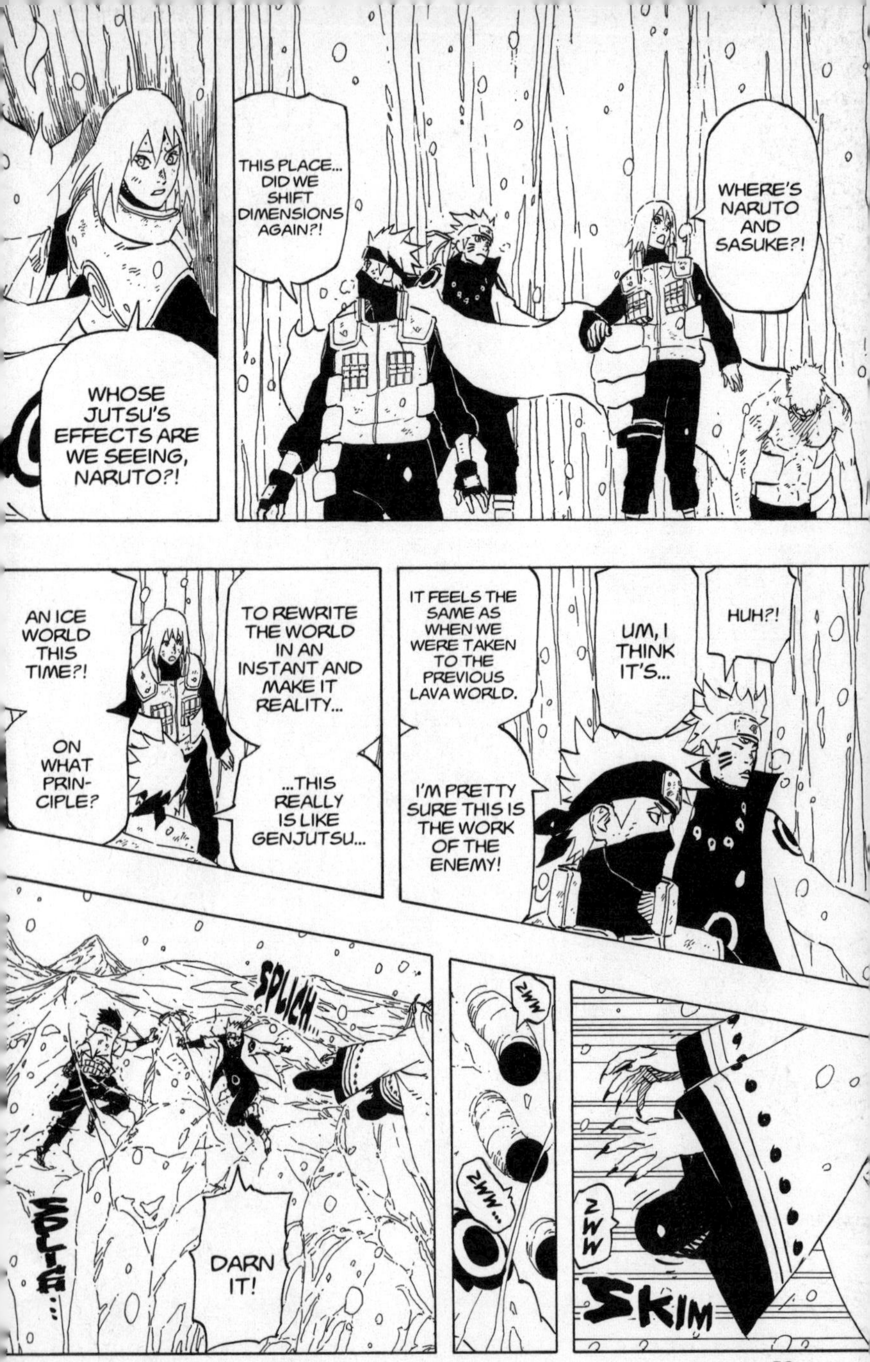
WHERE'S NARUTO AND SASUKE?!
THIS PLACE... DID WE SHIFT DIMENSIONS AGAIN?!
WHOSE JUTSU'S EFFECTS ARE WE SEEING, NARUTO?!
HUH?!
UM, I THINK IT'S...
IT FEELS THE SAME AS WHEN WE WERE TAKEN TO THE PREVIOUS LAVA WORLD.
I'M PRETTY SURE THIS IS THE WORK OF THE ENEMY!
TO REWRITE THE WORLD IN AN INSTANT AND MAKE IT REALITY...
...THIS REALLY IS LIKE GENJUTSU...
AN ICE WORLD THIS TIME?!
ON WHAT PRINCIPLE?
ZWW
SKIM
ZWW
ZWW...
SPLICH...
DARN IT!
SPLUG...

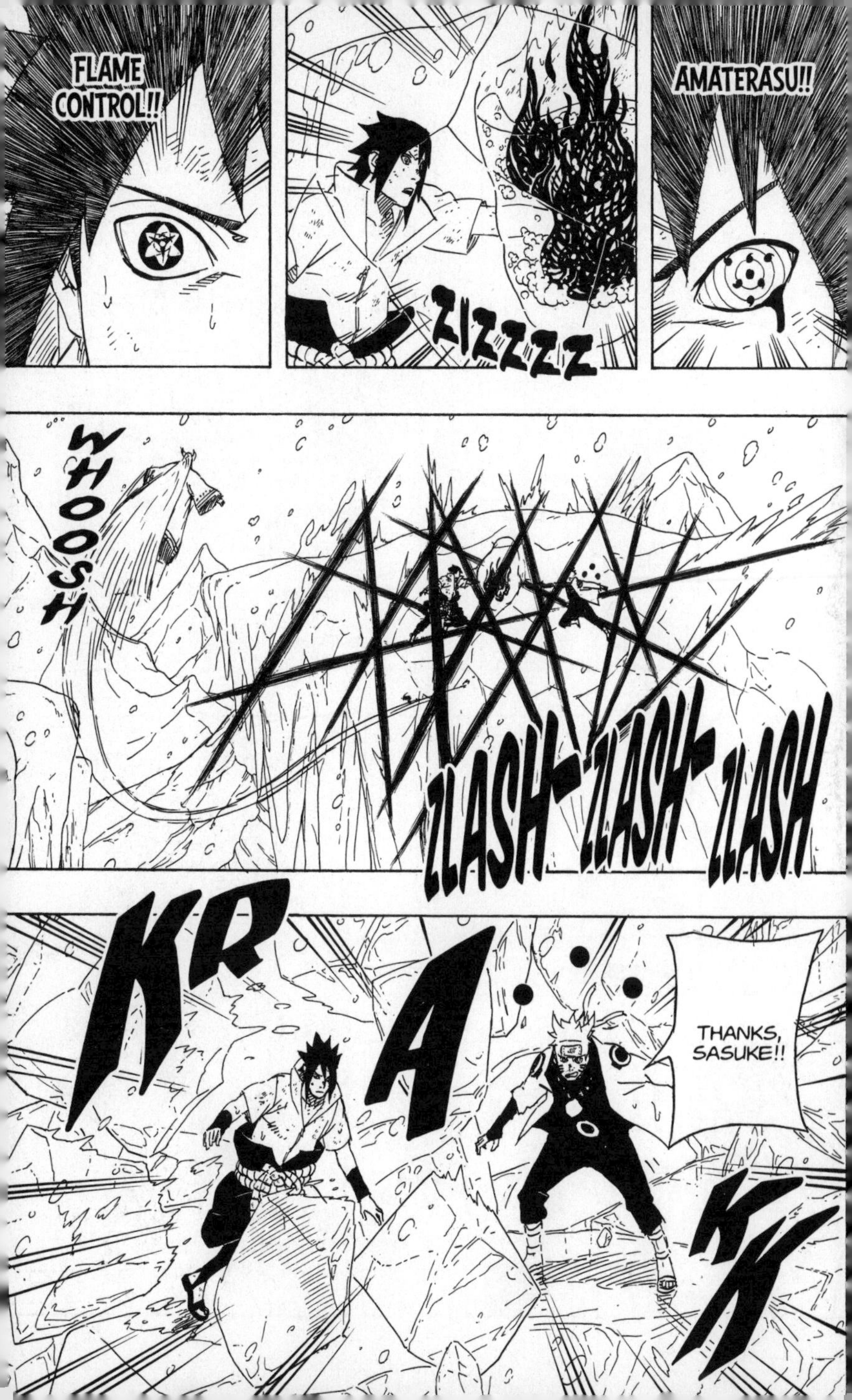
AMATERASU!!
ZIZZZZZ
FLAME CONTROL!!
WHOOSH
ZLASH ZLASH ZLASH
THANKS, SASUKE!!
KRAKK

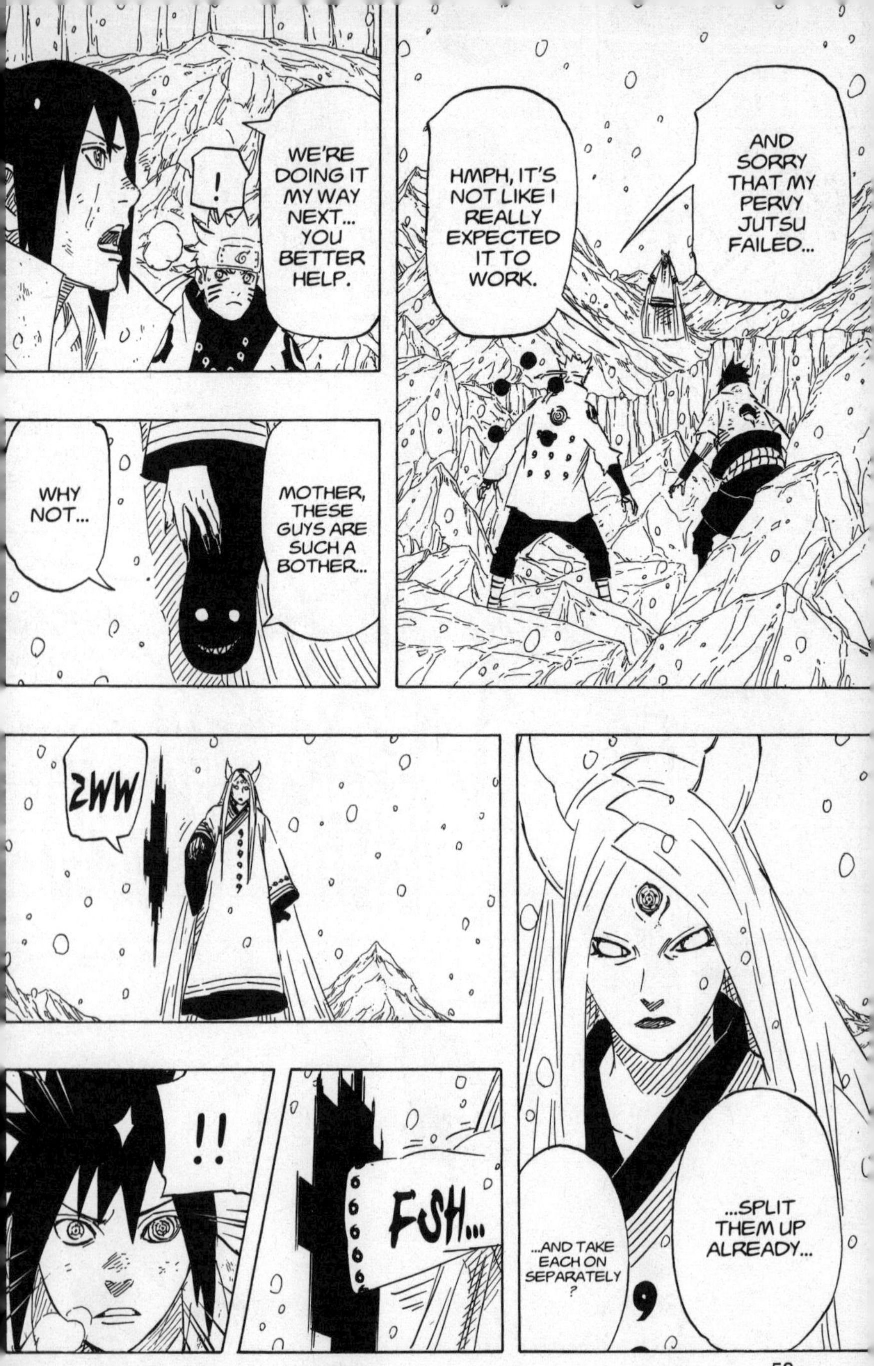
AND SORRY THAT MY PERVY JUTSU FAILED...
HMPH, IT'S NOT LIKE I REALLY EXPECTED IT TO WORK.
WE'RE DOING IT MY WAY NEXT... YOU BETTER HELP.
!
MOTHER, THESE GUYS ARE SUCH A BOTHER...
WHY NOT...
...SPLIT THEM UP ALREADY...
...AND TAKE EACH ON SEPARATELY?
ZWW
FSH...
!!

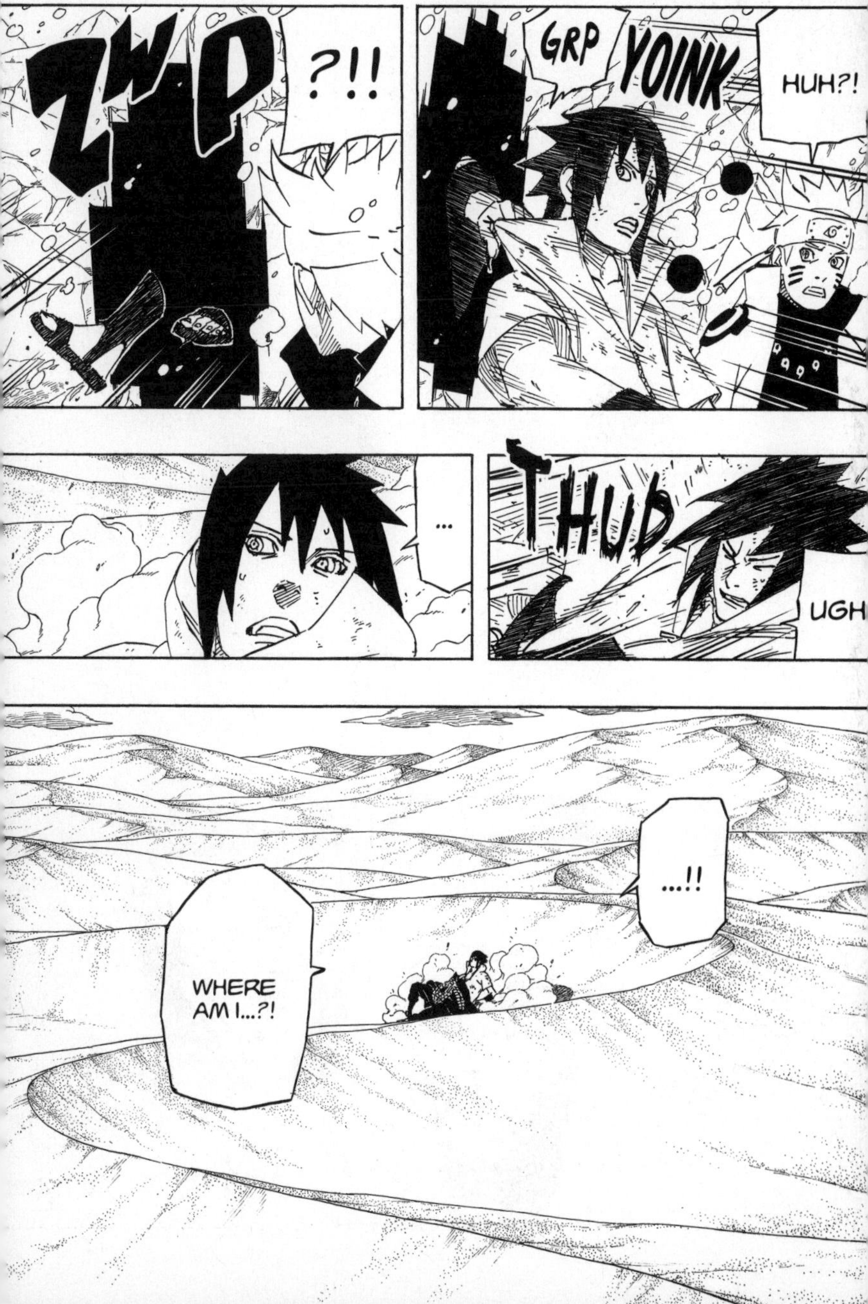
GRP
YOINK
HUH?!
ZWP
?!!
THUD
UGH
...
...!!
WHERE AM I...?!

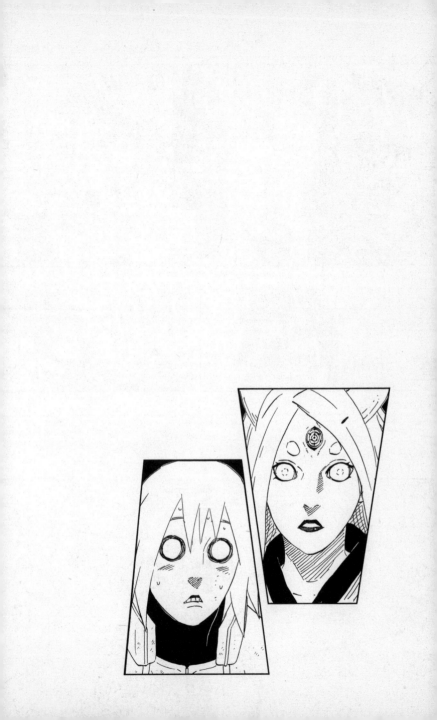

Number 683: I Dreamt the Same Dream

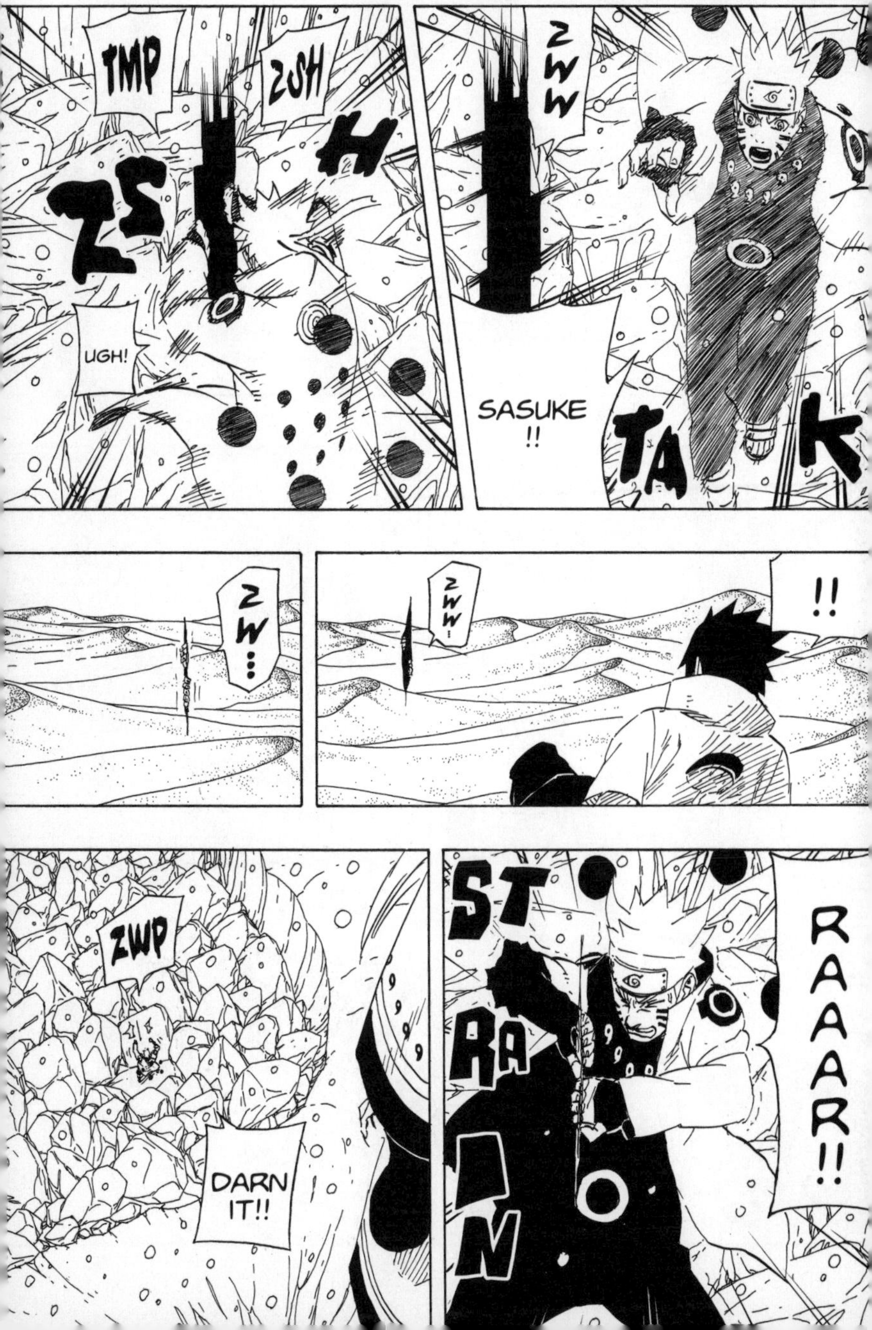

ZWW
SASUKE!!
TAK
TMP
ZSH
ZSH
UGH!
!!
ZWW...
ZW...
RAAAR!!
STRAIN
ZWP
DARN IT!!

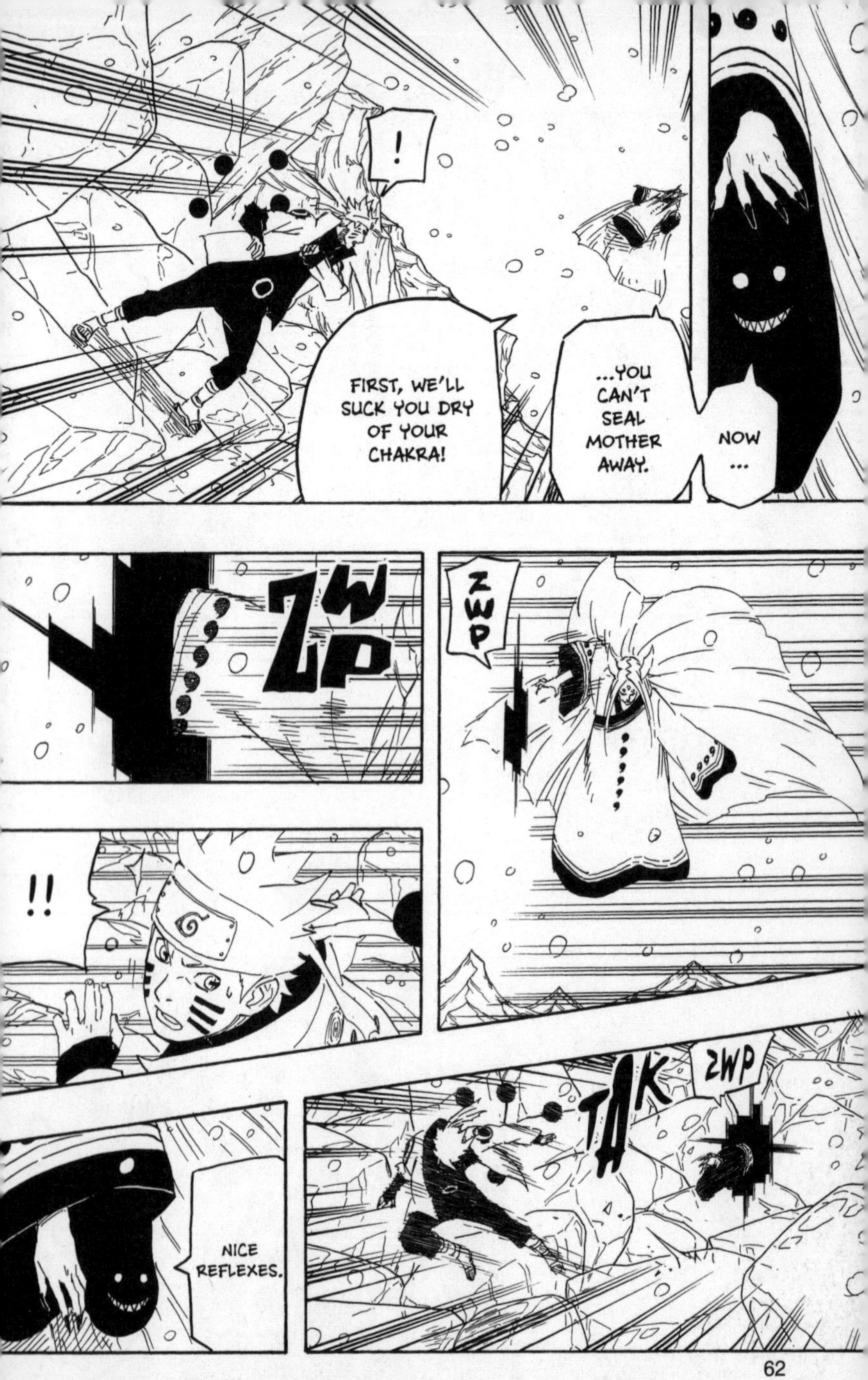
NOW ...
...YOU CAN'T SEAL MOTHER AWAY.
!
FIRST, WE'LL SUCK YOU DRY OF YOUR CHAKRA!
ZWP
ZWP
!!
ZWP
TAK
NICE REFLEXES.

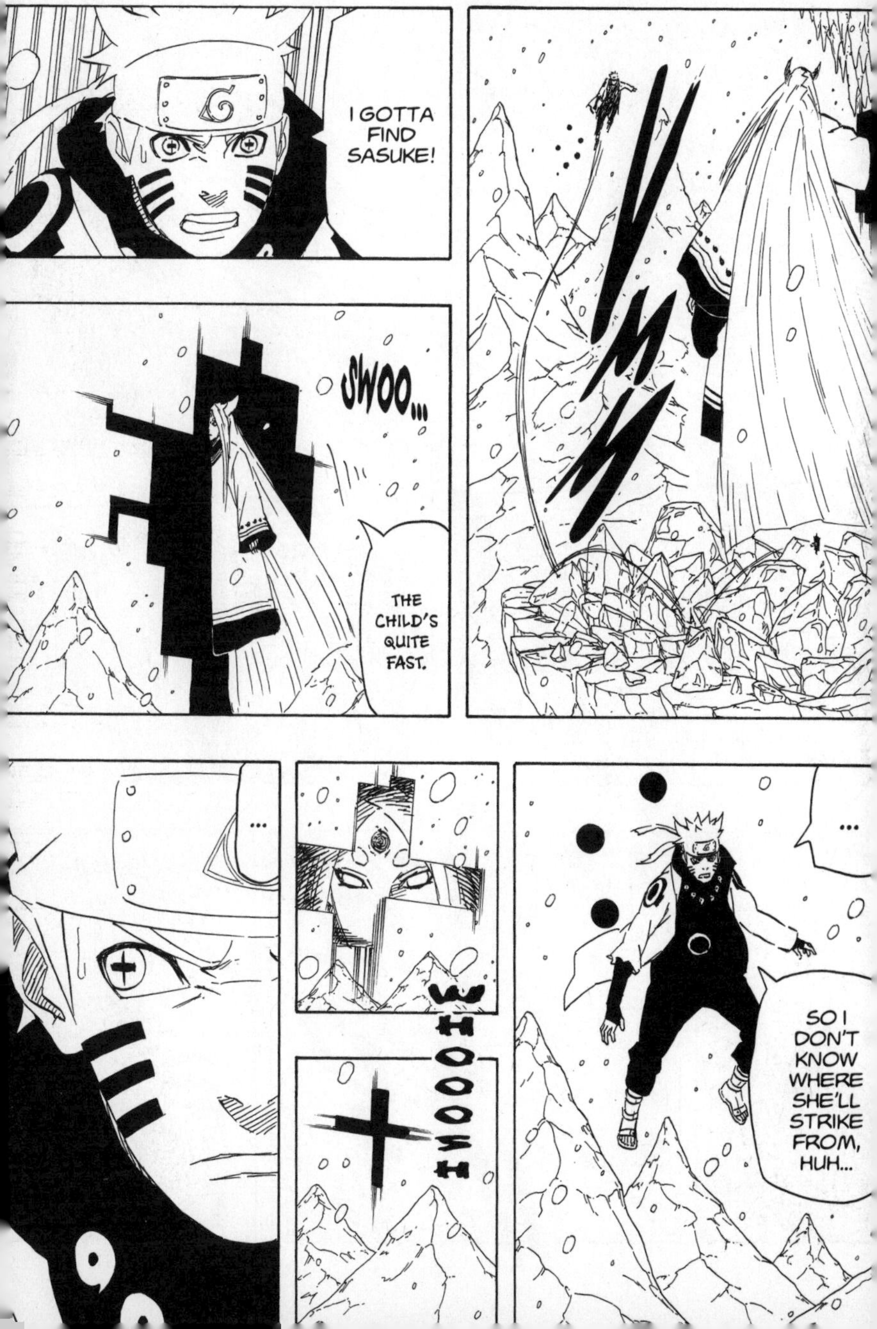
I GOTTA FIND SASUKE!
SWOO...
THE CHILD'S QUITE FAST.
...
SO I DON'T KNOW WHERE SHE'LL STRIKE FROM, HUH...
WHOOOOSH
...

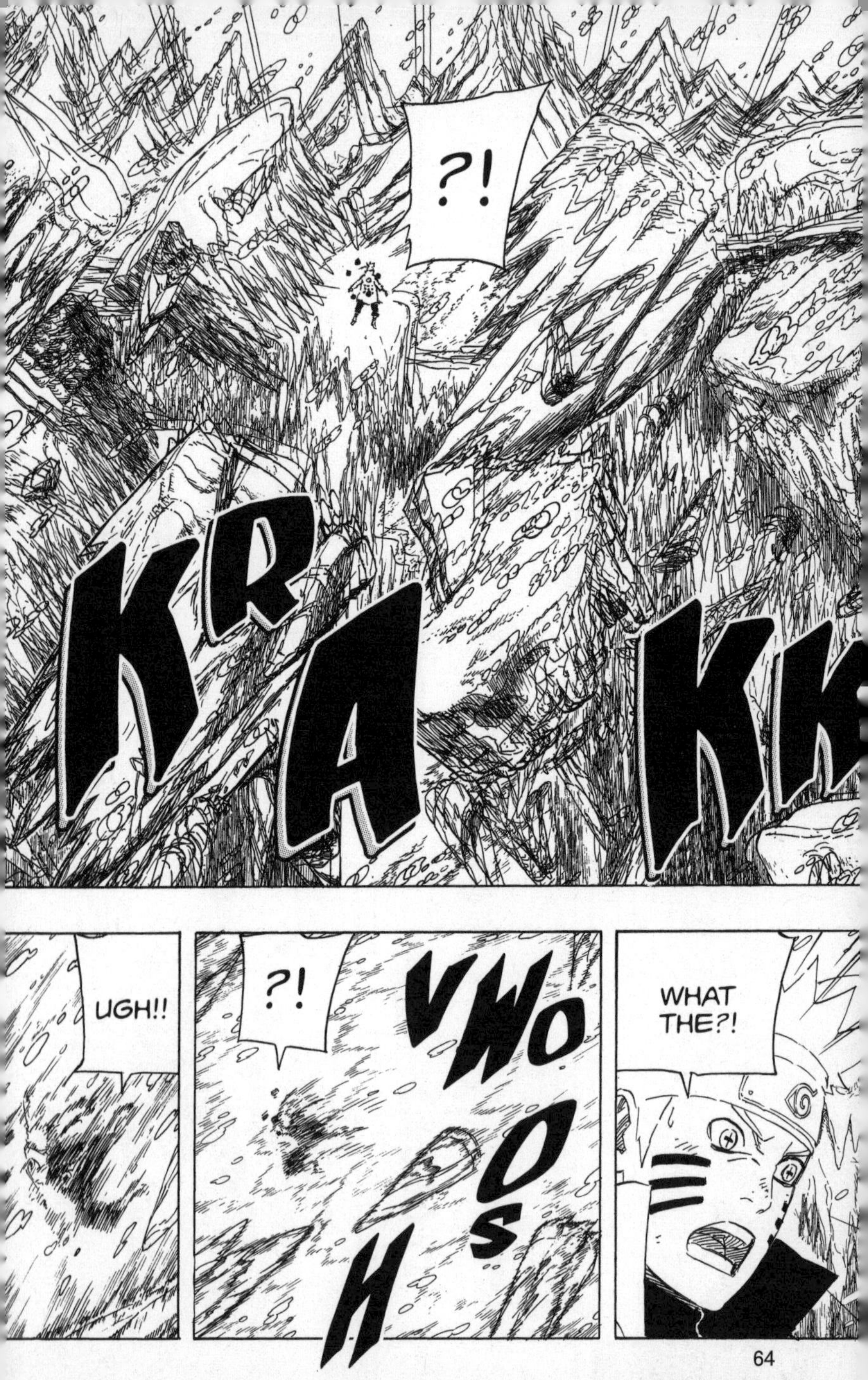
?!
KRAKK
WHAT THE?!
?!
WHOOSH
UGH!!

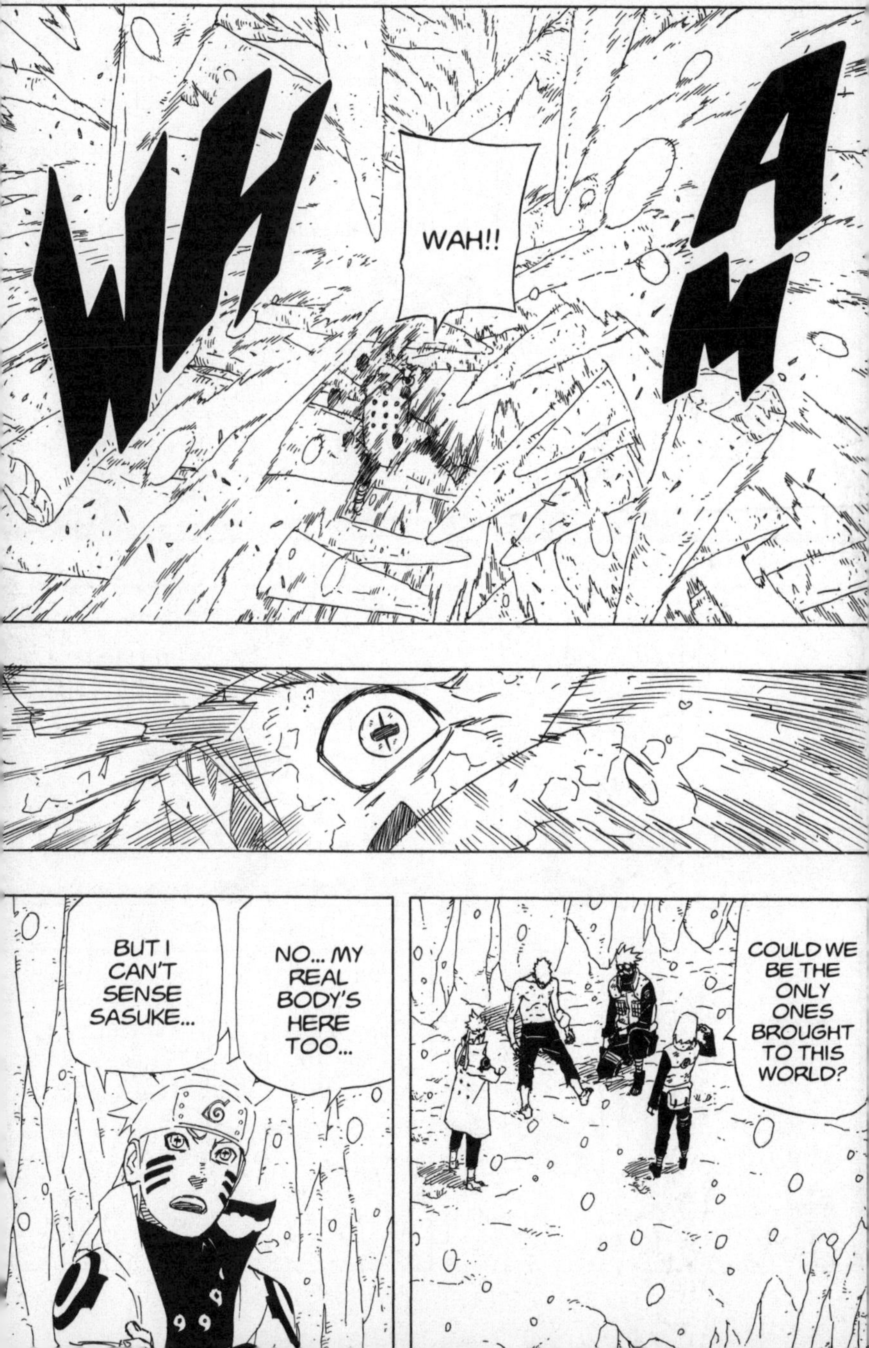
WHAM
WAH!!
COULD WE BE THE ONLY ONES BROUGHT TO THIS WORLD?
NO... MY REAL BODY'S HERE TOO...
BUT I CAN'T SENSE SASUKE...

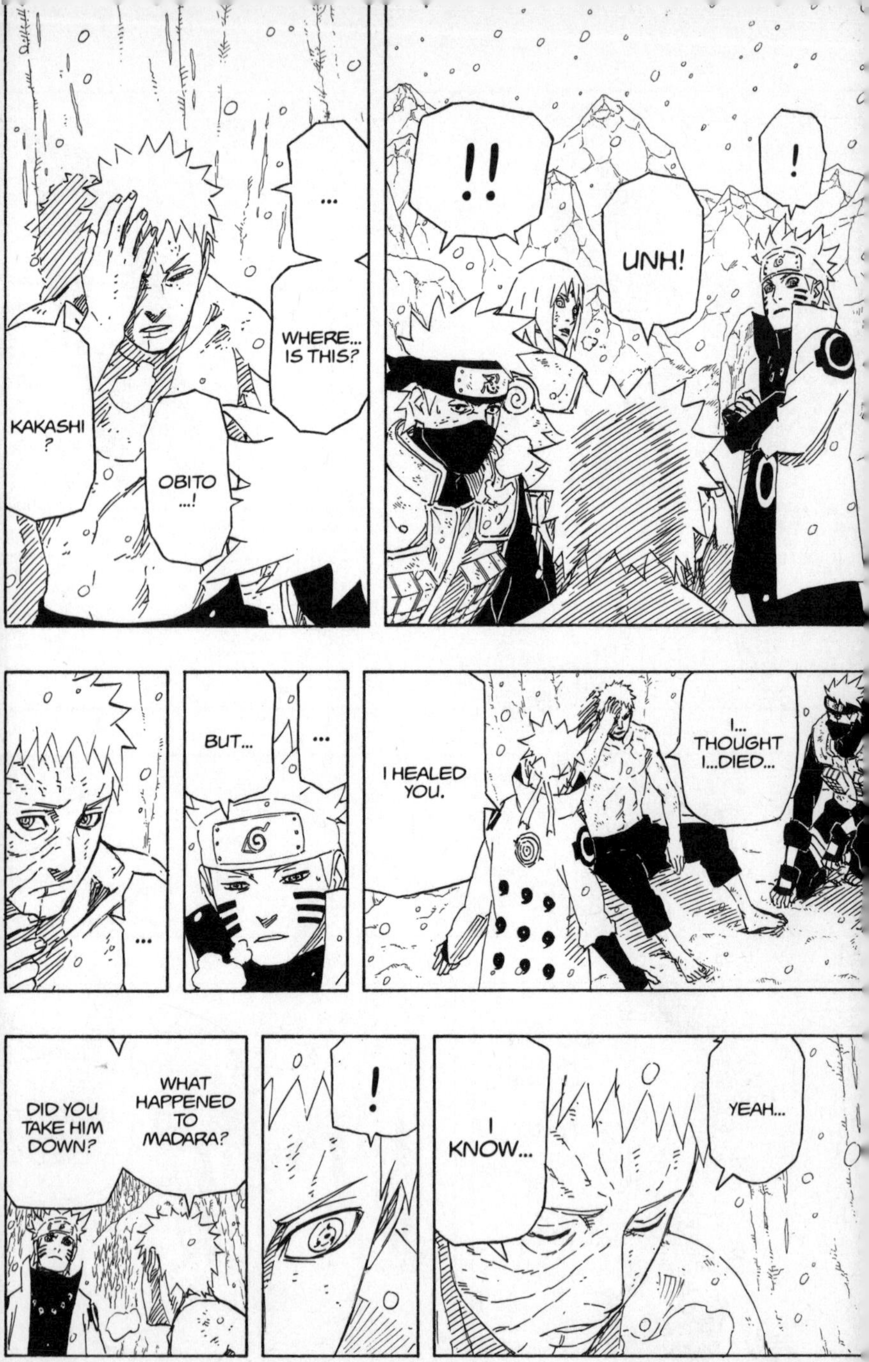
!
UNH!
!!
...
WHERE... IS THIS?
OBITO ...!
KAKASHI ?
I... THOUGHT I...DIED...
I HEALED YOU.
...
BUT...
...
YEAH...
I KNOW...
!
WHAT HAPPENED TO MADARA?
DID YOU TAKE HIM DOWN?

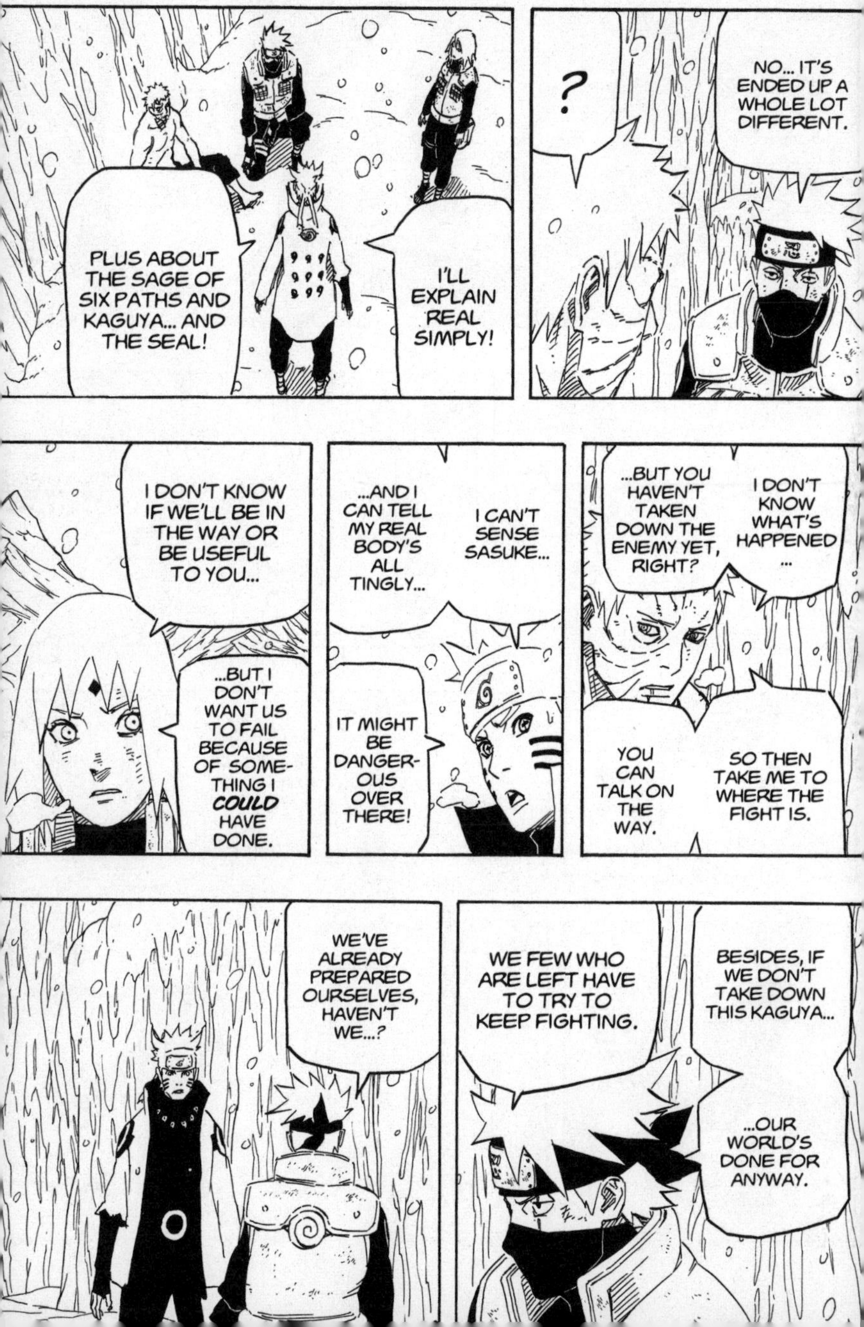

NO... IT'S ENDED UP A WHOLE LOT DIFFERENT.
?
I'LL EXPLAIN REAL SIMPLY!
PLUS ABOUT THE SAGE OF SIX PATHS AND KAGUYA... AND THE SEAL!
I DON'T KNOW WHAT'S HAPPENED ...
...BUT YOU HAVEN'T TAKEN DOWN THE ENEMY YET, RIGHT?
SO THEN TAKE ME TO WHERE THE FIGHT IS.
YOU CAN TALK ON THE WAY.
I CAN'T SENSE SASUKE...
...AND I CAN TELL MY REAL BODY'S ALL TINGLY...
IT MIGHT BE DANGEROUS OVER THERE!
I DON'T KNOW IF WE'LL BE IN THE WAY OR BE USEFUL TO YOU...
...BUT I DON'T WANT US TO FAIL BECAUSE OF SOMETHING I **COULD** HAVE DONE.
BESIDES, IF WE DON'T TAKE DOWN THIS KAGUYA...
...OUR WORLD'S DONE FOR ANYWAY.
WE FEW WHO ARE LEFT HAVE TO TRY TO KEEP FIGHTING.
WE'VE ALREADY PREPARED OURSELVES, HAVEN'T WE...?

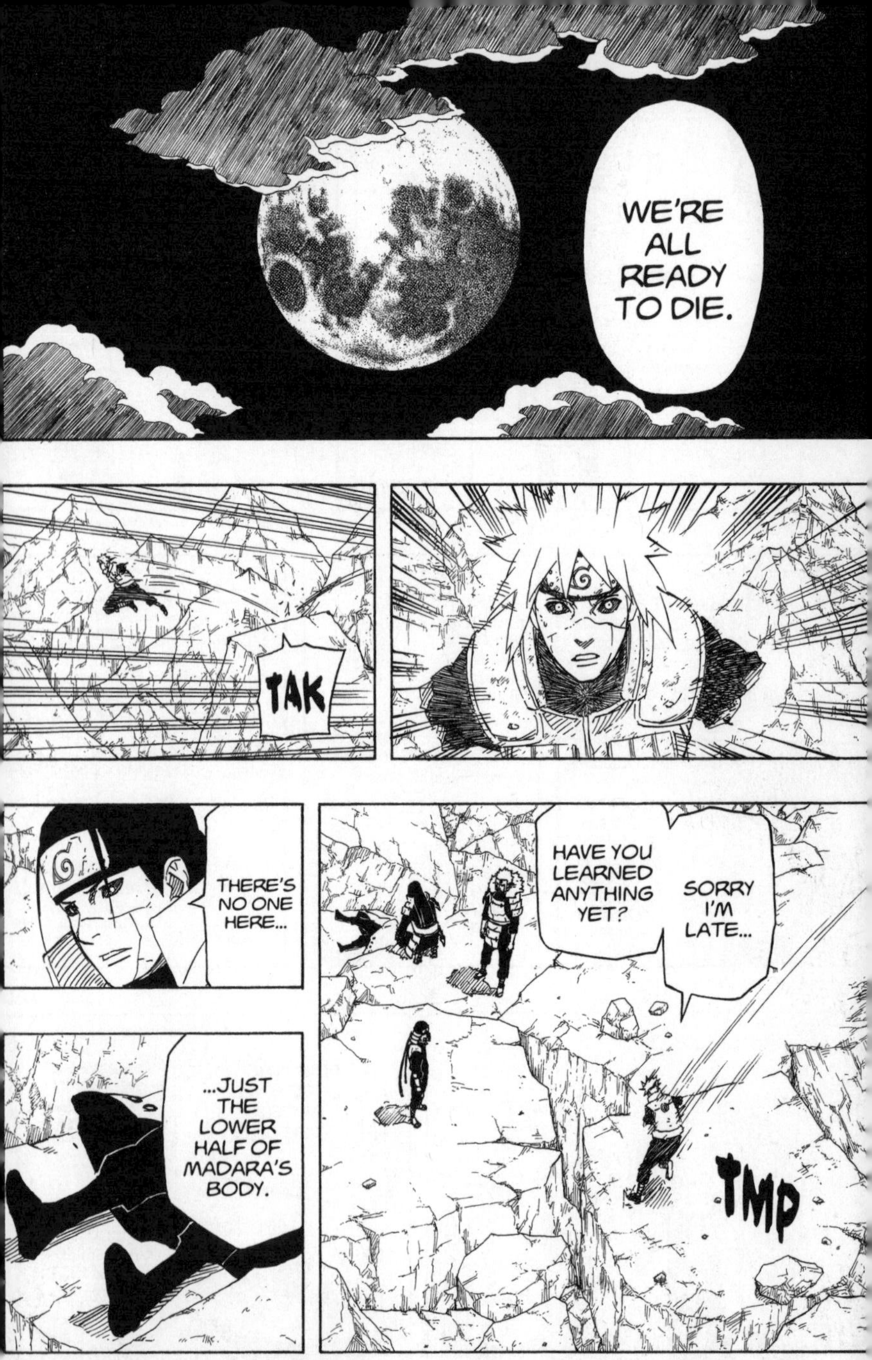
WE'RE ALL READY TO DIE.
TAK
SORRY I'M LATE...
HAVE YOU LEARNED ANYTHING YET?
TMP
THERE'S NO ONE HERE...
...JUST THE LOWER HALF OF MADARA'S BODY.

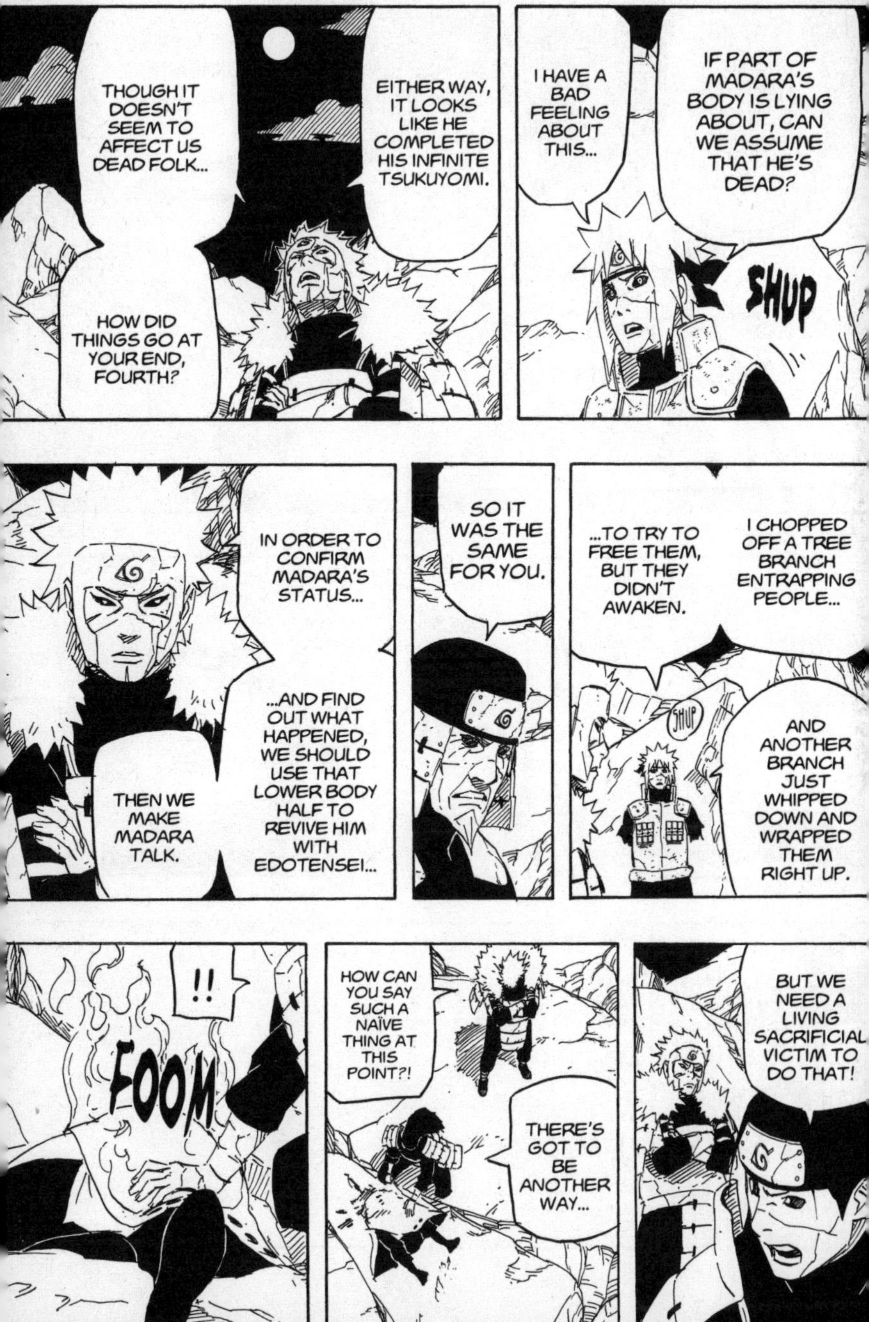
IF PART OF MADARA'S BODY IS LYING ABOUT, CAN WE ASSUME THAT HE'S DEAD?
SHUP
I HAVE A BAD FEELING ABOUT THIS...
EITHER WAY, IT LOOKS LIKE HE COMPLETED HIS INFINITE TSUKUYOMI.
THOUGH IT DOESN'T SEEM TO AFFECT US DEAD FOLK...
HOW DID THINGS GO AT YOUR END, FOURTH?
I CHOPPED OFF A TREE BRANCH ENTRAPPING PEOPLE...
...TO TRY TO FREE THEM, BUT THEY DIDN'T AWAKEN.
SHUP
AND ANOTHER BRANCH JUST WHIPPED DOWN AND WRAPPED THEM RIGHT UP.
SO IT WAS THE SAME FOR YOU.
IN ORDER TO CONFIRM MADARA'S STATUS...
...AND FIND OUT WHAT HAPPENED, WE SHOULD USE THAT LOWER BODY HALF TO REVIVE HIM WITH EDOTENSEI...
THEN WE MAKE MADARA TALK.
BUT WE NEED A LIVING SACRIFICIAL VICTIM TO DO THAT!
HOW CAN YOU SAY SUCH A NAÏVE THING AT THIS POINT?!
THERE'S GOT TO BE ANOTHER WAY...
!!
FOOM

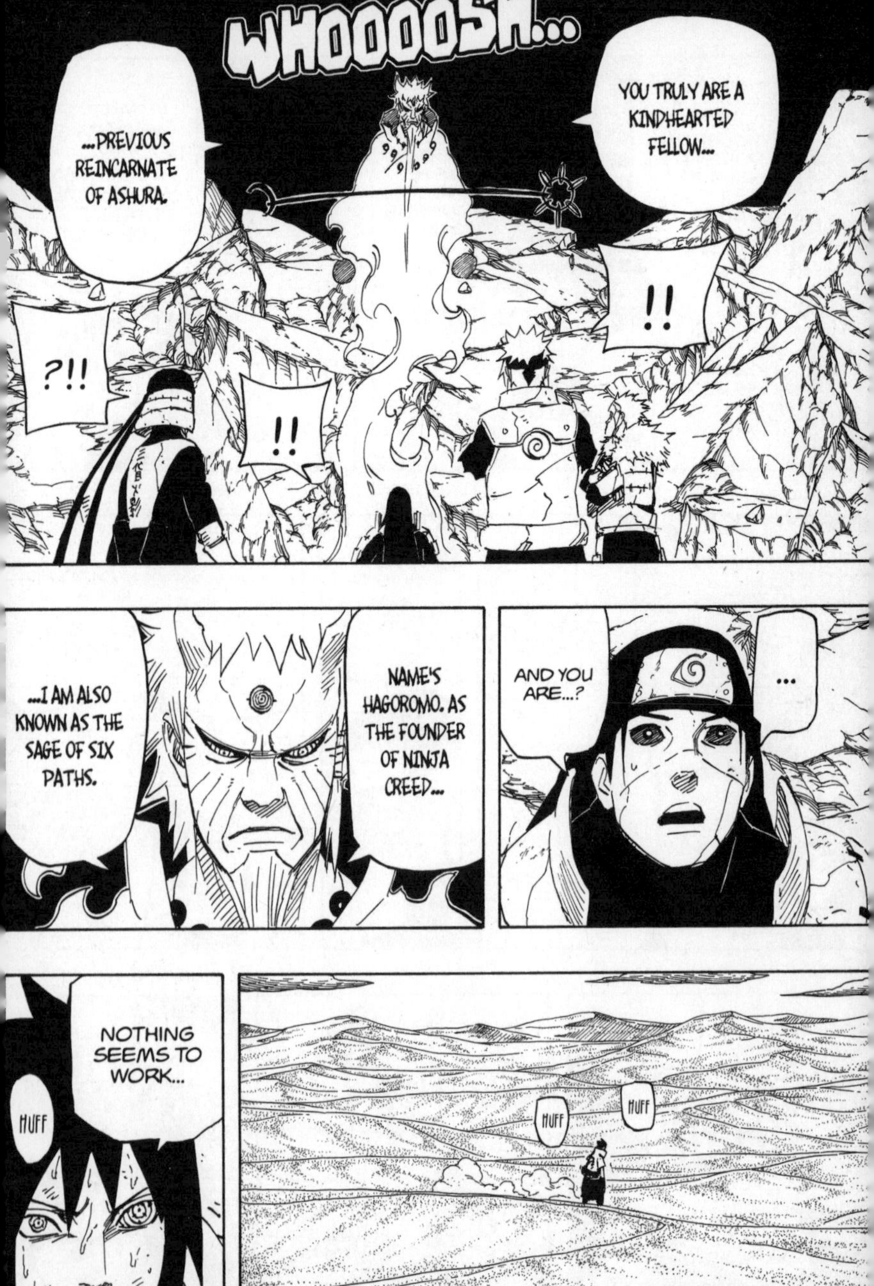
WHOOOOSH...
YOU TRULY ARE A KINDHEARTED FELLOW...
...PREVIOUS REINCARNATE OF ASHURA.
!!
!!
?!!
...
AND YOU ARE...?
NAME'S HAGOROMO. AS THE FOUNDER OF NINJA CREED...
...I AM ALSO KNOWN AS THE SAGE OF SIX PATHS.
HUFF
HUFF
NOTHING SEEMS TO WORK...
HUFF

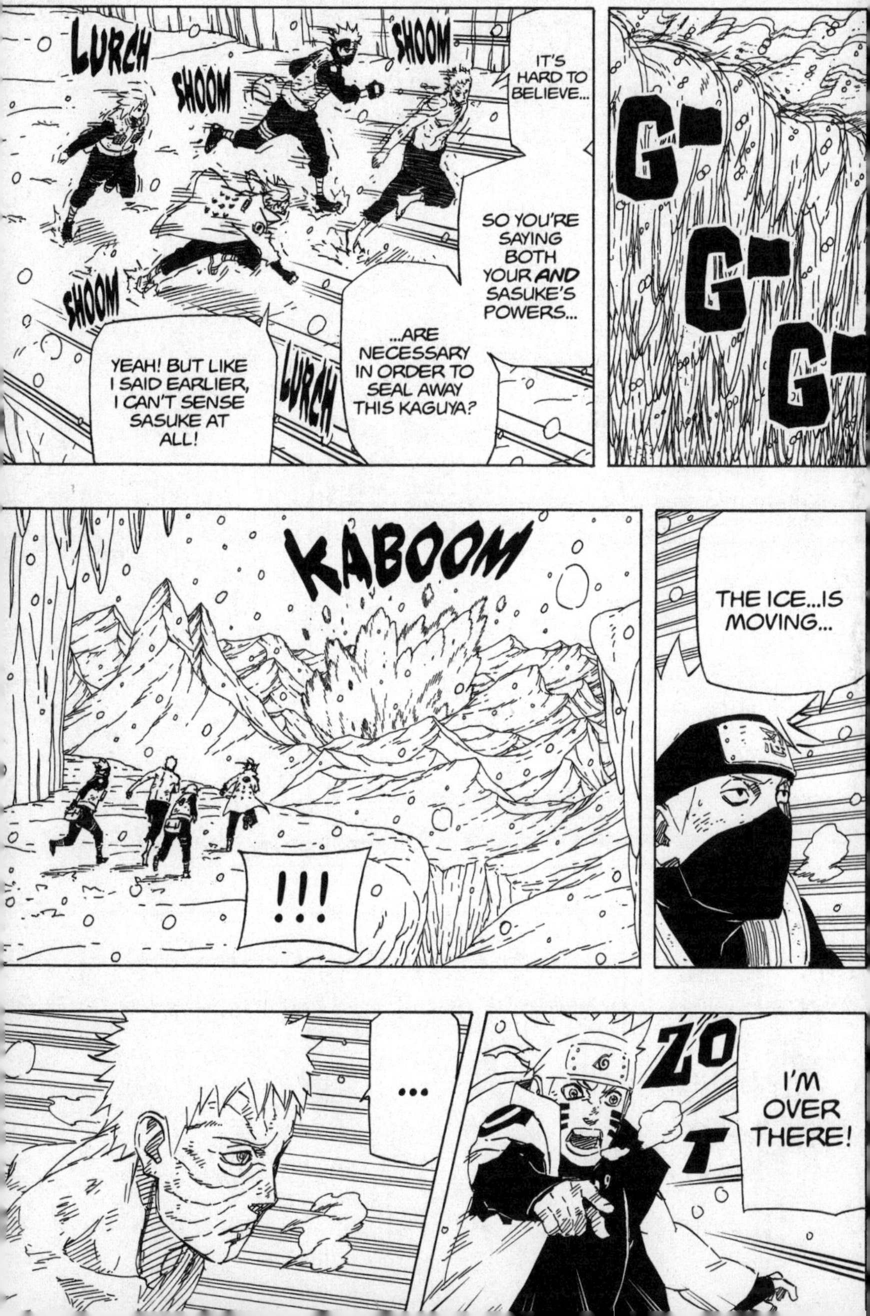
G-
G-
G-
IT'S HARD TO BELIEVE...
SO YOU'RE SAYING BOTH YOUR *AND* SASUKE'S POWERS...
SHOOM
...ARE NECESSARY IN ORDER TO SEAL AWAY THIS KAGUYA?
SHOOM
LURCH
YEAH! BUT LIKE I SAID EARLIER, I CAN'T SENSE SASUKE AT ALL!
LURCH
SHOOM
THE ICE...IS MOVING...
KABOOM
!!!
I'M OVER THERE!
ZOT
...

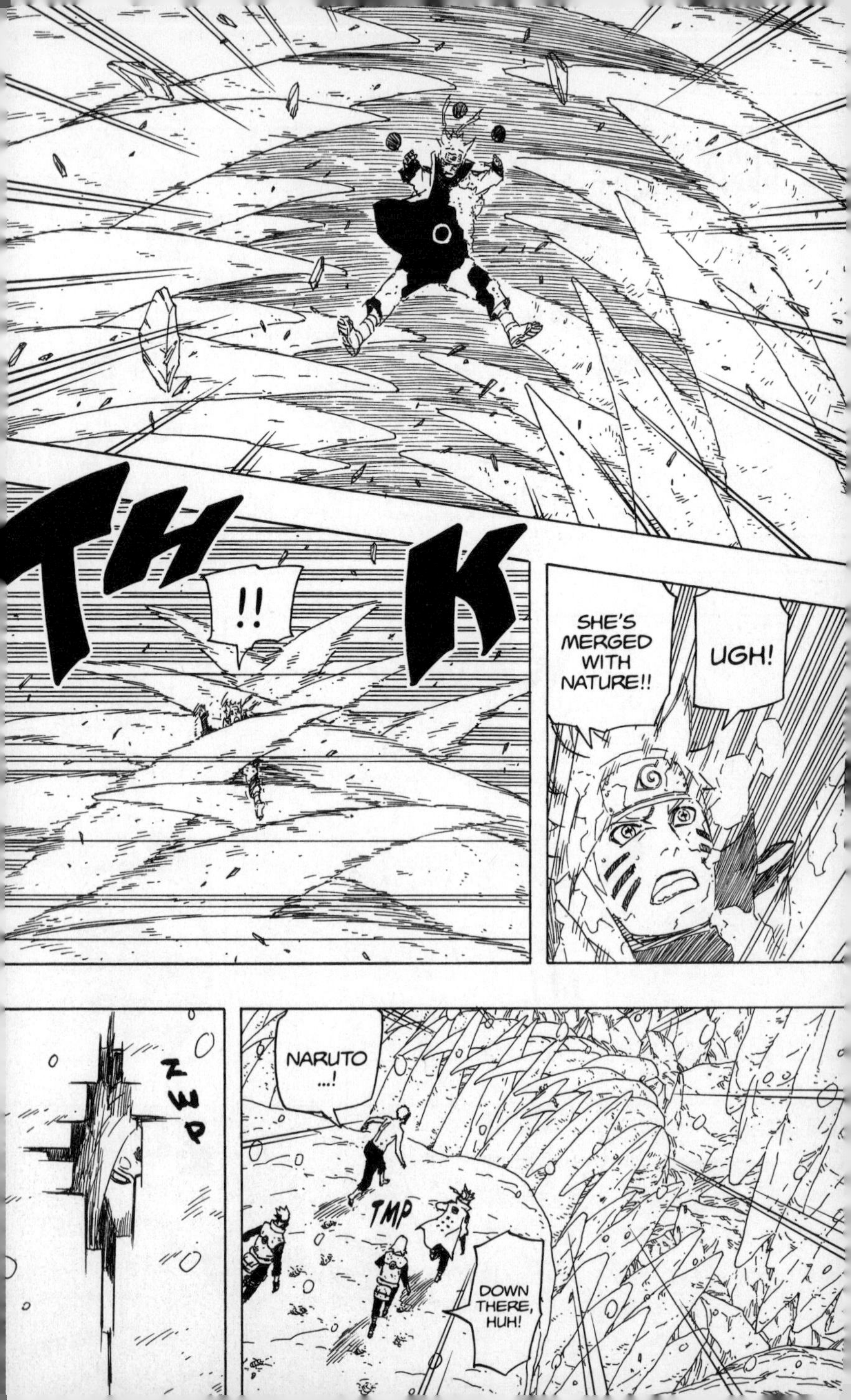
UGH!
SHE'S MERGED WITH NATURE!!
THK
!!
NARUTO ...!
TMP
DOWN THERE, HUH!
ZWP

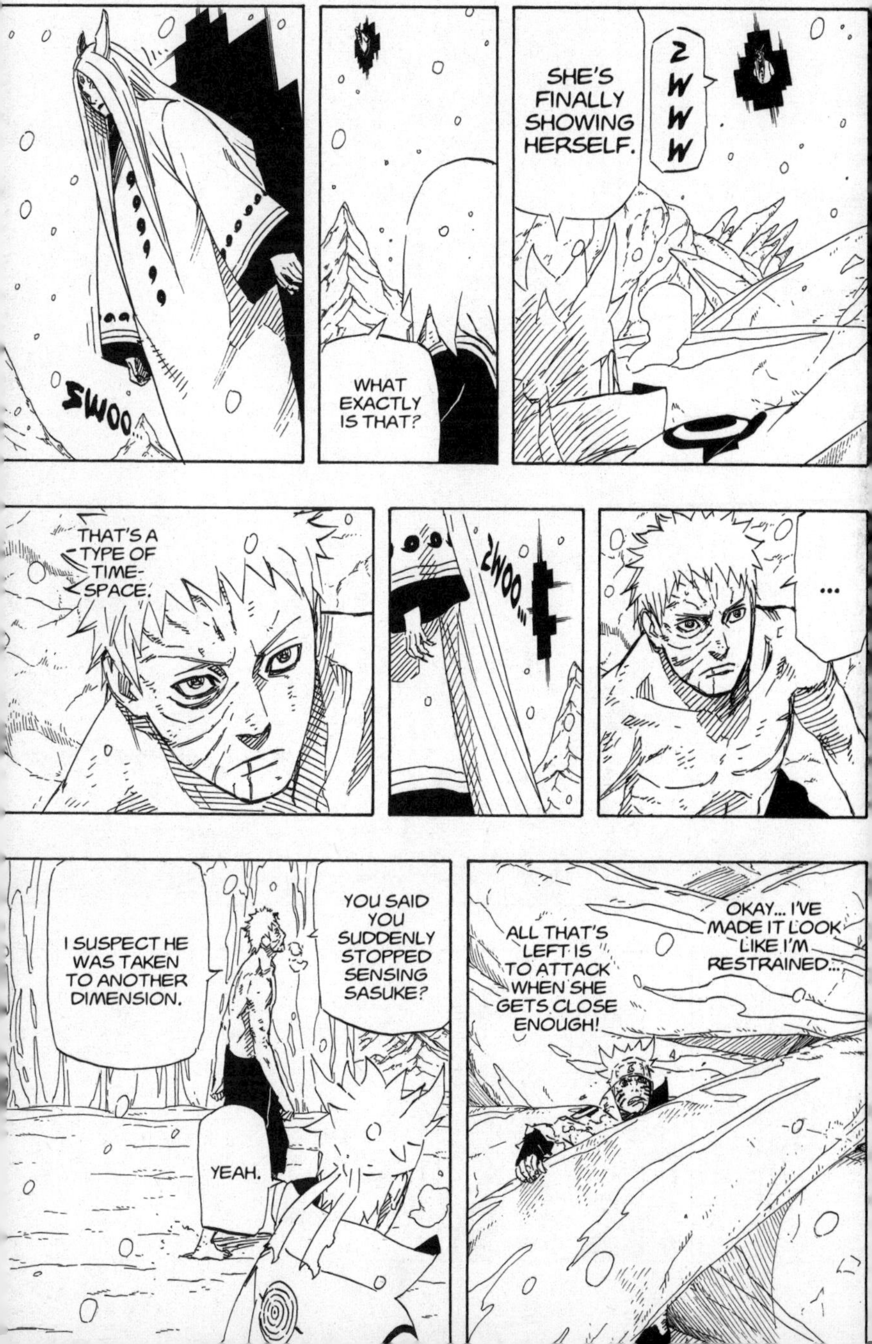
ZWWW
SHE'S FINALLY SHOWING HERSELF.
WHAT EXACTLY IS THAT?
SWOO
...
SWOO...
THAT'S A TYPE OF TIME-SPACE.
OKAY... I'VE MADE IT LOOK LIKE I'M RESTRAINED...
ALL THAT'S LEFT IS TO ATTACK WHEN SHE GETS CLOSE ENOUGH!
YOU SAID YOU SUDDENLY STOPPED SENSING SASUKE?
YEAH.
I SUSPECT HE WAS TAKEN TO ANOTHER DIMENSION.

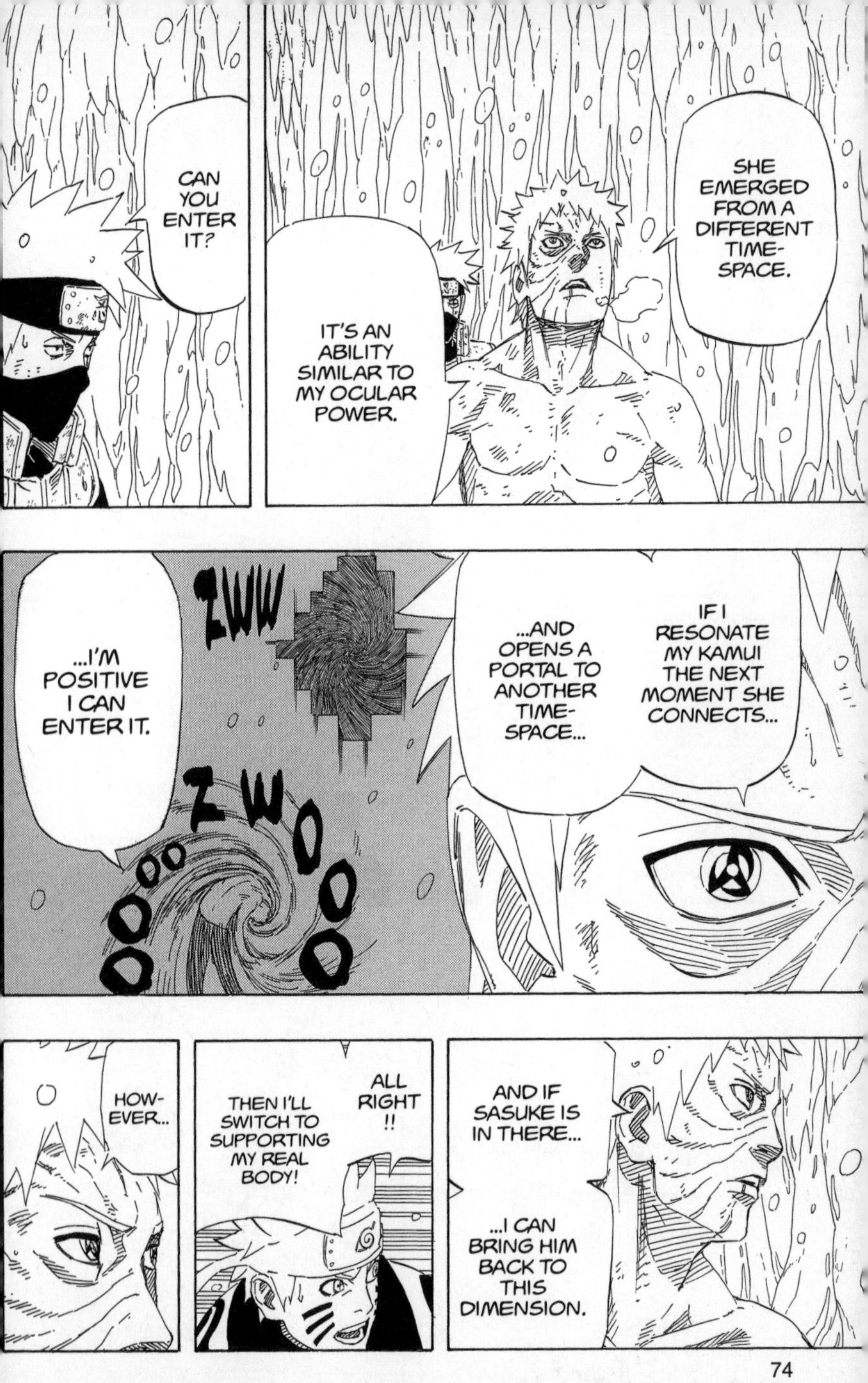
SHE EMERGED FROM A DIFFERENT TIME-SPACE.
IT'S AN ABILITY SIMILAR TO MY OCULAR POWER.
CAN YOU ENTER IT?
IF I RESONATE MY KAMUI THE NEXT MOMENT SHE CONNECTS...
...AND OPENS A PORTAL TO ANOTHER TIME-SPACE...
ZWW
ZWOOOO
...I'M POSITIVE I CAN ENTER IT.
AND IF SASUKE IS IN THERE...
...I CAN BRING HIM BACK TO THIS DIMENSION.
ALL RIGHT!!
THEN I'LL SWITCH TO SUPPORTING MY REAL BODY!
HOW-EVER...

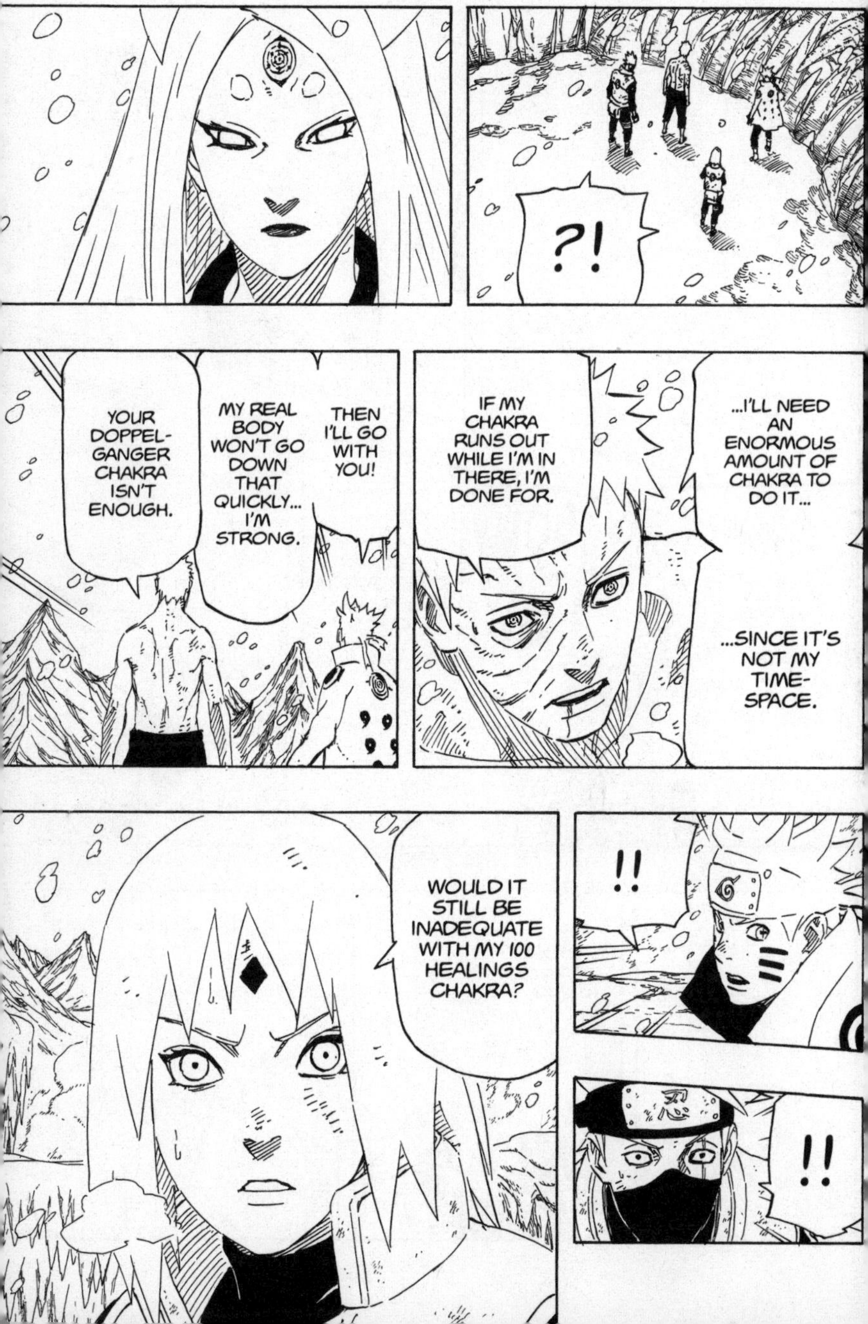
?!
...I'LL NEED AN ENORMOUS AMOUNT OF CHAKRA TO DO IT...
...SINCE IT'S NOT MY TIME-SPACE.
IF MY CHAKRA RUNS OUT WHILE I'M IN THERE, I'M DONE FOR.
THEN I'LL GO WITH YOU!
MY REAL BODY WON'T GO DOWN THAT QUICKLY... I'M STRONG.
YOUR DOPPEL-GANGER CHAKRA ISN'T ENOUGH.
!!
!!
WOULD IT STILL BE INADEQUATE WITH MY 100 HEALINGS CHAKRA?

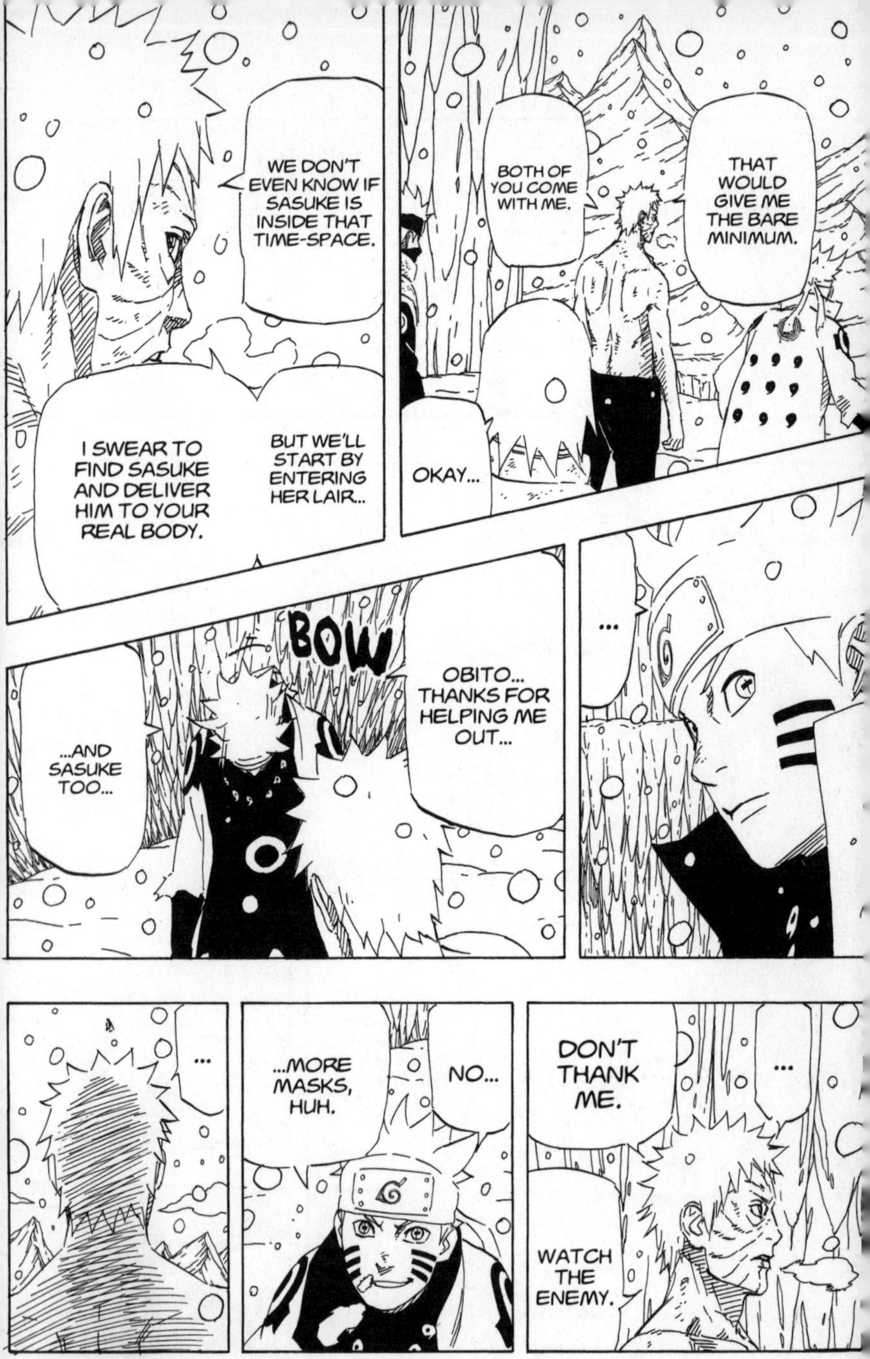
THAT WOULD GIVE ME THE BARE MINIMUM.
BOTH OF YOU COME WITH ME.
OKAY...
WE DON'T EVEN KNOW IF SASUKE IS INSIDE THAT TIME-SPACE.
BUT WE'LL START BY ENTERING HER LAIR...
I SWEAR TO FIND SASUKE AND DELIVER HIM TO YOUR REAL BODY.
...
OBITO... THANKS FOR HELPING ME OUT...
BOW
...AND SASUKE TOO...
...
DON'T THANK ME.
WATCH THE ENEMY.
NO...
...MORE MASKS, HUH.
...

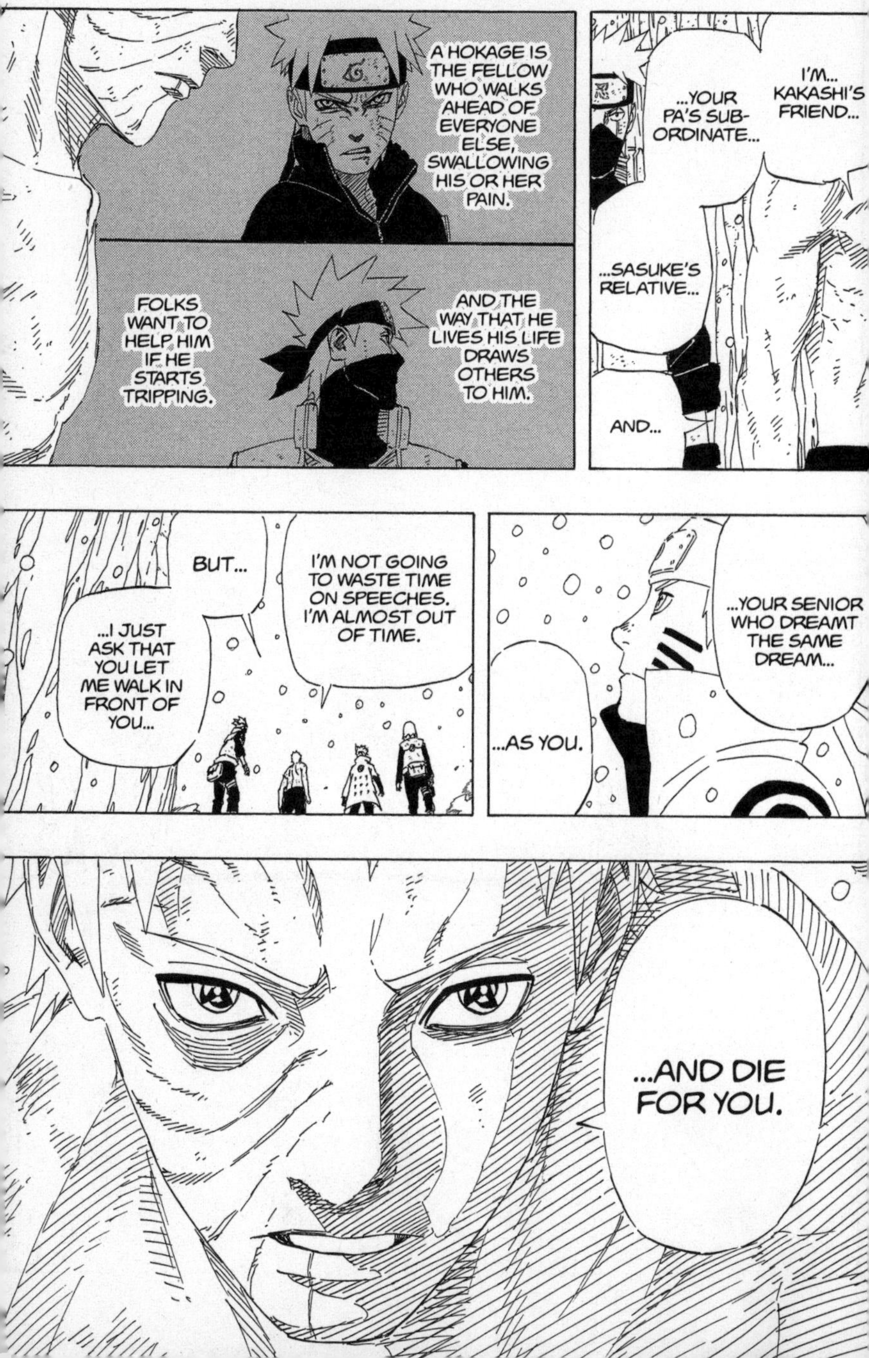
I'M... KAKASHI'S FRIEND...
...YOUR PA'S SUB-ORDINATE...
...SASUKE'S RELATIVE...
AND...
A HOKAGE IS THE FELLOW WHO WALKS AHEAD OF EVERYONE ELSE, SWALLOWING HIS OR HER PAIN.
AND THE WAY THAT HE LIVES HIS LIFE DRAWS OTHERS TO HIM.
FOLKS WANT TO HELP HIM IF HE STARTS TRIPPING.
...YOUR SENIOR WHO DREAMT THE SAME DREAM...
...AS YOU.
I'M NOT GOING TO WASTE TIME ON SPEECHES. I'M ALMOST OUT OF TIME.
BUT...
...I JUST ASK THAT YOU LET ME WALK IN FRONT OF YOU...
...AND DIE FOR YOU.

Number 684: We Ought to Kill Him

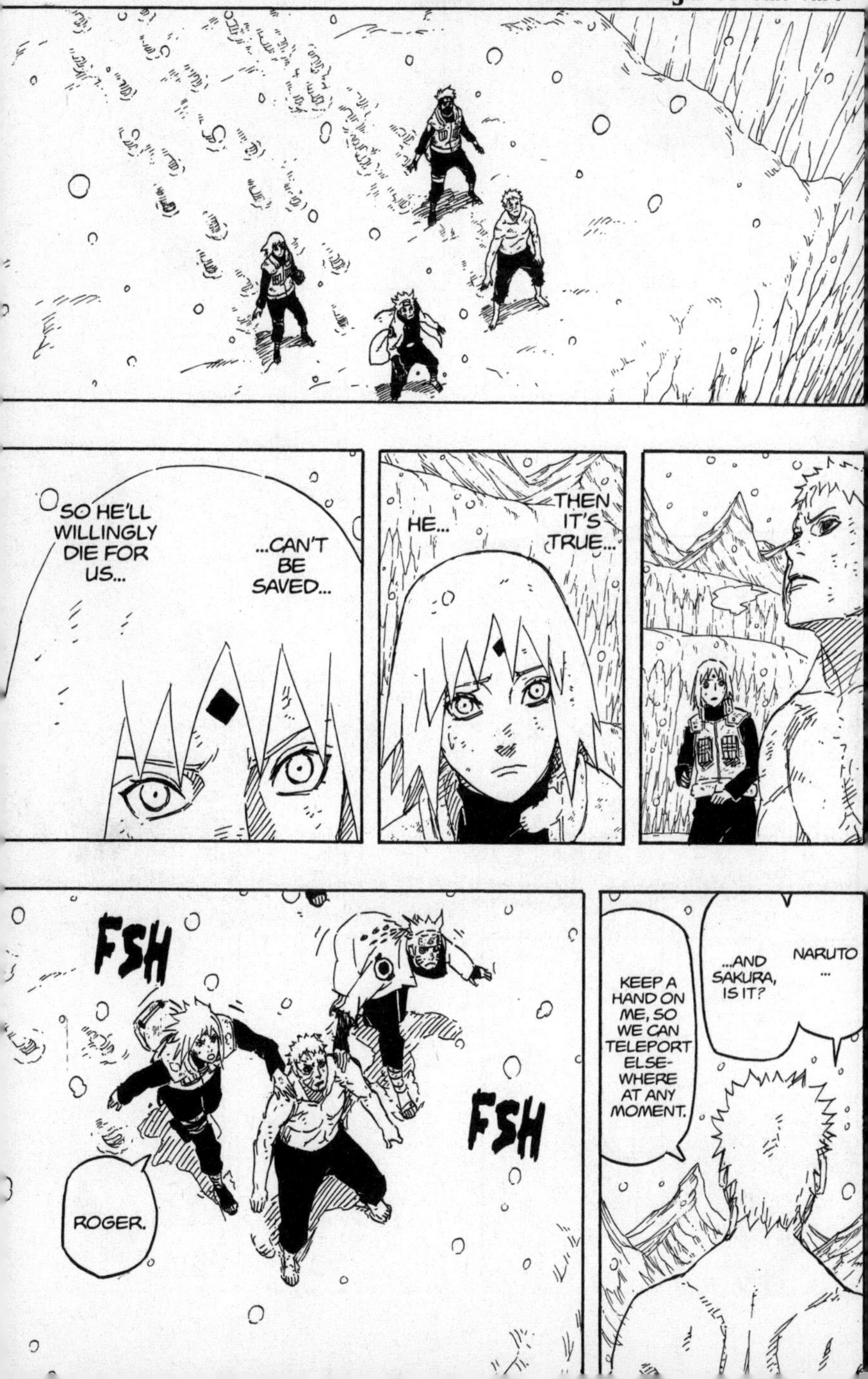
THEN IT'S TRUE...
HE...
...CAN'T BE SAVED...
SO HE'LL WILLINGLY DIE FOR US...
NARUTO ...
...AND SAKURA, IS IT?
KEEP A HAND ON ME, SO WE CAN TELEPORT ELSEWHERE AT ANY MOMENT.
FSH
FSH
ROGER.

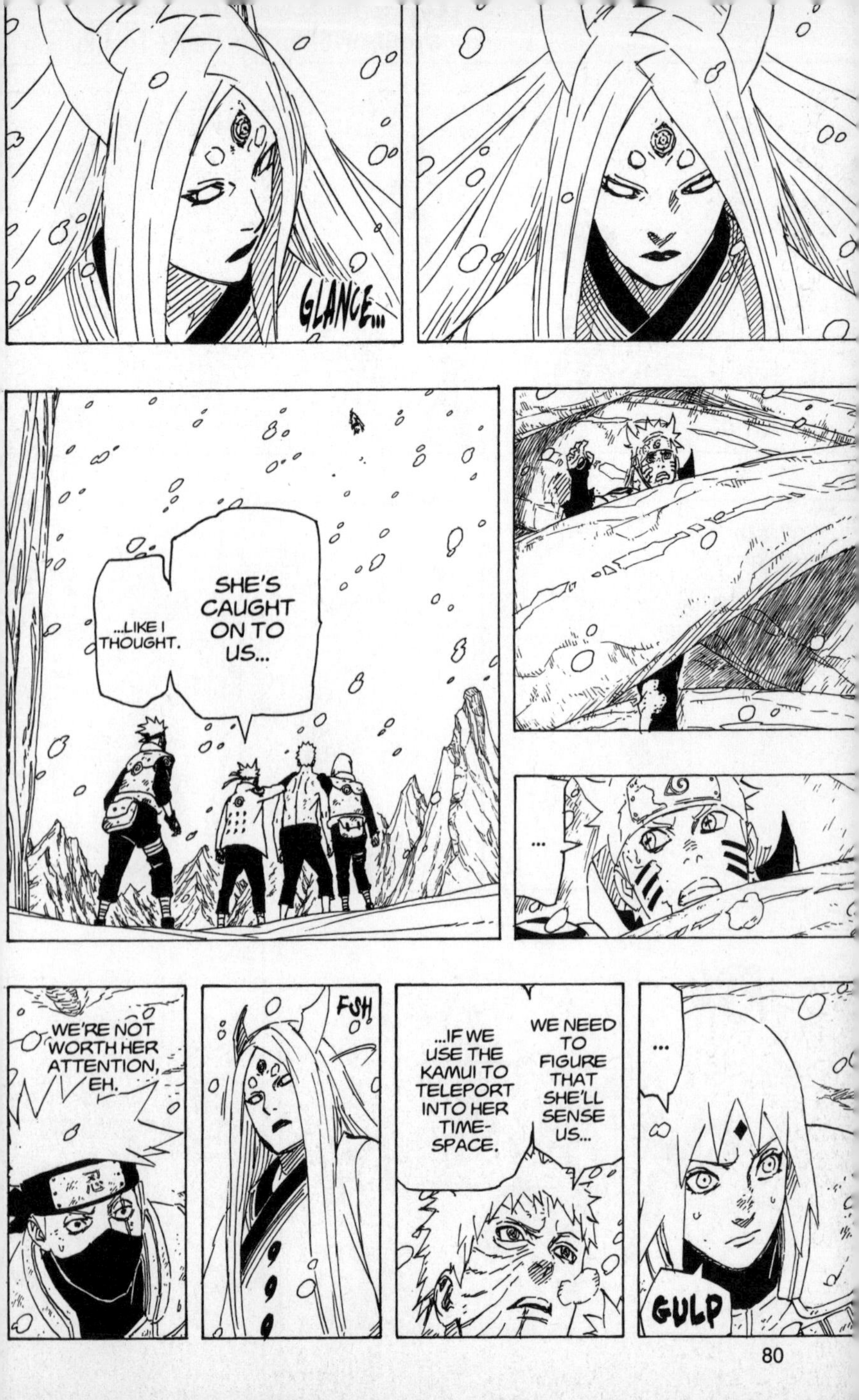
GLANCE...
...
SHE'S CAUGHT ON TO US...
...LIKE I THOUGHT.
...
GULP
WE NEED TO FIGURE THAT SHE'LL SENSE US...
...IF WE USE THE KAMUI TO TELEPORT INTO HER TIME-SPACE.
FSH
WE'RE NOT WORTH HER ATTENTION, EH.

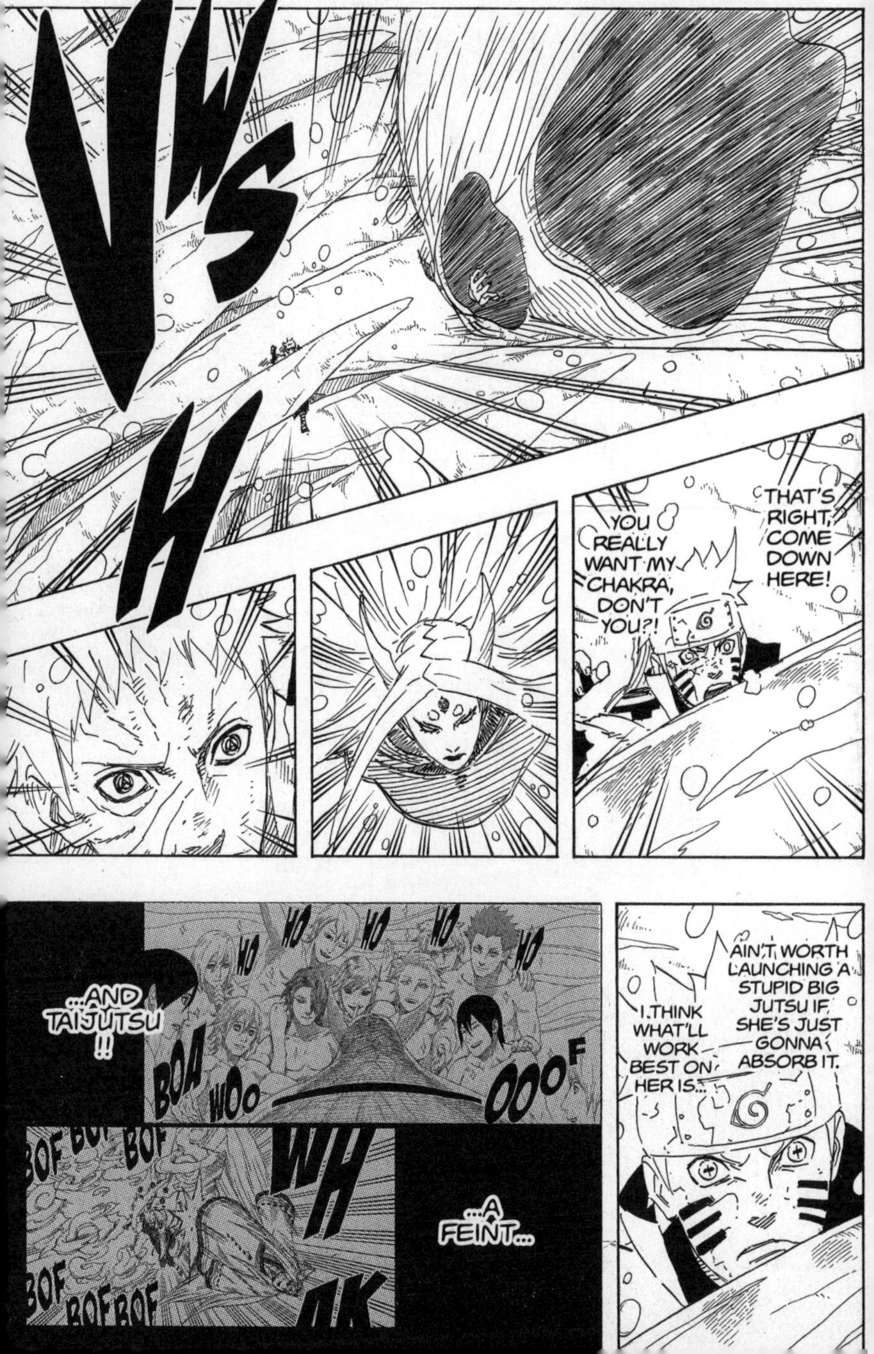
VWSH
THAT'S RIGHT, COME DOWN HERE!
YOU REALLY WANT MY CHAKRA, DON'T YOU?!
AIN'T WORTH LAUNCHING A STUPID BIG JUTSU IF SHE'S JUST GONNA ABSORB IT.
I THINK WHAT'LL WORK BEST ON HER IS...
HO HO HO HO HO
...AND TAIJUTSU!!
BOA WOO OOOF
...A FEINT...
WHAK
BOF BOF BOF
BOF BOF BOF

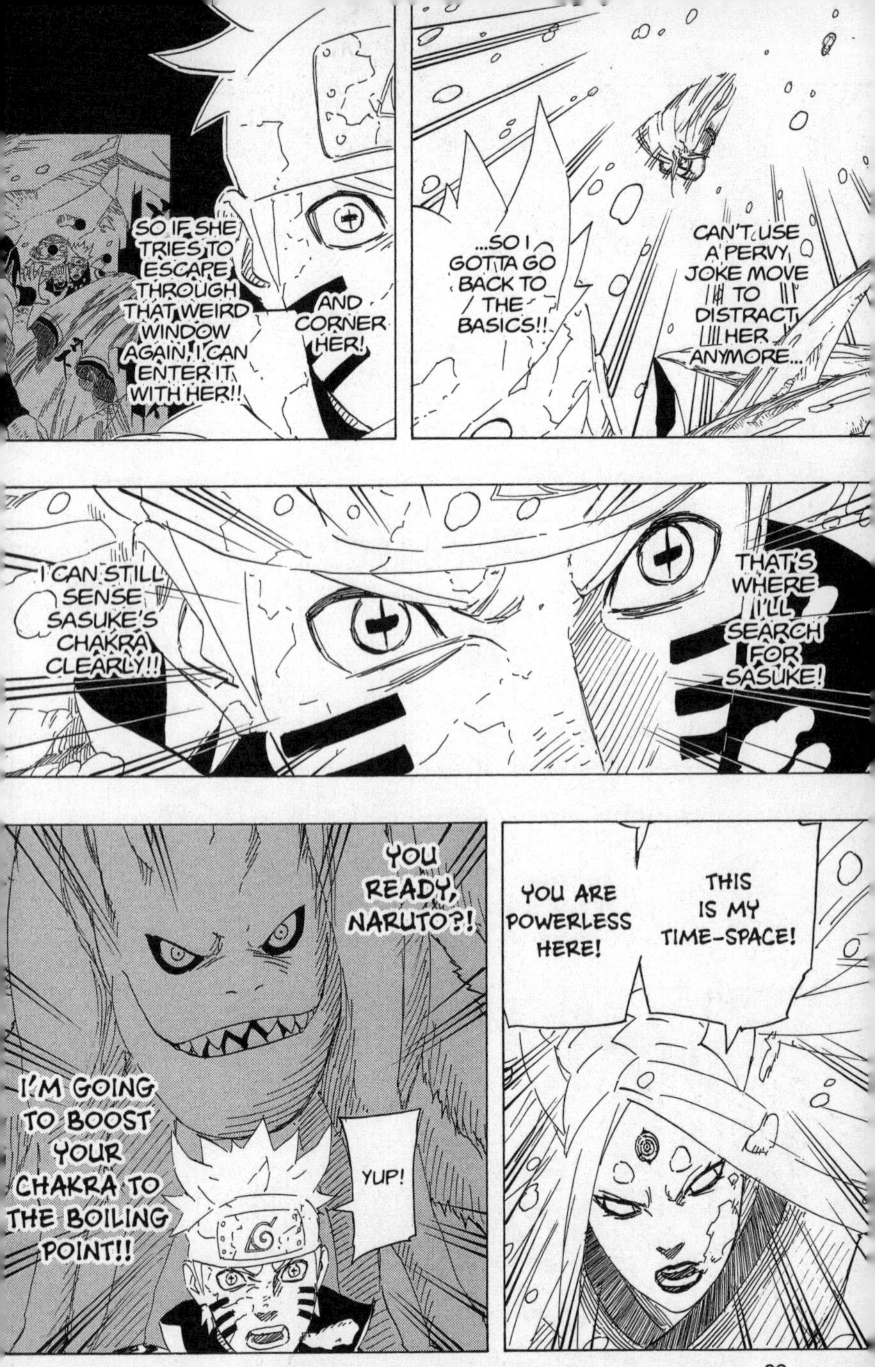

CAN'T USE A PERVY JOKE MOVE TO DISTRACT HER ANYMORE...
...SO I GOTTA GO BACK TO THE BASICS!!
SO IF SHE TRIES TO ESCAPE THROUGH THAT WEIRD WINDOW AGAIN, I CAN ENTER IT WITH HER!!
AND CORNER HER!
THAT'S WHERE I'LL SEARCH FOR SASUKE!
I CAN STILL SENSE SASUKE'S CHAKRA CLEARLY!!
THIS IS MY TIME-SPACE!
YOU ARE POWERLESS HERE!
YOU READY, NARUTO?!
I'M GOING TO BOOST YOUR CHAKRA TO THE BOILING POINT!!
YUP!

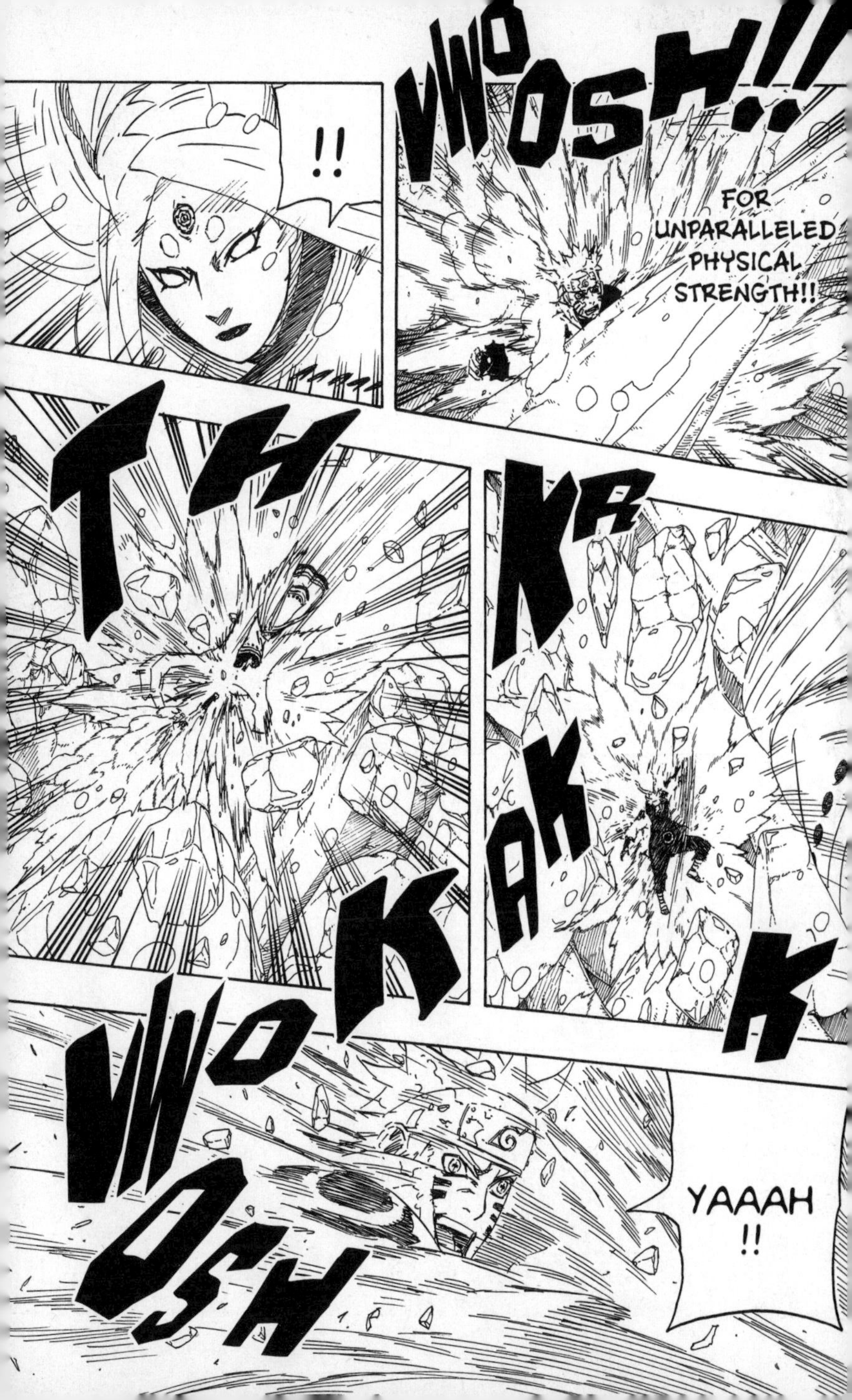
WOOSH!!
FOR UNPARALLELED PHYSICAL STRENGTH!!
!!
WOOSH
YAAAH!!

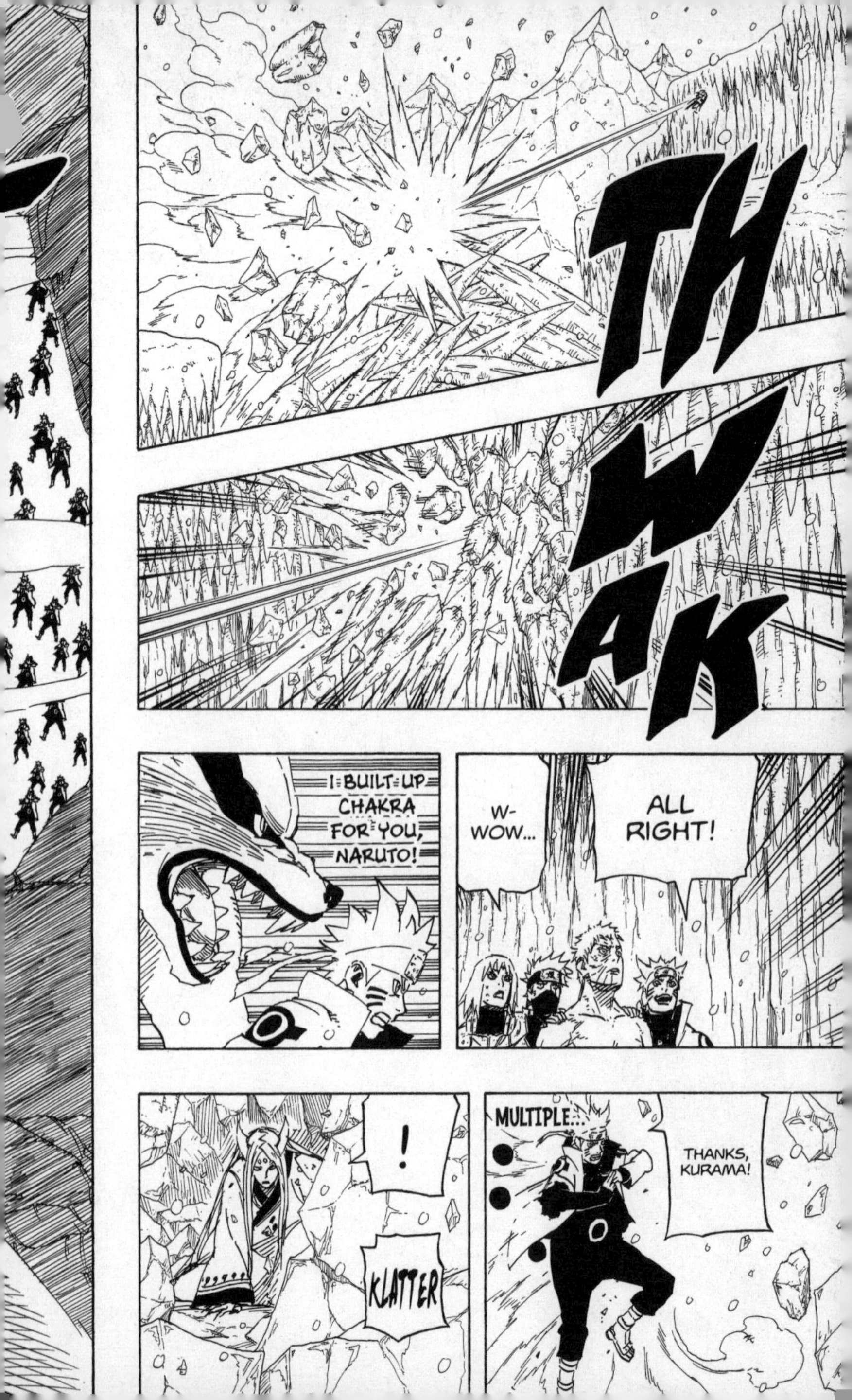
THWAK
ALL RIGHT!
W- WOW...
I BUILT UP CHAKRA FOR YOU, NARUTO!
THANKS, KURAMA!
MULTIPLE...
!
KLATTER

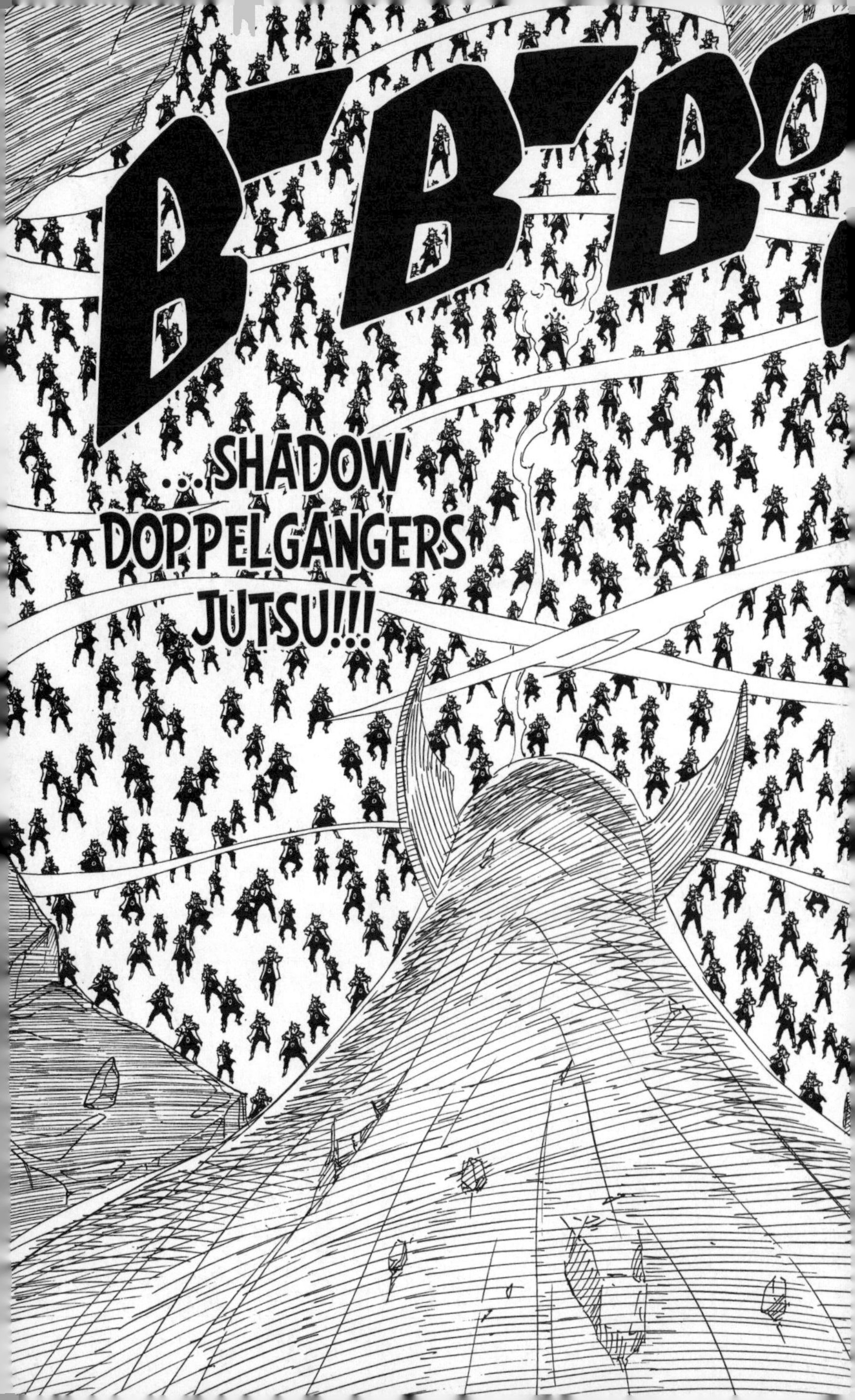
B-B-B...
...SHADOW DOPPELGANGERS JUTSU!!!

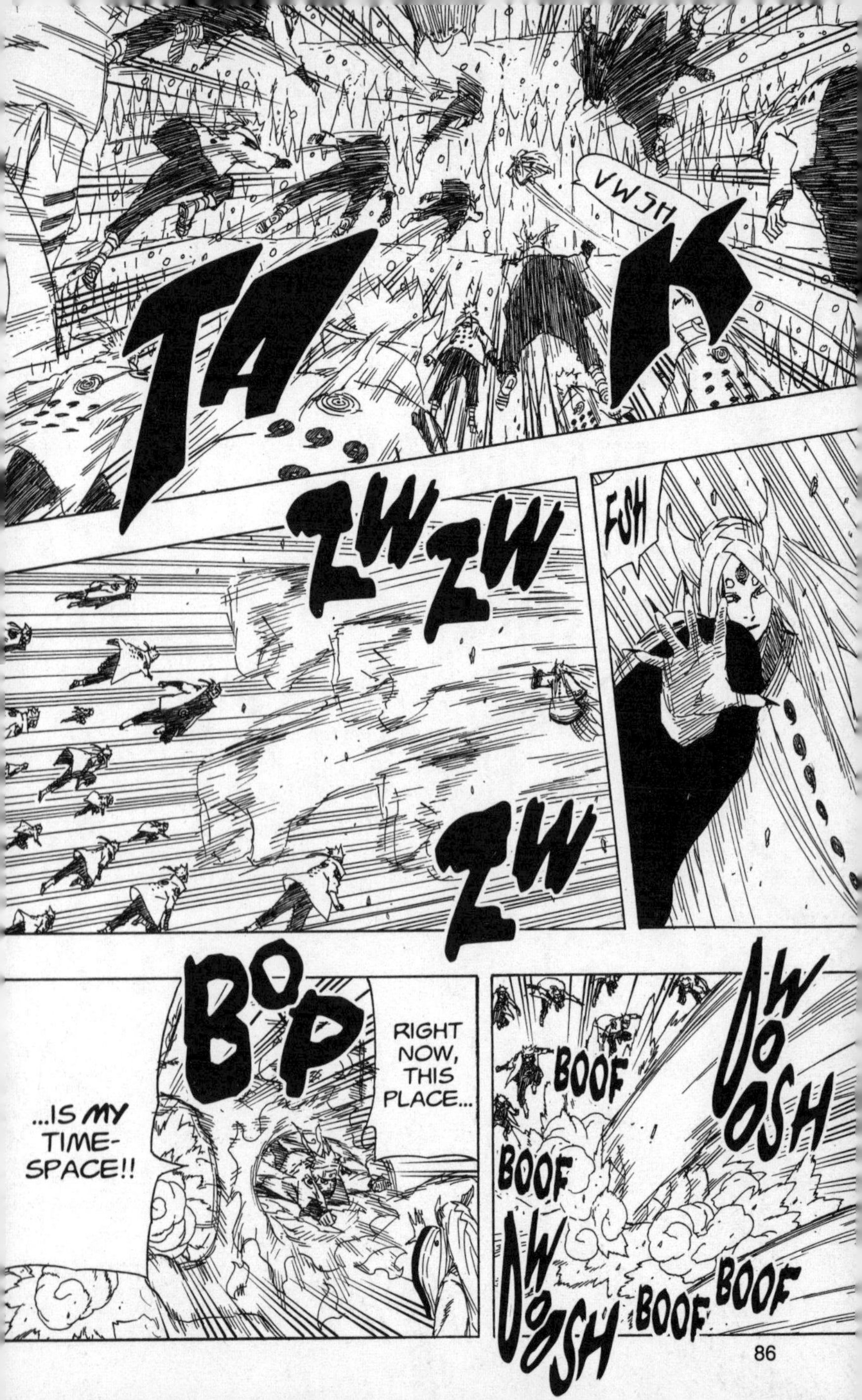
VWJSH
TAK
FSH
ZW ZW ZW
WOOSH
BOOF
BOOF
WOOSH
BOOF
BOOF
BOP
RIGHT NOW, THIS PLACE...
...IS MY TIME-SPACE!!

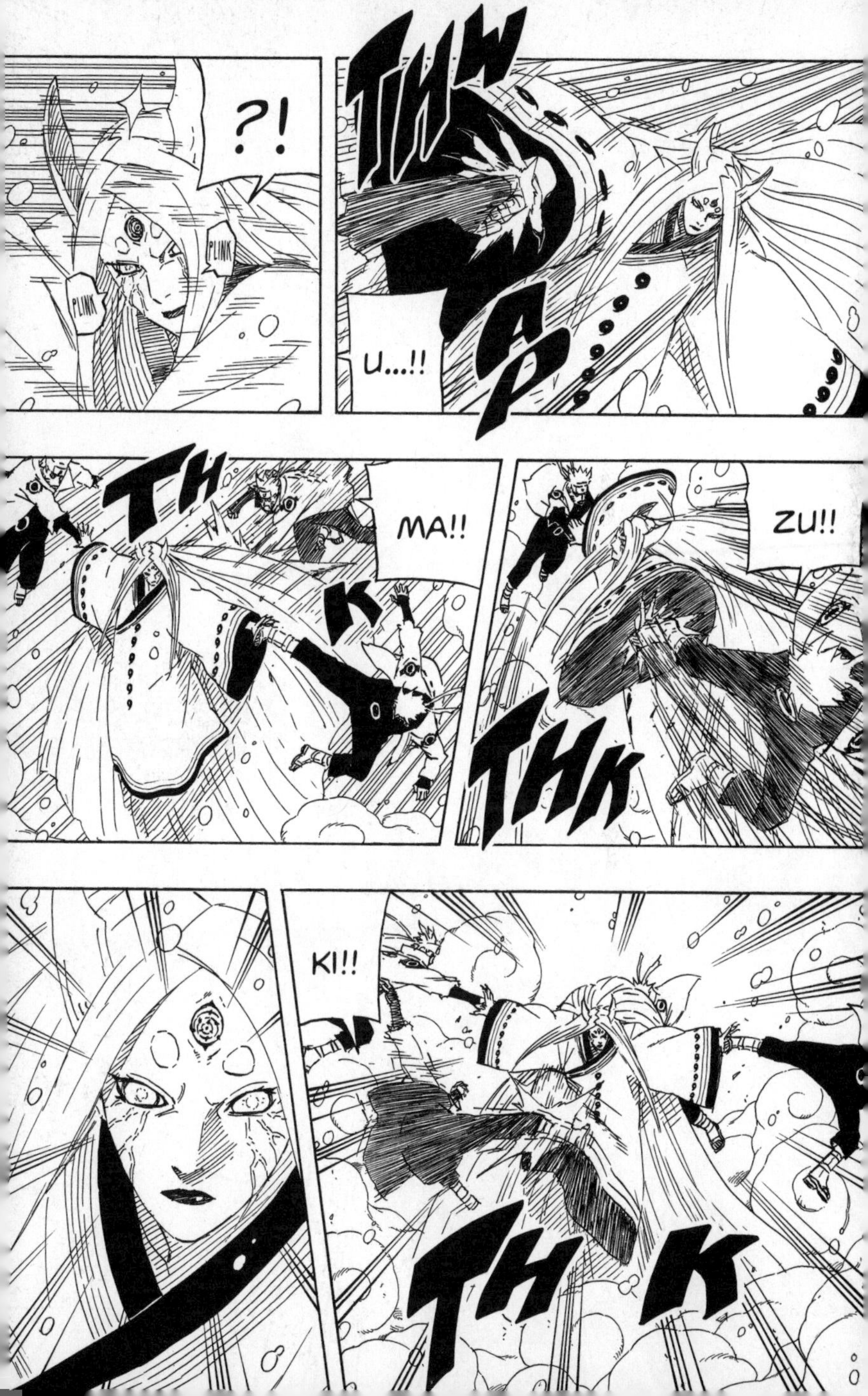
THWAP
U...!!
?!
PLINK
PLINK
ZU!!
THK
MA!!
THK
KI!!
THK

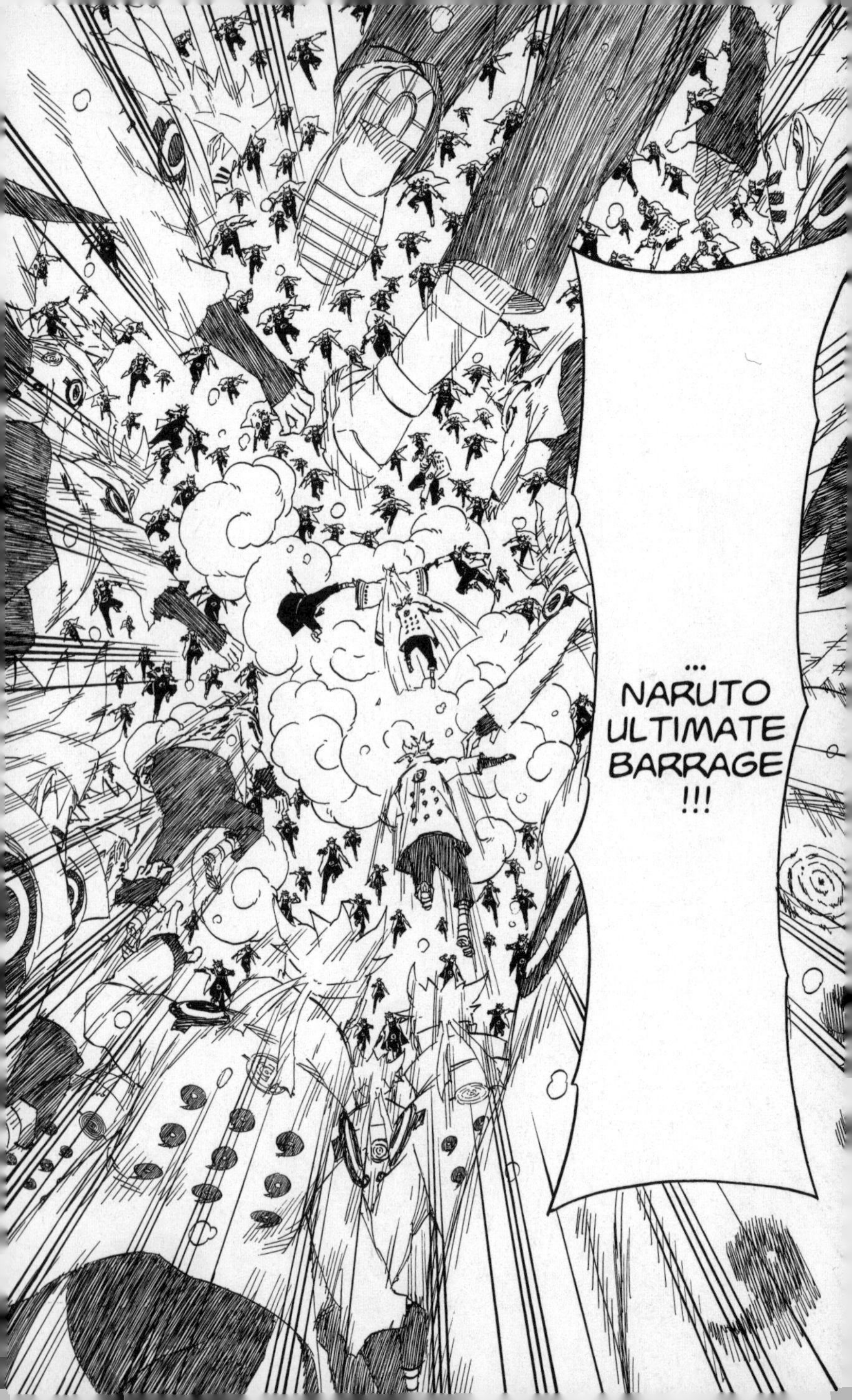
...
NARUTO ULTIMATE BARRAGE !!!

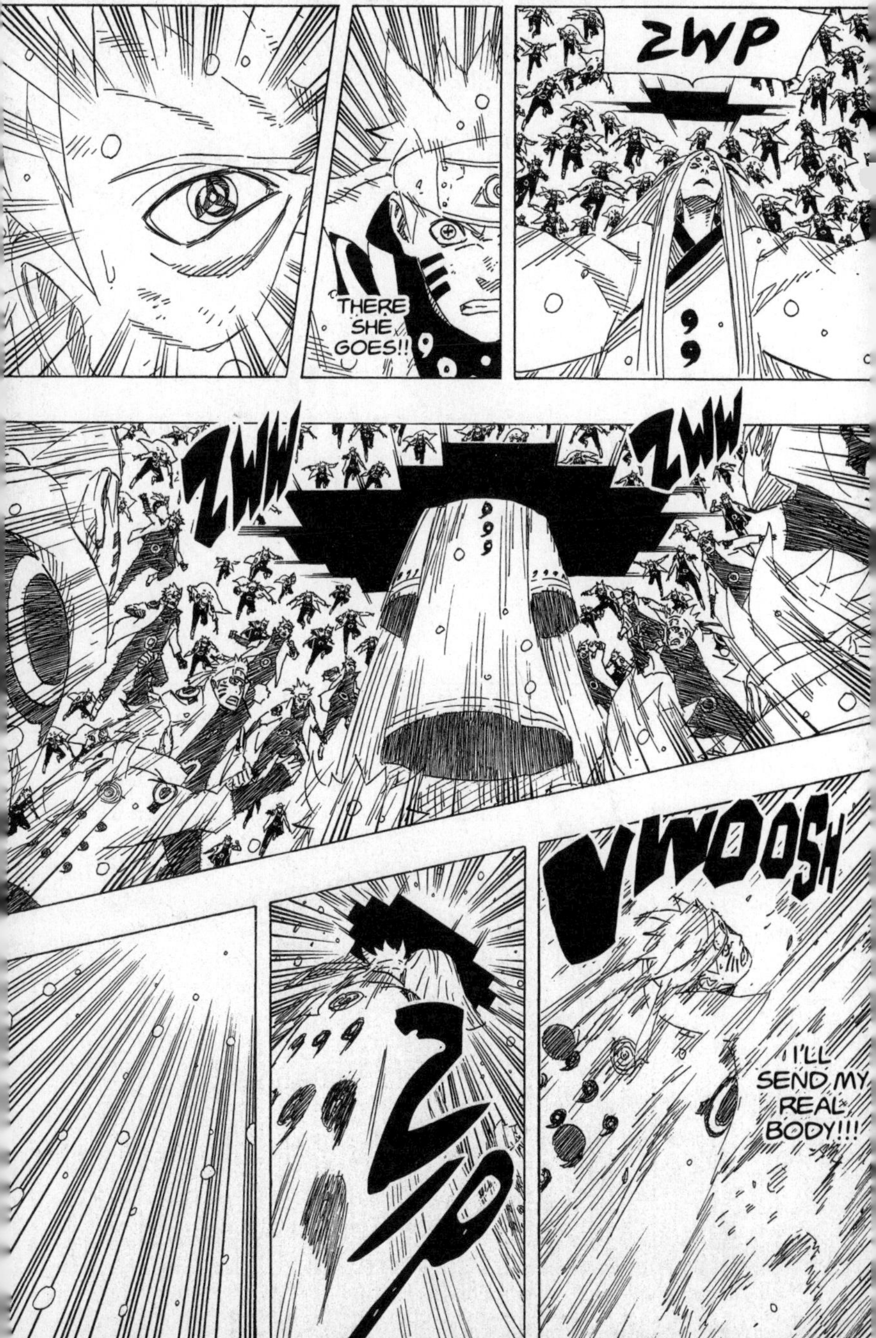
ZWP
THERE SHE GOES!!
ZWW
ZWW
VWOOSH
I'LL SEND MY REAL BODY!!!!

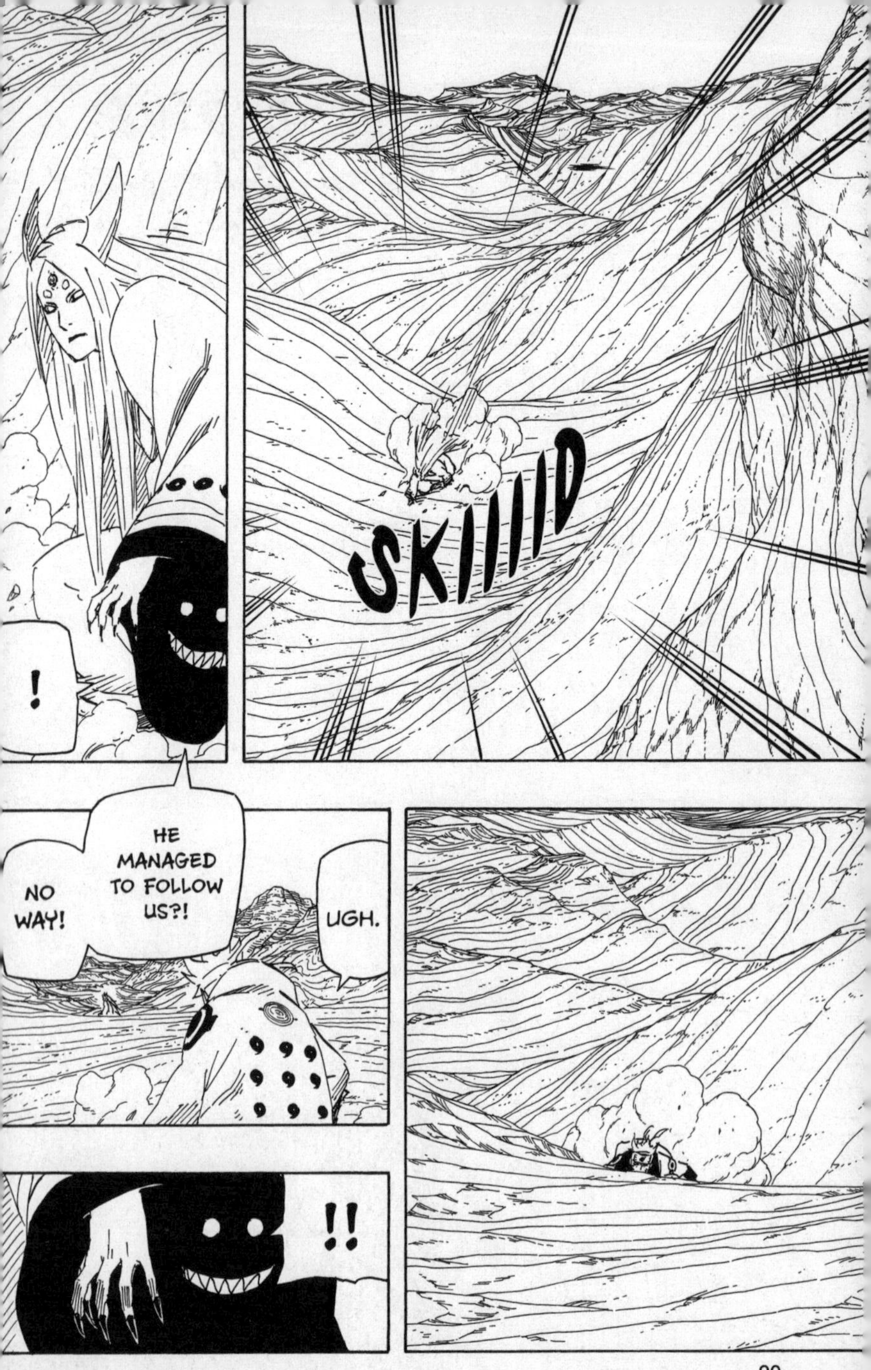
SKIIIID
!
UGH.
HE MANAGED TO FOLLOW US?!
NO WAY!
!!

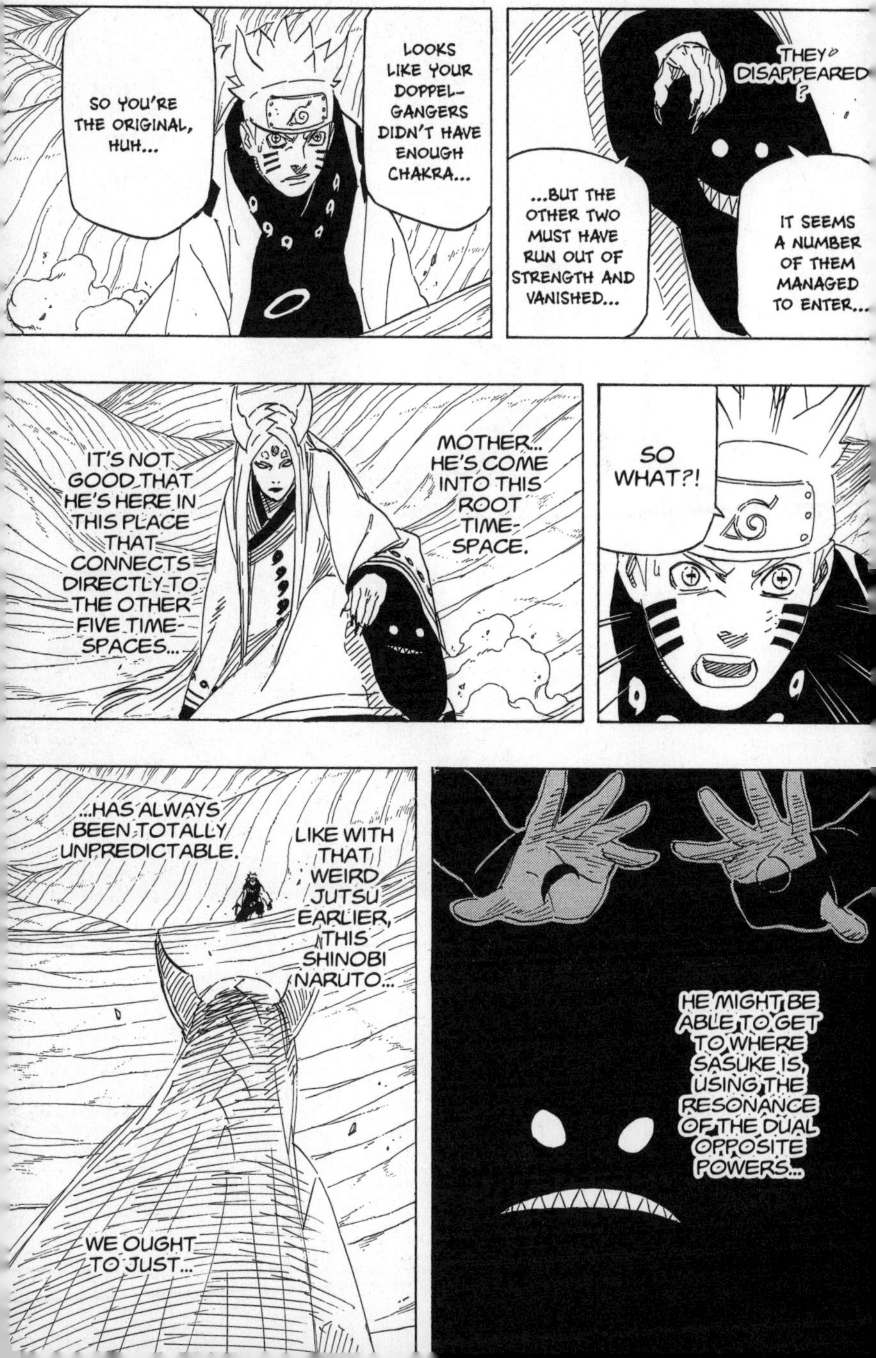
THEY DISAPPEARED?
IT SEEMS A NUMBER OF THEM MANAGED TO ENTER...
...BUT THE OTHER TWO MUST HAVE RUN OUT OF STRENGTH AND VANISHED...
LOOKS LIKE YOUR DOPPEL-GANGERS DIDN'T HAVE ENOUGH CHAKRA...
SO YOU'RE THE ORIGINAL, HUH...
SO WHAT?!
MOTHER... HE'S COME INTO THIS ROOT TIME-SPACE.
IT'S NOT GOOD THAT HE'S HERE IN THIS PLACE THAT CONNECTS DIRECTLY TO THE OTHER FIVE TIME-SPACES...
HE MIGHT BE ABLE TO GET TO WHERE SASUKE IS, USING THE RESONANCE OF THE DUAL OPPOSITE POWERS...
LIKE WITH THAT WEIRD JUTSU EARLIER, THIS SHINOBI NARUTO...
...HAS ALWAYS BEEN TOTALLY UNPREDICTABLE.
WE OUGHT TO JUST...

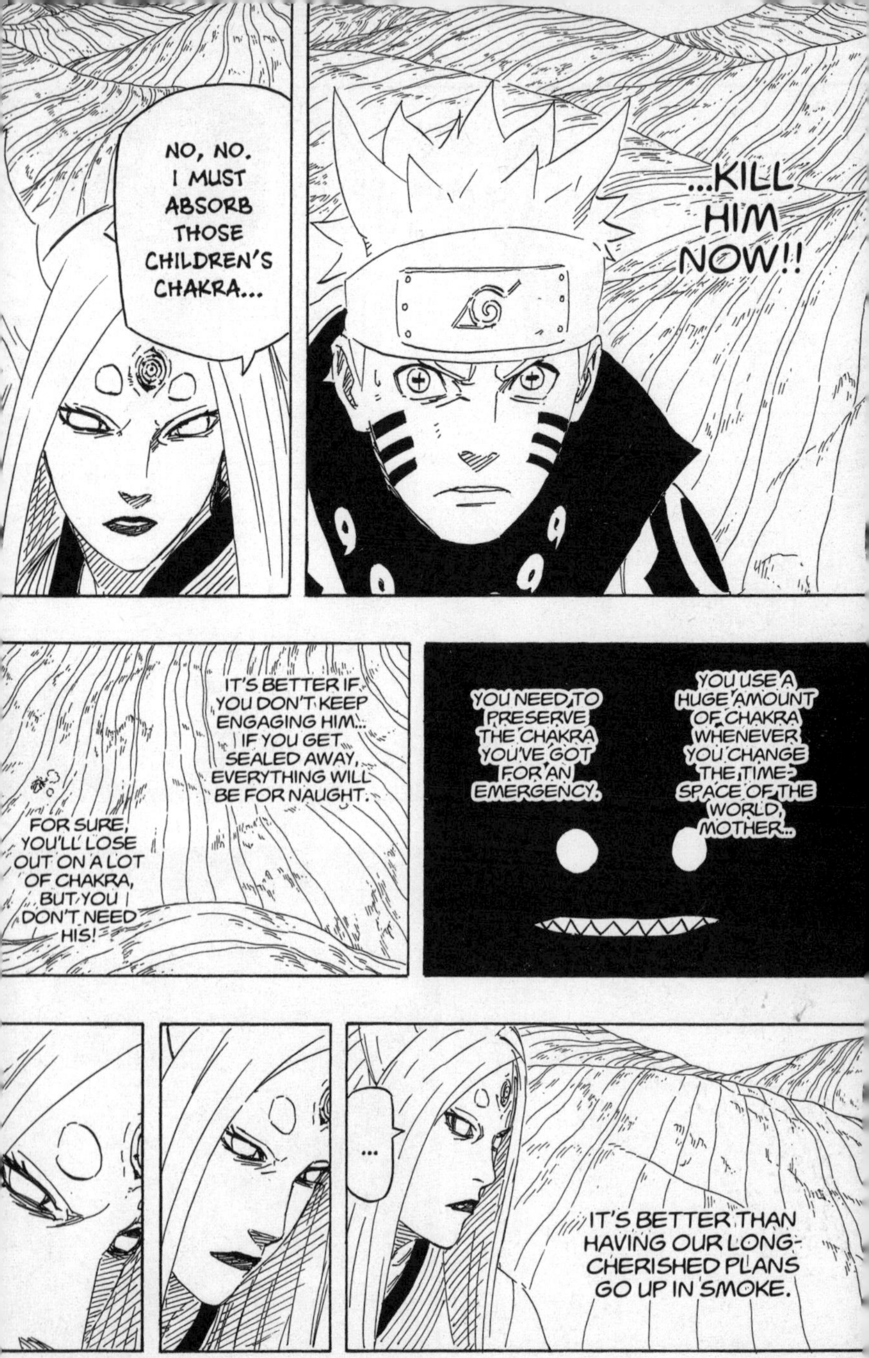
...KILL HIM NOW!!
NO, NO. I MUST ABSORB THOSE CHILDREN'S CHAKRA...
YOU USE A HUGE AMOUNT OF CHAKRA WHENEVER YOU CHANGE THE TIME-SPACE OF THE WORLD, MOTHER...
YOU NEED TO PRESERVE THE CHAKRA YOU'VE GOT FOR AN EMERGENCY.
IT'S BETTER IF YOU DON'T KEEP ENGAGING HIM... IF YOU GET SEALED AWAY, EVERYTHING WILL BE FOR NAUGHT.
FOR SURE, YOU'LL LOSE OUT ON A LOT OF CHAKRA, BUT YOU DON'T NEED HIS!
...
IT'S BETTER THAN HAVING OUR LONG-CHERISHED PLANS GO UP IN SMOKE.

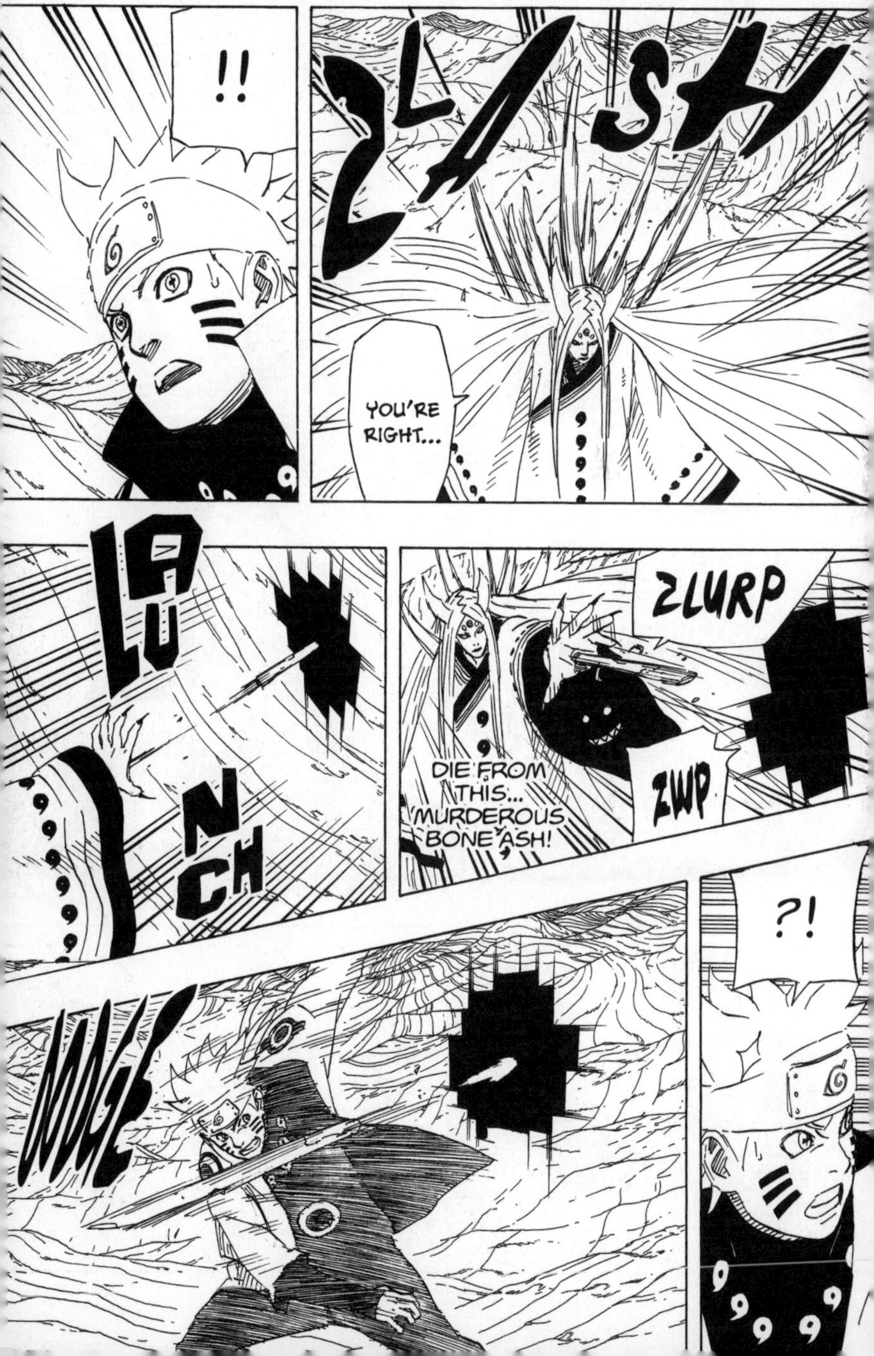

ZLASH
YOU'RE RIGHT...
!!
ZLURP
DIE FROM THIS... MURDEROUS BONE ASH!
ZWP
LAUNCH
?!

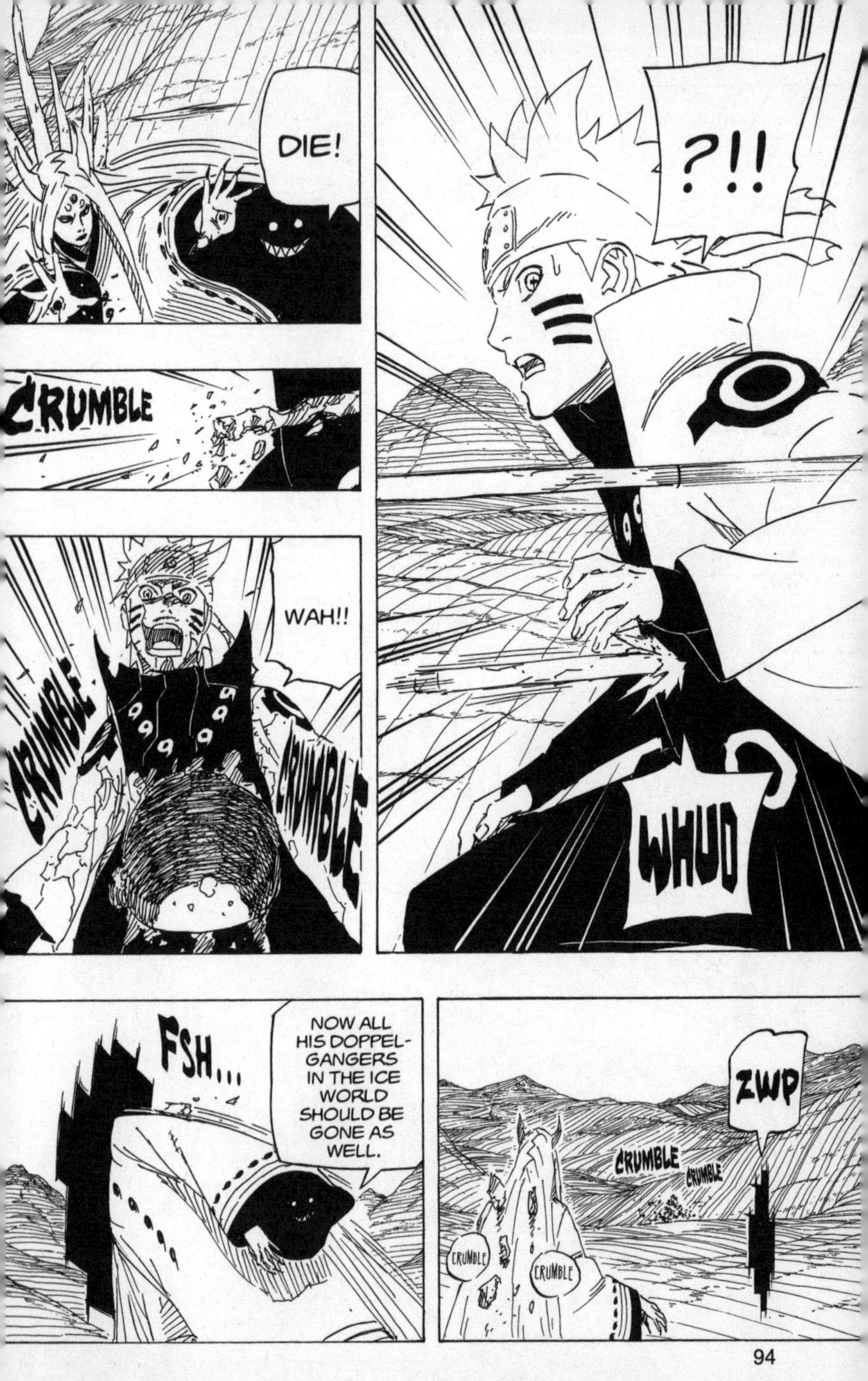
?!!
WHUD
DIE!
CRUMBLE
WAH!!
CRUMBLE
CRUMBLE
ZWP
CRUMBLE
CRUMBLE
CRUMBLE
CRUMBLE
FSH...
NOW ALL HIS DOPPEL-GANGERS IN THE ICE WORLD SHOULD BE GONE AS WELL.

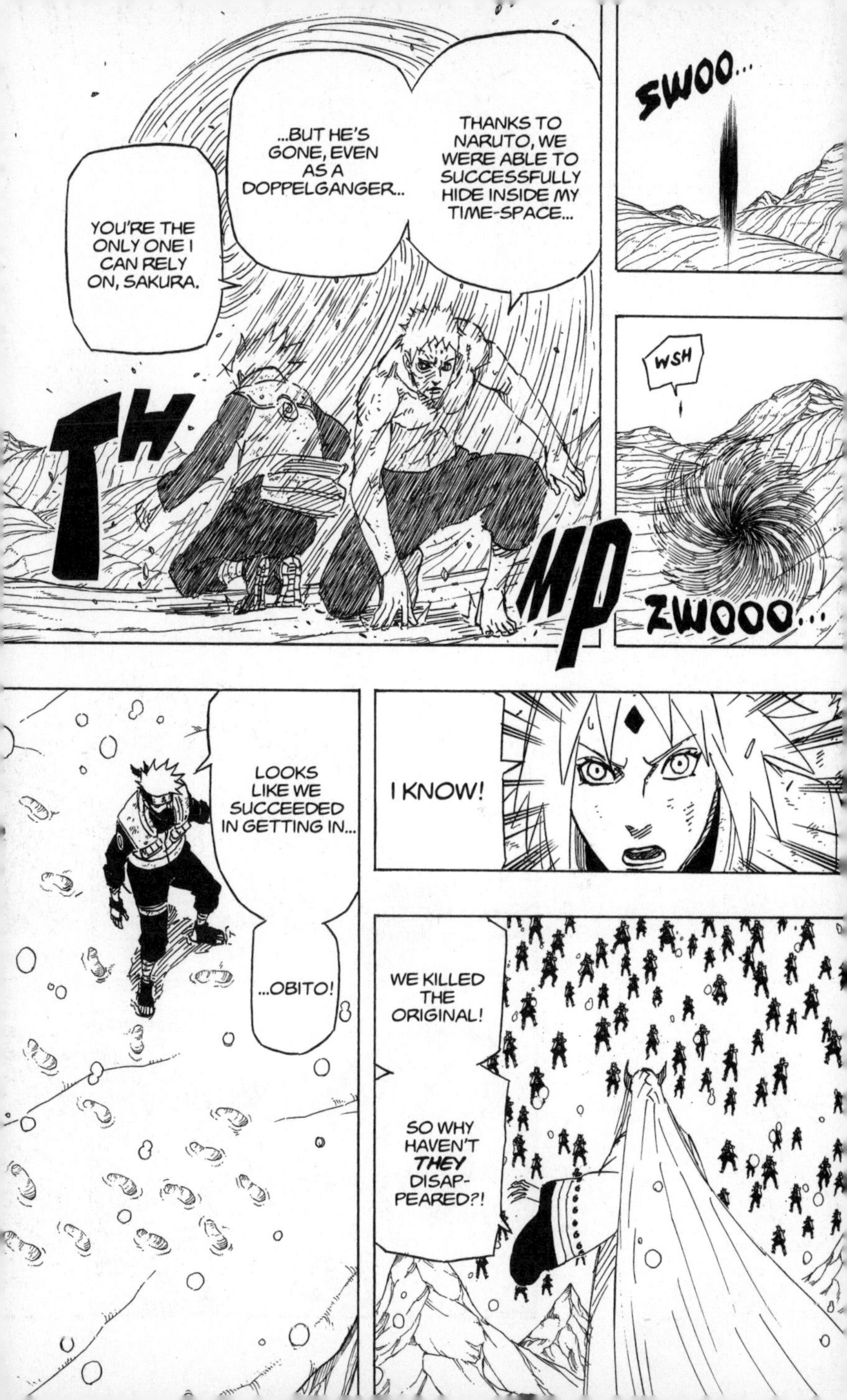
SWOO...
WSH
ZWOOO...
THANKS TO NARUTO, WE WERE ABLE TO SUCCESSFULLY HIDE INSIDE MY TIME-SPACE...
...BUT HE'S GONE, EVEN AS A DOPPELGANGER...
YOU'RE THE ONLY ONE I CAN RELY ON, SAKURA.
THMP
I KNOW!
WE KILLED THE ORIGINAL!
SO WHY HAVEN'T *THEY* DISAPPEARED?!
LOOKS LIKE WE SUCCEEDED IN GETTING IN...
...OBITO!

Number 685: All That I've Got

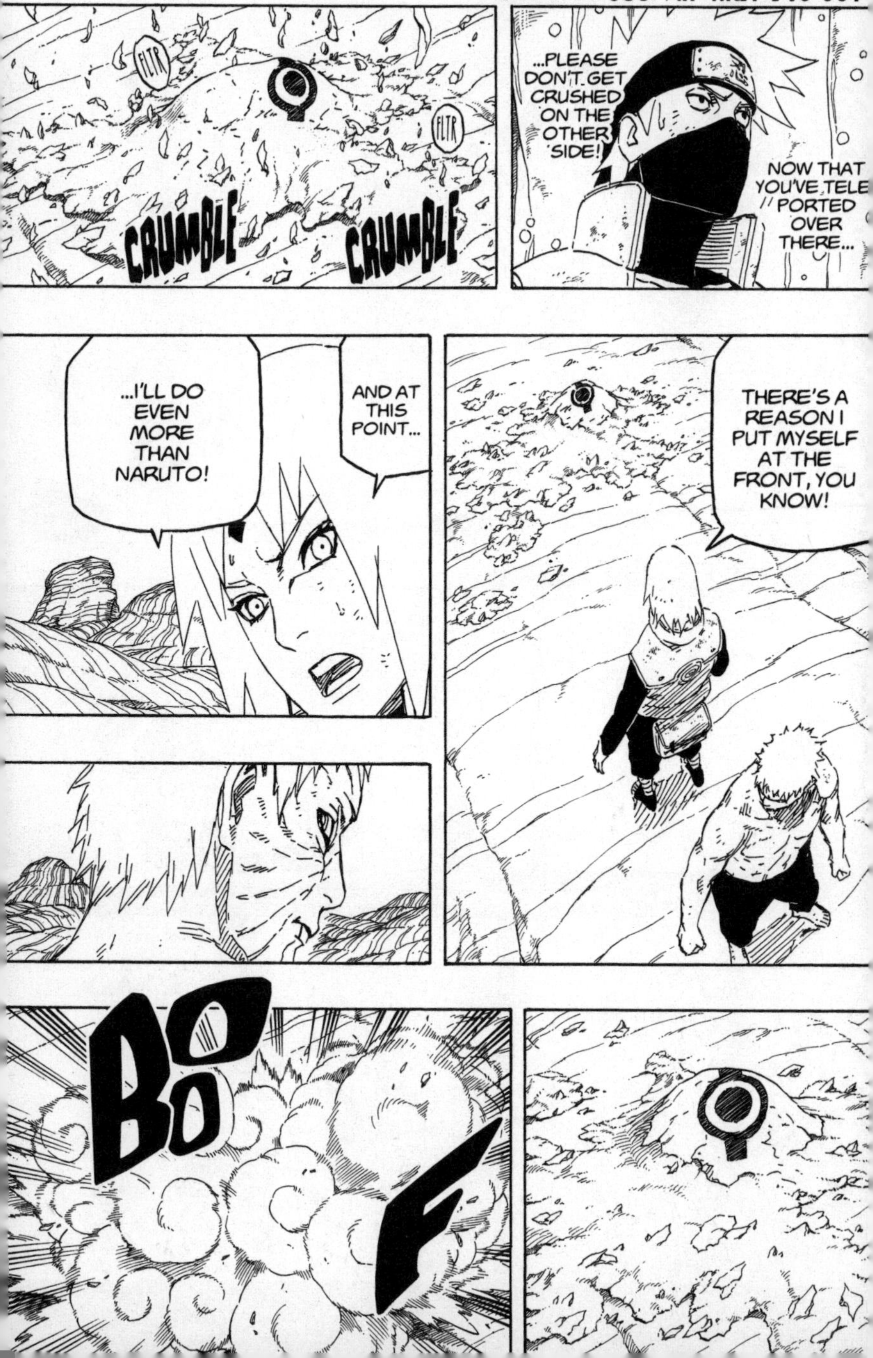
NOW THAT YOU'VE TELEPORTED OVER THERE...
...PLEASE DON'T GET CRUSHED ON THE OTHER SIDE!
FLTR
FLTR
CRUMBLE
CRUMBLE
THERE'S A REASON I PUT MYSELF AT THE FRONT, YOU KNOW!
AND AT THIS POINT...
...I'LL DO EVEN MORE THAN NARUTO!
BOOOF

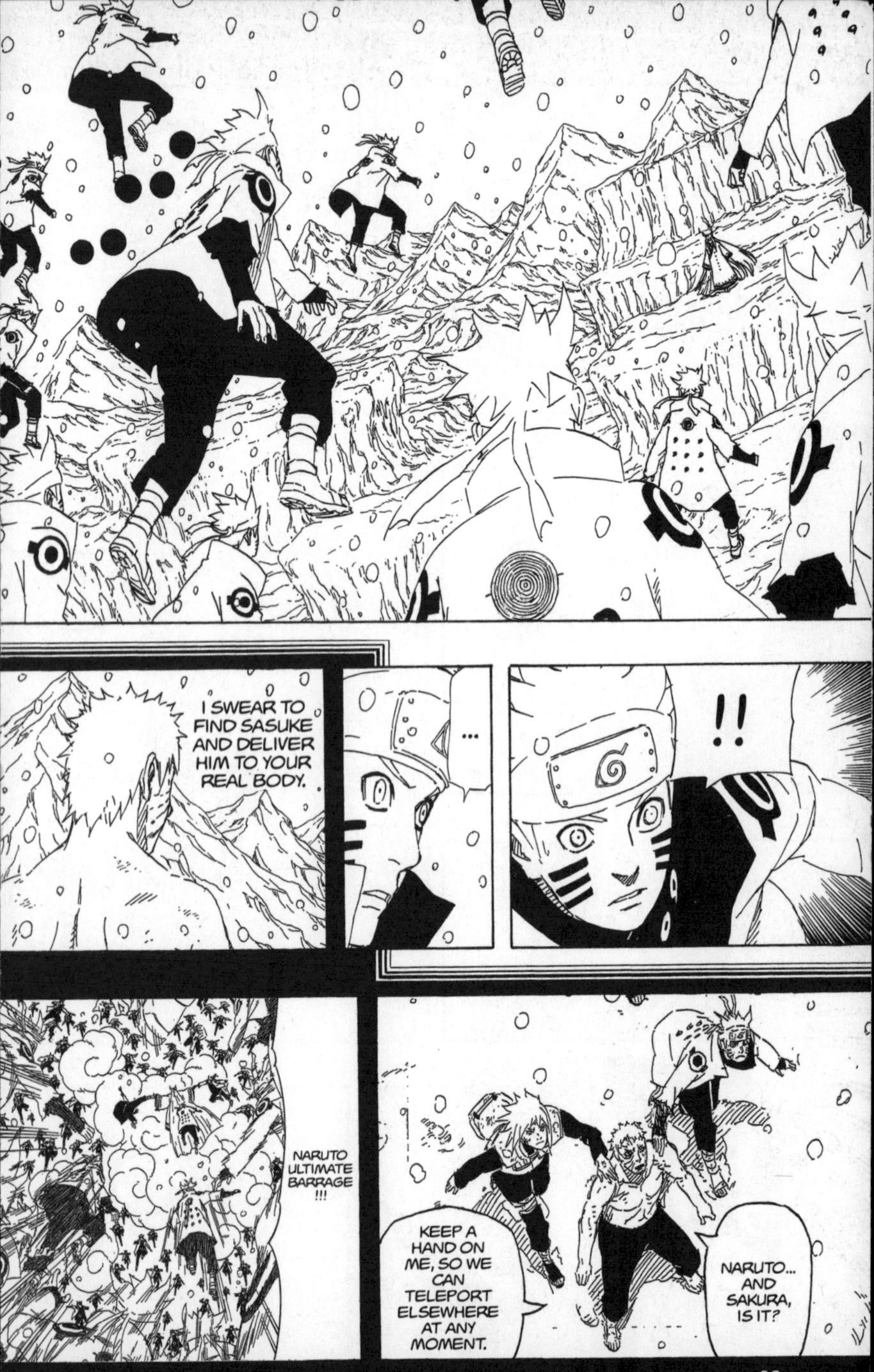
!!
...
I SWEAR TO FIND SASUKE AND DELIVER HIM TO YOUR REAL BODY.
NARUTO... AND SAKURA, IS IT?
KEEP A HAND ON ME, SO WE CAN TELEPORT ELSEWHERE AT ANY MOMENT.
NARUTO ULTIMATE BARRAGE !!!

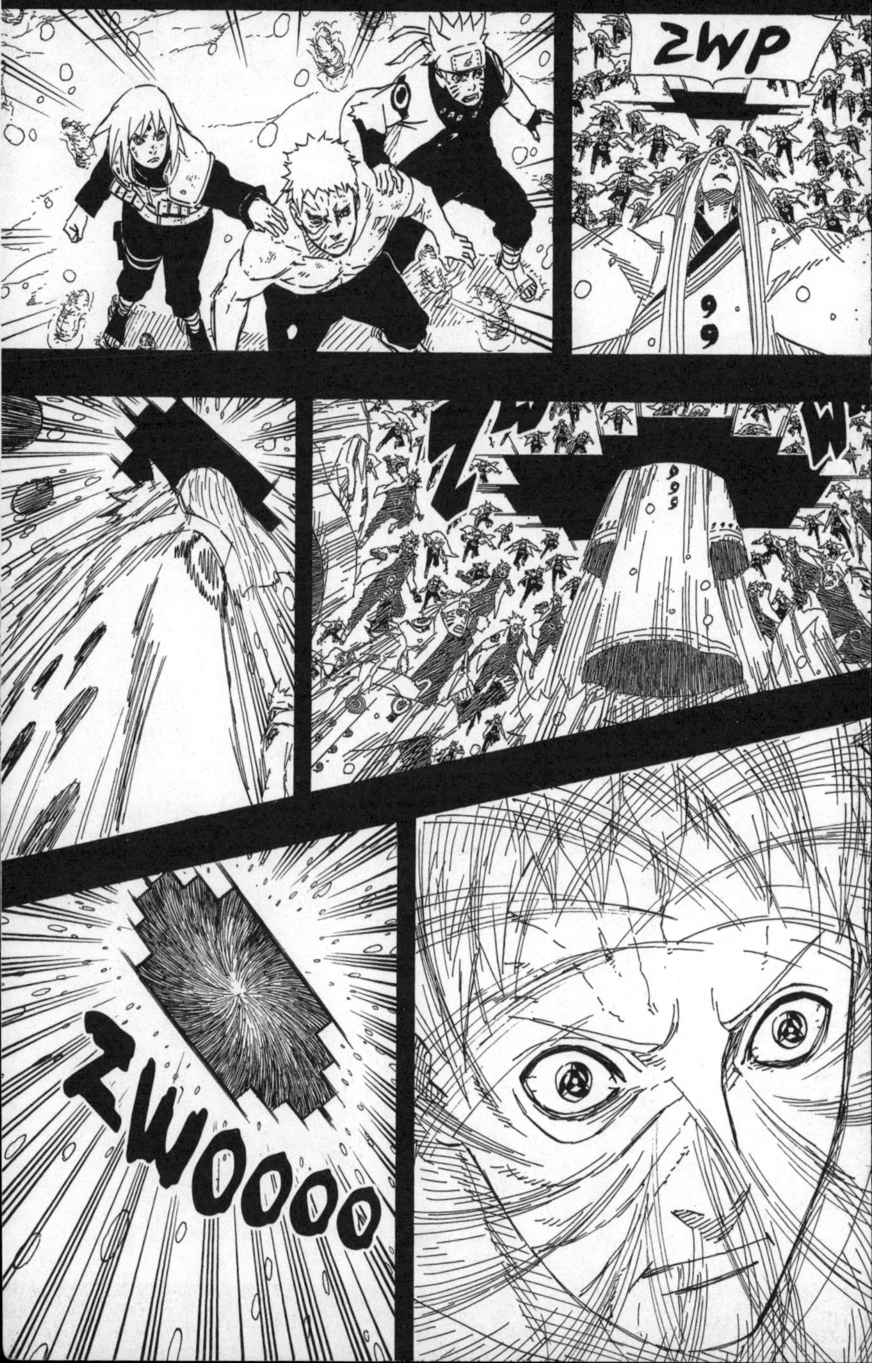
ZWP
ZWOOOO

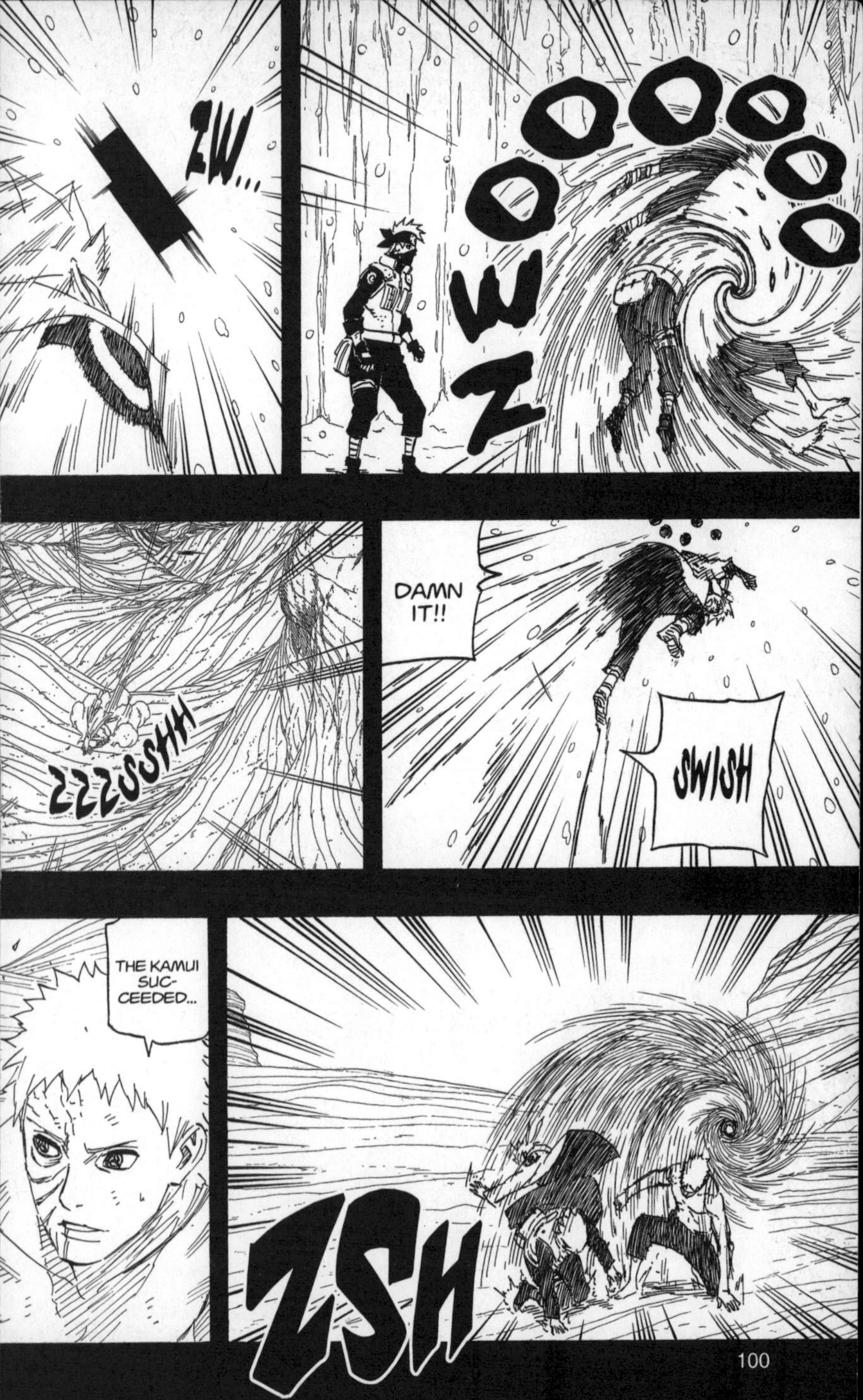
ZWOOOOOOOO
ZW...
DAMN IT!!
SWISH
ZZZZSSHH
ZSH
THE KAMUI SUC-CEEDED...

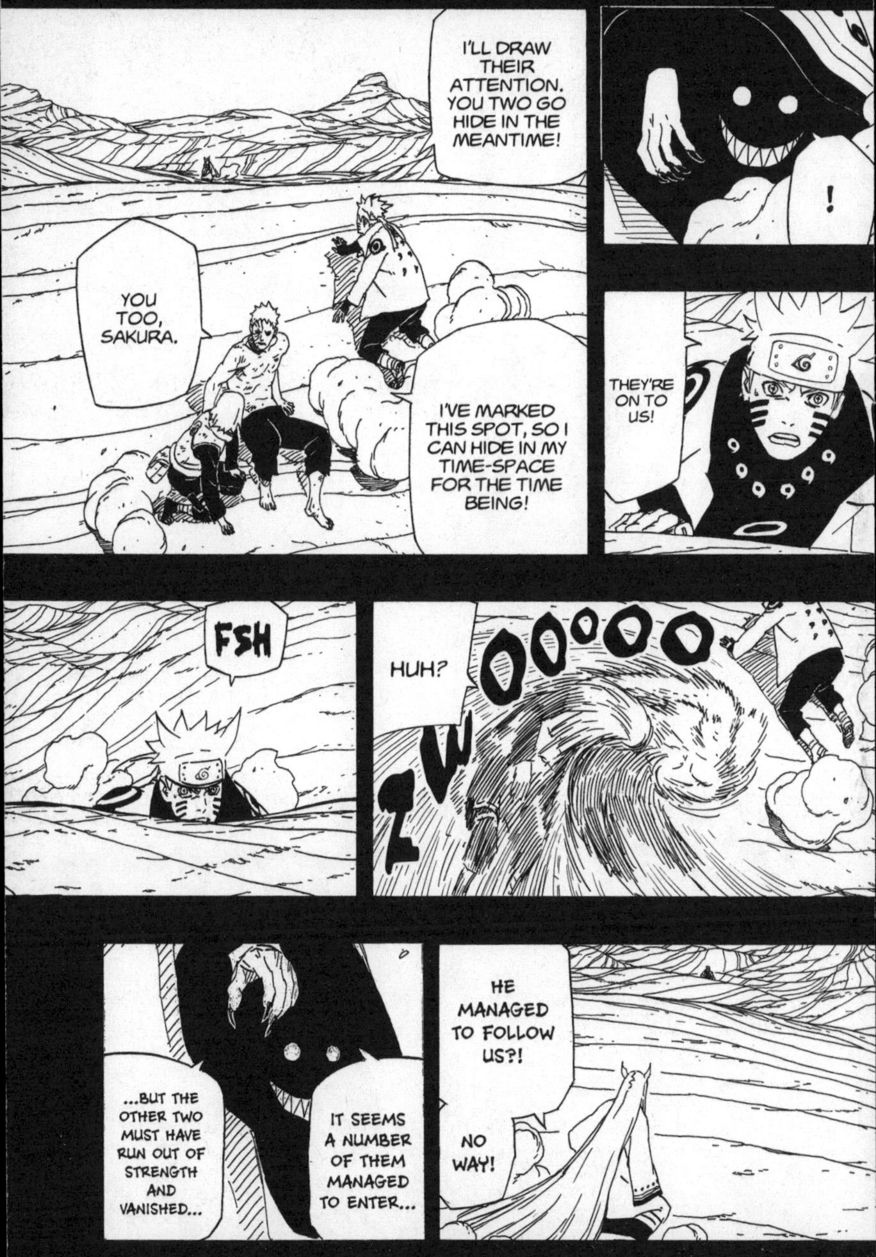
!
THEY'RE ON TO US!
I'LL DRAW THEIR ATTENTION. YOU TWO GO HIDE IN THE MEANTIME!
YOU TOO, SAKURA.
I'VE MARKED THIS SPOT, SO I CAN HIDE IN MY TIME-SPACE FOR THE TIME BEING!
HUH?
ZWOOOOOO
FSH
HE MANAGED TO FOLLOW US?!
NO WAY!
IT SEEMS A NUMBER OF THEM MANAGED TO ENTER...
...BUT THE OTHER TWO MUST HAVE RUN OUT OF STRENGTH AND VANISHED...

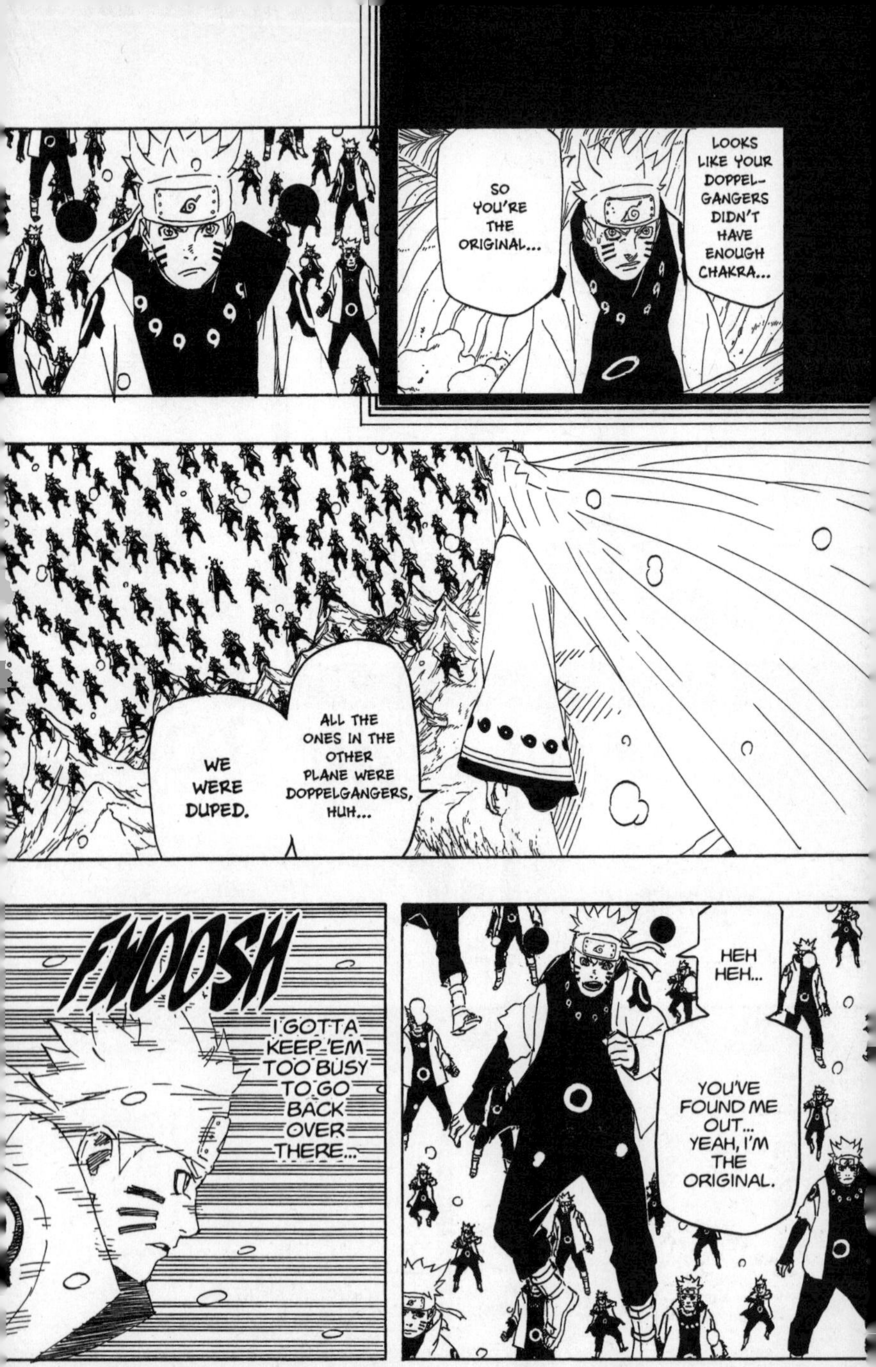
LOOKS LIKE YOUR DOPPEL-GANGERS DIDN'T HAVE ENOUGH CHAKRA...
SO YOU'RE THE ORIGINAL...
ALL THE ONES IN THE OTHER PLANE WERE DOPPELGANGERS, HUH...
WE WERE DUPED.
HEH HEH...
YOU'VE FOUND ME OUT... YEAH, I'M THE ORIGINAL.
FWOOSH
I GOTTA KEEP 'EM TOO BUSY TO GO BACK OVER THERE...

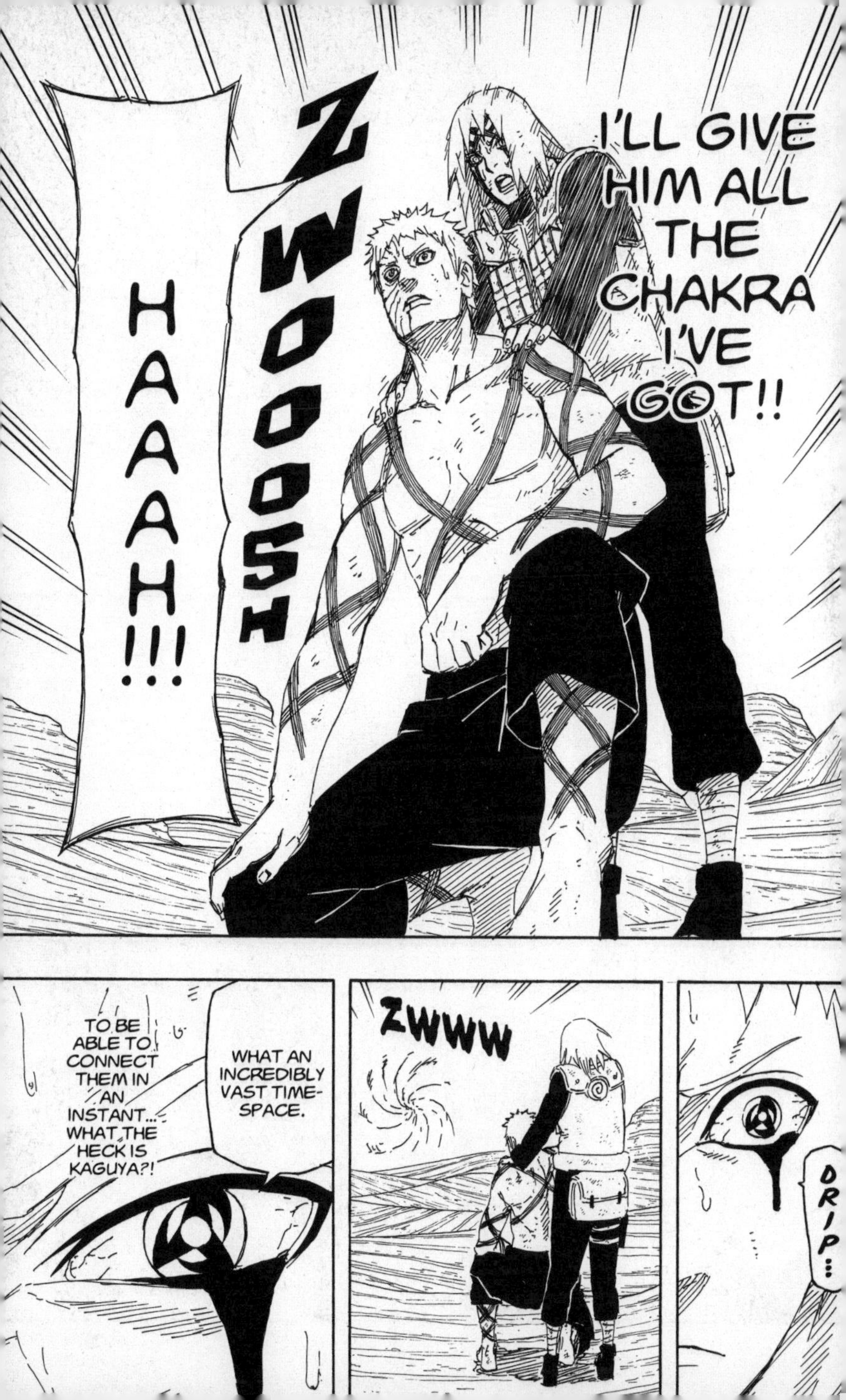
I'LL GIVE HIM ALL THE CHAKRA I'VE GOT!!
ZWOOOSH
HAAAAH!!!
DRIP...
ZWWW
WHAT AN INCREDIBLY VAST TIME-SPACE.
TO BE ABLE TO CONNECT THEM IN AN INSTANT... WHAT THE HECK IS KAGUYA?!

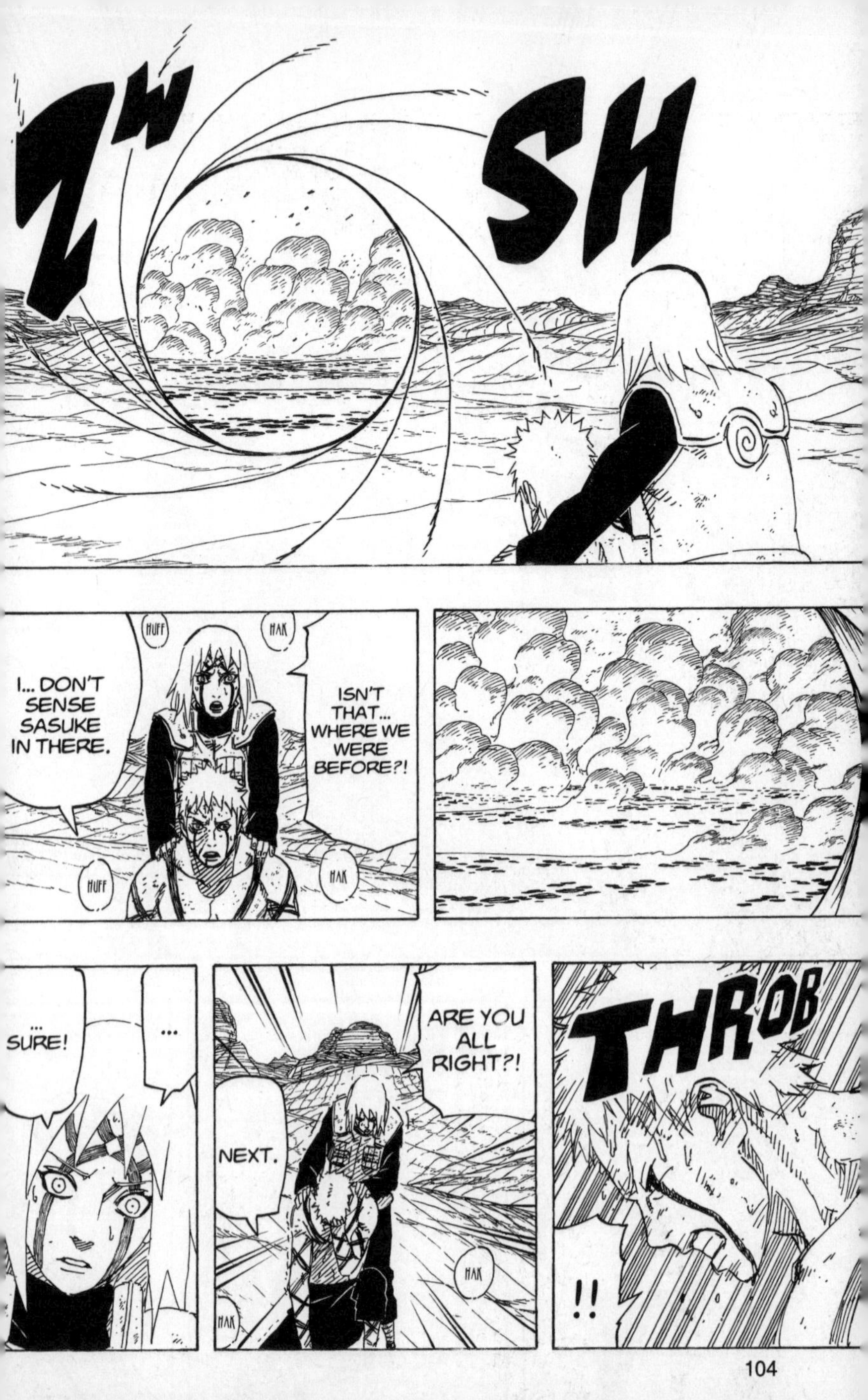
ZWSH
ISN'T THAT... WHERE WE WERE BEFORE?!
HAK
HUFF
I... DON'T SENSE SASUKE IN THERE.
HAK
HUFF
THROB
!!
ARE YOU ALL RIGHT?!
NEXT.
HAK
HAK
...
... SURE!

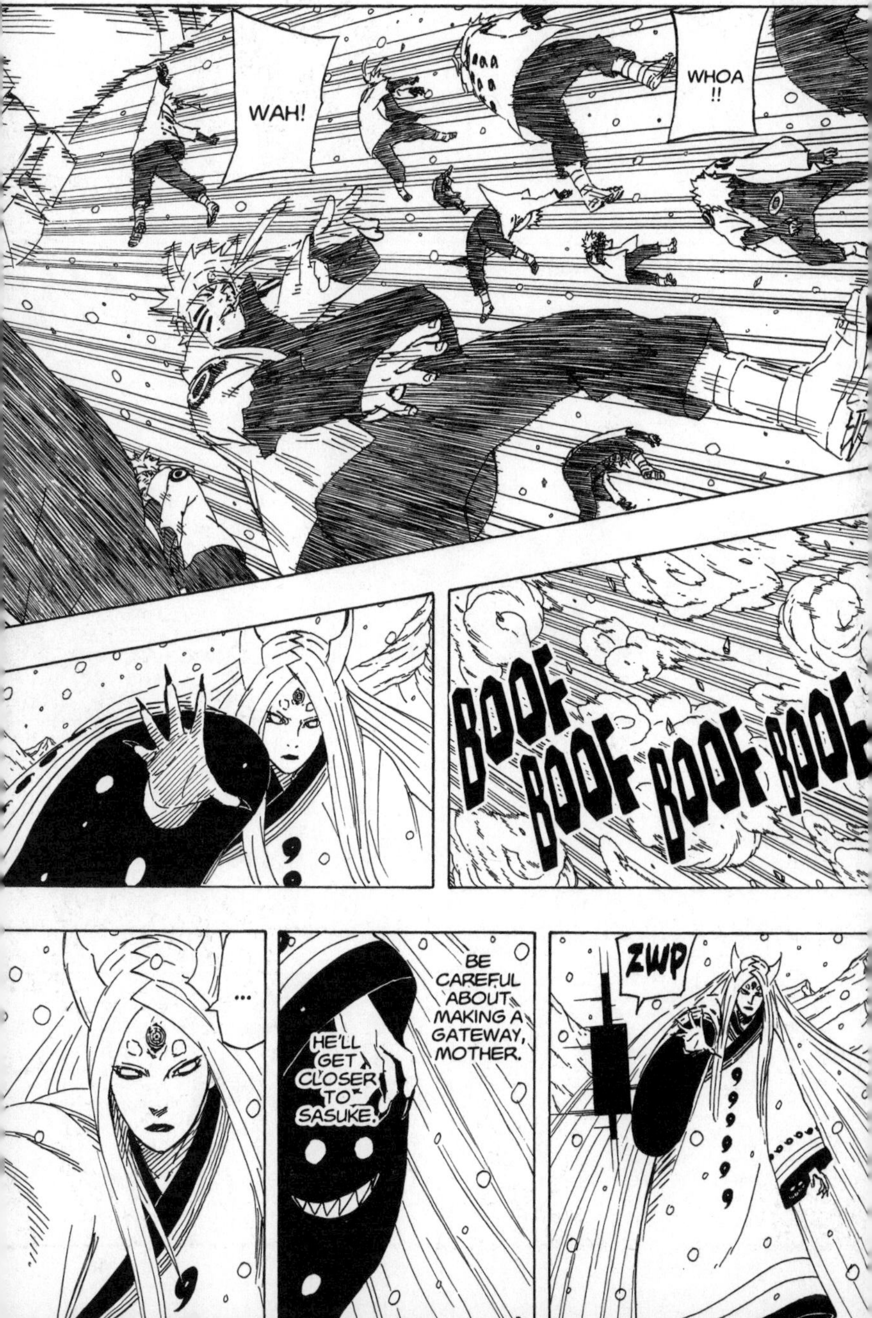
WHOA!!
WAH!
BOOF BOOF BOOF BOOF
ZWP
BE CAREFUL ABOUT MAKING A GATEWAY, MOTHER.
HE'LL GET CLOSER TO SASUKE.
...

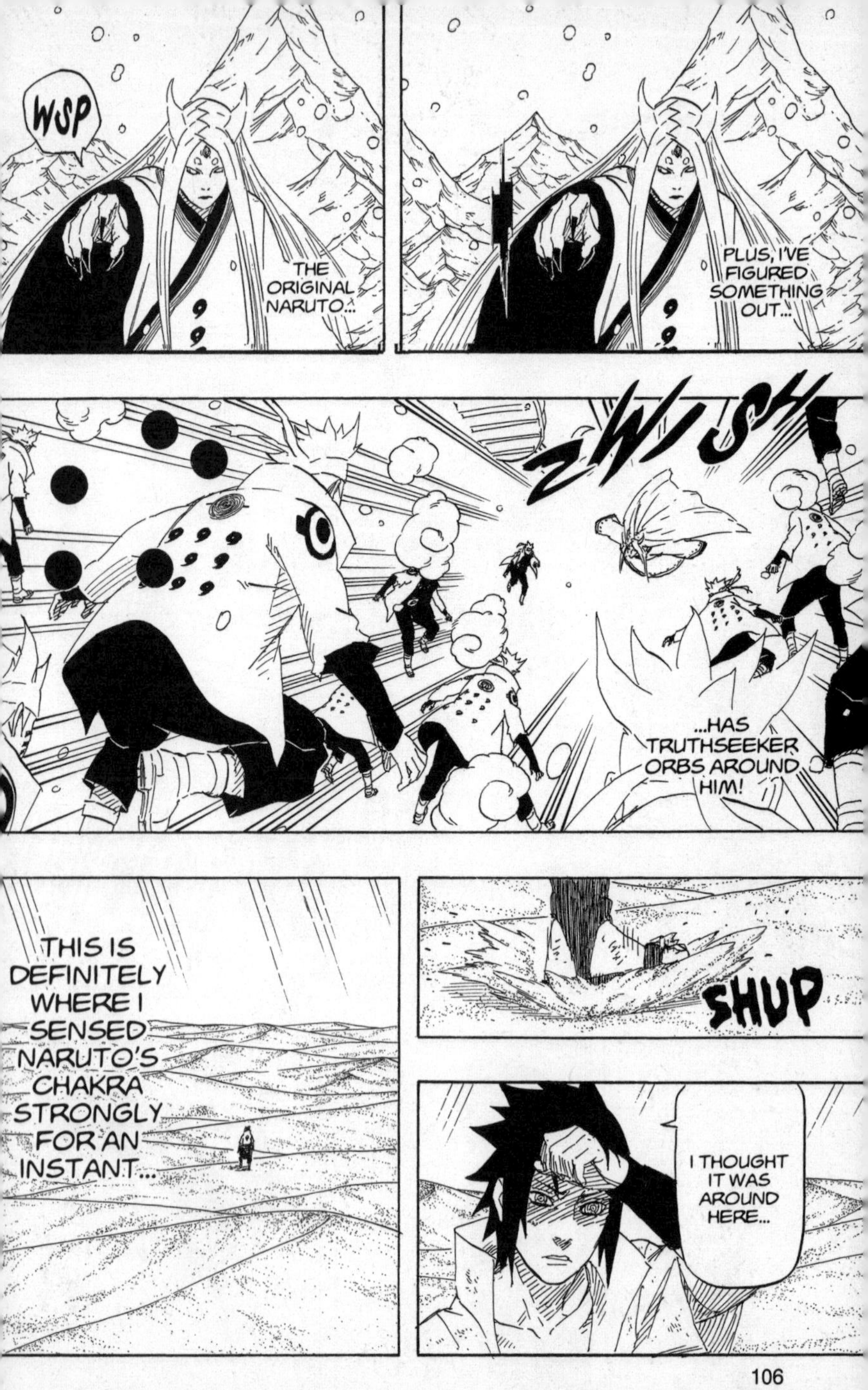

PLUS, I'VE FIGURED SOMETHING OUT...
WSP
THE ORIGINAL NARUTO...
ZWISH
...HAS TRUTHSEEKER ORBS AROUND HIM!
SHUP
I THOUGHT IT WAS AROUND HERE...
THIS IS DEFINITELY WHERE I SENSED NARUTO'S CHAKRA STRONGLY FOR AN INSTANT...

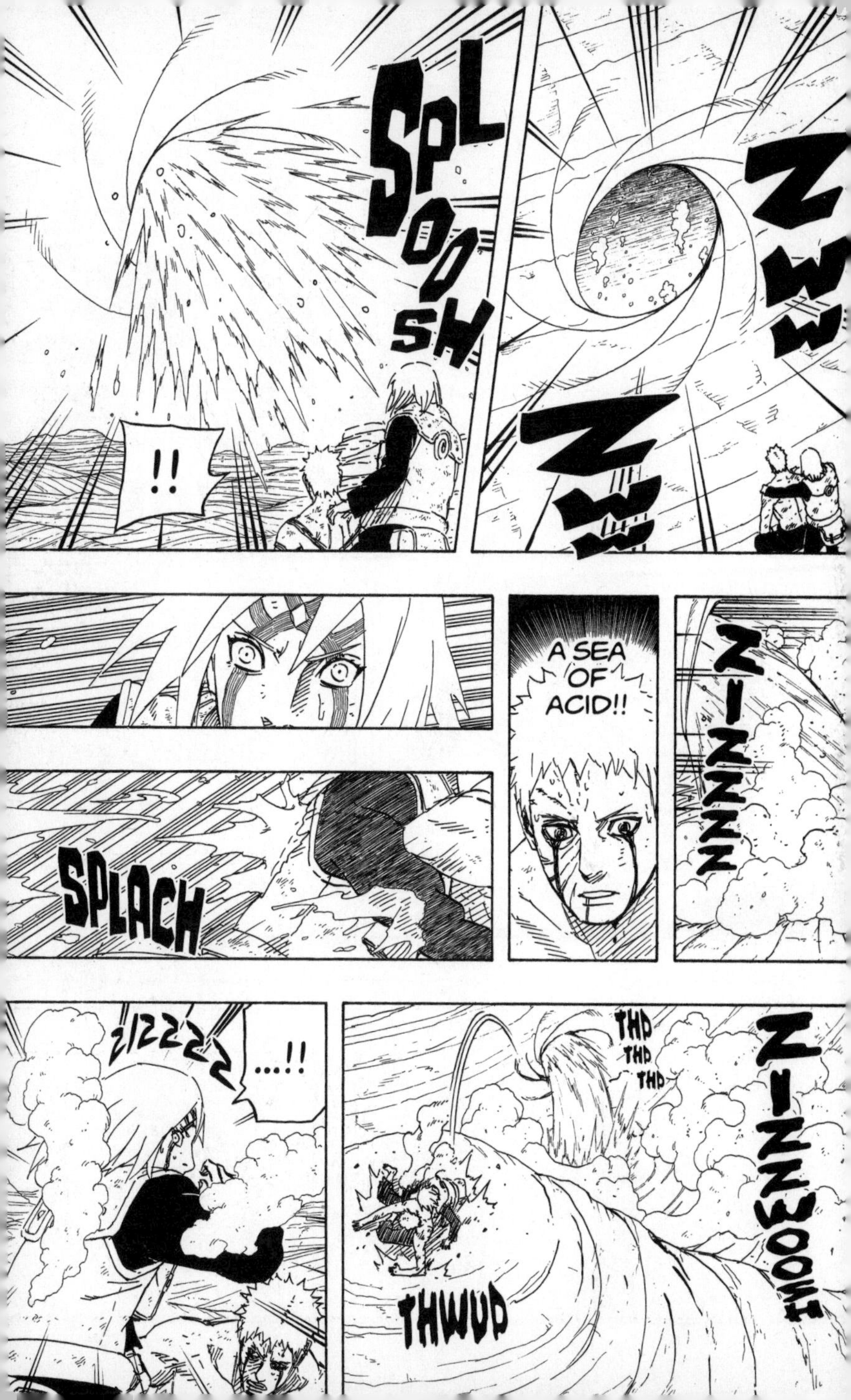
ZWWW
ZWW
SPLOOOSH
!!
ZIZZZZZ
A SEA OF ACID!!
SPLACH
ZIZZWOOOH
THD THD THD
THWUD
ZIZZZZ
...!!

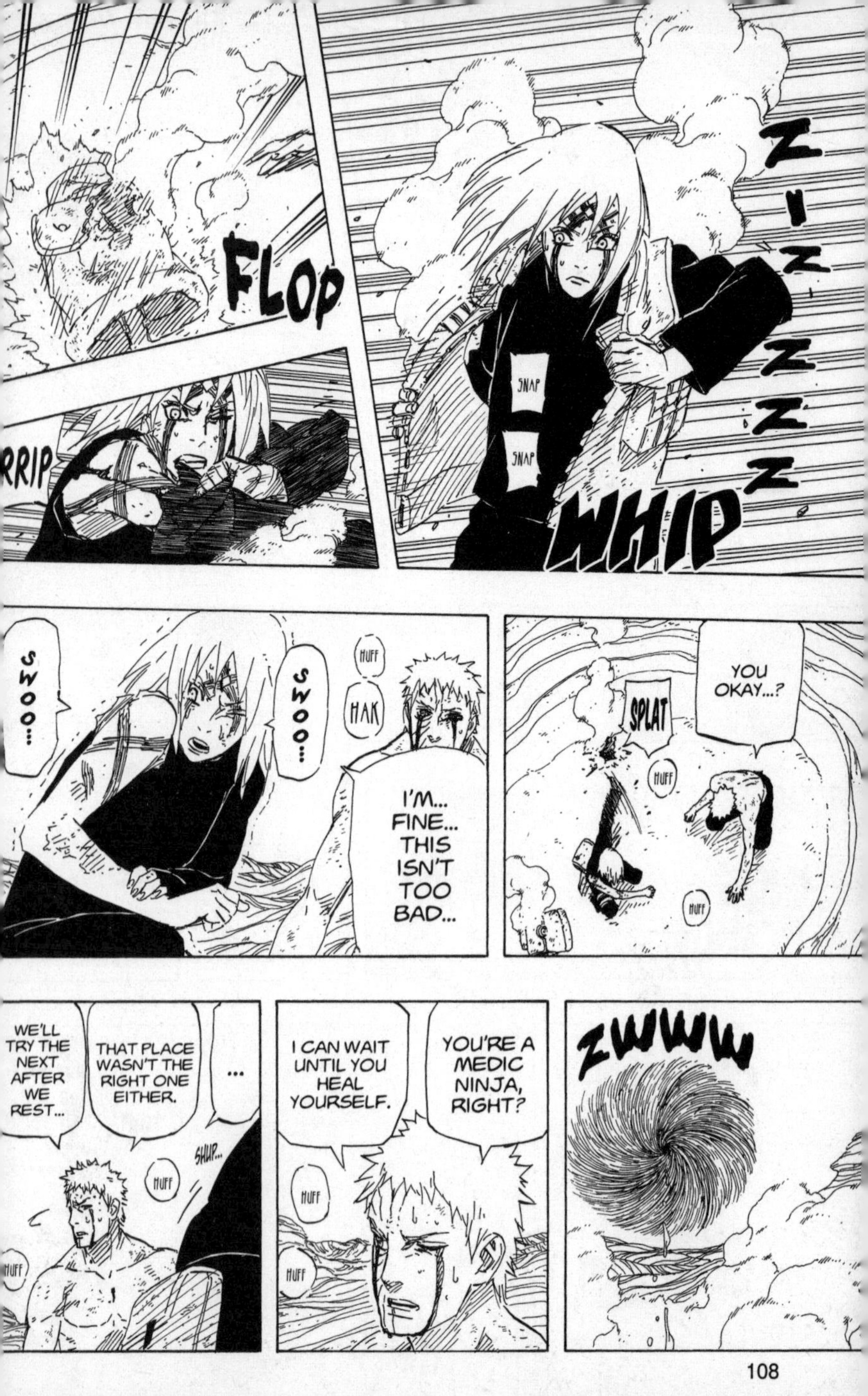
ZZZZZZ
SNAP
SNAP
WHIP
FLOP
RRIP
SPLAT
YOU OKAY...?
HUFF
HUFF
HUFF
HAK
SWOO...
I'M... FINE... THIS ISN'T TOO BAD...
SWOO...
ZWWW
YOU'RE A MEDIC NINJA, RIGHT?
I CAN WAIT UNTIL YOU HEAL YOURSELF.
HUFF
HUFF
...
THAT PLACE WASN'T THE RIGHT ONE EITHER.
WE'LL TRY THE NEXT AFTER WE REST...
SHUP...
HUFF
HUFF

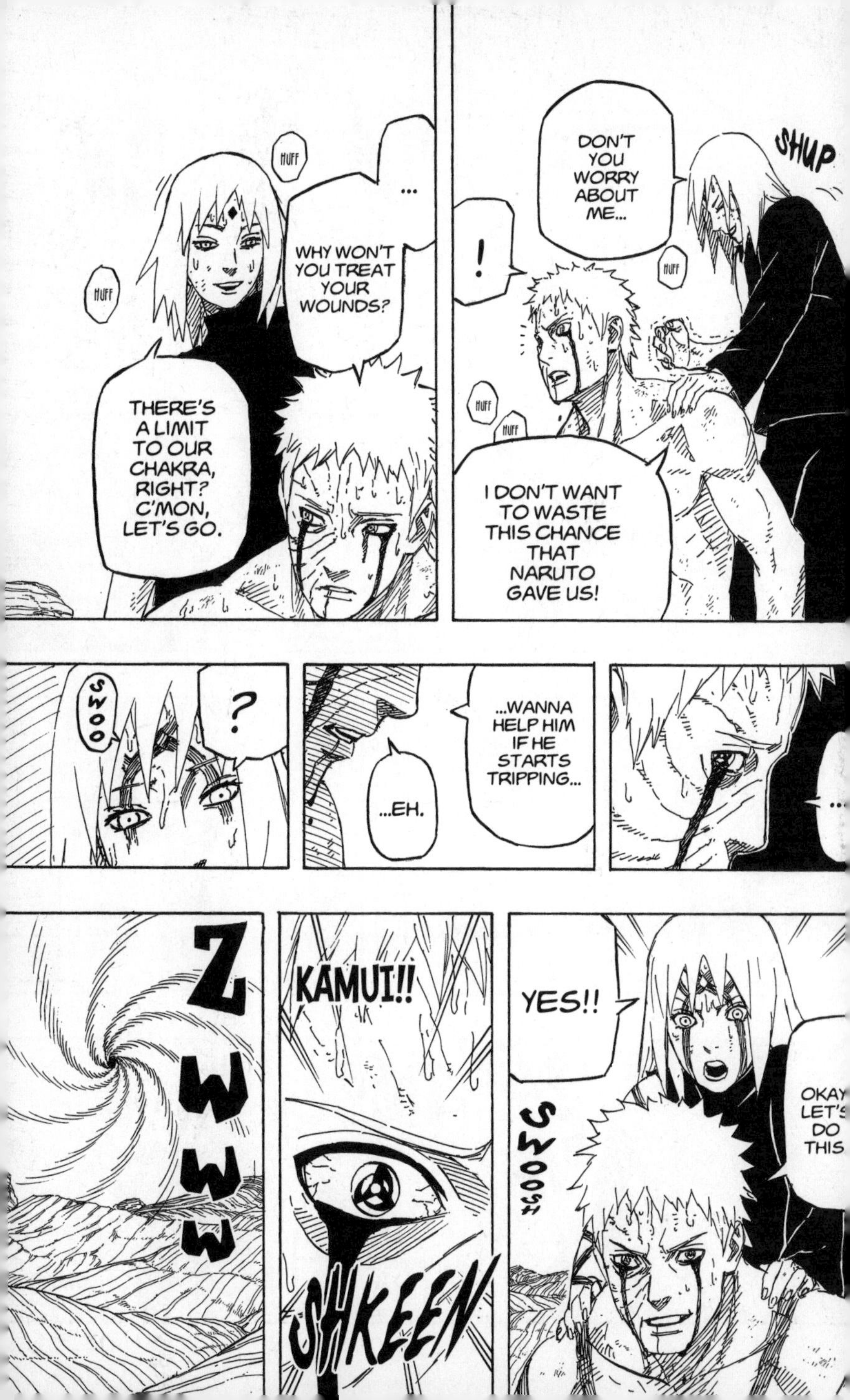
SHUP
DON'T YOU WORRY ABOUT ME...
HUFF
!
HUFF
HUFF
I DON'T WANT TO WASTE THIS CHANCE THAT NARUTO GAVE US!
...
HUFF
WHY WON'T YOU TREAT YOUR WOUNDS?
HUFF
THERE'S A LIMIT TO OUR CHAKRA, RIGHT? C'MON, LET'S GO.
...
...WANNA HELP HIM IF HE STARTS TRIPPING...
...EH.
?
SWOO
OKAY LET'S DO THIS
YES!!
SWOOSH
KAMUI!!
SHKEEN
ZWWWW

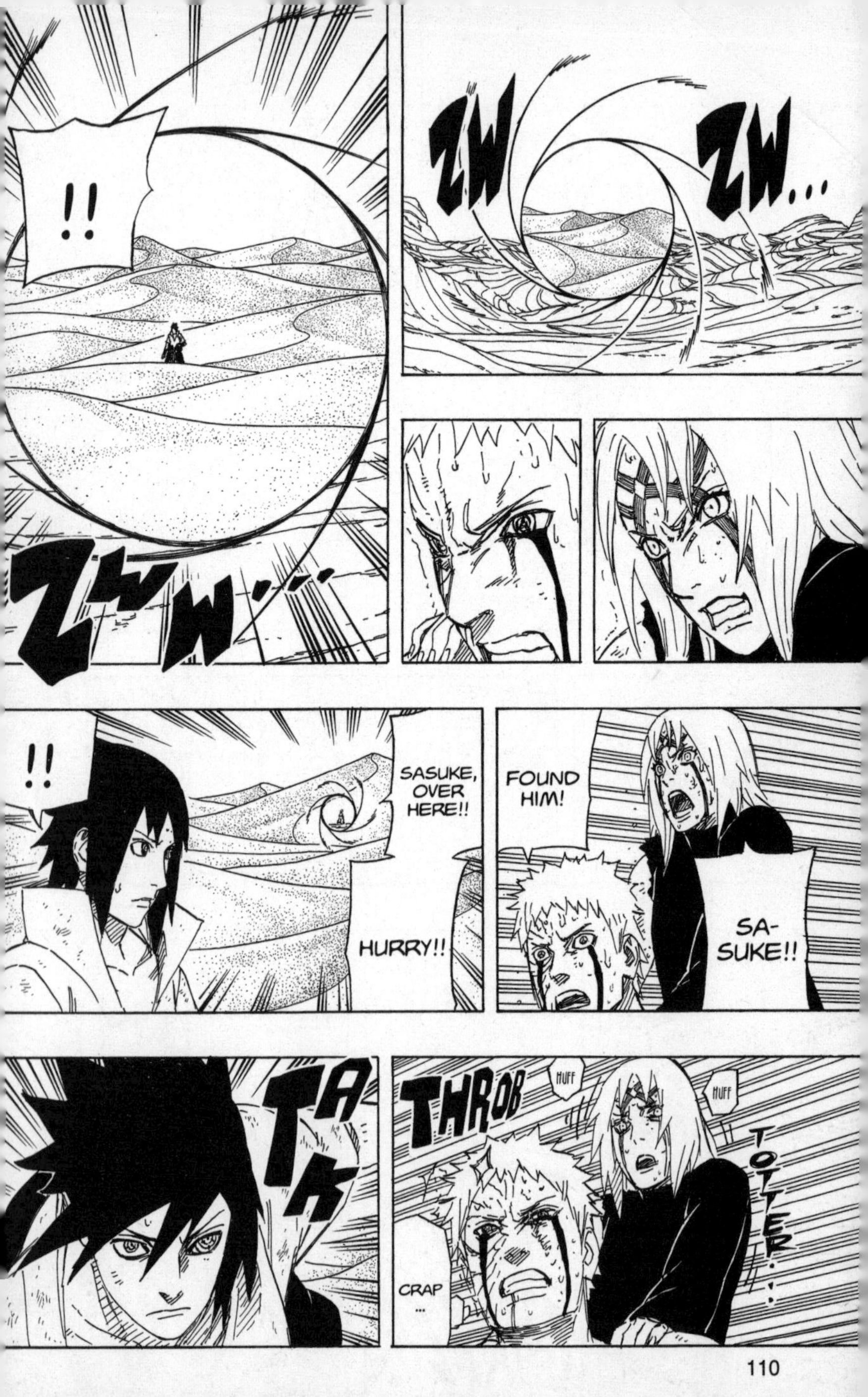
ZW
ZW...
!!
ZWWW...
FOUND HIM!
SA-
SUKE!!
SASUKE,
OVER
HERE!!
HURRY!!
!!
HUFF
HUFF
THROB
TOTTER...
CRAP
...
TAK

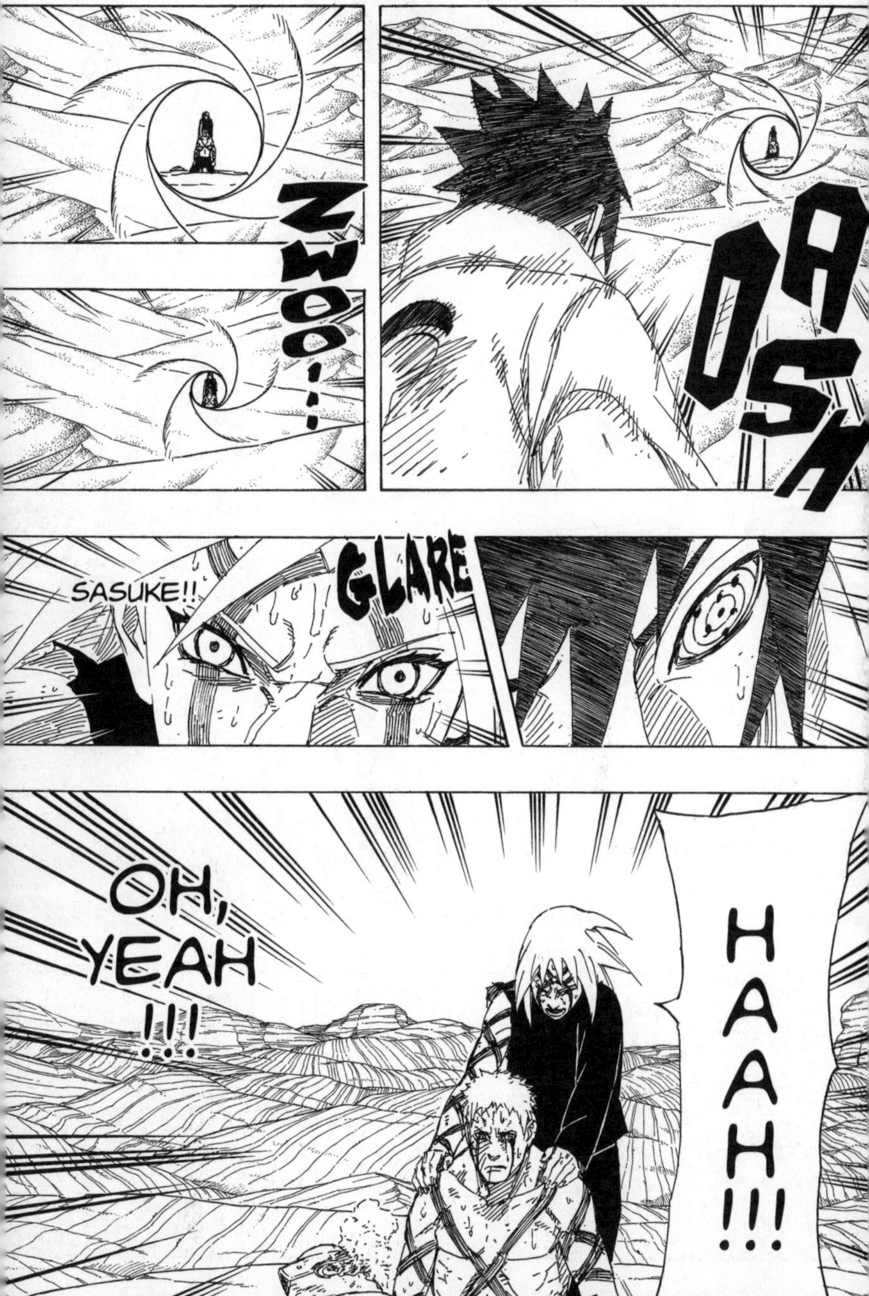
DOSH
ZWOO...
GLARE
SASUKE!!
HAAH!!!
OH, YEAH!!!

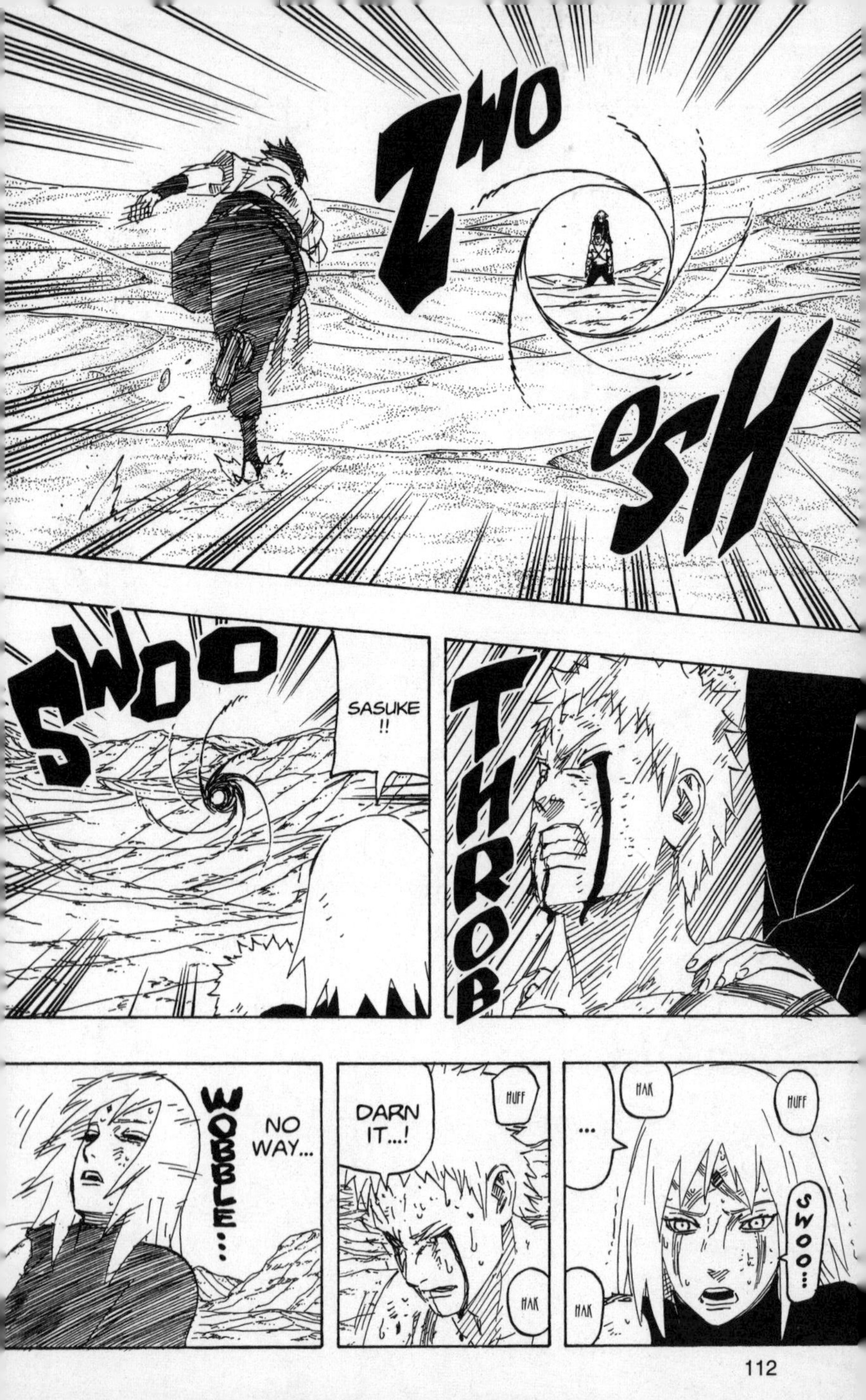
ZWOOSH
THROB
SASUKE!!
SWOO
HUFF
HAK
...
SWOO...
HAK
HUFF
DARN IT...!
HAK
NO WAY...
WOBBLE...

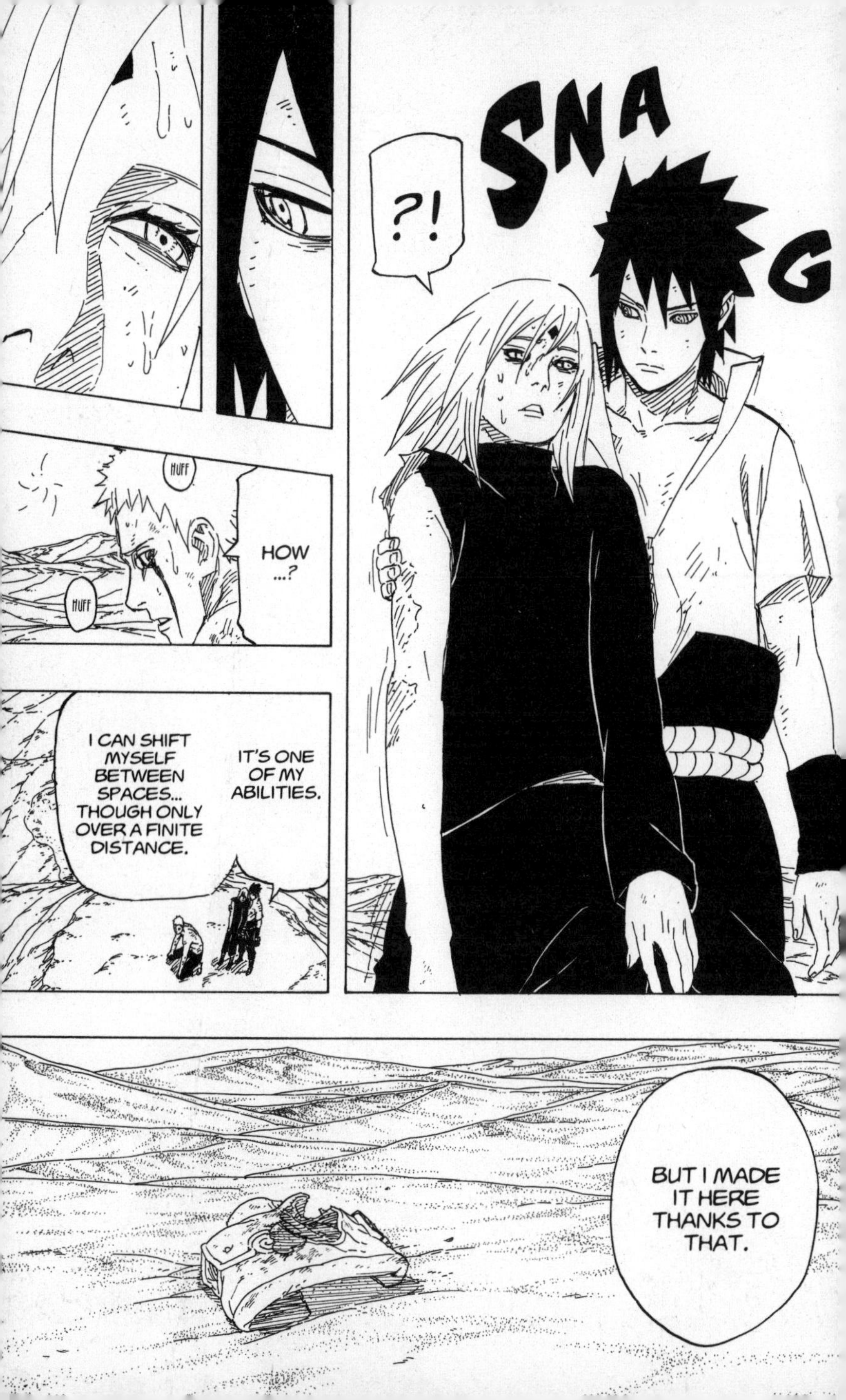

?!
SNAG
HUFF
HOW ...?
HUFF
IT'S ONE OF MY ABILITIES.
I CAN SHIFT MYSELF BETWEEN SPACES... THOUGH ONLY OVER A FINITE DISTANCE.
BUT I MADE IT HERE THANKS TO THAT.

Number 686: Bequeath and Inherit

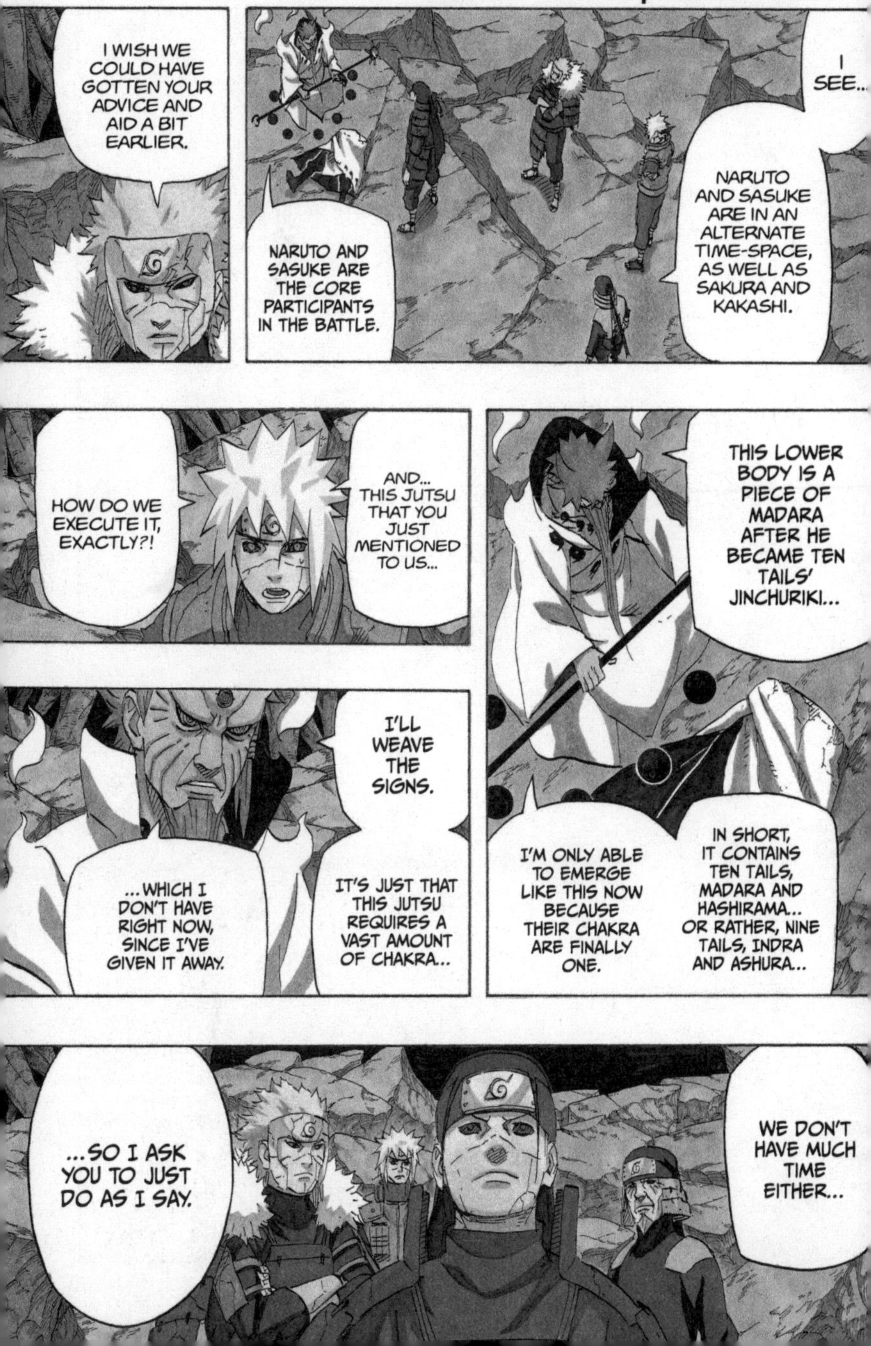
I SEE...
NARUTO AND SASUKE ARE IN AN ALTERNATE TIME-SPACE, AS WELL AS SAKURA AND KAKASHI.
NARUTO AND SASUKE ARE THE CORE PARTICIPANTS IN THE BATTLE.
I WISH WE COULD HAVE GOTTEN YOUR ADVICE AND AID A BIT EARLIER.
THIS LOWER BODY IS A PIECE OF MADARA AFTER HE BECAME TEN TAILS' JINCHURIKI...
IN SHORT, IT CONTAINS TEN TAILS, MADARA AND HASHIRAMA... OR RATHER, NINE TAILS, INDRA AND ASHURA...
I'M ONLY ABLE TO EMERGE LIKE THIS NOW BECAUSE THEIR CHAKRA ARE FINALLY ONE.
AND... THIS JUTSU THAT YOU JUST MENTIONED TO US...
HOW DO WE EXECUTE IT, EXACTLY?!
I'LL WEAVE THE SIGNS.
IT'S JUST THAT THIS JUTSU REQUIRES A VAST AMOUNT OF CHAKRA...
...WHICH I DON'T HAVE RIGHT NOW, SINCE I'VE GIVEN IT AWAY.
WE DON'T HAVE MUCH TIME EITHER...
...SO I ASK YOU TO JUST DO AS I SAY.

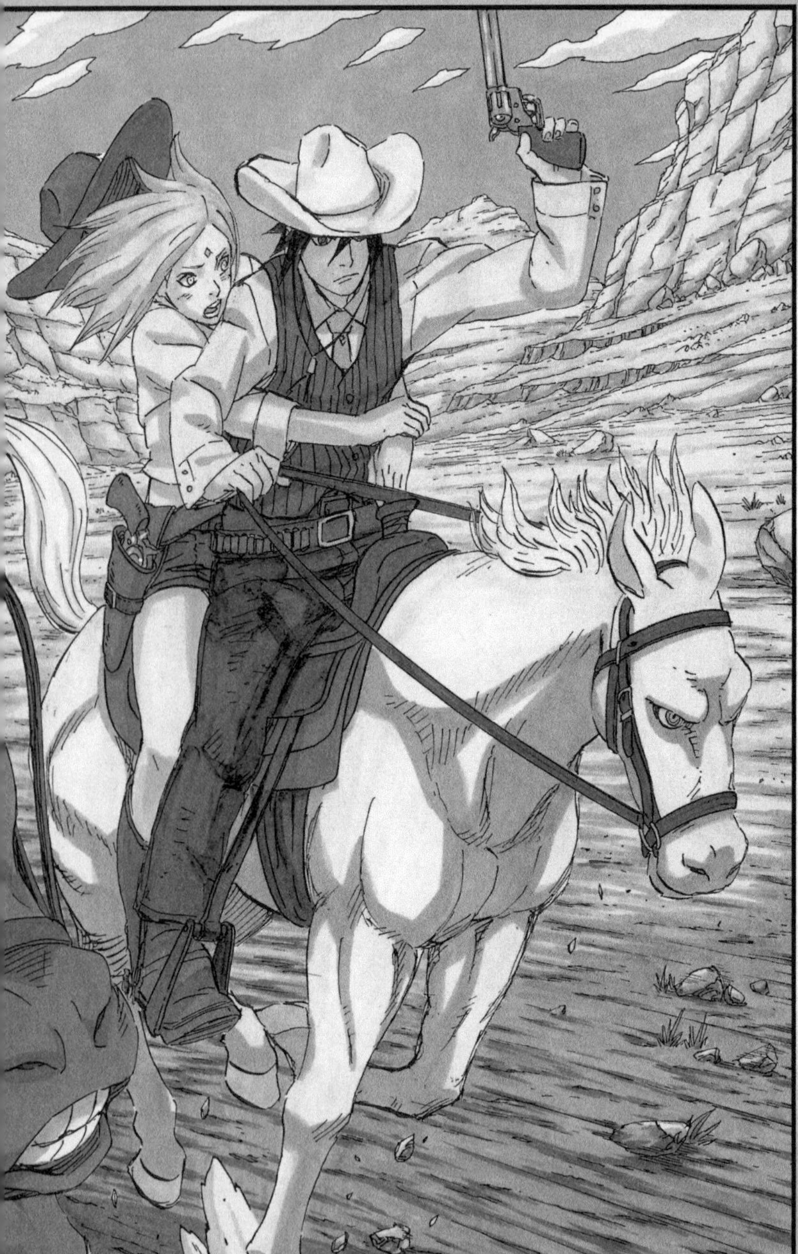

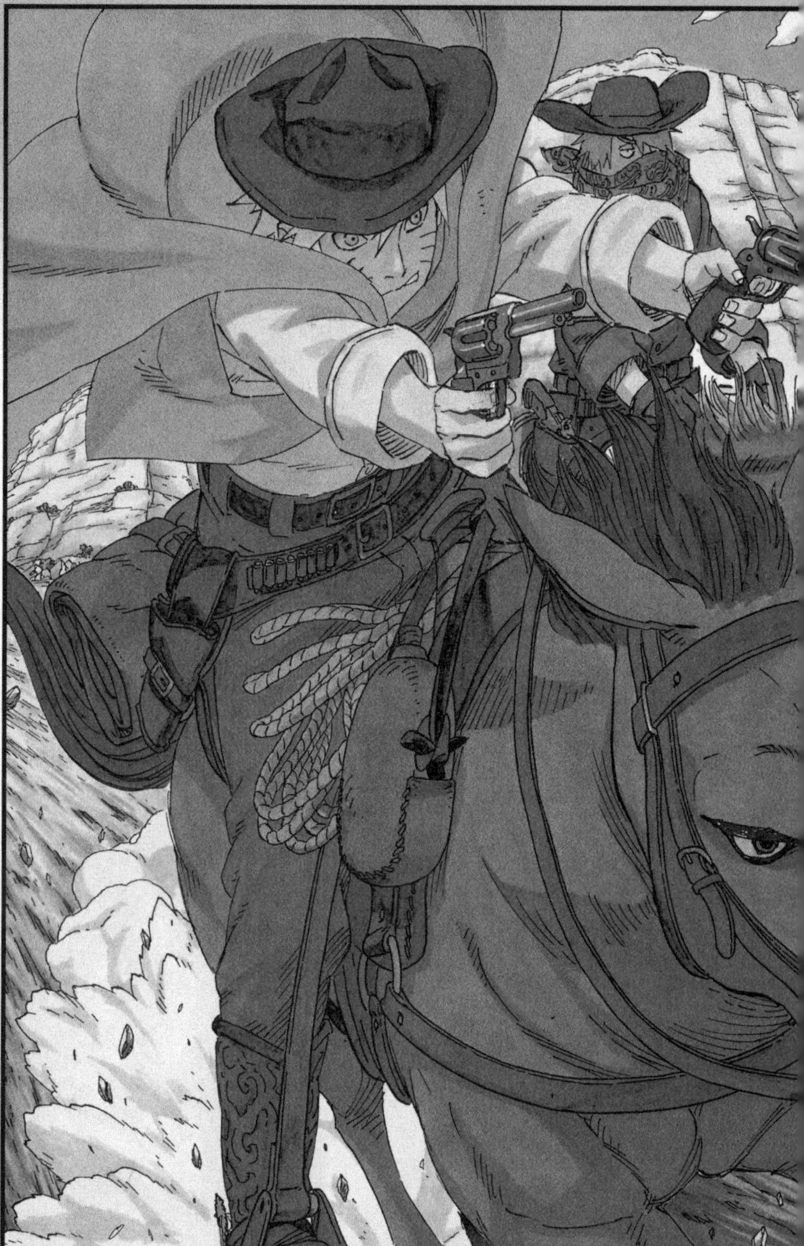

Number 686: Bequeath and Inherit

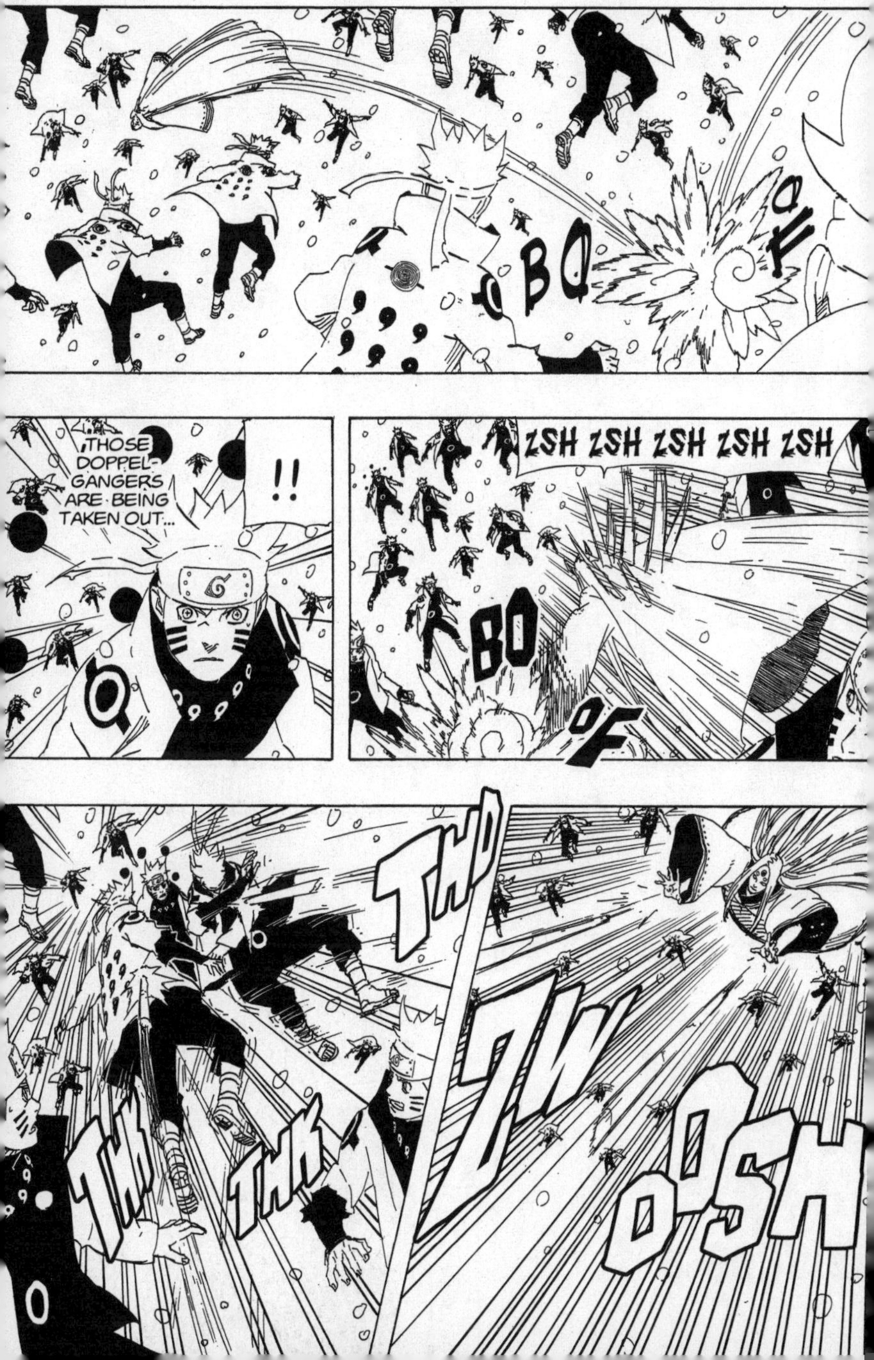
BOOF
ZSH ZSH ZSH ZSH ZSH
BOOF
THOSE DOPPEL-GANGERS ARE BEING TAKEN OUT...
!!
ZWOOSH
THD
THK
THK

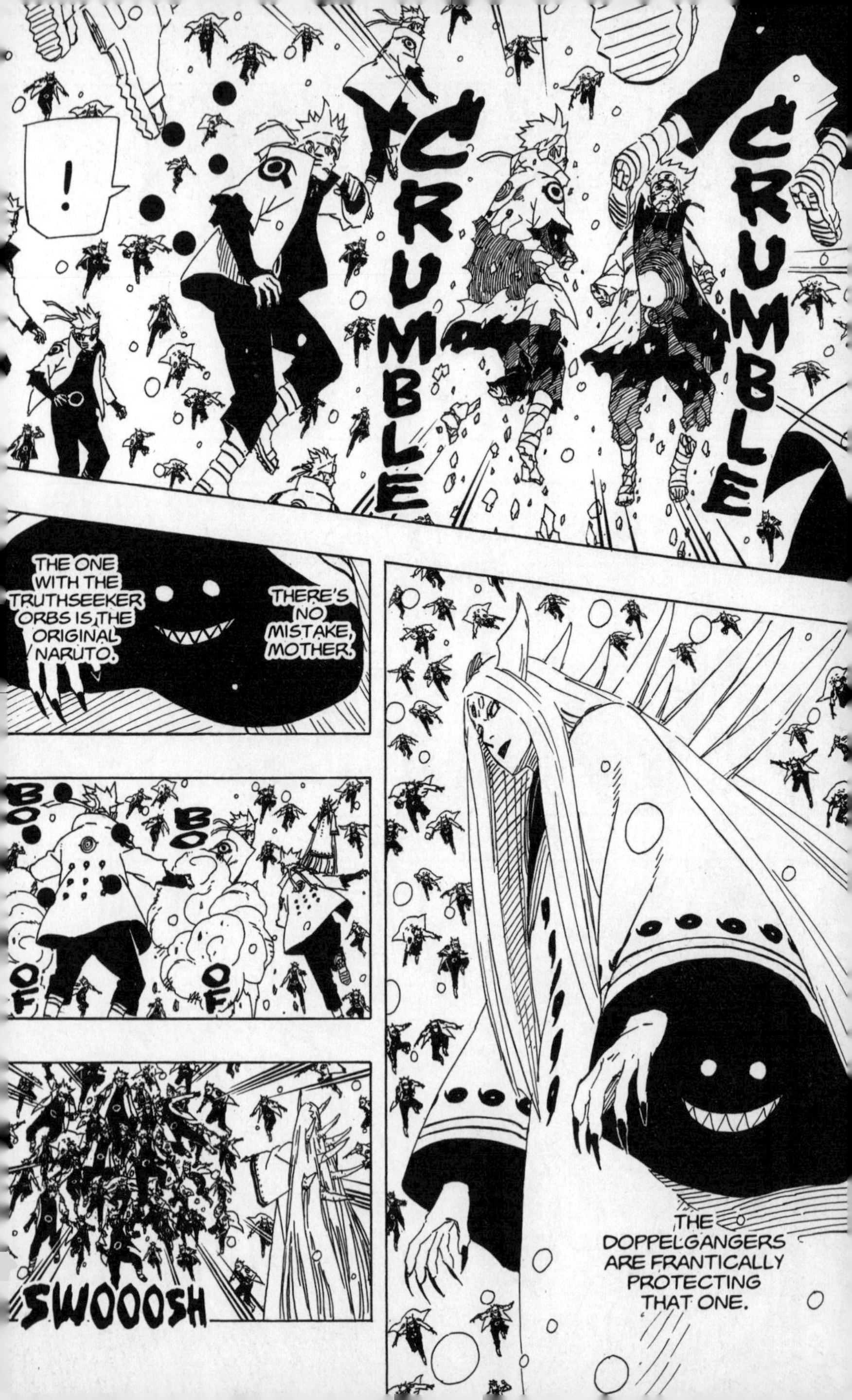
CRUMBLE
CRUMBLE
!
THE DOPPELGANGERS ARE FRANTICALLY PROTECTING THAT ONE.
THERE'S NO MISTAKE, MOTHER.
THE ONE WITH THE TRUTHSEEKER ORBS IS THE ORIGINAL NARUTO.
BOOF
BOOF
SWOOOSH

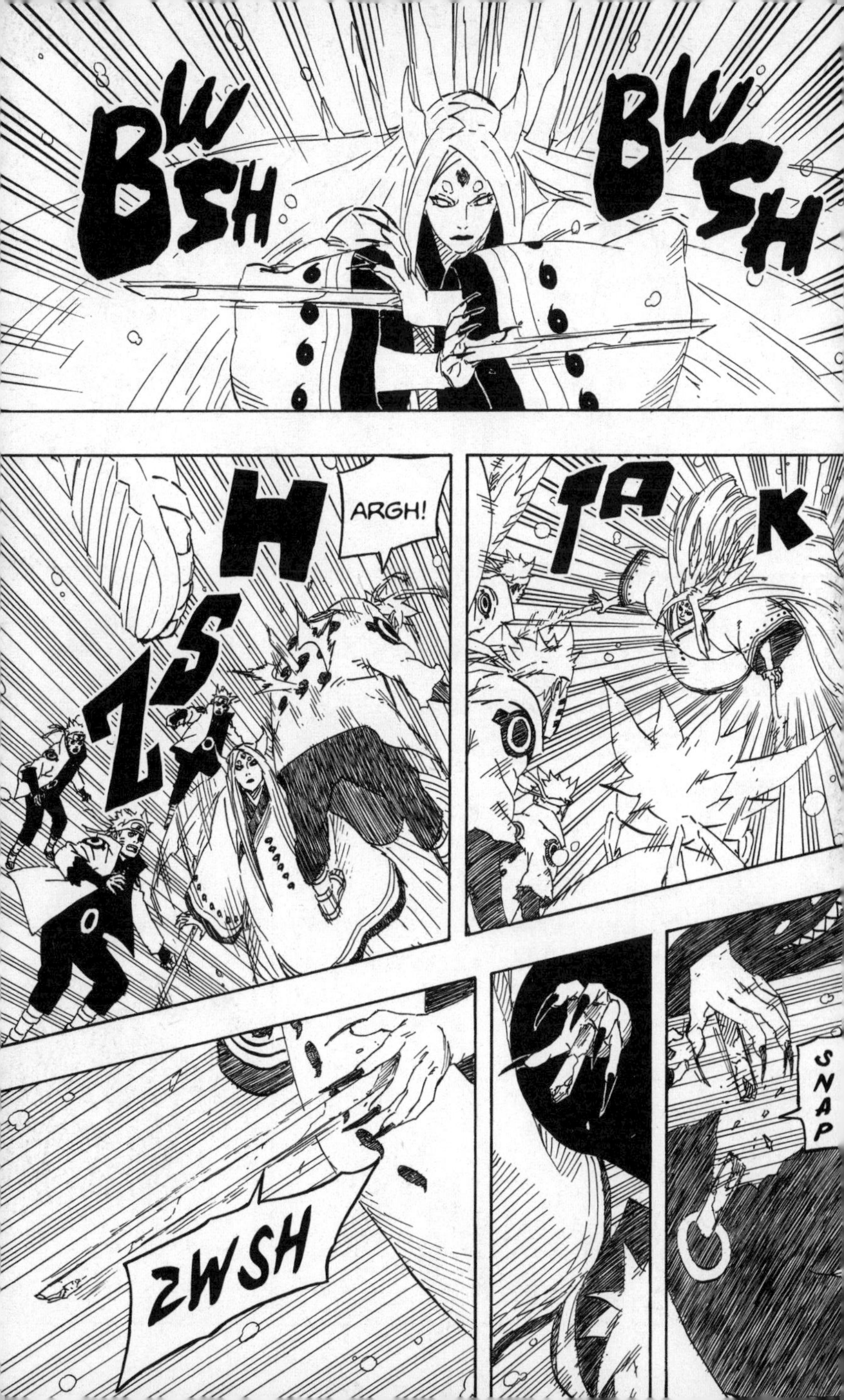
BWSH
BWSH
TAK
ZSH
ARGH!
SNAP
ZWSH

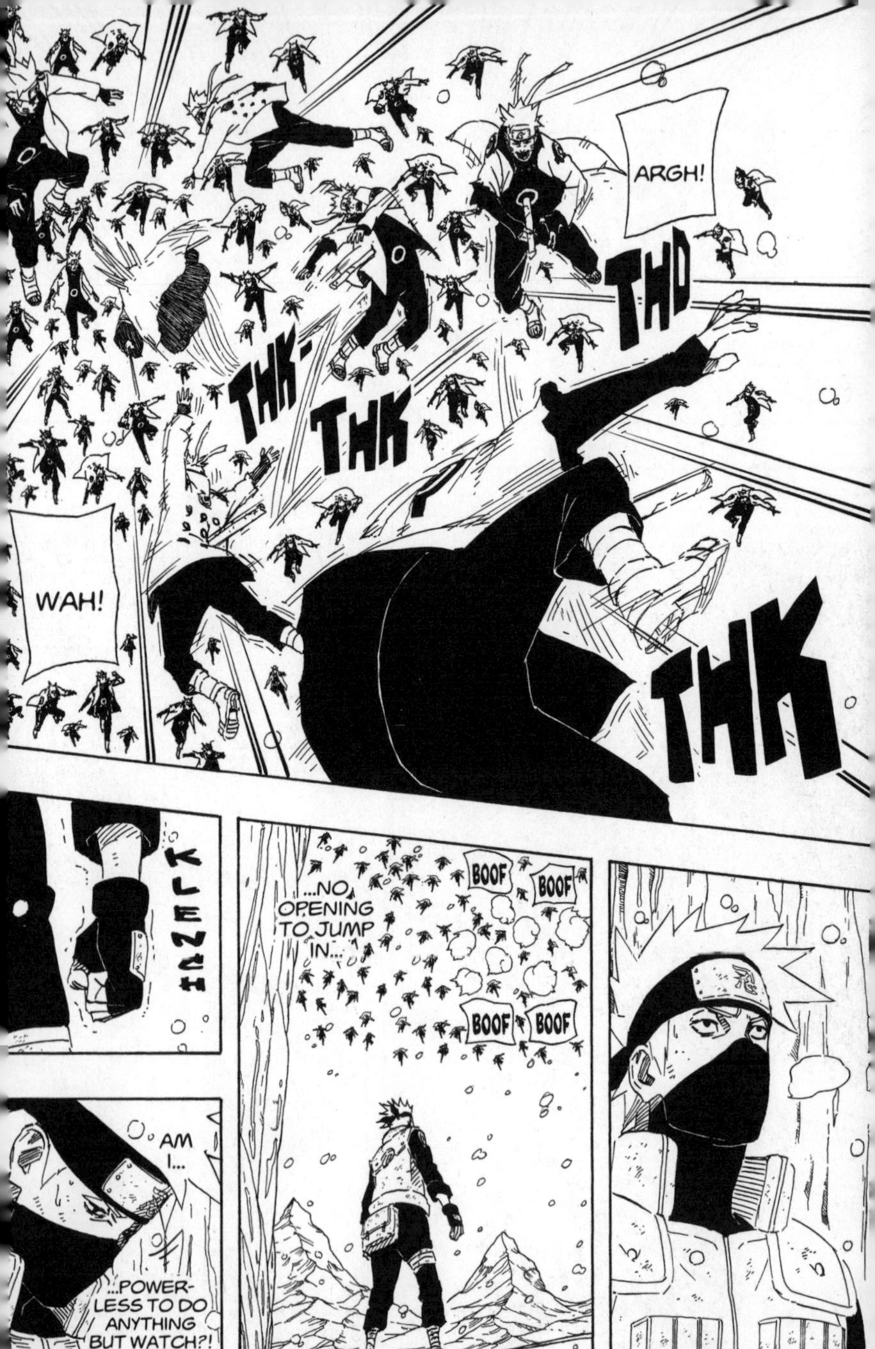
ARGH!
THD
THK
THK-THK
WAH!
BOOF
BOOF
BOOF
BOOF
...NO OPENING TO JUMP IN...
KLENCH
AM I...
...POWER-LESS TO DO ANYTHING BUT WATCH?!

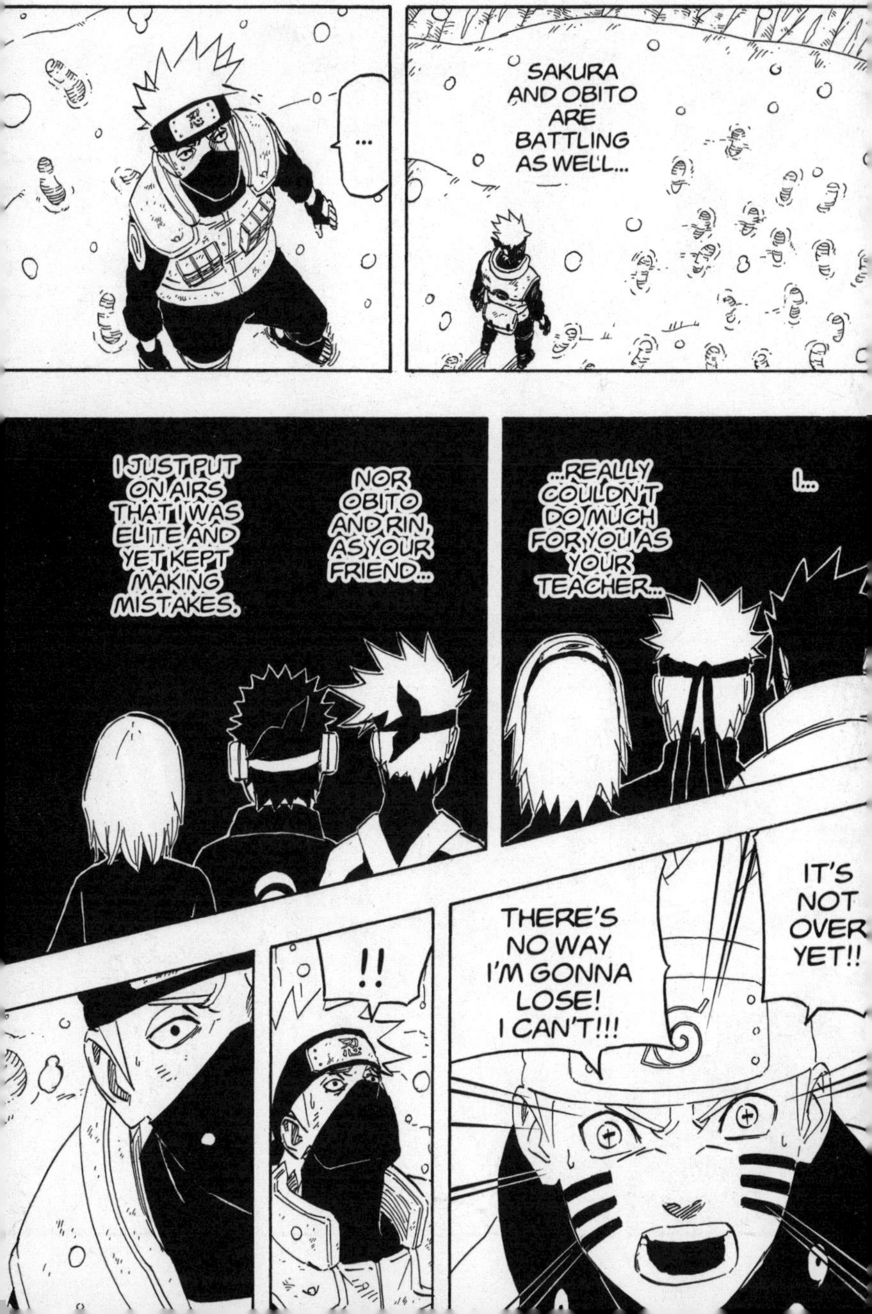
SAKURA AND OBITO ARE BATTLING AS WELL...
...
I...
...REALLY COULDN'T DO MUCH FOR YOU AS YOUR TEACHER...
NOR OBITO AND RIN, AS YOUR FRIEND...
I JUST PUT ON AIRS THAT I WAS ELITE AND YET KEPT MAKING MISTAKES.
IT'S NOT OVER YET!!
THERE'S NO WAY I'M GONNA LOSE! I CAN'T!!!
!!

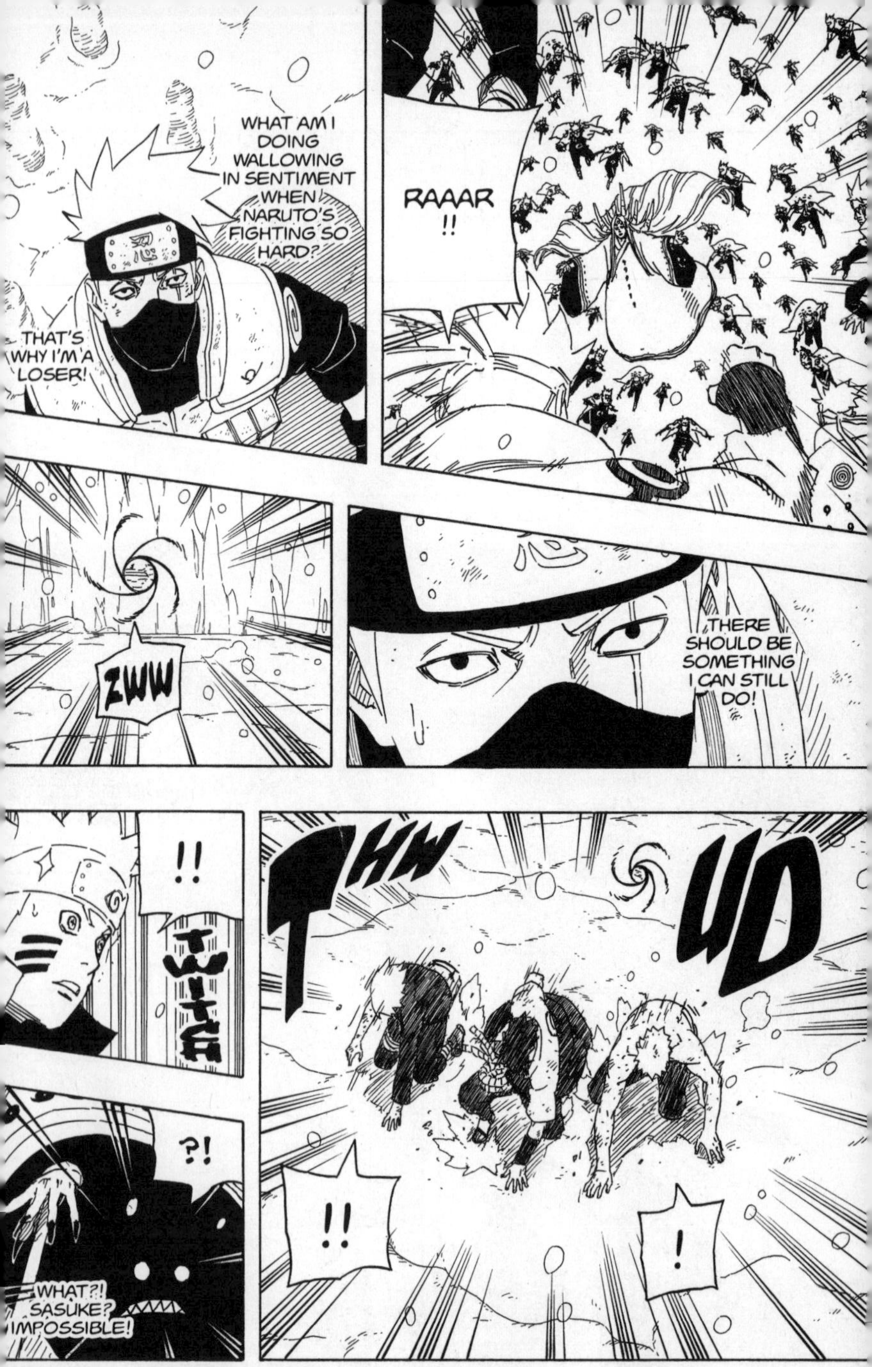
RAAAR !!
WHAT AM I DOING WALLOWING IN SENTIMENT WHEN NARUTO'S FIGHTING SO HARD?
THAT'S WHY I'M A LOSER!
THERE SHOULD BE SOMETHING I CAN STILL DO!
ZWW
THWUD
!
!!
!!
TWITCH
?!
WHAT?! SASUKE? IMPOSSIBLE!

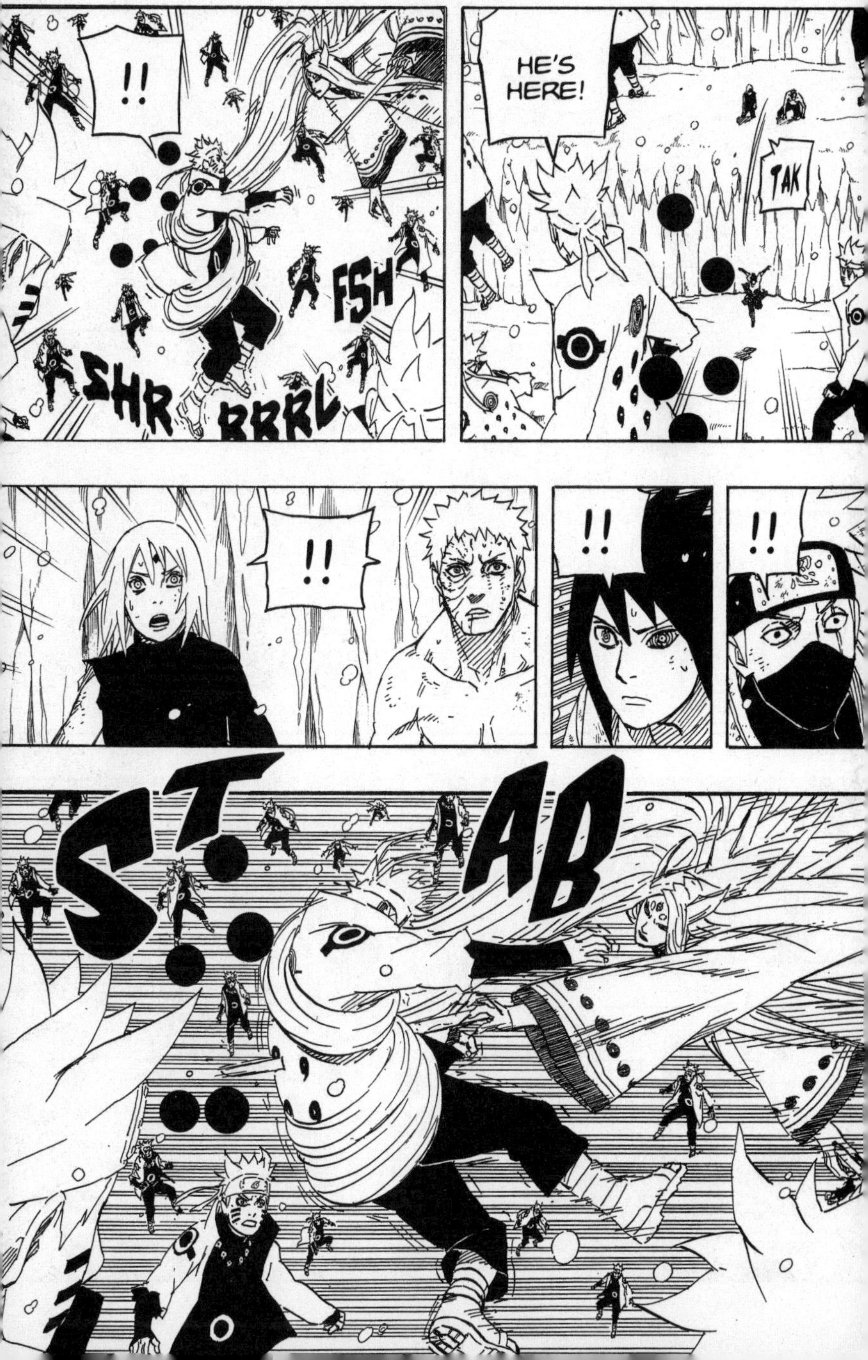
HE'S HERE!
TAK
!!
FSH
SHR
RRRL
!!
!!
!!
STAB

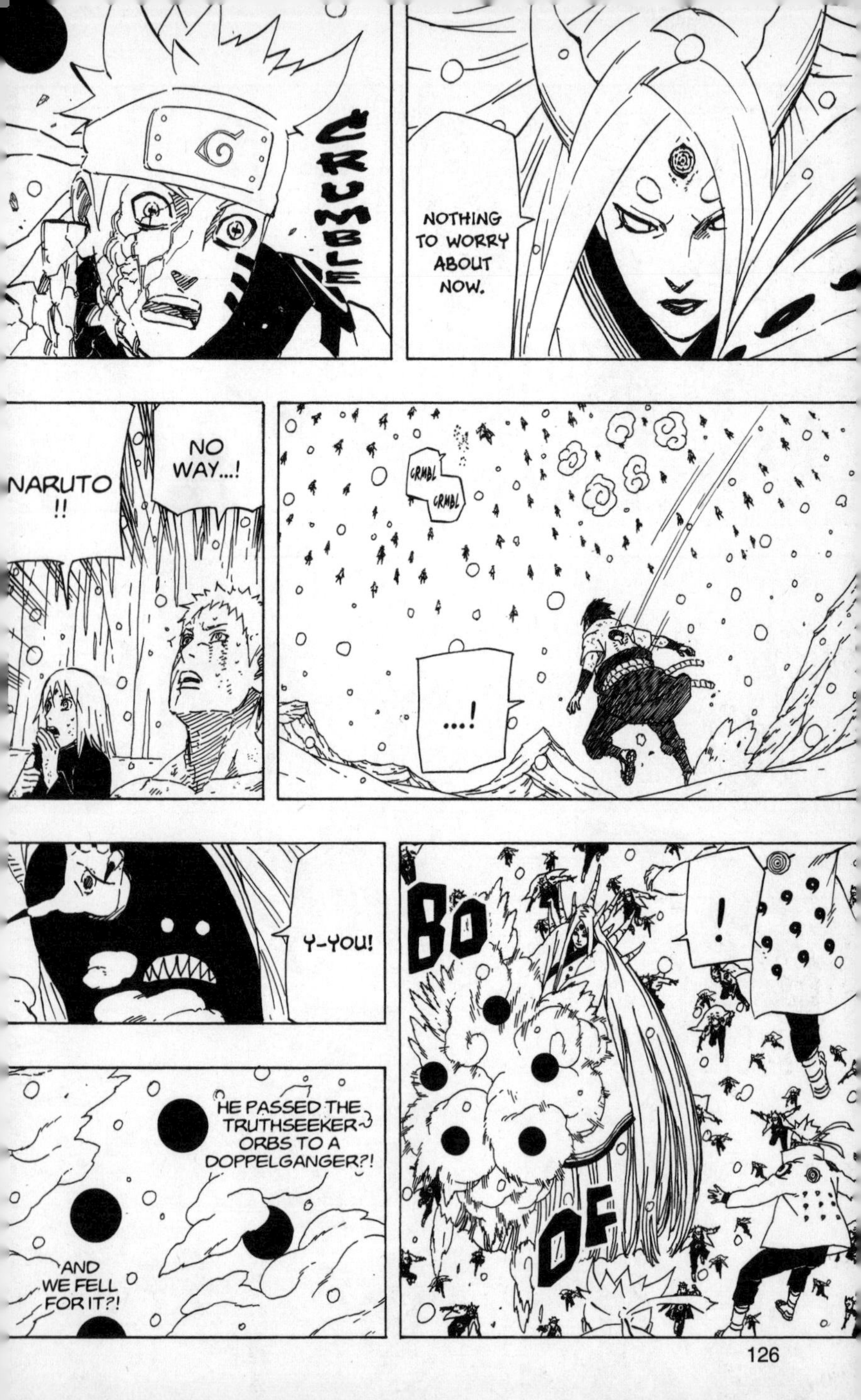
NOTHING TO WORRY ABOUT NOW.
CRUMBLE
CRMBL
CRMBL
...!
NO WAY...!
NARUTO !!
!
BOOF
Y-YOU!
HE PASSED THE TRUTHSEEKER ORBS TO A DOPPELGANGER?!
AND WE FELL FOR IT?!

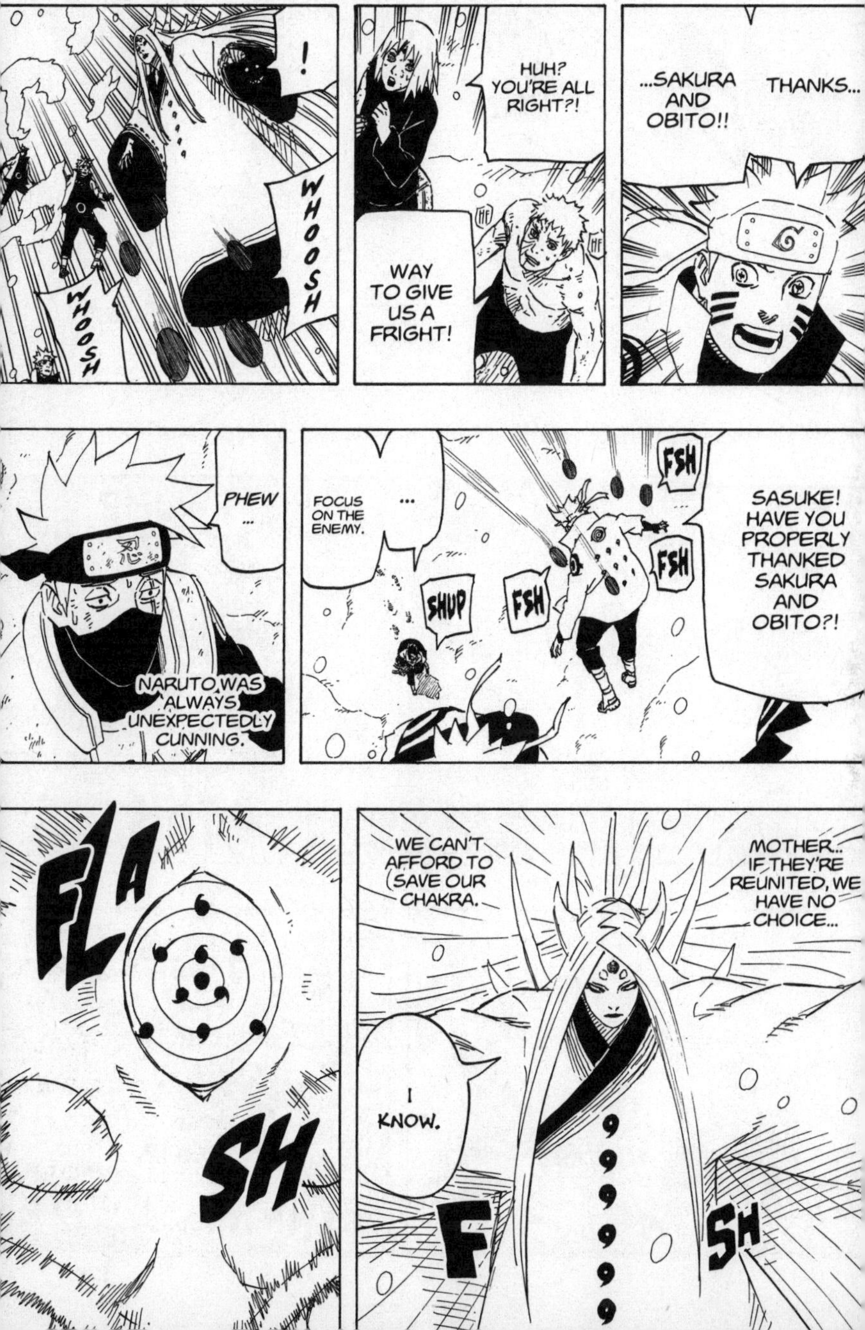
THANKS...
...SAKURA AND OBITO!!
HUH? YOU'RE ALL RIGHT?!
HF
HF
WAY TO GIVE US A FRIGHT!
!
WHOOSH
WHOOSH
SASUKE! HAVE YOU PROPERLY THANKED SAKURA AND OBITO?!
FSH
FSH
...
...
FOCUS ON THE ENEMY.
FSH
SHUP
PHEW...
NARUTO WAS ALWAYS UNEXPECTEDLY CUNNING.
MOTHER... IF THEY'RE REUNITED, WE HAVE NO CHOICE...
WE CAN'T AFFORD TO SAVE OUR CHAKRA.
I KNOW.
SH
F
FLA
SH

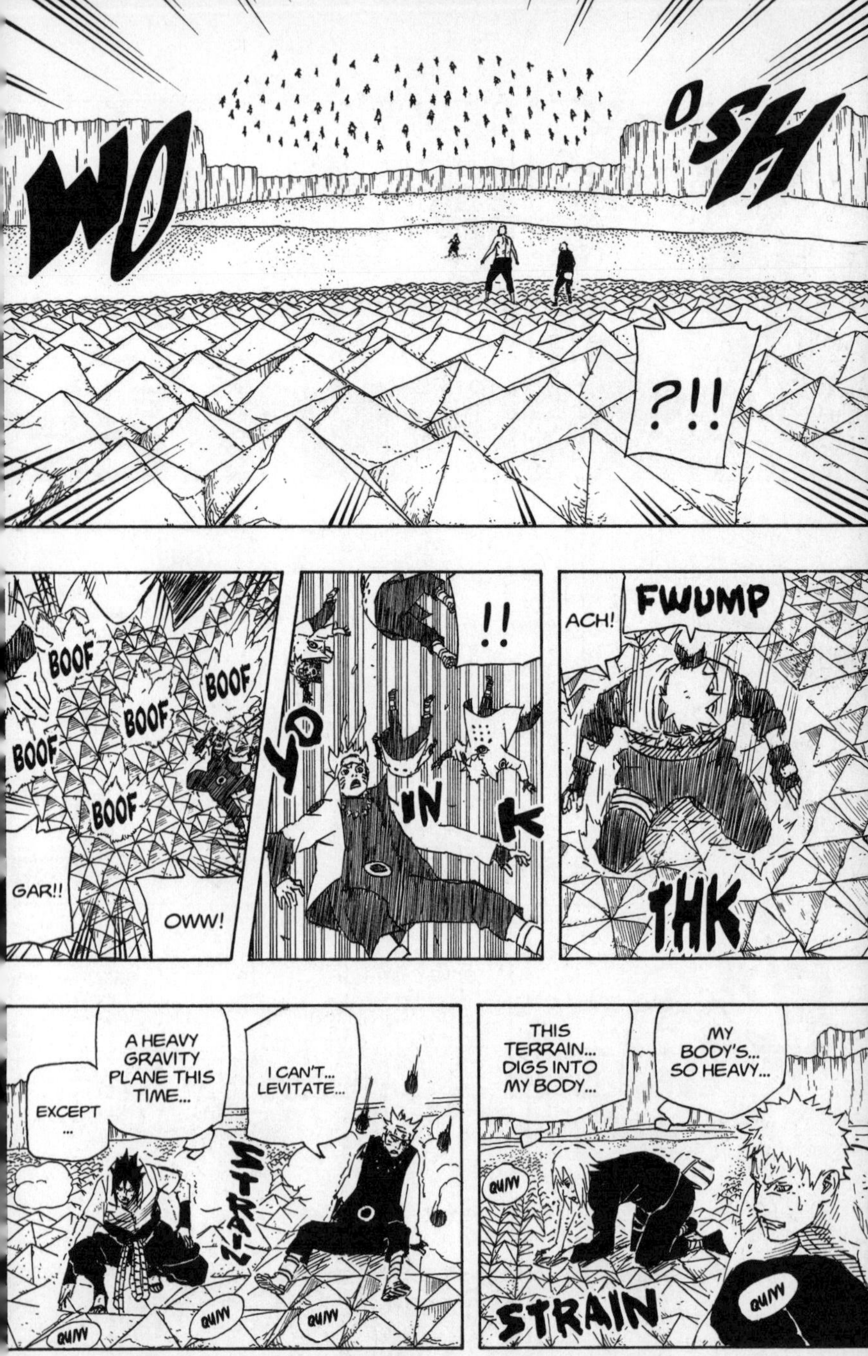
WO
OSH
?!!
FWUMP
ACH!
THK
!!
SINK
BOOF
BOOF
BOOF
BOOF
BOOF
GAR!!
OWW!
MY BODY'S... SO HEAVY...
THIS TERRAIN... DIGS INTO MY BODY...
QUIVV
STRAIN
QUIVV
I CAN'T... LEVITATE...
A HEAVY GRAVITY PLANE THIS TIME...
EXCEPT ...
STRAIN
QUIVV
QUIVV
QUIVV

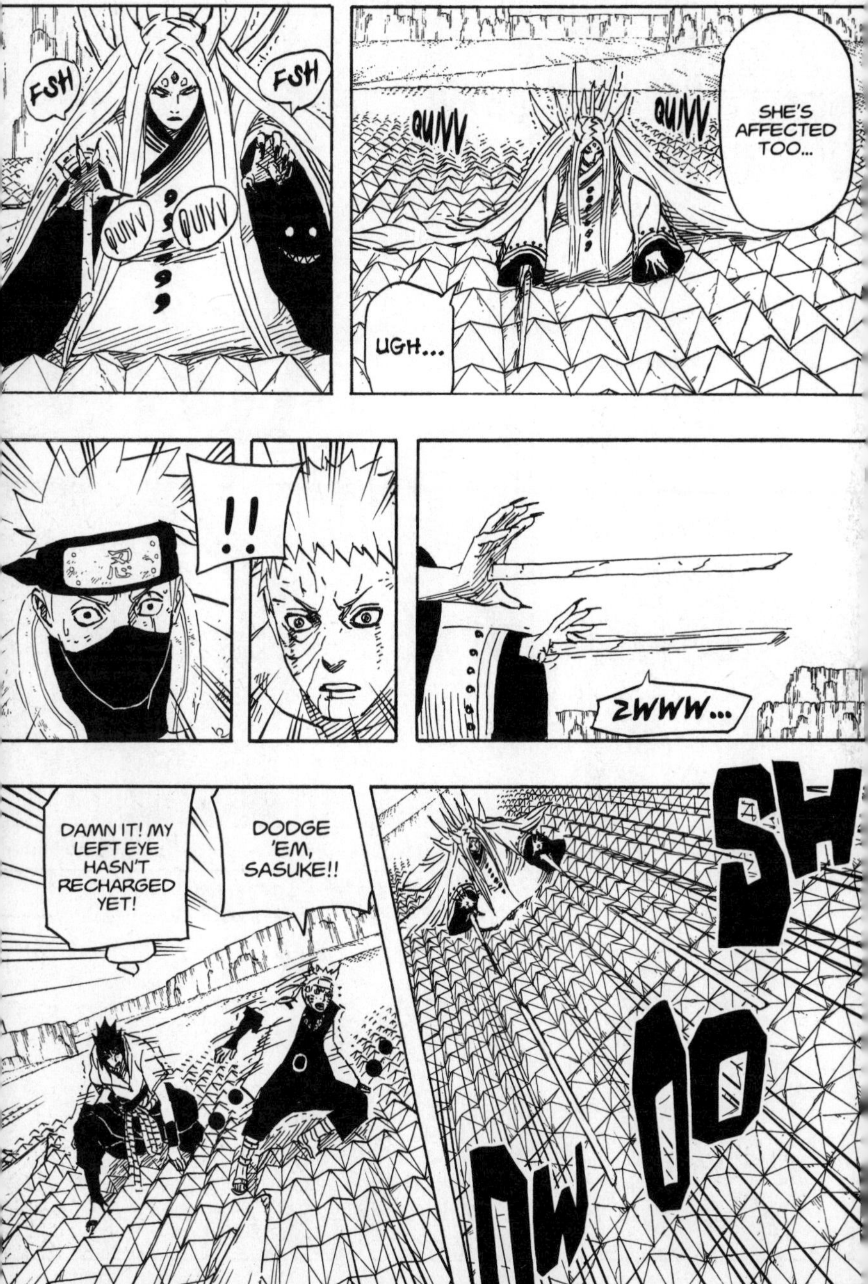
QUIVV
QUIVV
SHE'S AFFECTED TOO...
UGH...
FSH
FSH
QUIVV
QUIVV
ZWWW...
!!
SH
DWOO
DODGE 'EM, SASUKE!!
DAMN IT! MY LEFT EYE HASN'T RECHARGED YET!

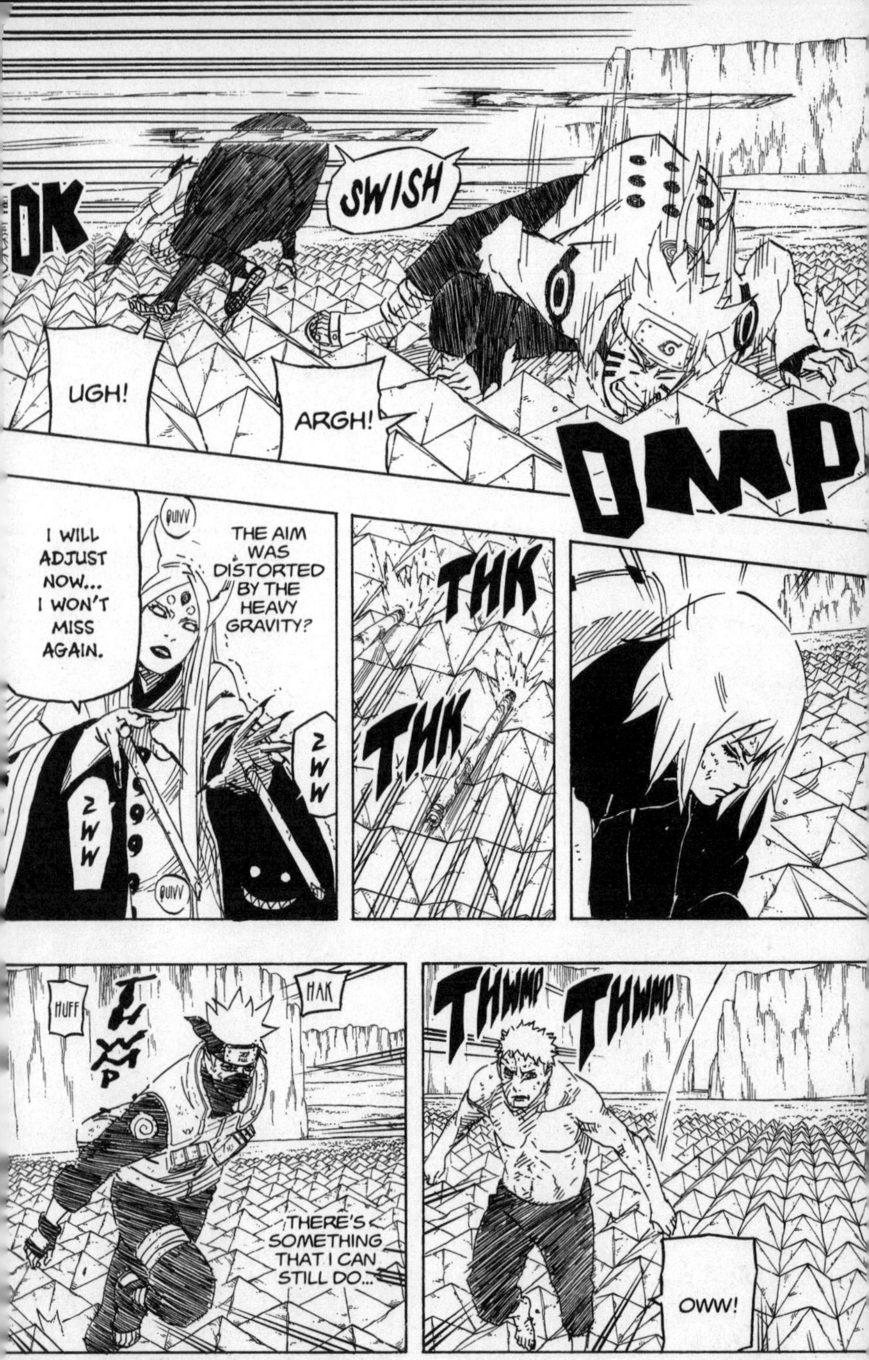

SWISH
DK
ARGH!
UGH!
DMP
THK
THK
QUIVV
THE AIM WAS DISTORTED BY THE HEAVY GRAVITY?
I WILL ADJUST NOW... I WON'T MISS AGAIN.
ZWW
ZWW
QUIVV
THWMP
THWMP
OWW!
HAK
THUMP
HUFF
THERE'S SOMETHING THAT I CAN STILL DO...

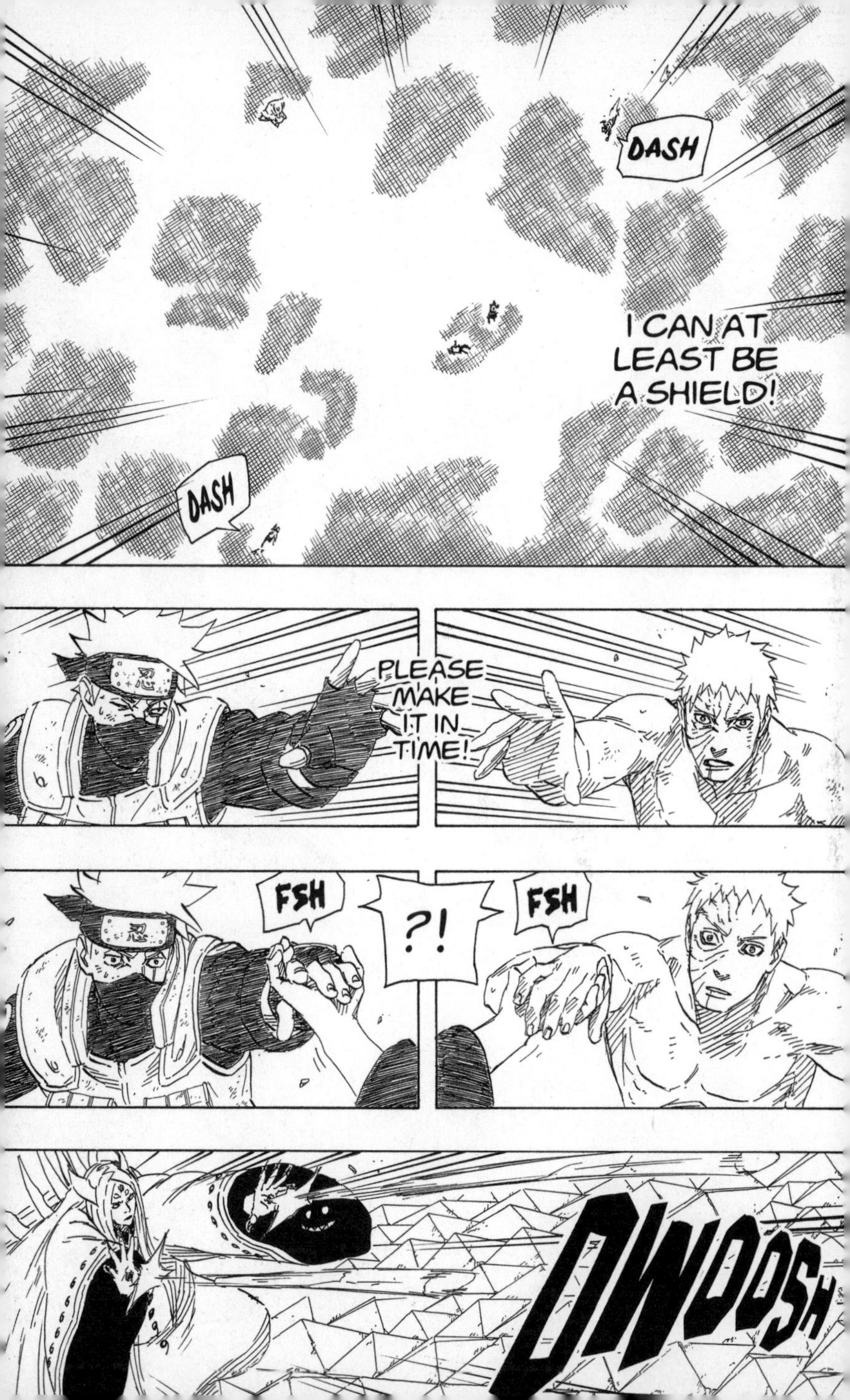
DASH
I CAN AT LEAST BE A SHIELD!
DASH
PLEASE MAKE IT IN TIME!
FSH
?!
FSH
DWOOSH

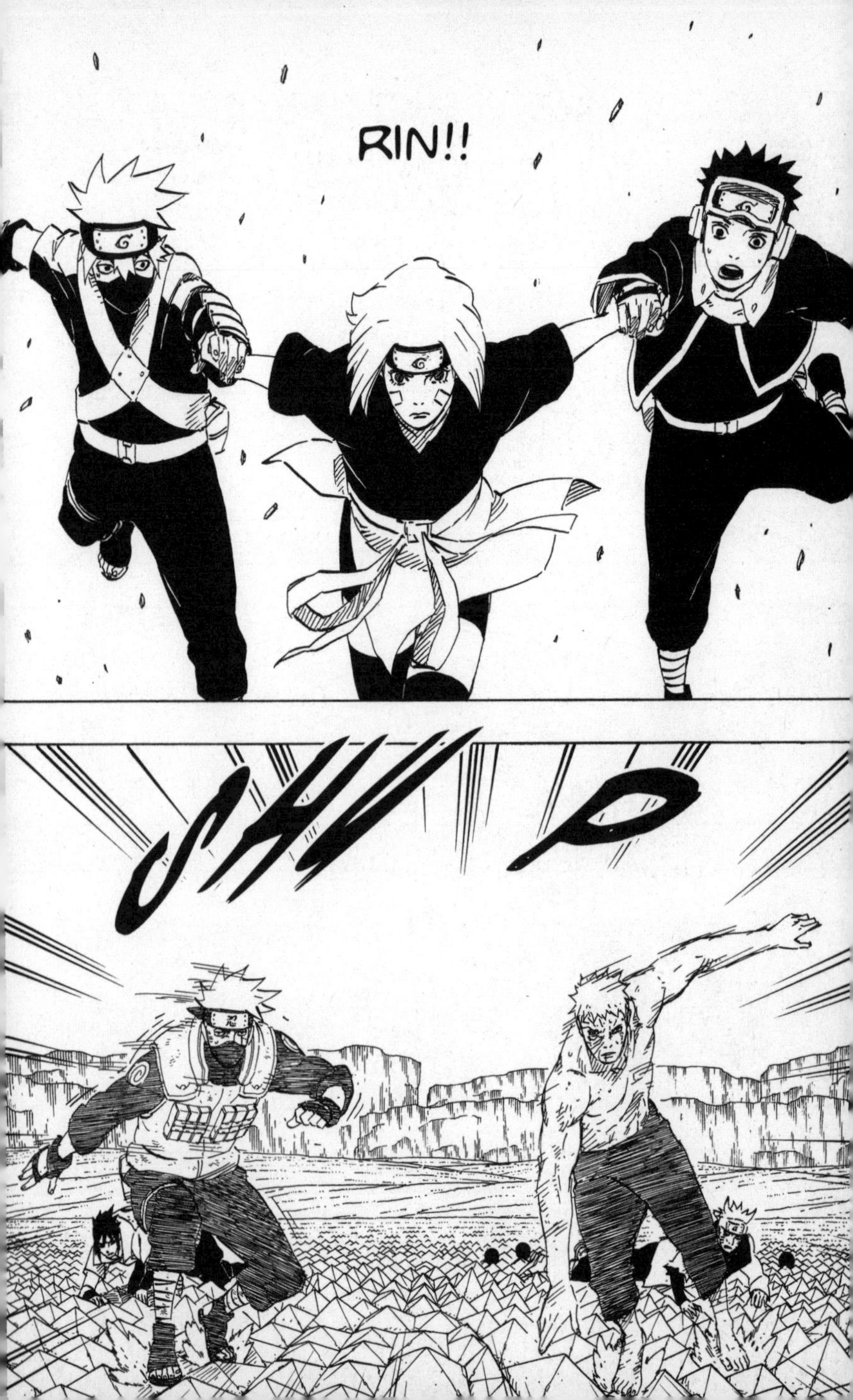
RIN!!
SHUP

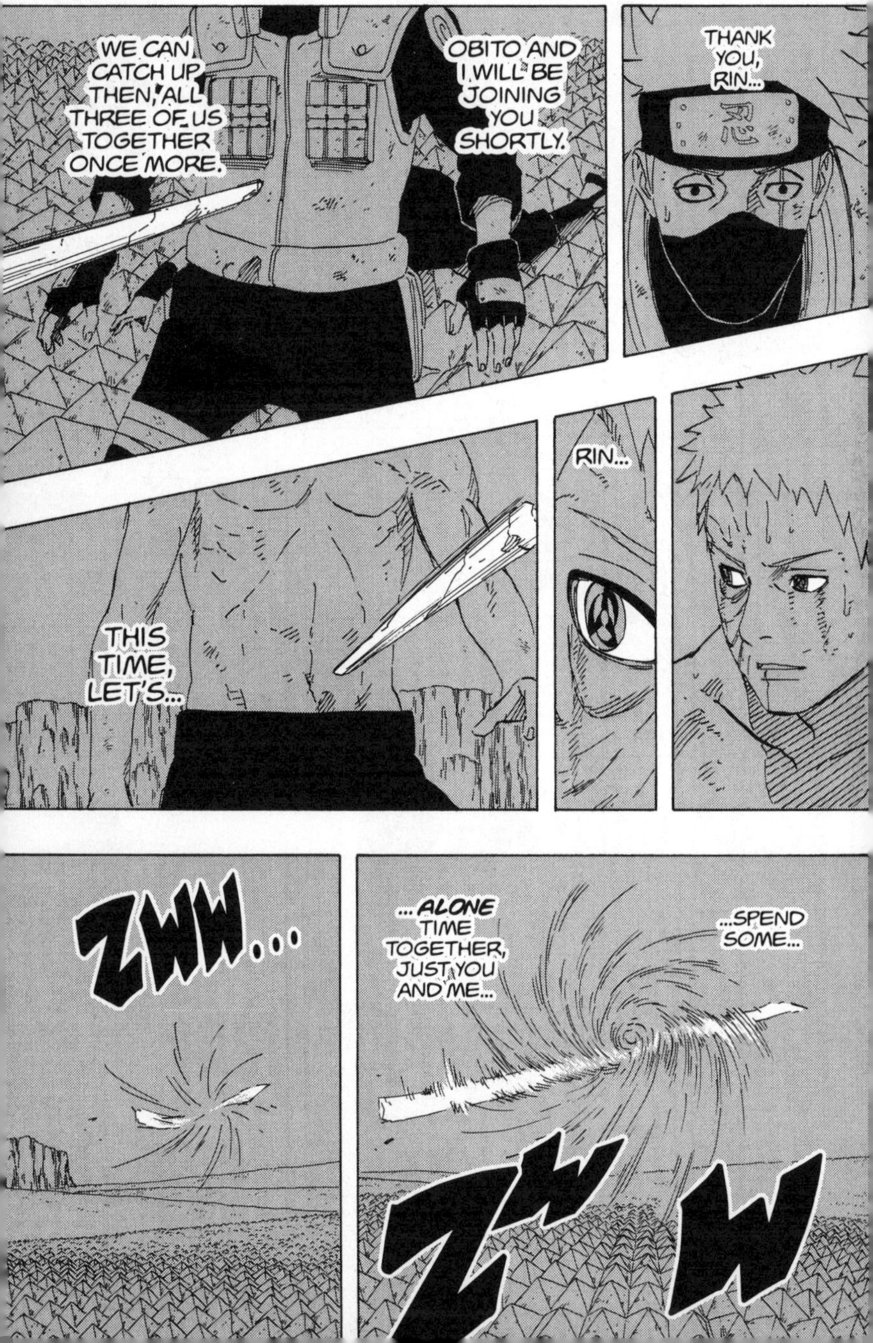
THANK YOU, RIN...
OBITO AND I WILL BE JOINING YOU SHORTLY.
WE CAN CATCH UP THEN, ALL THREE OF US TOGETHER ONCE MORE.
RIN...
THIS TIME, LET'S...
...SPEND SOME...
...*ALONE* TIME TOGETHER, JUST YOU AND ME...
ZWW
ZWW...

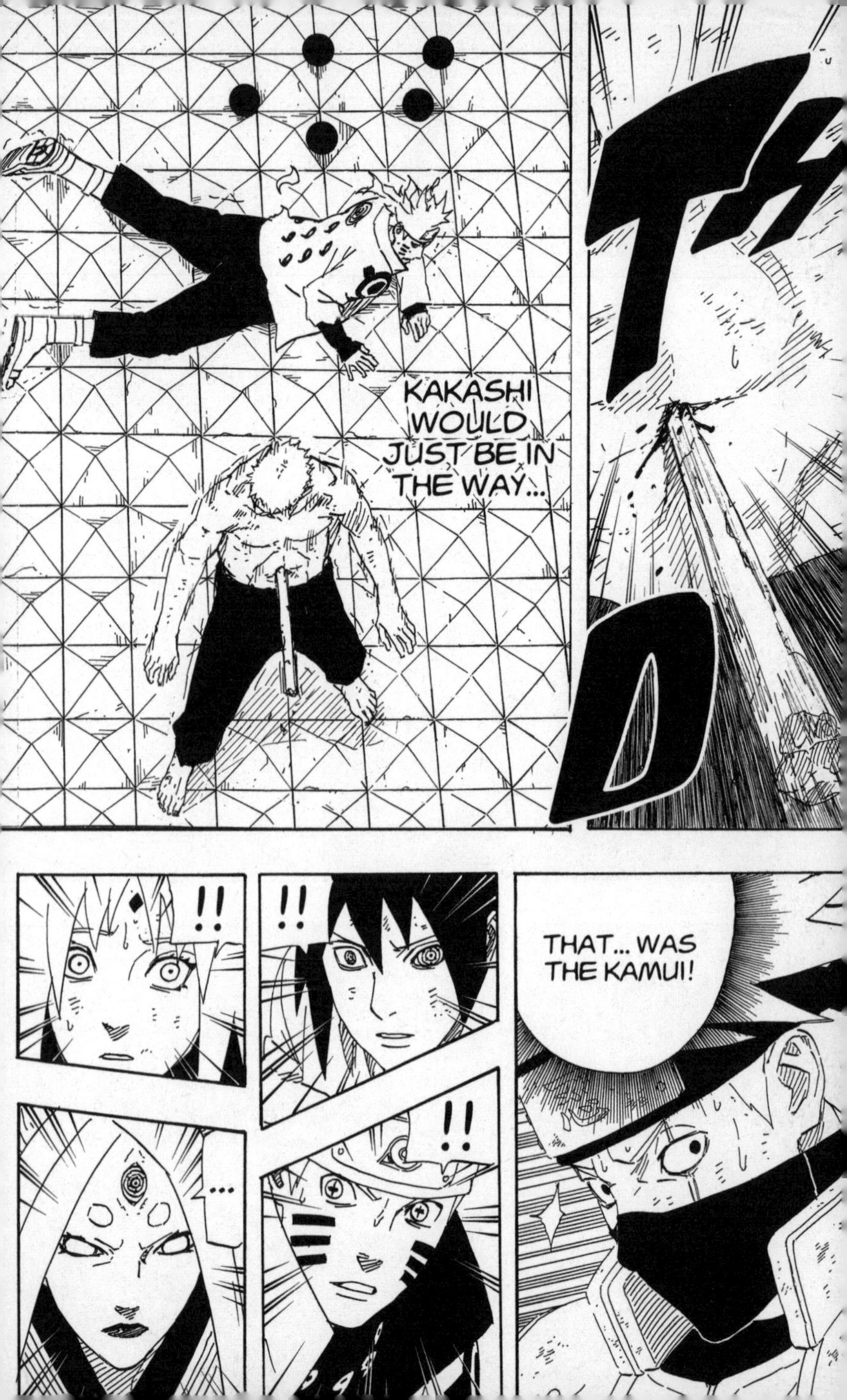
TH
D
KAKASHI WOULD JUST BE IN THE WAY...
THAT... WAS THE KAMUI!
!!
!!
!!
...

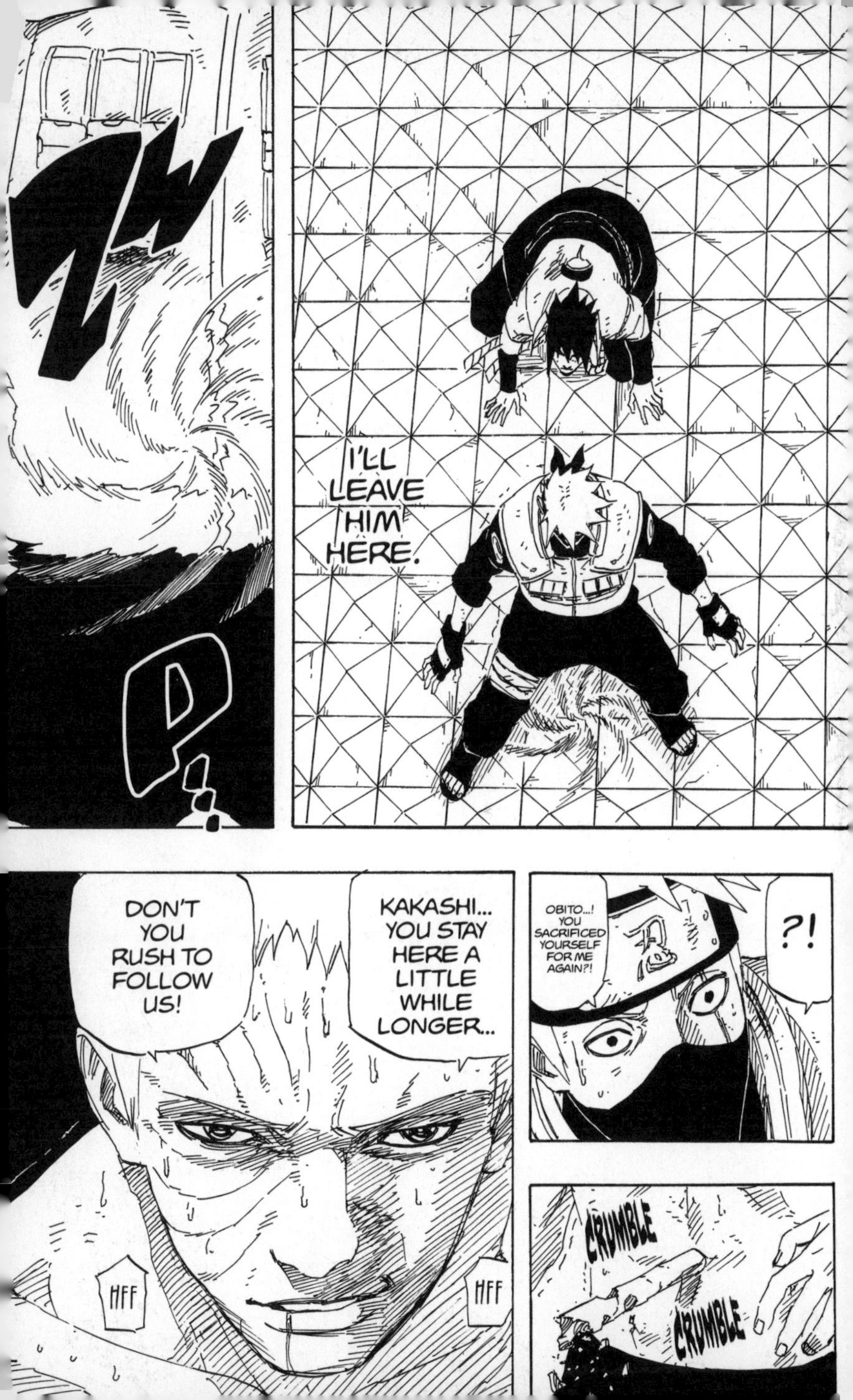
I'LL LEAVE HIM HERE.
ZW
P
?!
OBITO...! YOU SACRIFICED YOURSELF FOR ME AGAIN?!
CRUMBLE
CRUMBLE
KAKASHI... YOU STAY HERE A LITTLE WHILE LONGER...
DON'T YOU RUSH TO FOLLOW US!
HFF
HFF

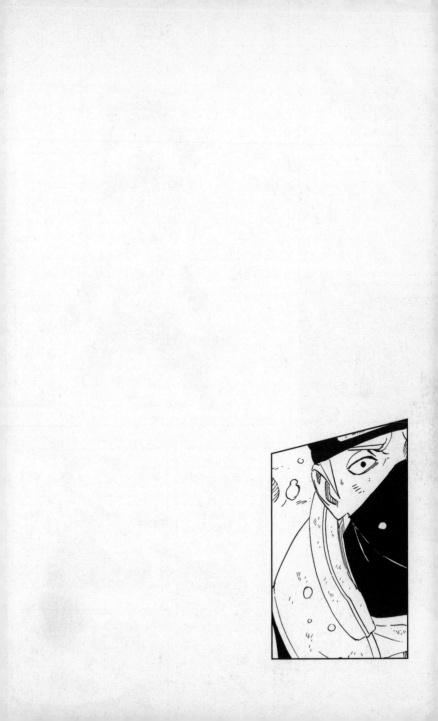

Number 687: You Better

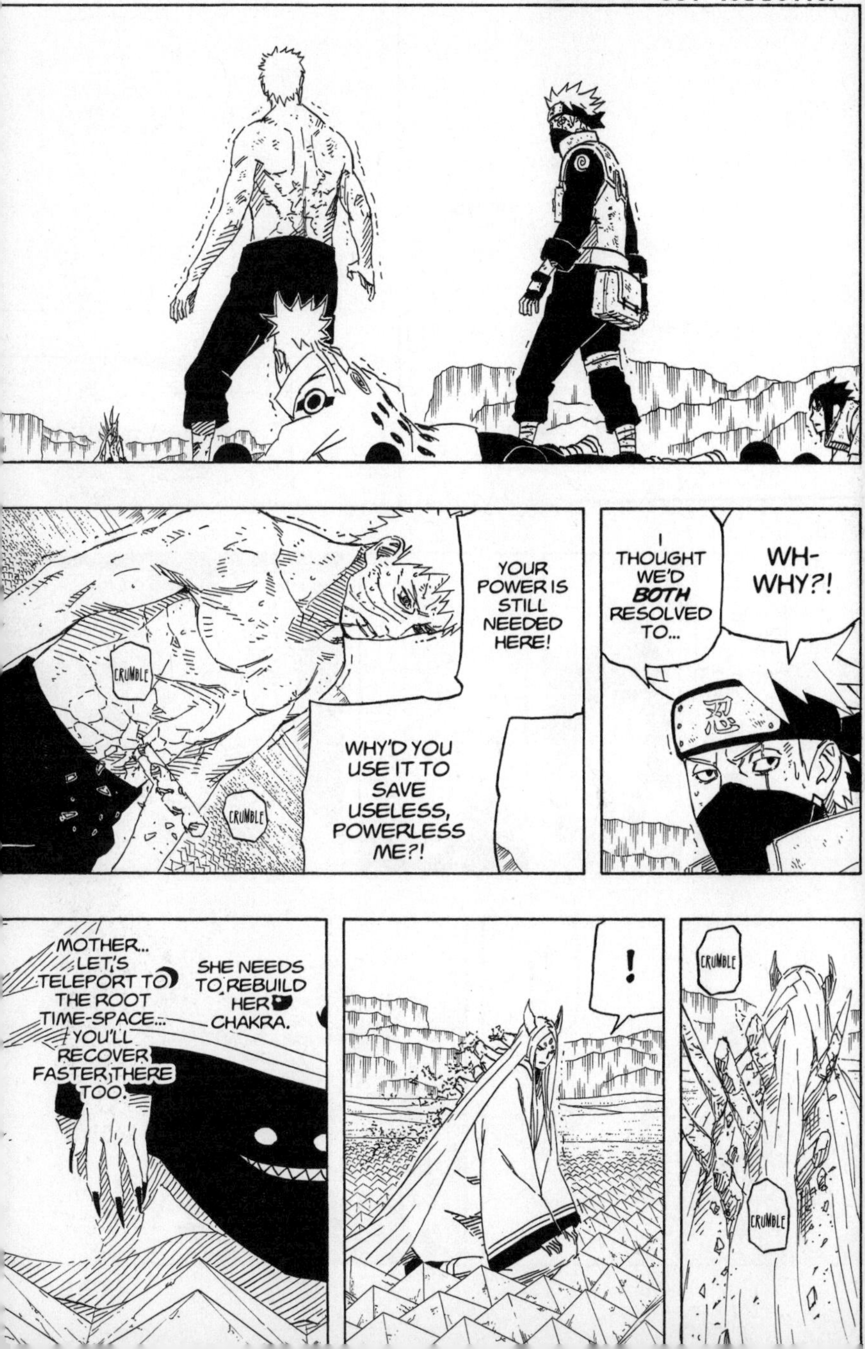
WH- WHY?!
I THOUGHT WE'D BOTH RESOLVED TO...
YOUR POWER IS STILL NEEDED HERE!
CRUMBLE
WHY'D YOU USE IT TO SAVE USELESS, POWERLESS ME?!
CRUMBLE
CRUMBLE
CRUMBLE
!
SHE NEEDS TO REBUILD HER CHAKRA.
MOTHER... LET'S TELEPORT TO THE ROOT TIME-SPACE... YOU'LL RECOVER FASTER THERE TOO.

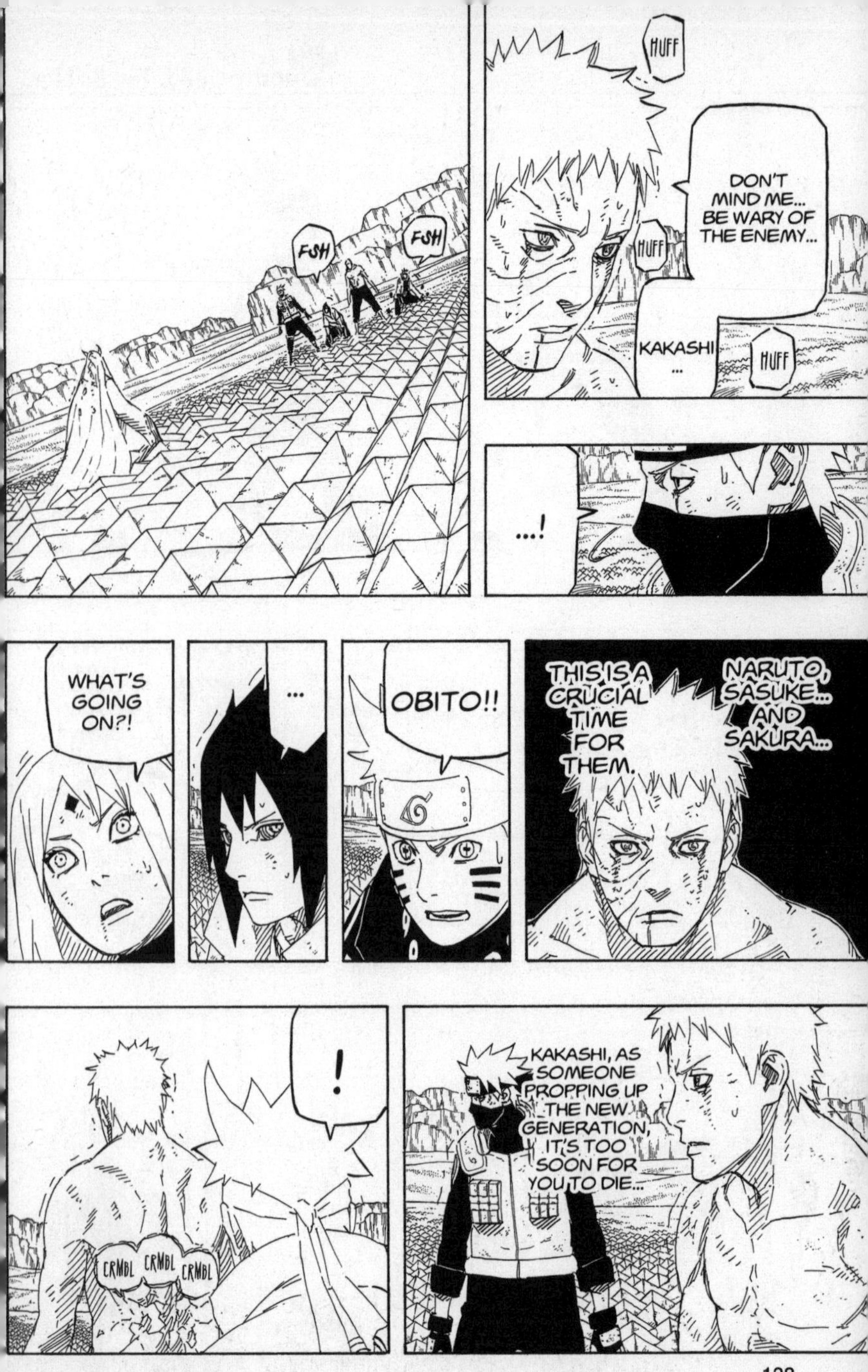
HUFF
DON'T MIND ME... BE WARY OF THE ENEMY...
HUFF
KAKASHI ...
HUFF
...!
FSH
FSH
NARUTO, SASUKE... AND SAKURA...
THIS IS A CRUCIAL TIME FOR THEM.
OBITO!!
...
WHAT'S GOING ON?!
KAKASHI, AS SOMEONE PROPPING UP THE NEW GENERATION, IT'S TOO SOON FOR YOU TO DIE...
!
CRMBL
CRMBL
CRMBL

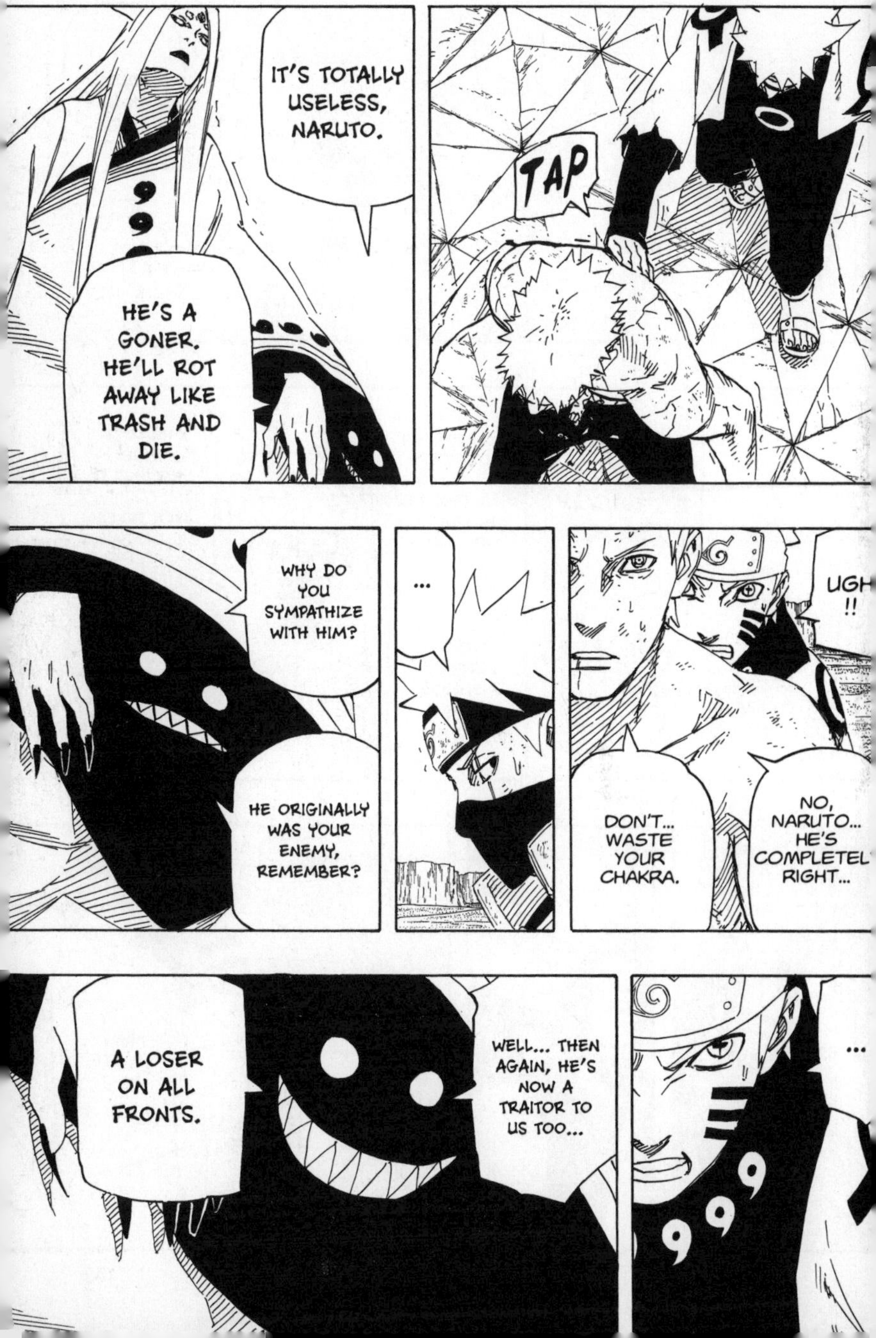
TAP
IT'S TOTALLY USELESS, NARUTO.
HE'S A GONER. HE'LL ROT AWAY LIKE TRASH AND DIE.
UGH !!
NO, NARUTO... HE'S COMPLETEL RIGHT...
DON'T... WASTE YOUR CHAKRA.
...
WHY DO YOU SYMPATHIZE WITH HIM?
HE ORIGINALLY WAS YOUR ENEMY, REMEMBER?
...
WELL... THEN AGAIN, HE'S NOW A TRAITOR TO US TOO...
A LOSER ON ALL FRONTS.

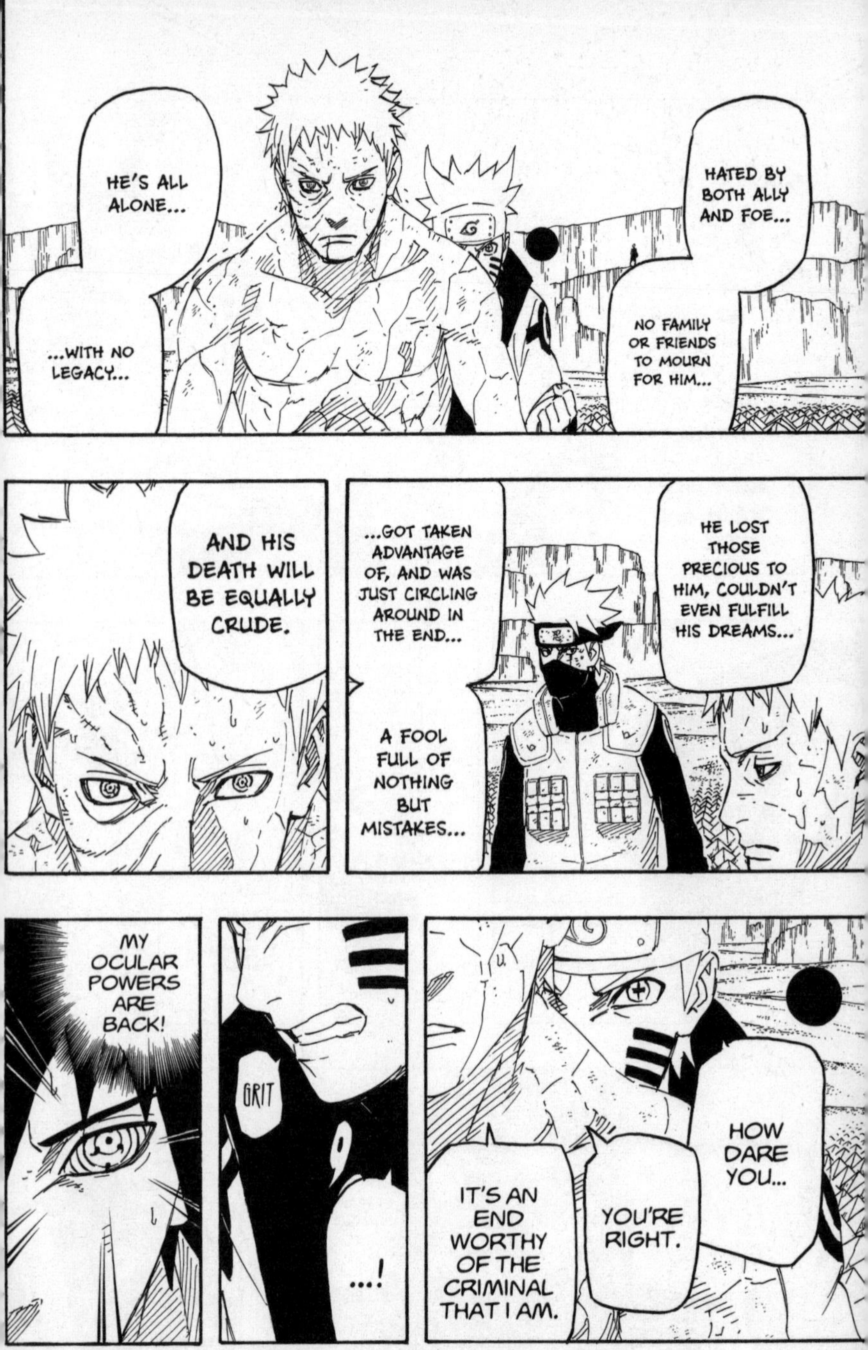

HATED BY BOTH ALLY AND FOE...
NO FAMILY OR FRIENDS TO MOURN FOR HIM...
HE'S ALL ALONE...
...WITH NO LEGACY...
HE LOST THOSE PRECIOUS TO HIM, COULDN'T EVEN FULFILL HIS DREAMS...
...GOT TAKEN ADVANTAGE OF, AND WAS JUST CIRCLING AROUND IN THE END...
A FOOL FULL OF NOTHING BUT MISTAKES...
AND HIS DEATH WILL BE EQUALLY CRUDE.
HOW DARE YOU...
YOU'RE RIGHT.
IT'S AN END WORTHY OF THE CRIMINAL THAT I AM.
GRIT
...!
MY OCULAR POWERS ARE BACK!

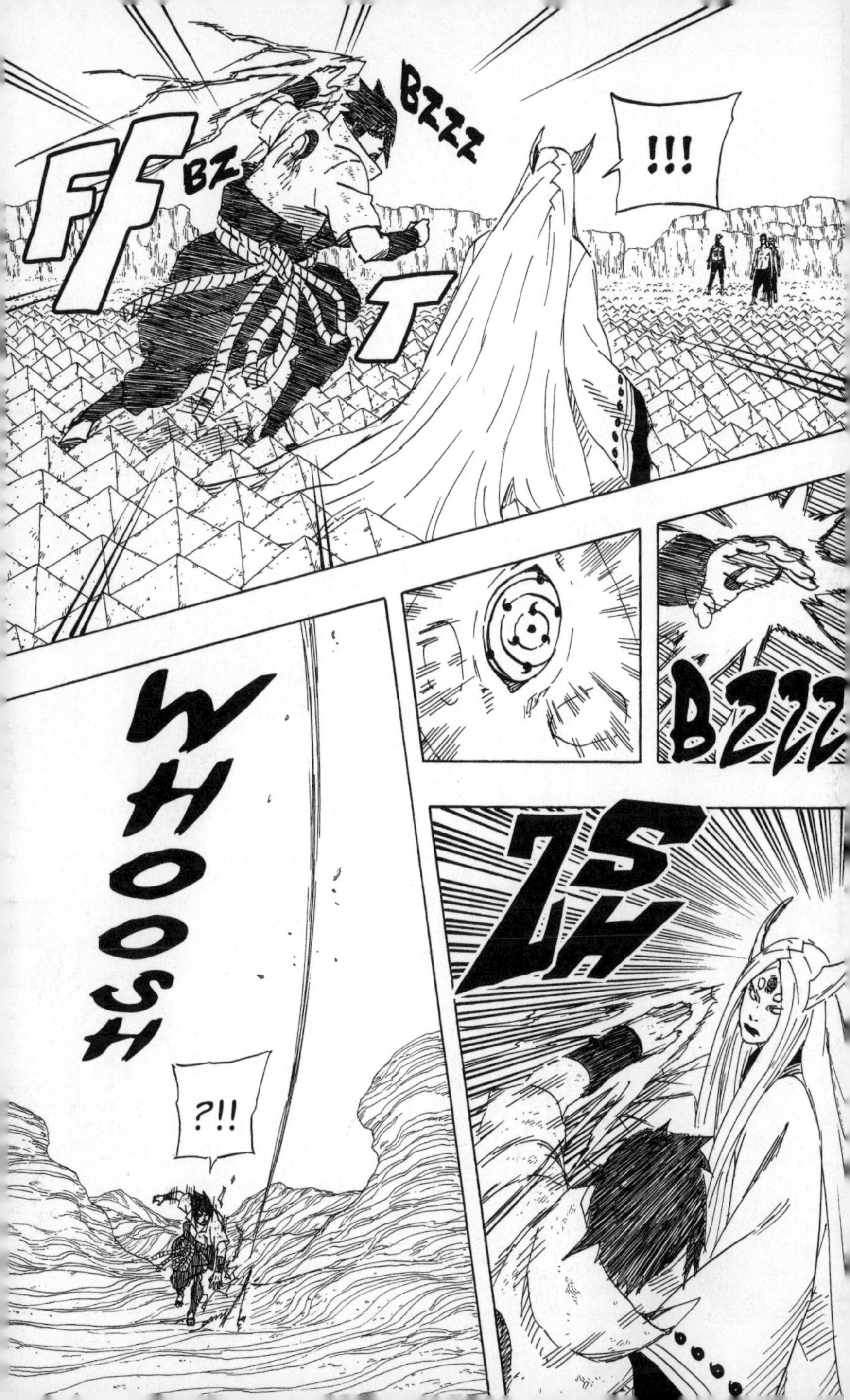
!!!
BZZZ
BZ
FF
T
BZZZ
ZSH
WHOOSH
?!!

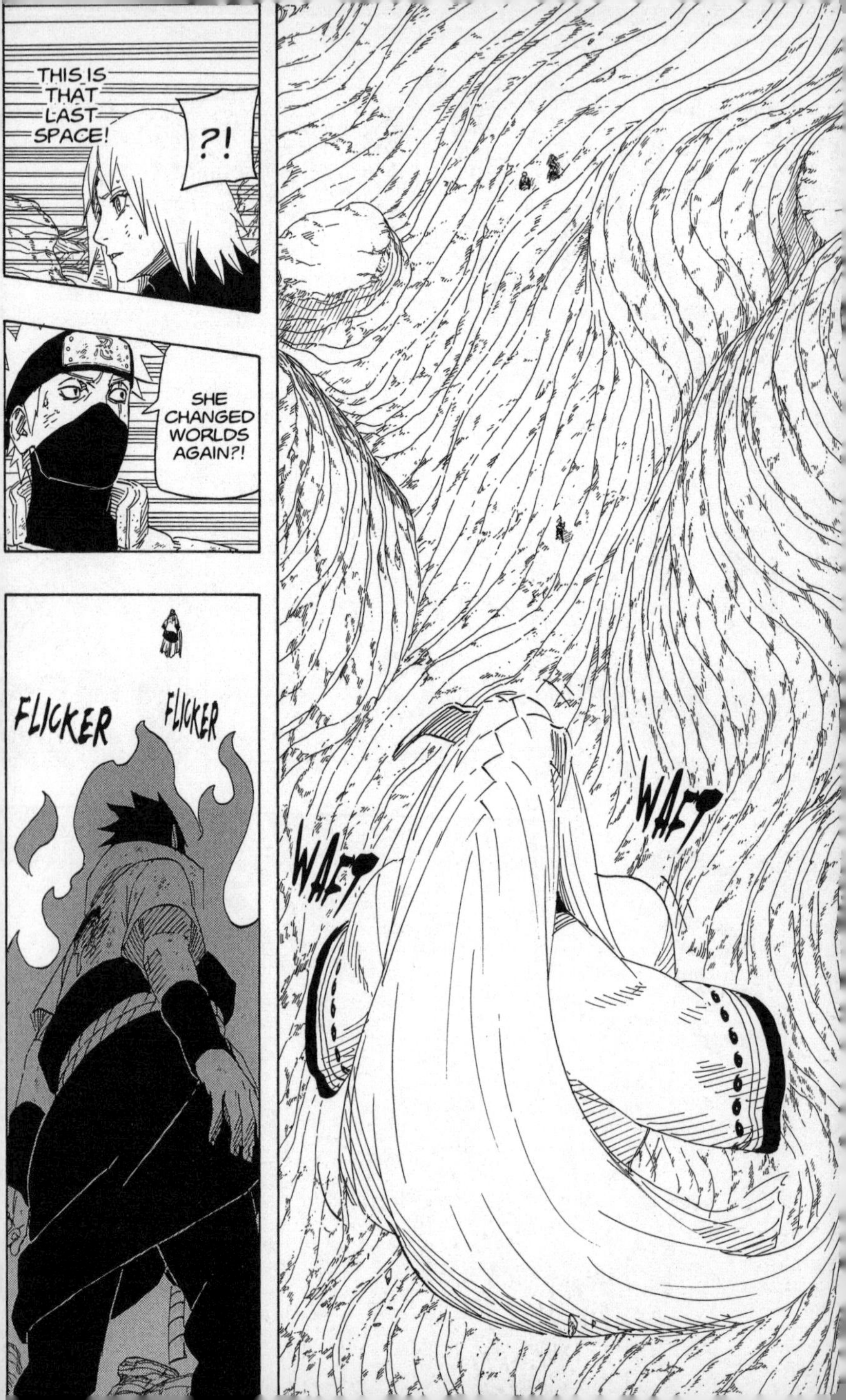
WAFT
WAFT
?!
THIS IS THAT LAST SPACE!
SHE CHANGED WORLDS AGAIN?!
FLICKER
FLICKER

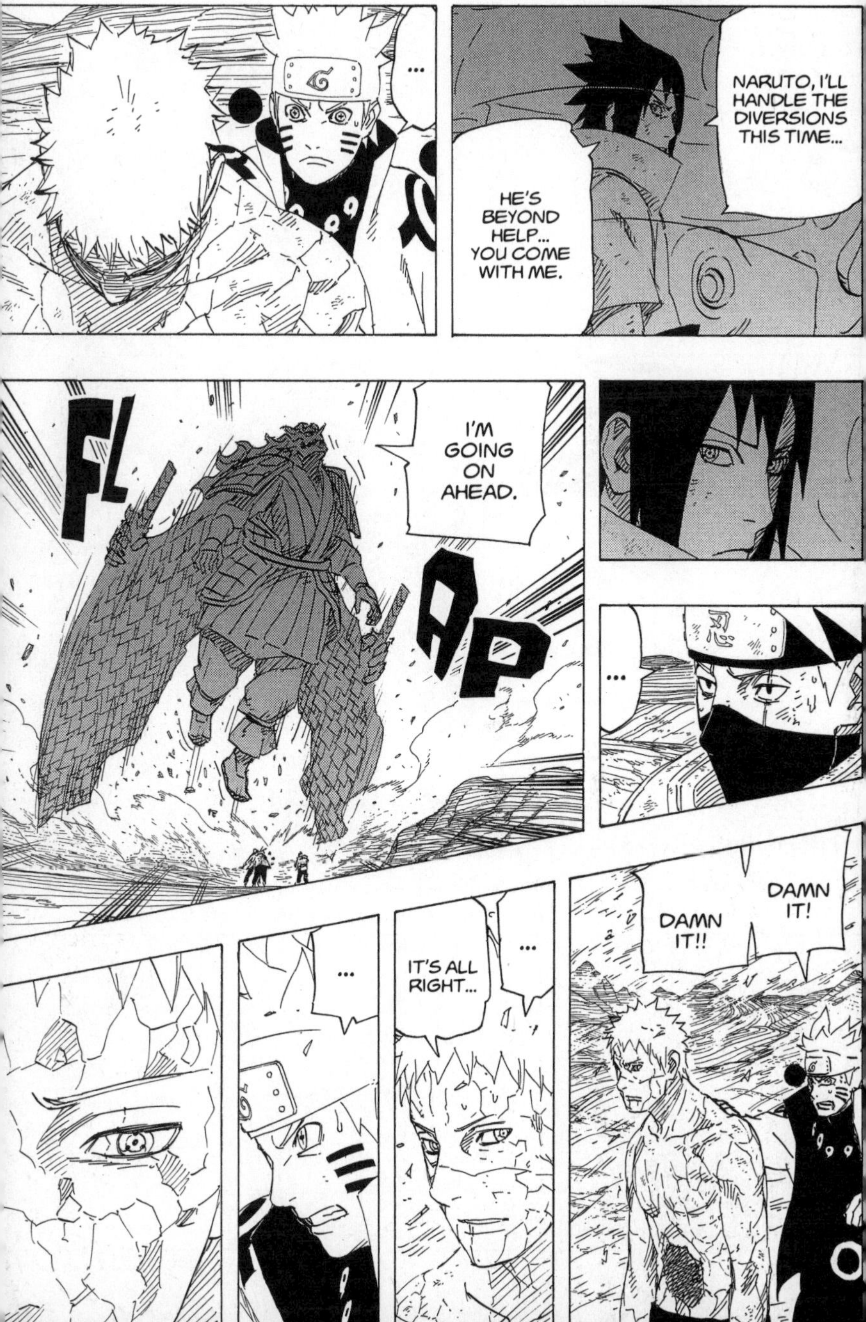
NARUTO, I'LL HANDLE THE DIVERSIONS THIS TIME...
HE'S BEYOND HELP... YOU COME WITH ME.
...
...
I'M GOING ON AHEAD.
FLAP
DAMN IT!
DAMN IT!!
...
IT'S ALL RIGHT...
...

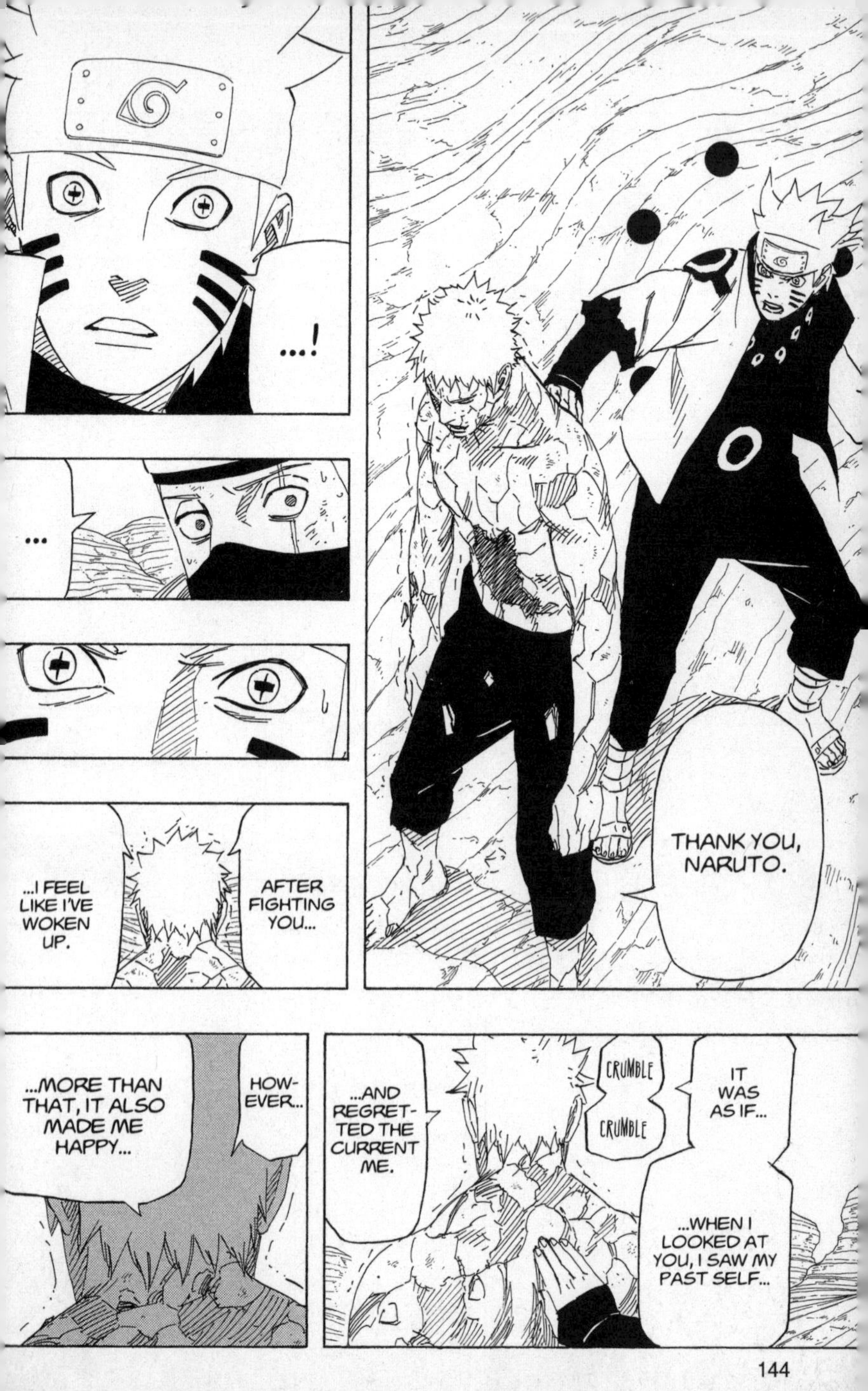
THANK YOU, NARUTO.
...!
...
AFTER FIGHTING YOU...
...I FEEL LIKE I'VE WOKEN UP.
IT WAS AS IF...
CRUMBLE
CRUMBLE
...WHEN I LOOKED AT YOU, I SAW MY PAST SELF...
...AND REGRETTED THE CURRENT ME.
HOWEVER...
...MORE THAN THAT, IT ALSO MADE ME HAPPY...

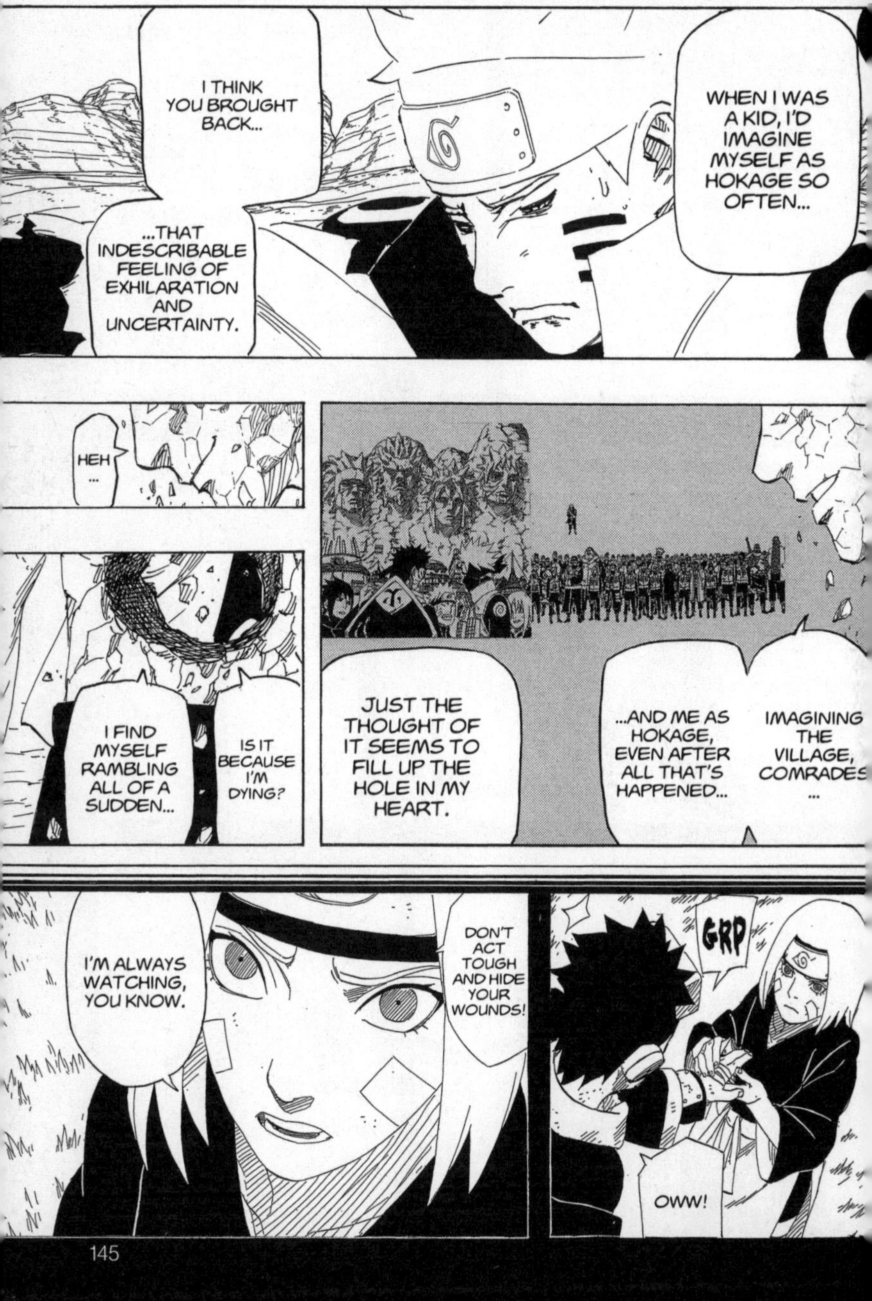
WHEN I WAS A KID, I'D IMAGINE MYSELF AS HOKAGE SO OFTEN...
I THINK YOU BROUGHT BACK...
...THAT INDESCRIBABLE FEELING OF EXHILARATION AND UNCERTAINTY.
IMAGINING THE VILLAGE, COMRADES...
...AND ME AS HOKAGE, EVEN AFTER ALL THAT'S HAPPENED...
JUST THE THOUGHT OF IT SEEMS TO FILL UP THE HOLE IN MY HEART.
HEH...
IS IT BECAUSE I'M DYING?
I FIND MYSELF RAMBLING ALL OF A SUDDEN...
GRP
OWW!
DON'T ACT TOUGH AND HIDE YOUR WOUNDS!
I'M ALWAYS WATCHING, YOU KNOW.

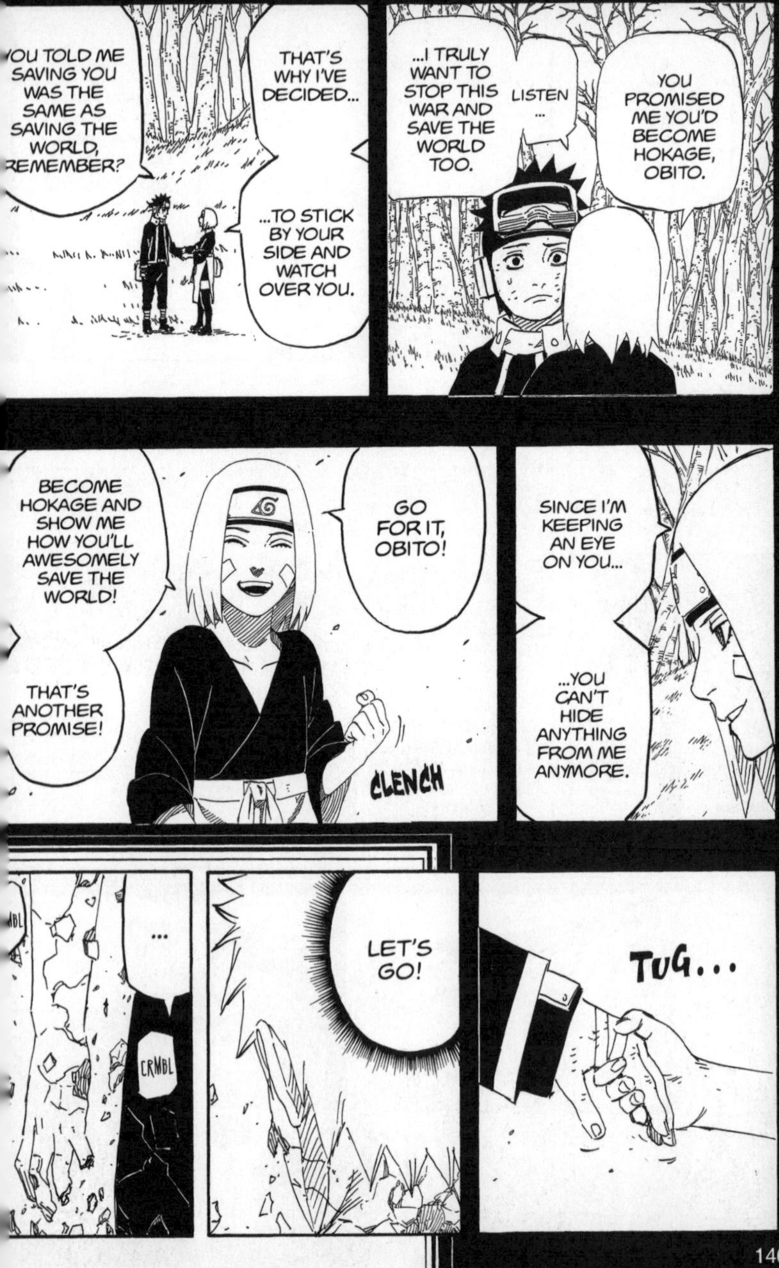
YOU PROMISED ME YOU'D BECOME HOKAGE, OBITO.
LISTEN ...
...I TRULY WANT TO STOP THIS WAR AND SAVE THE WORLD TOO.
YOU TOLD ME SAVING YOU WAS THE SAME AS SAVING THE WORLD, REMEMBER?
THAT'S WHY I'VE DECIDED...
...TO STICK BY YOUR SIDE AND WATCH OVER YOU.
SINCE I'M KEEPING AN EYE ON YOU...
...YOU CAN'T HIDE ANYTHING FROM ME ANYMORE.
GO FOR IT, OBITO!
BECOME HOKAGE AND SHOW ME HOW YOU'LL AWESOMELY SAVE THE WORLD!
CLENCH
THAT'S ANOTHER PROMISE!
TUG...
LET'S GO!
...
CRMBL

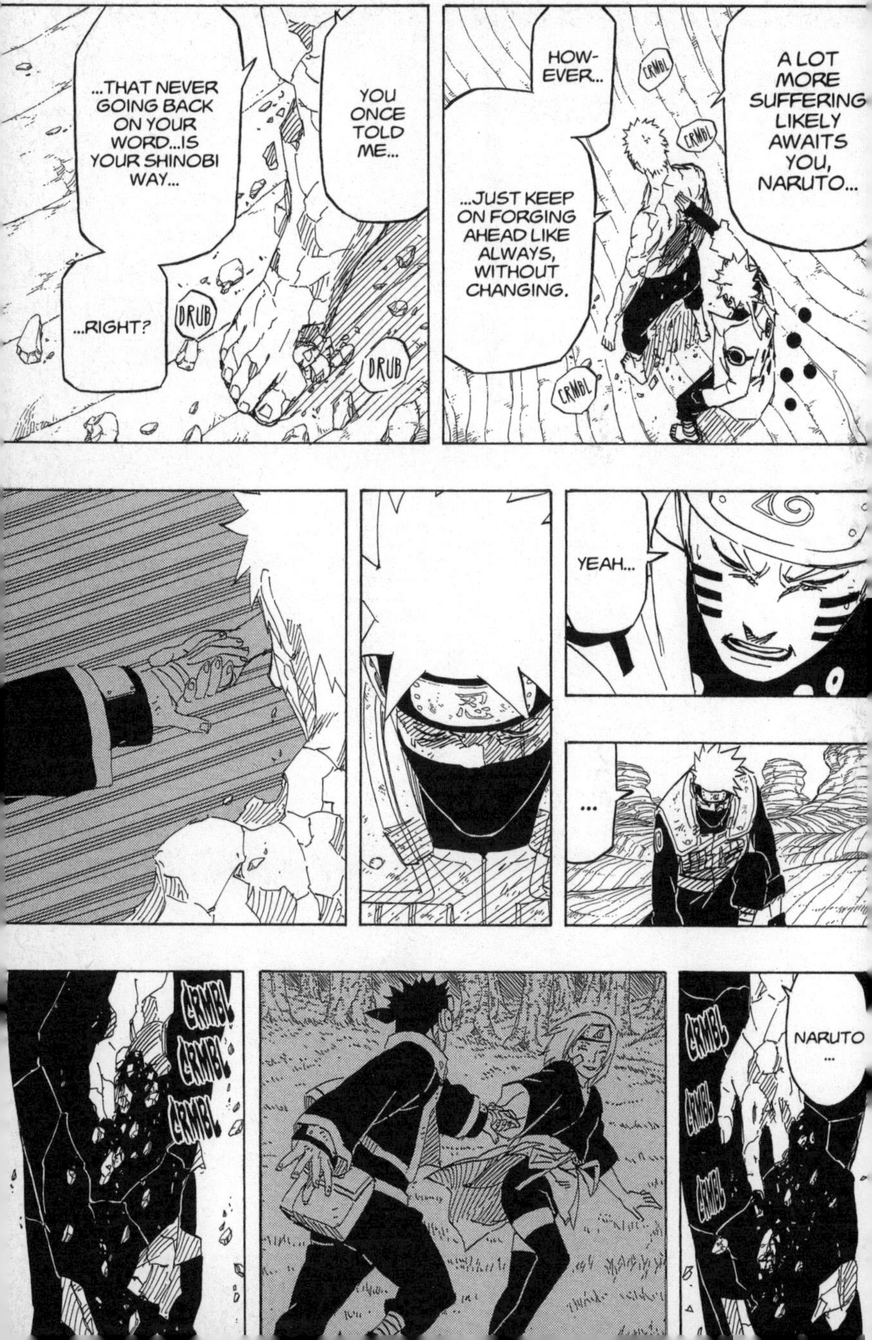
A LOT MORE SUFFERING LIKELY AWAITS YOU, NARUTO...
HOW-EVER...
CRMBL
CRMBL
...JUST KEEP ON FORGING AHEAD LIKE ALWAYS, WITHOUT CHANGING.
CRMBL
YOU ONCE TOLD ME...
...THAT NEVER GOING BACK ON YOUR WORD...IS YOUR SHINOBI WAY...
...RIGHT?
DRUB
DRUB
YEAH...
...
CRMBL
CRMBL
CRMBL
NARUTO ...
CRMBL
CRMBL
CRMBL

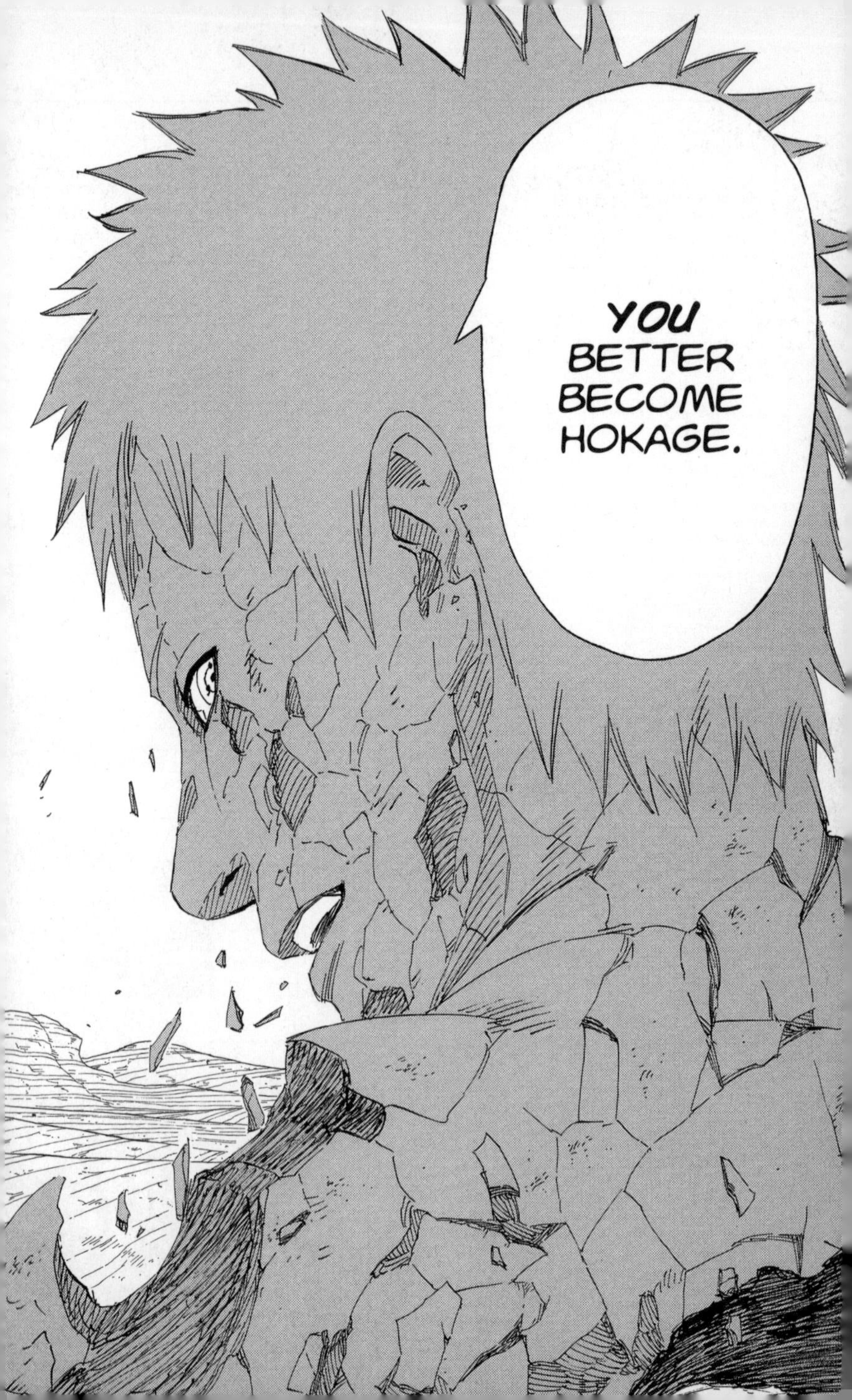
YOU BETTER BECOME HOKAGE.

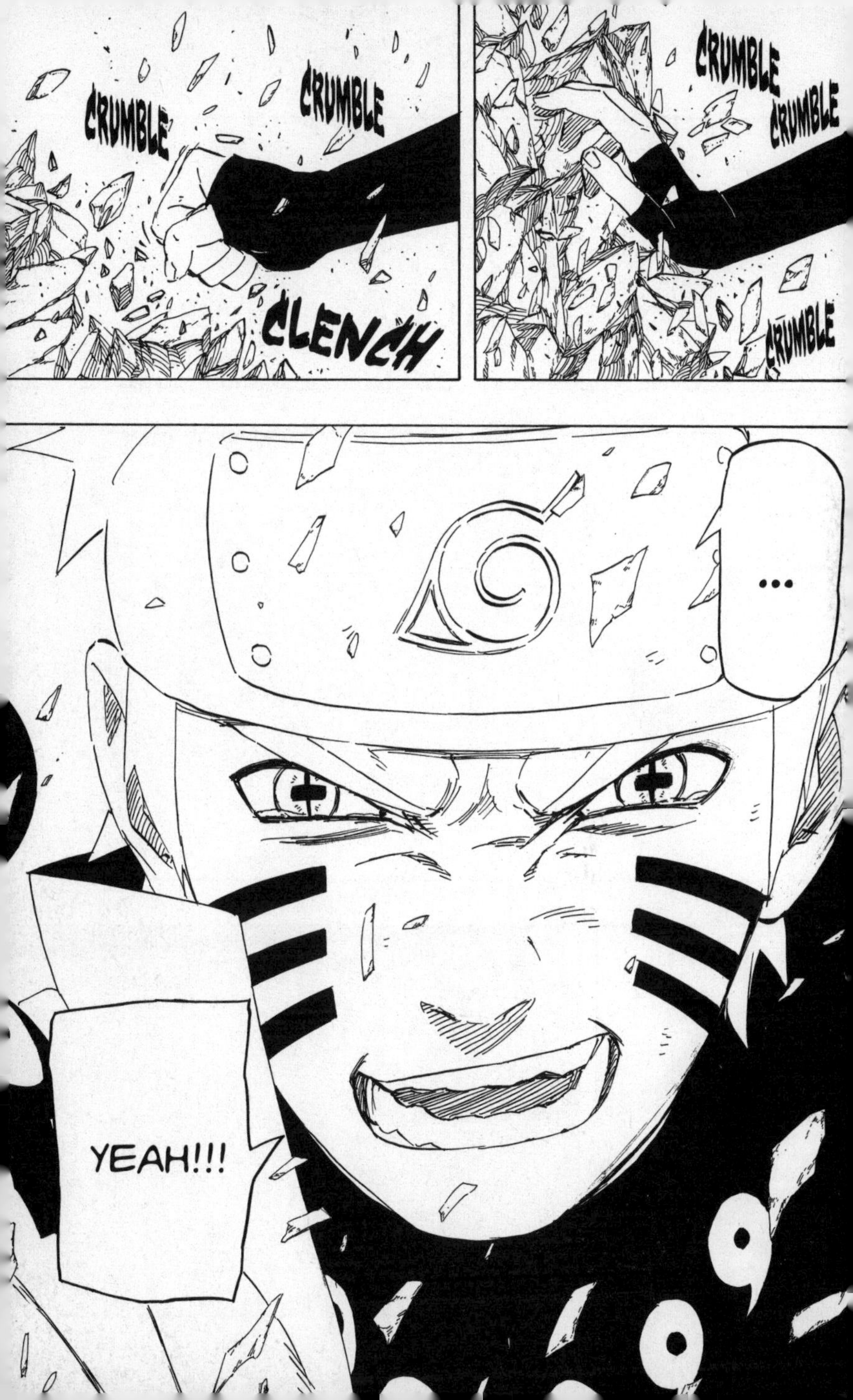
CRUMBLE
CRUMBLE
CRUMBLE
CRUMBLE
CRUMBLE
CLENCH
...
YEAH!!!

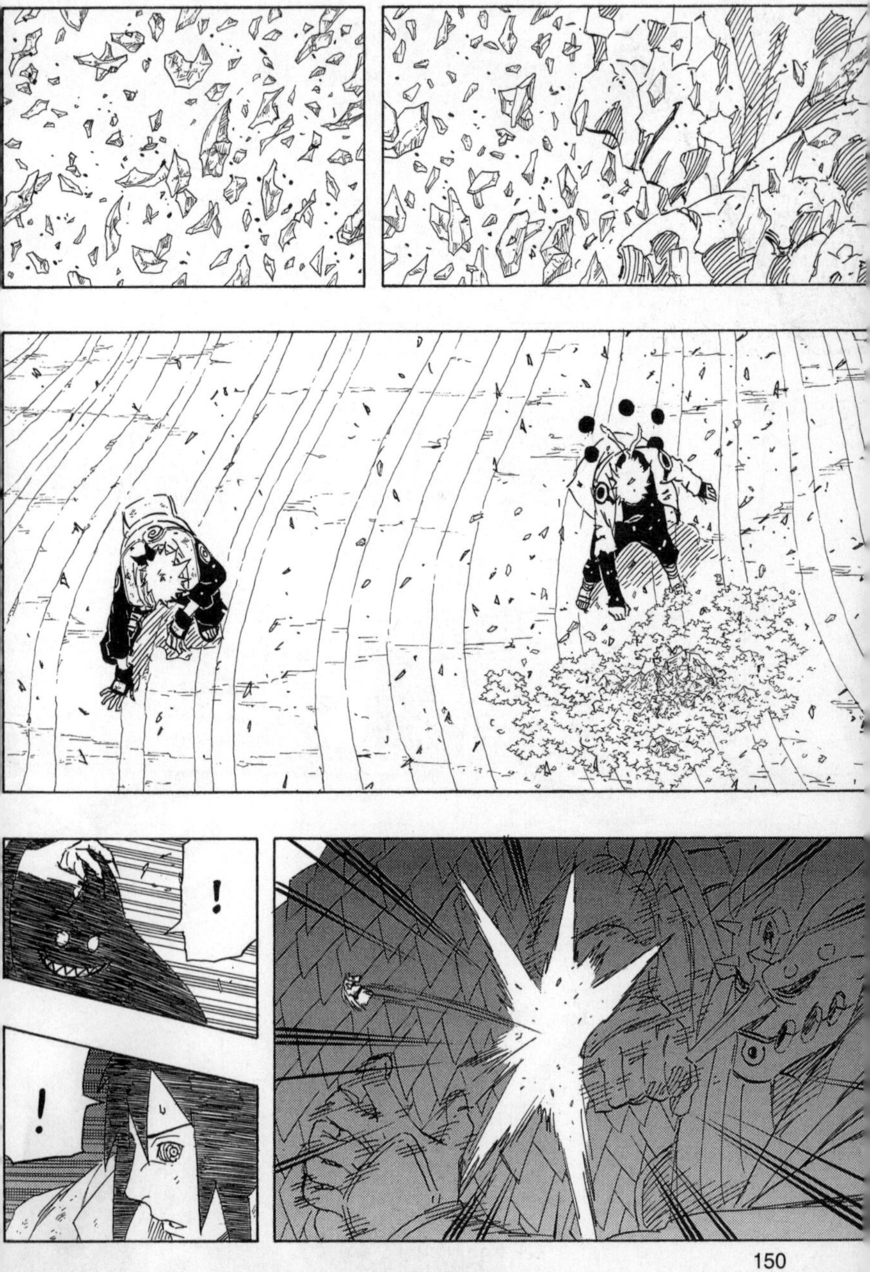
!
!

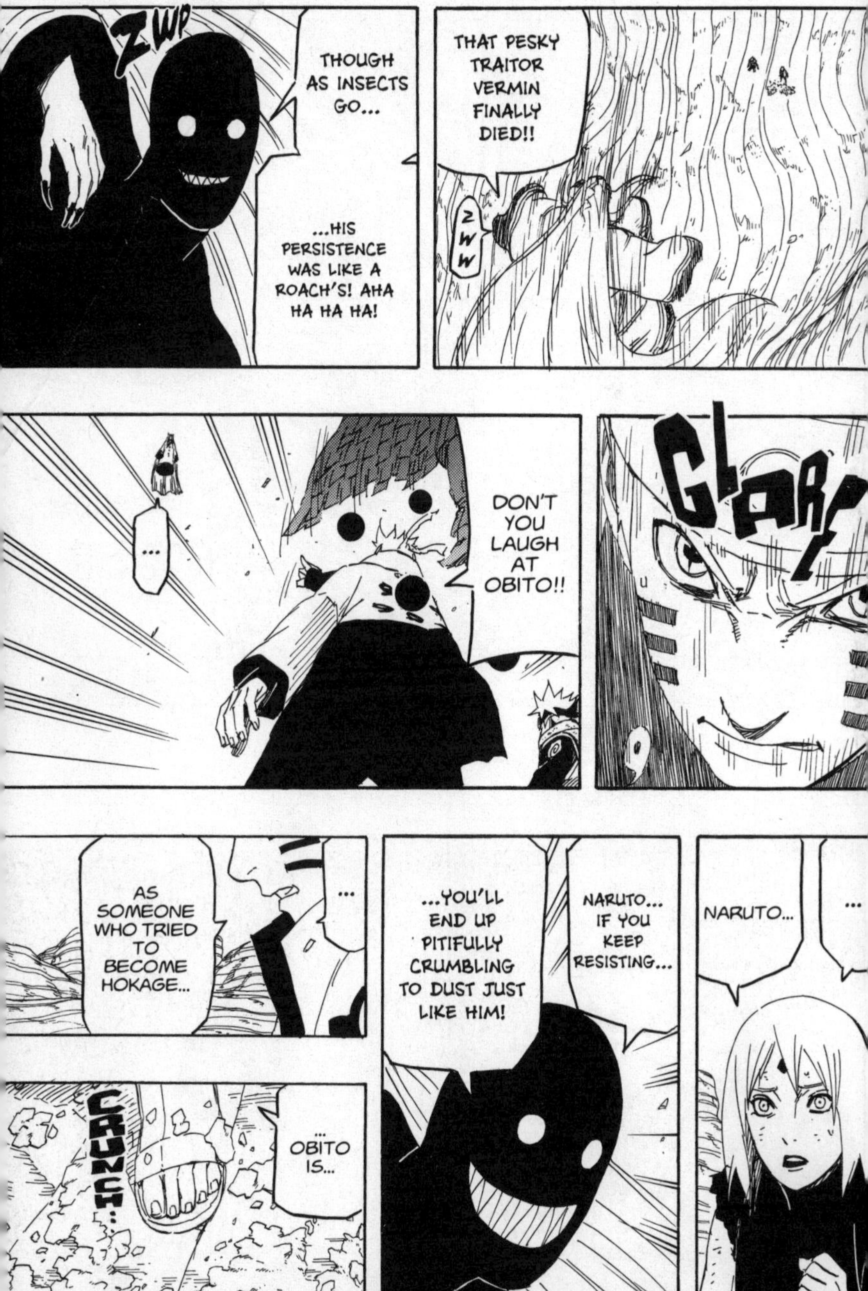
THAT PESKY TRAITOR VERMIN FINALLY DIED!!
ZWW
ZWP
THOUGH AS INSECTS GO...
...HIS PERSISTENCE WAS LIKE A ROACH'S! AHA HA HA HA!
GLAR
DON'T YOU LAUGH AT OBITO!!
...
...
NARUTO...
NARUTO... IF YOU KEEP RESISTING...
...YOU'LL END UP PITIFULLY CRUMBLING TO DUST JUST LIKE HIM!
...
AS SOMEONE WHO TRIED TO BECOME HOKAGE...
CRUNCH...
... OBITO IS...

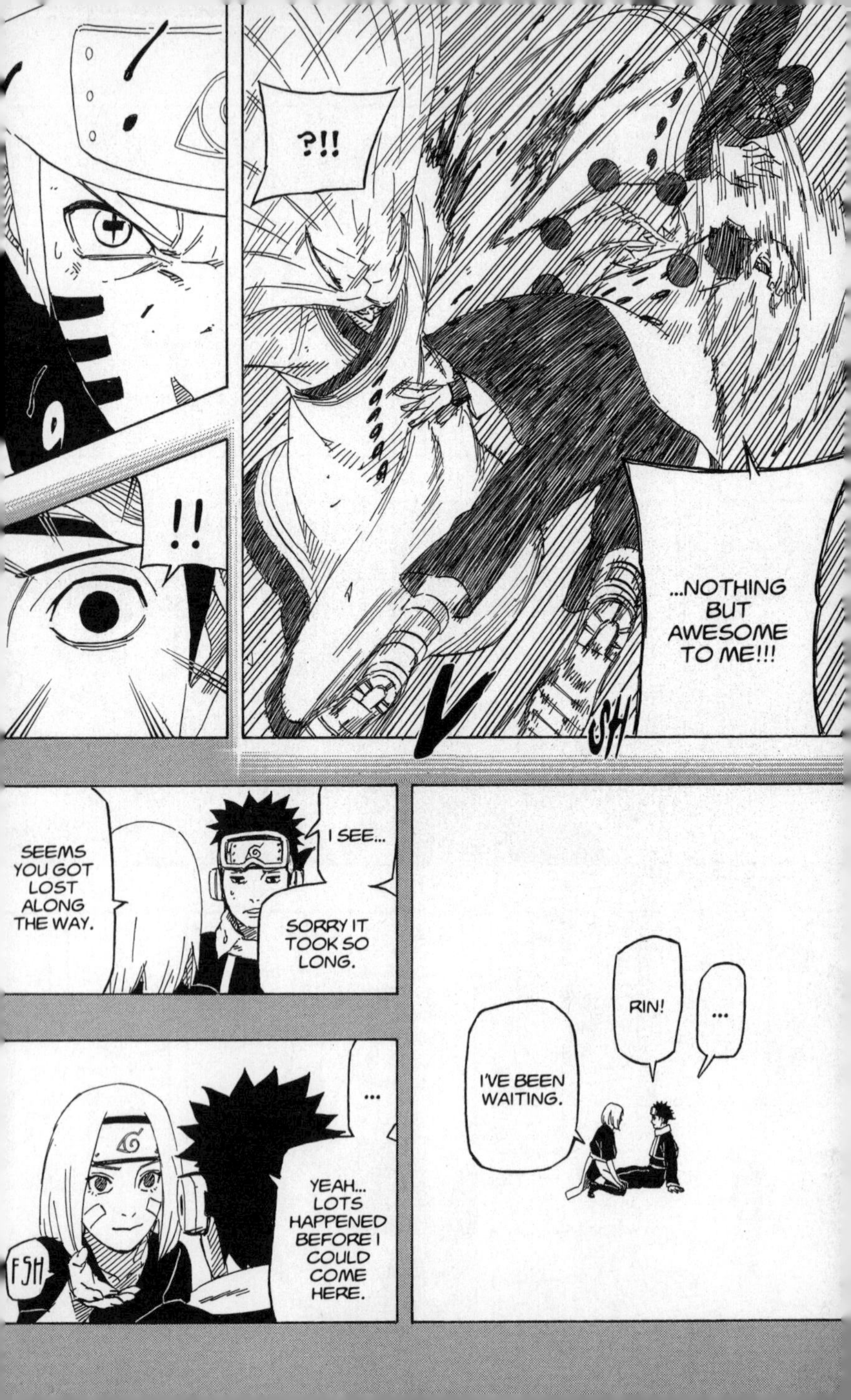
?!!
...NOTHING BUT AWESOME TO ME!!!
SH
!!
...
RIN!
I'VE BEEN WAITING.
I SEE...
SORRY IT TOOK SO LONG.
SEEMS YOU GOT LOST ALONG THE WAY.
...
YEAH... LOTS HAPPENED BEFORE I COULD COME HERE.
FSH

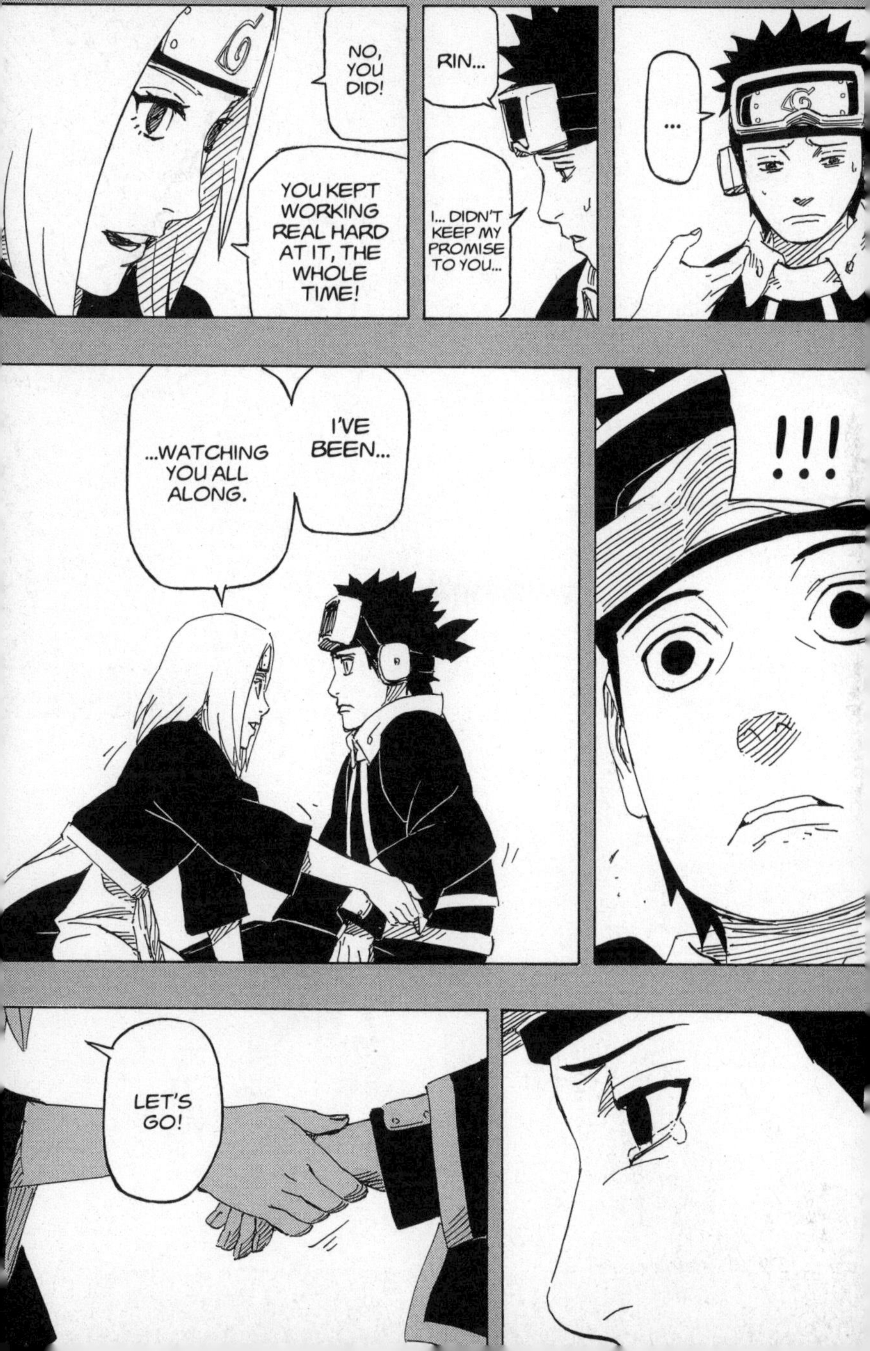
...
RIN...
I... DIDN'T KEEP MY PROMISE TO YOU...
NO, YOU DID!
YOU KEPT WORKING REAL HARD AT IT, THE WHOLE TIME!
!!!
I'VE BEEN...
...WATCHING YOU ALL ALONG.
LET'S GO!

Number 688: He of the Sharingan!!

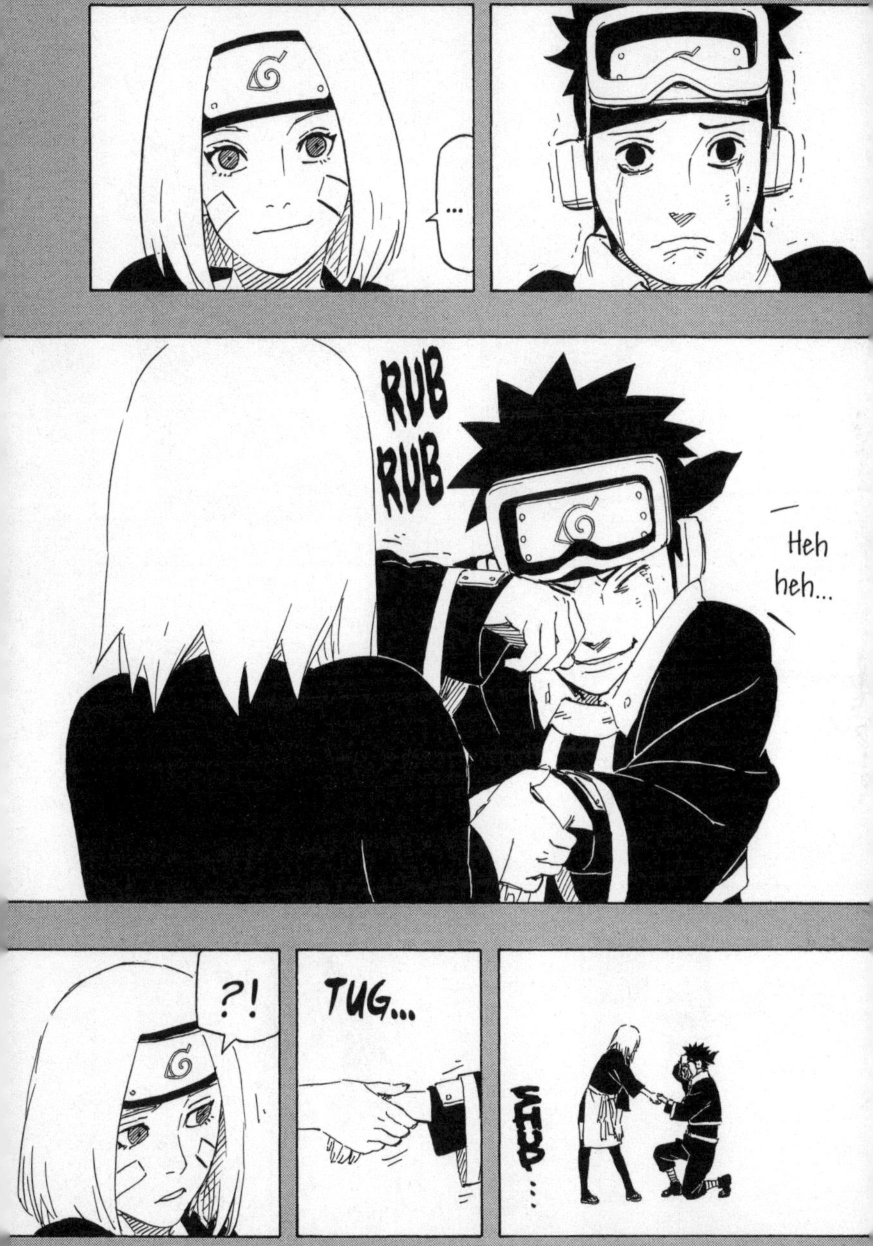
...
RUB RUB
Heh heh...
SHUP...
TUG...
?!

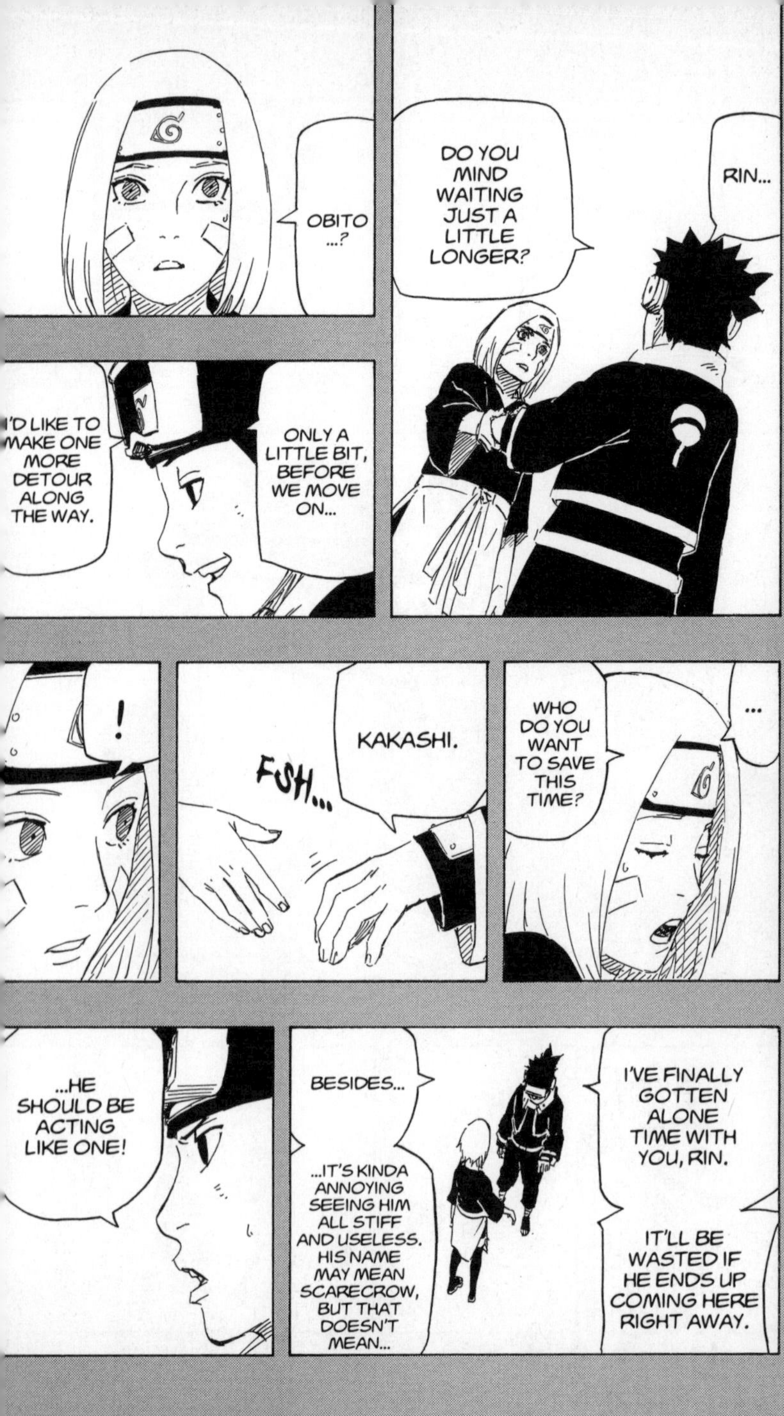
RIN...
DO YOU MIND WAITING JUST A LITTLE LONGER?
OBITO ...?
ONLY A LITTLE BIT, BEFORE WE MOVE ON...
I'D LIKE TO MAKE ONE MORE DETOUR ALONG THE WAY.
...
WHO DO YOU WANT TO SAVE THIS TIME?
KAKASHI.
FSH...
!
I'VE FINALLY GOTTEN ALONE TIME WITH YOU, RIN.
IT'LL BE WASTED IF HE ENDS UP COMING HERE RIGHT AWAY.
BESIDES...
...IT'S KINDA ANNOYING SEEING HIM ALL STIFF AND USELESS. HIS NAME MAY MEAN SCARECROW, BUT THAT DOESN'T MEAN...
...HE SHOULD BE ACTING LIKE ONE!

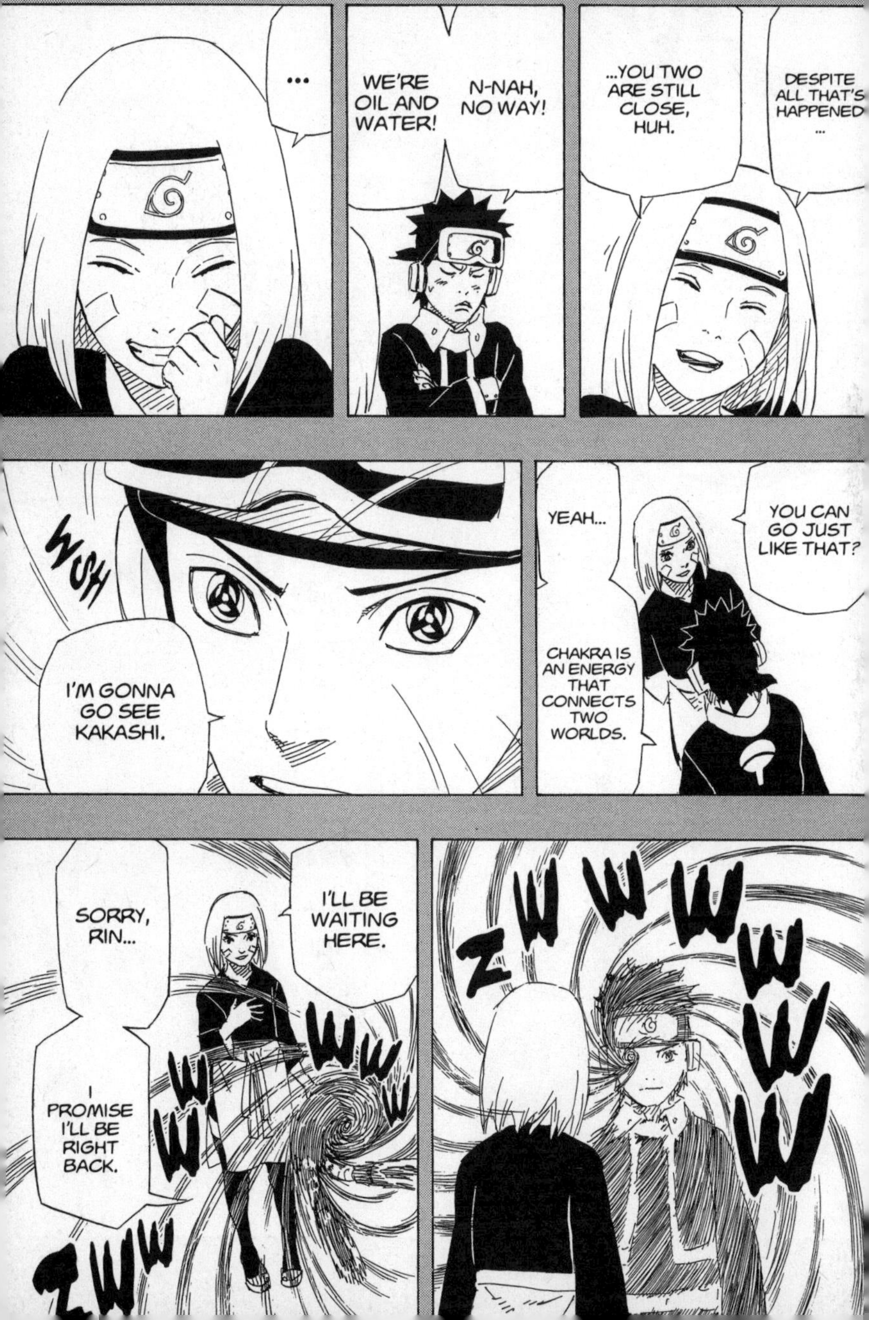
DESPITE ALL THAT'S HAPPENED ...
...YOU TWO ARE STILL CLOSE, HUH.
N-NAH, NO WAY!
WE'RE OIL AND WATER!
...
YOU CAN GO JUST LIKE THAT?
YEAH...
CHAKRA IS AN ENERGY THAT CONNECTS TWO WORLDS.
WSH
I'M GONNA GO SEE KAKASHI.
ZWWWWWWWWWW
I'LL BE WAITING HERE.
SORRY, RIN...
I PROMISE I'LL BE RIGHT BACK.
WWWWW
ZWW

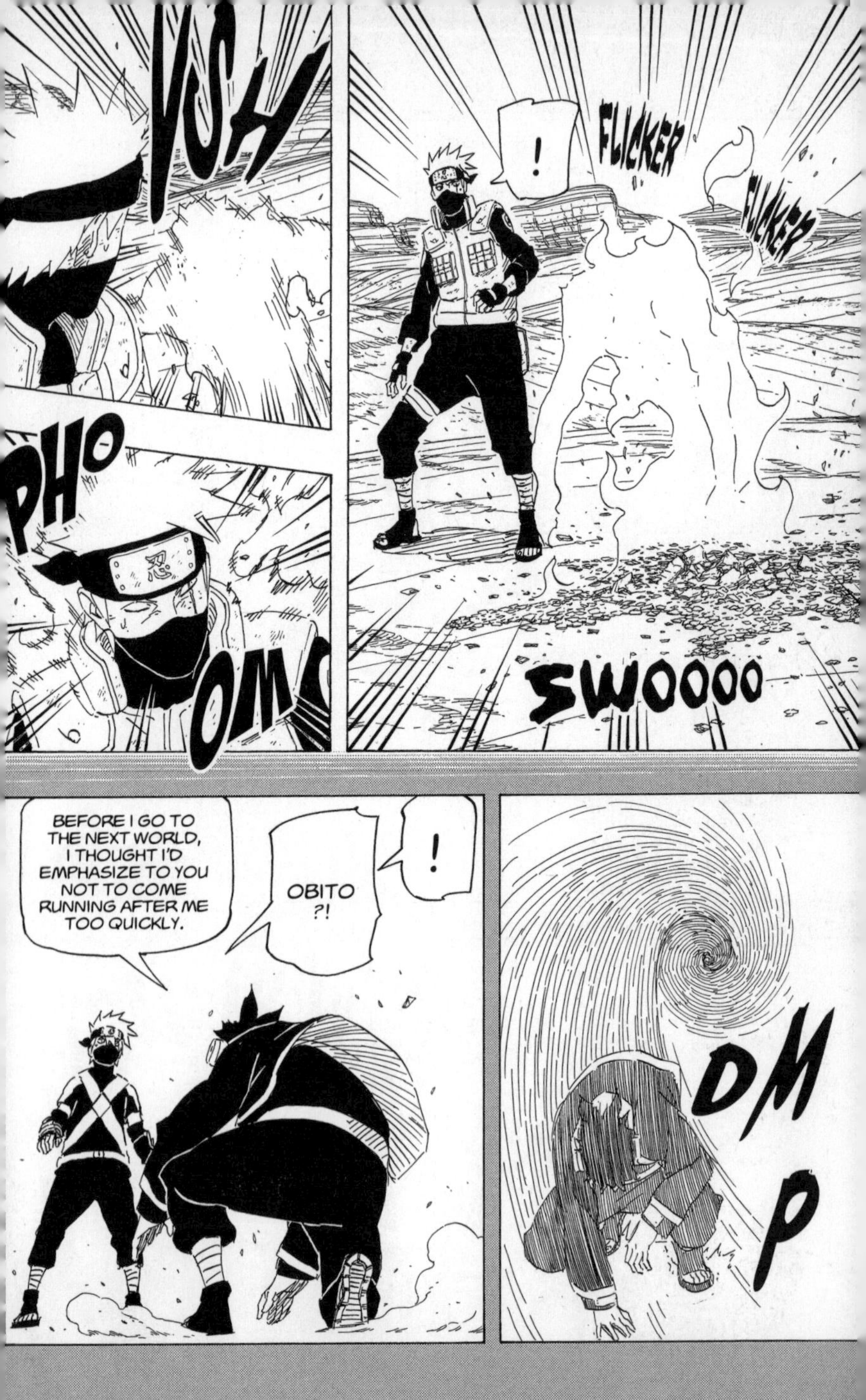
!
FLICKER
FLICKER
SWOOOO
VSH
PHOOM
DMP
!
OBITO ?!
BEFORE I GO TO THE NEXT WORLD, I THOUGHT I'D EMPHASIZE TO YOU NOT TO COME RUNNING AFTER ME TOO QUICKLY.

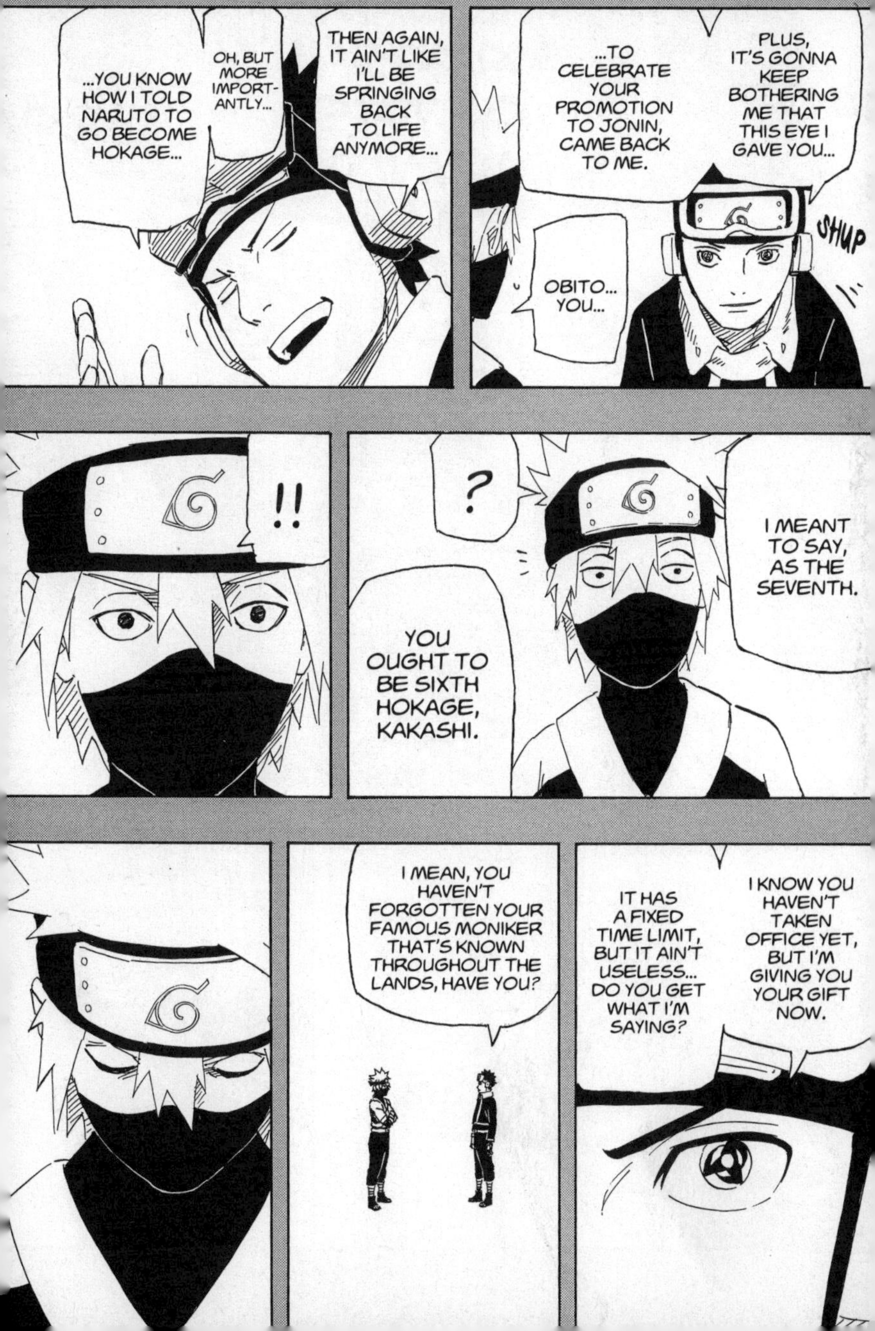
PLUS, IT'S GONNA KEEP BOTHERING ME THAT THIS EYE I GAVE YOU...
...TO CELEBRATE YOUR PROMOTION TO JONIN, CAME BACK TO ME.
SHUP
OBITO... YOU...
THEN AGAIN, IT AIN'T LIKE I'LL BE SPRINGING BACK TO LIFE ANYMORE...
OH, BUT MORE IMPORTANTLY...
...YOU KNOW HOW I TOLD NARUTO TO GO BECOME HOKAGE...
I MEANT TO SAY, AS THE SEVENTH.
?
YOU OUGHT TO BE SIXTH HOKAGE, KAKASHI.
!!
I KNOW YOU HAVEN'T TAKEN OFFICE YET, BUT I'M GIVING YOU YOUR GIFT NOW.
IT HAS A FIXED TIME LIMIT, BUT IT AIN'T USELESS... DO YOU GET WHAT I'M SAYING?
I MEAN, YOU HAVEN'T FORGOTTEN YOUR FAMOUS MONIKER THAT'S KNOWN THROUGHOUT THE LANDS, HAVE YOU?

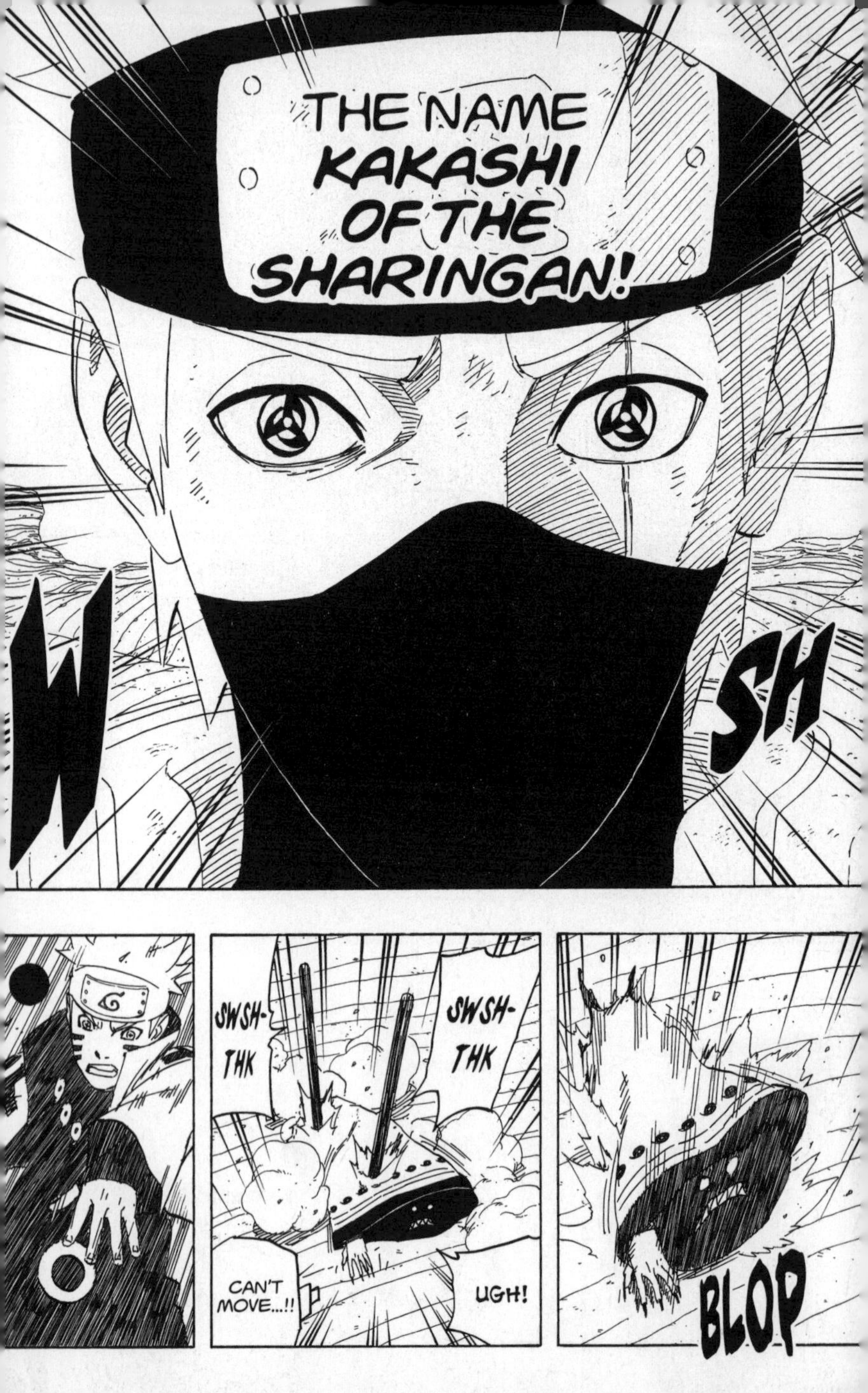
THE NAME KAKASHI OF THE SHARINGAN!
WH
SH
BLOP
SWSH-THK
SWSH-THK
UGH!
CAN'T MOVE...!!

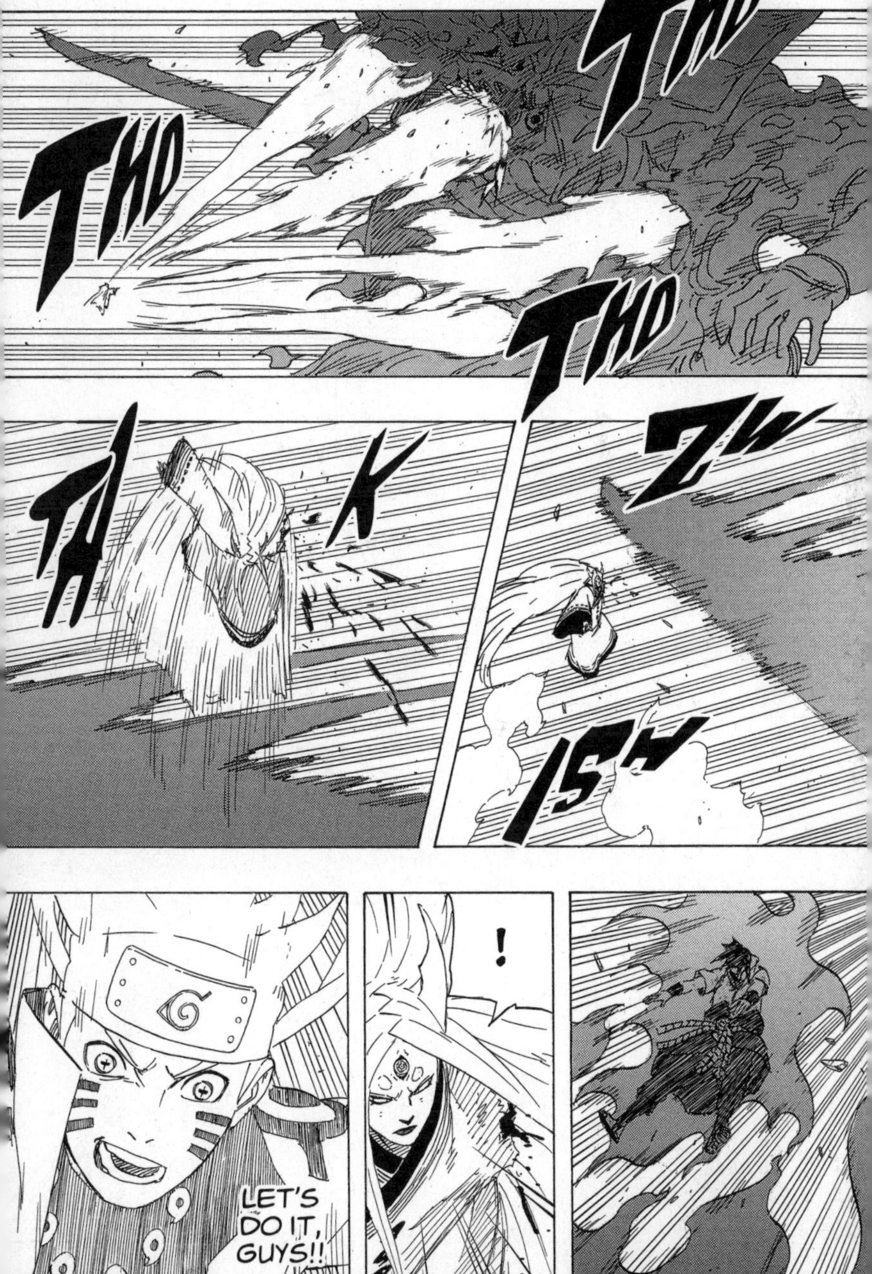
THD
THD
THD
ZW
ISH
TA
K
!
LET'S DO IT, GUYS!!

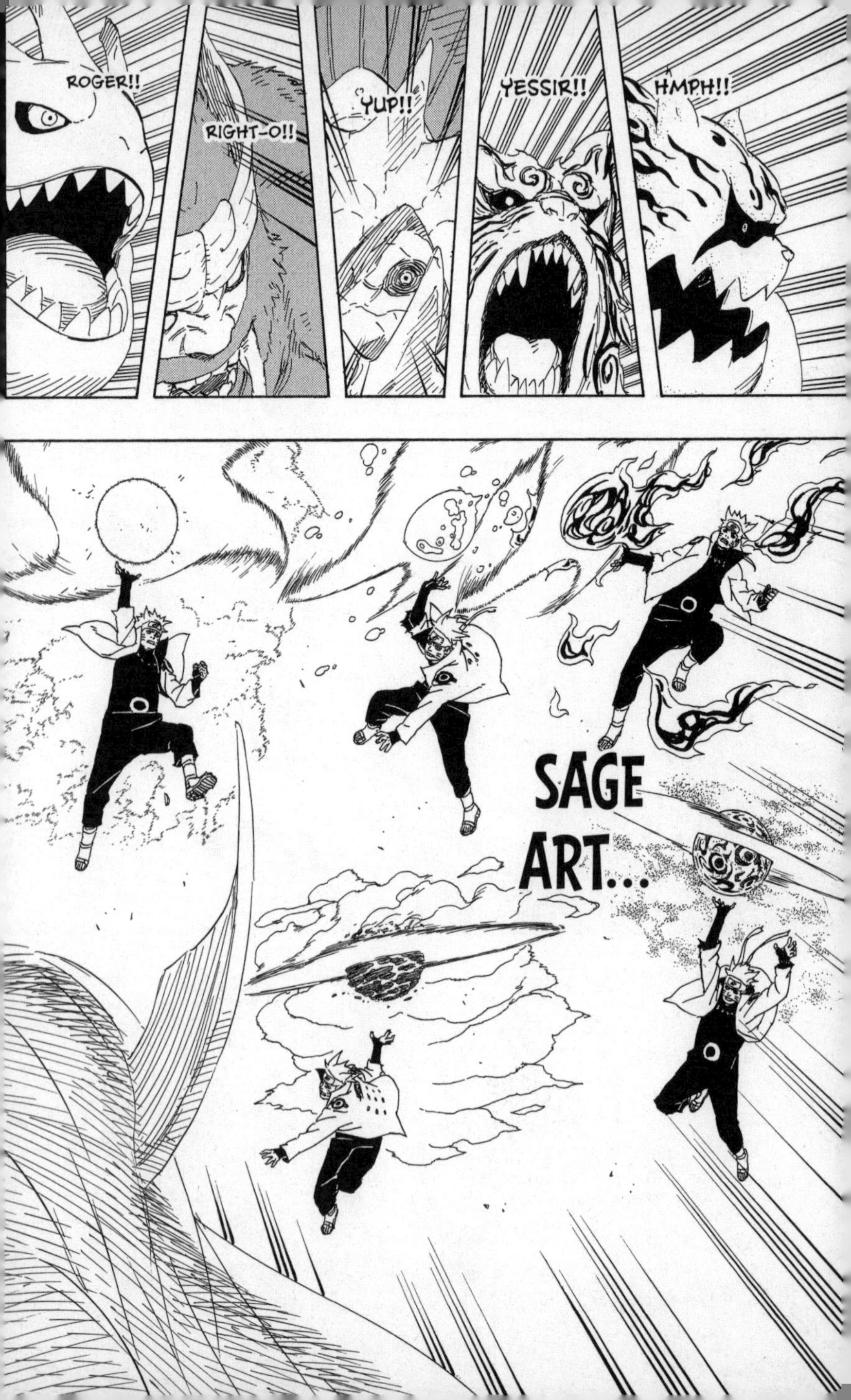
HMPH!!
YESSIR!!
YUP!!
RIGHT-O!!
ROGER!!
SAGE ART...

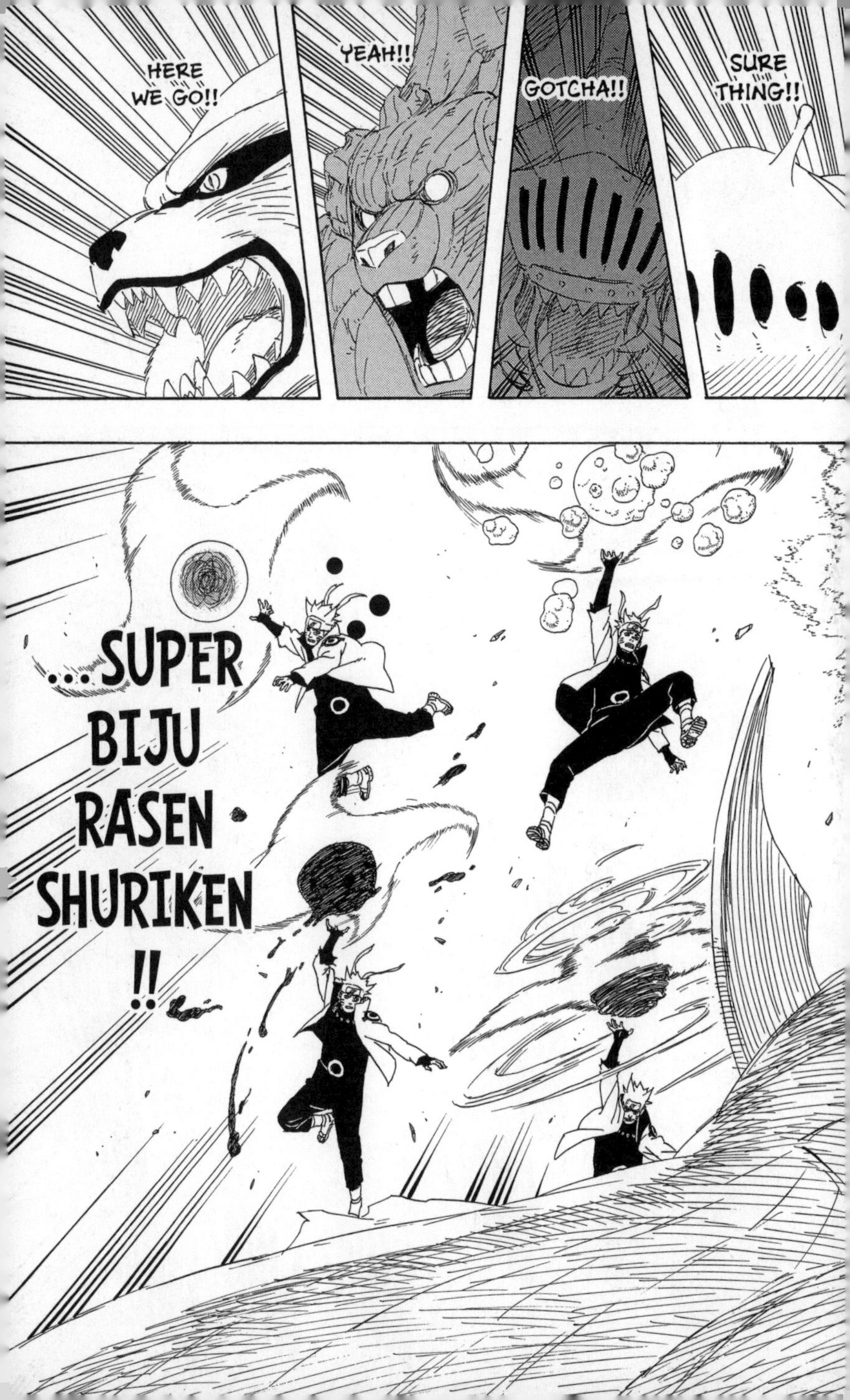
SURE THING!!
GOTCHA!!
YEAH!!
HERE WE GO!!
...SUPER BIJU RASEN SHURIKEN!!

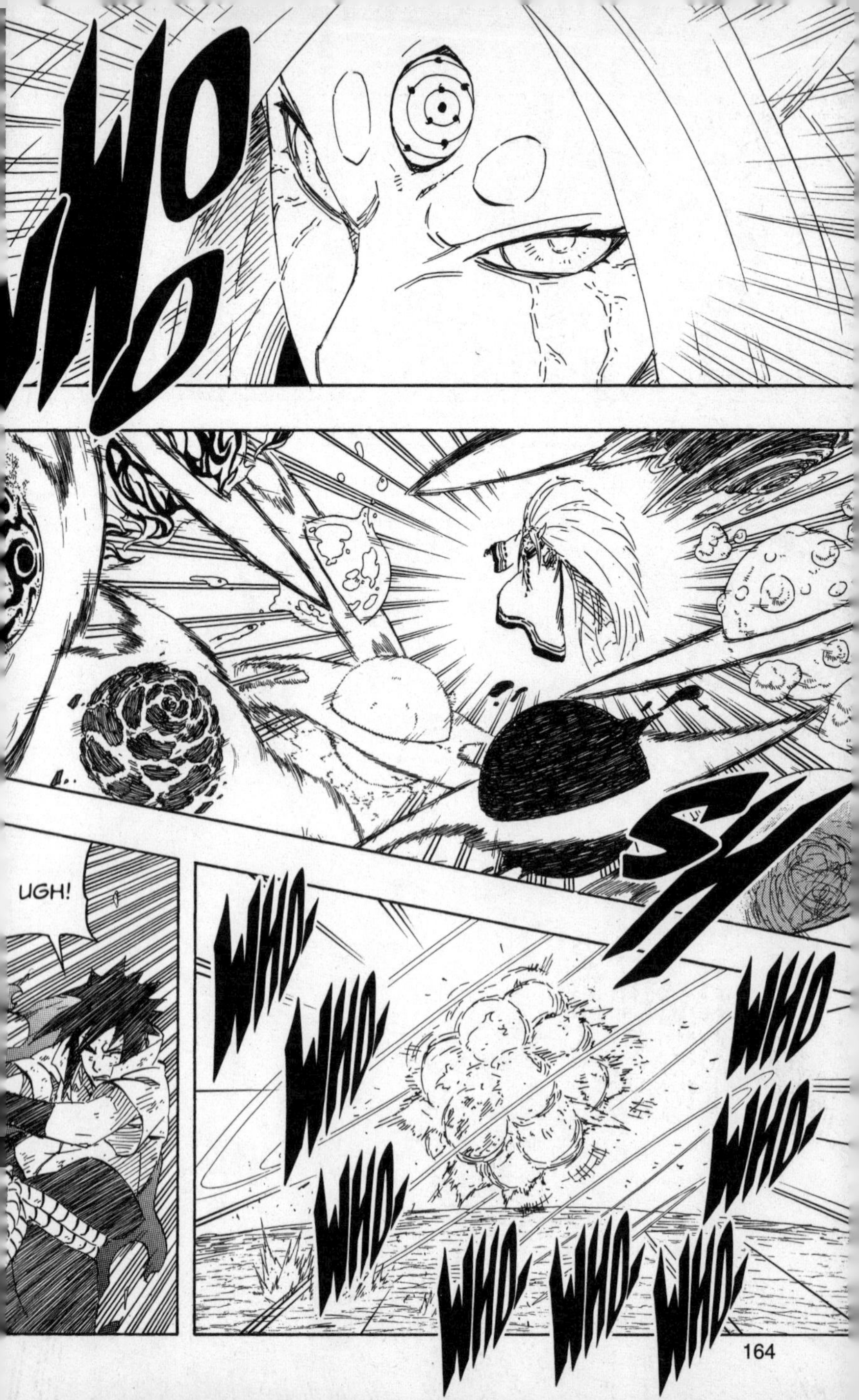
WHO
WHO
SH
WHO
WHO
WHO
WHO
WHO
WHO
WHO
WHO
UGH!

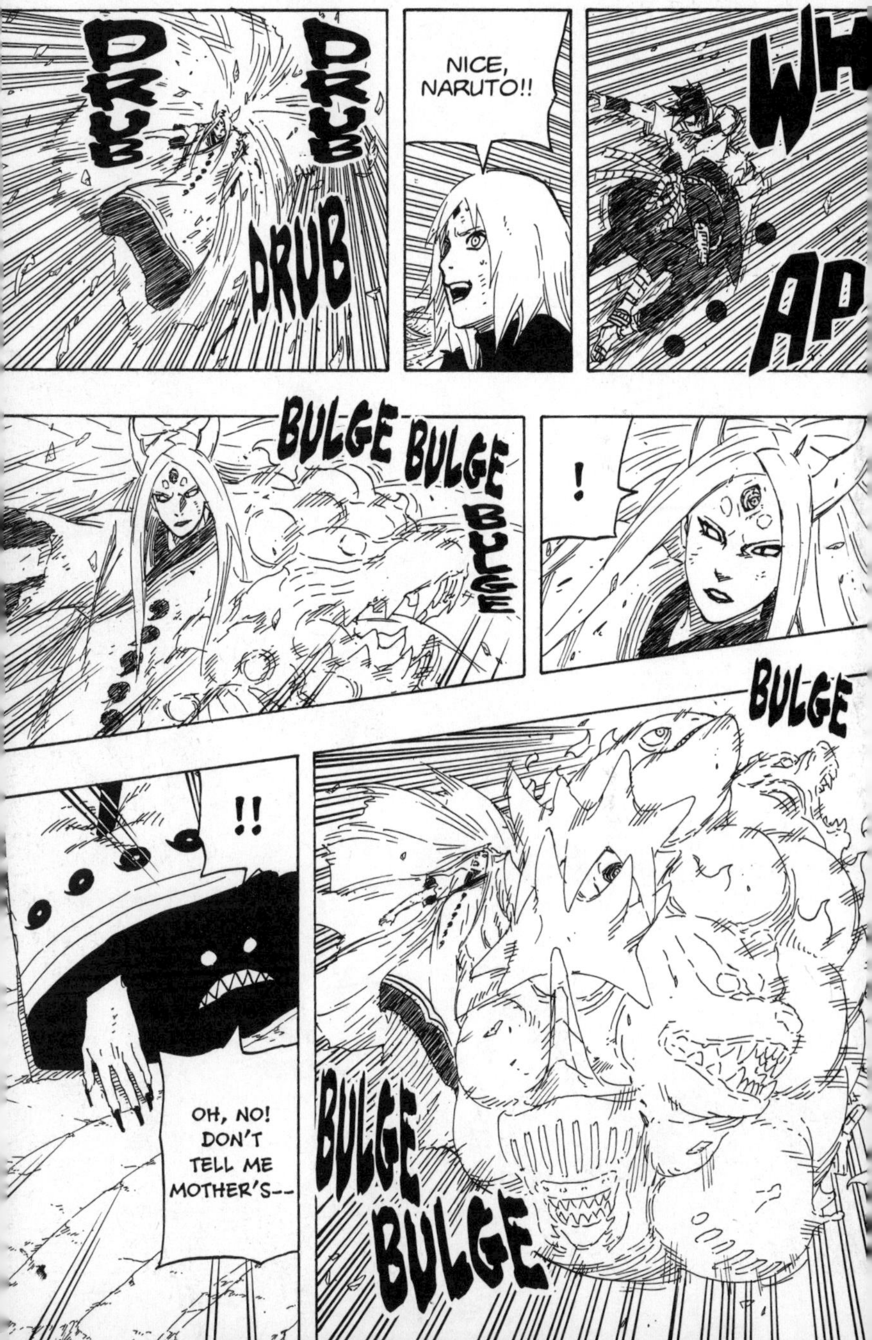
WHAP
NICE, NARUTO!!
DRUB
DRUB
DRUB
!
BULGE
BULGE
BULGE
BULGE
!!
OH, NO! DON'T TELL ME MOTHER'S--
BULGE
BULGE

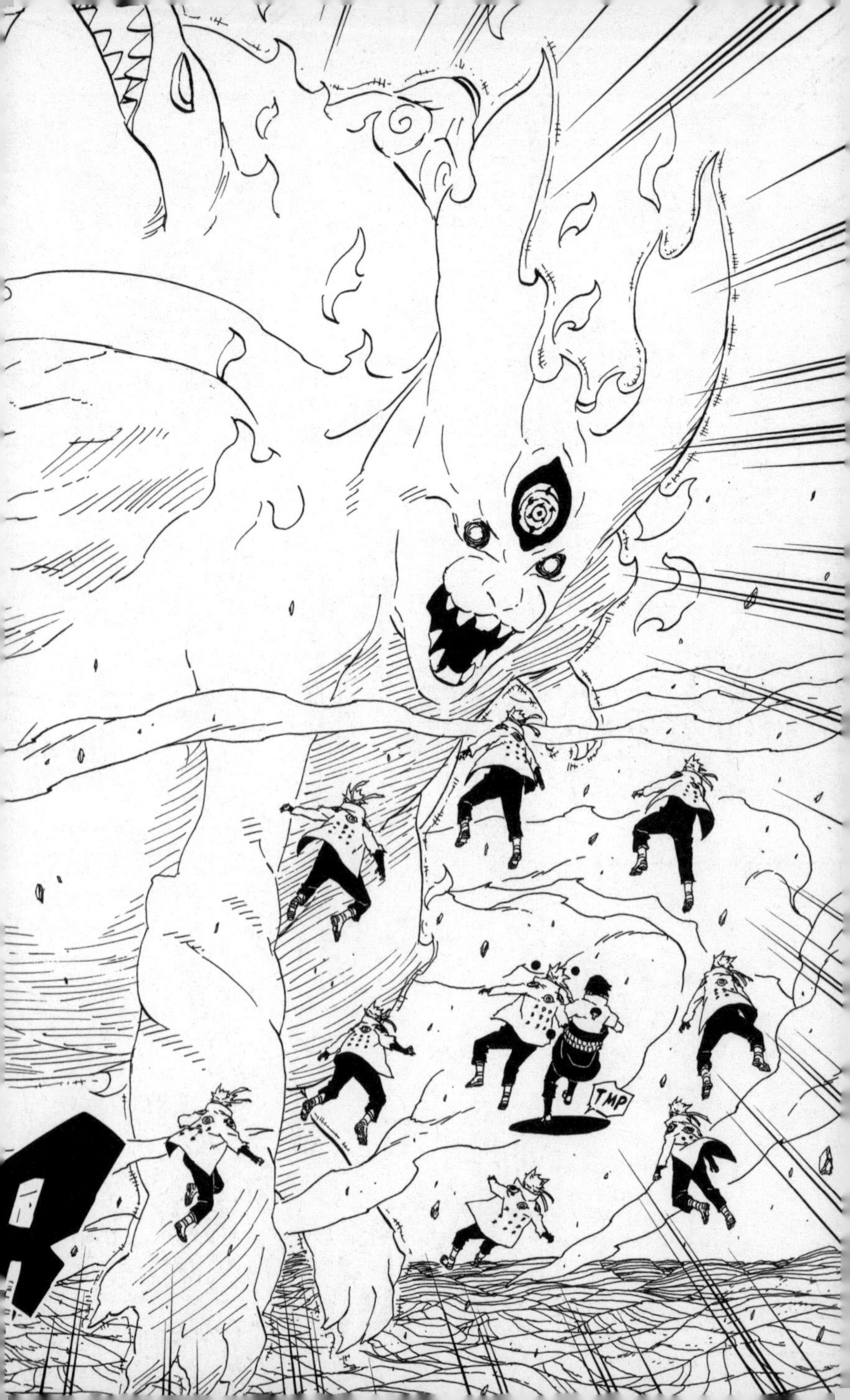
TMP

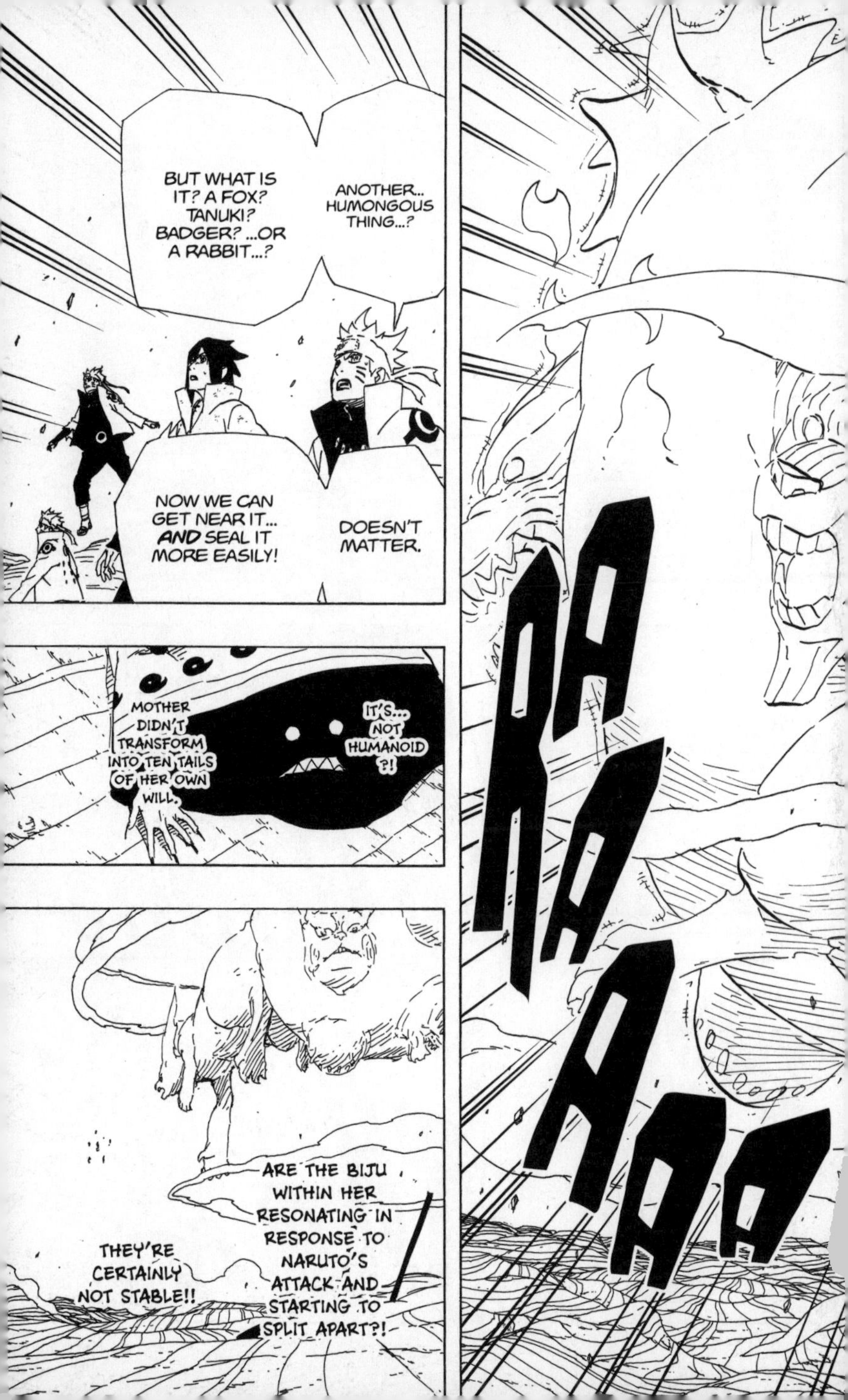
RAAAAAA
ANOTHER... HUMONGOUS THING...?
BUT WHAT IS IT? A FOX? TANUKI? BADGER? ...OR A RABBIT...?
DOESN'T MATTER.
NOW WE CAN GET NEAR IT... AND SEAL IT MORE EASILY!
IT'S... NOT HUMANOID?!
MOTHER DIDN'T TRANSFORM INTO TEN TAILS OF HER OWN WILL.
ARE THE BIJU WITHIN HER RESONATING IN RESPONSE TO NARUTO'S ATTACK AND STARTING TO SPLIT APART?!
THEY'RE CERTAINLY NOT STABLE!!

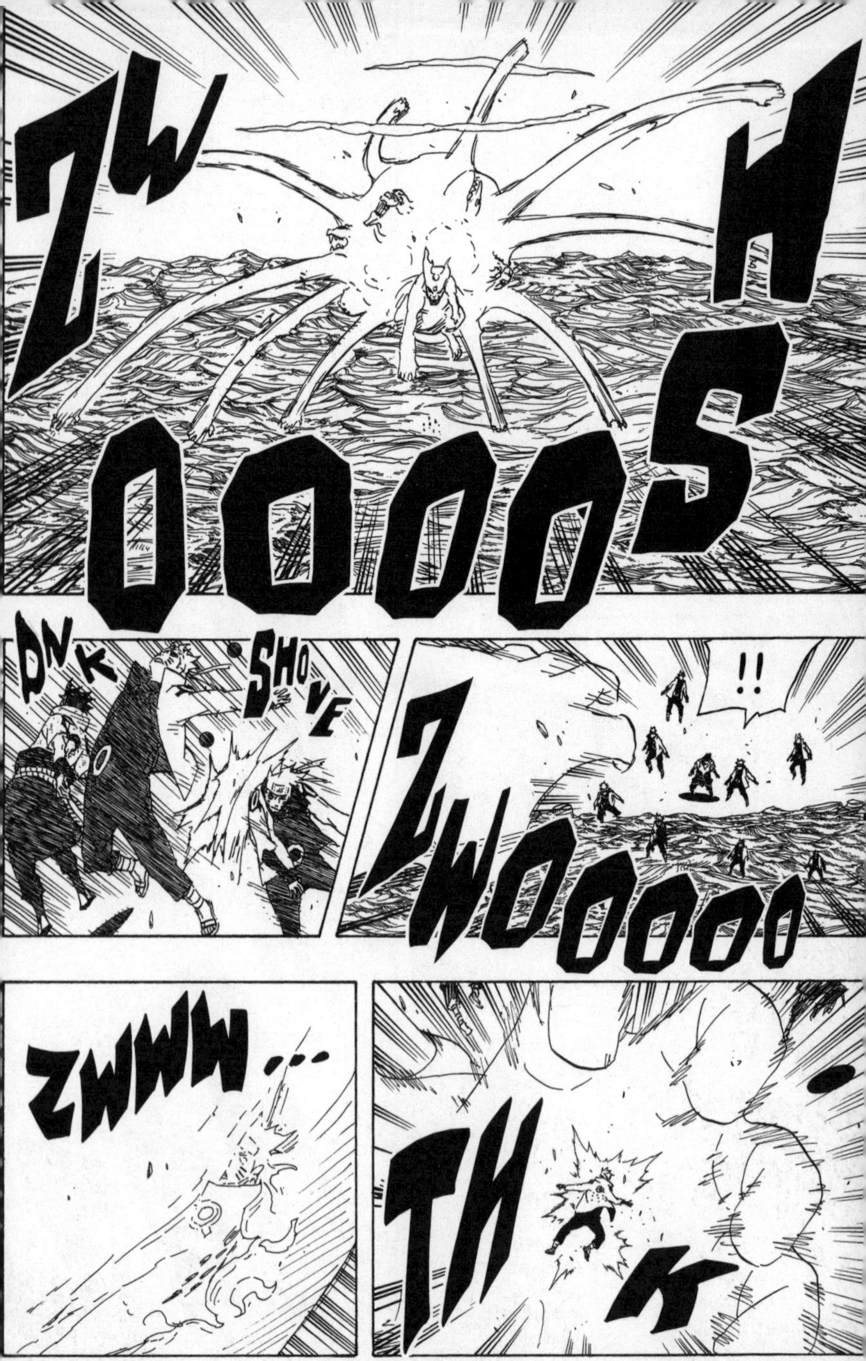
ZWOOOOSH
!!
ZWOOOOO
DNK
SHOVE
THK
ZWWW...

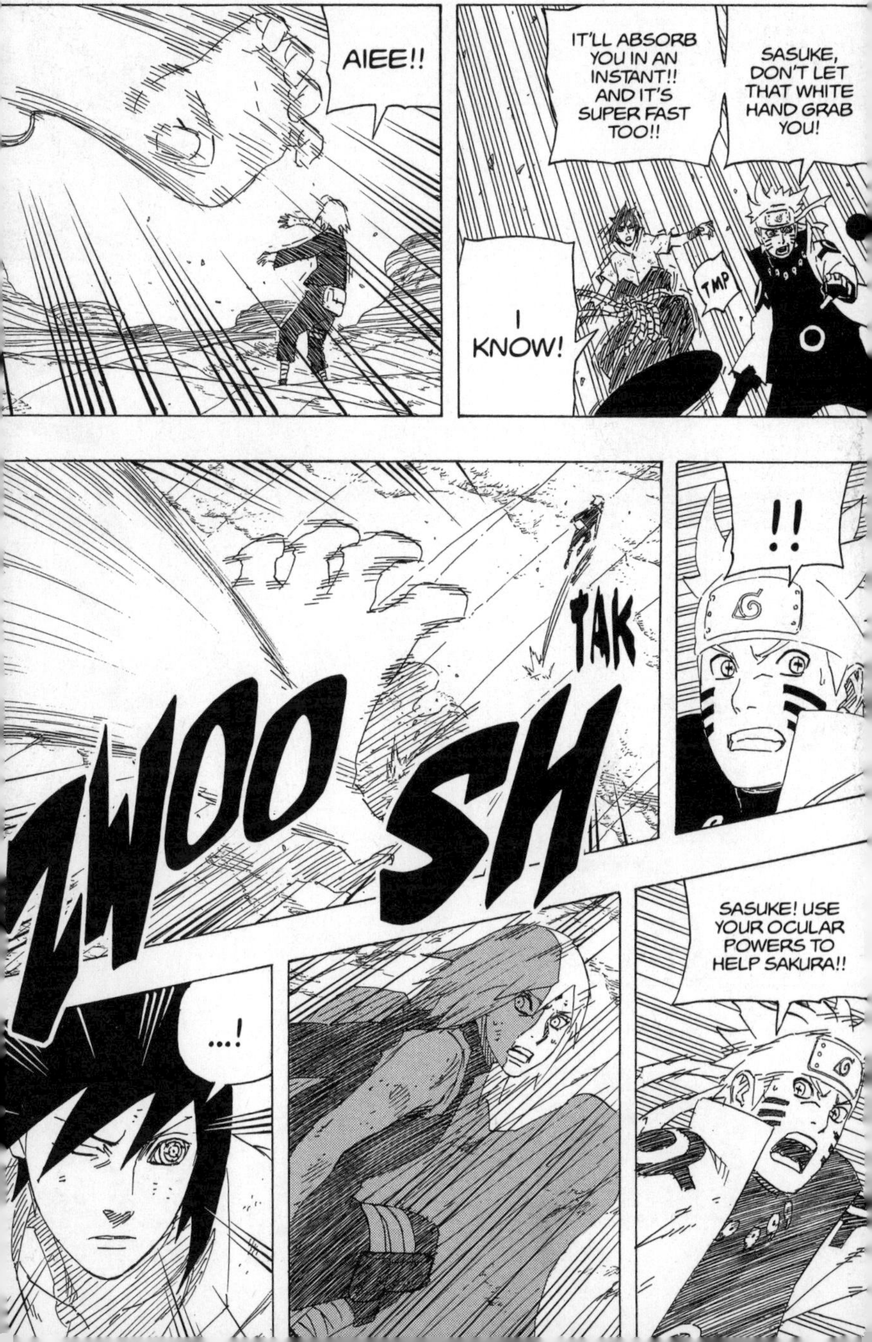
SASUKE, DON'T LET THAT WHITE HAND GRAB YOU!
IT'LL ABSORB YOU IN AN INSTANT!! AND IT'S SUPER FAST TOO!!
TMP
I KNOW!
AIEE!!
!!
TAK
ZWOOSH
SASUKE! USE YOUR OCULAR POWERS TO HELP SAKURA!!
...!

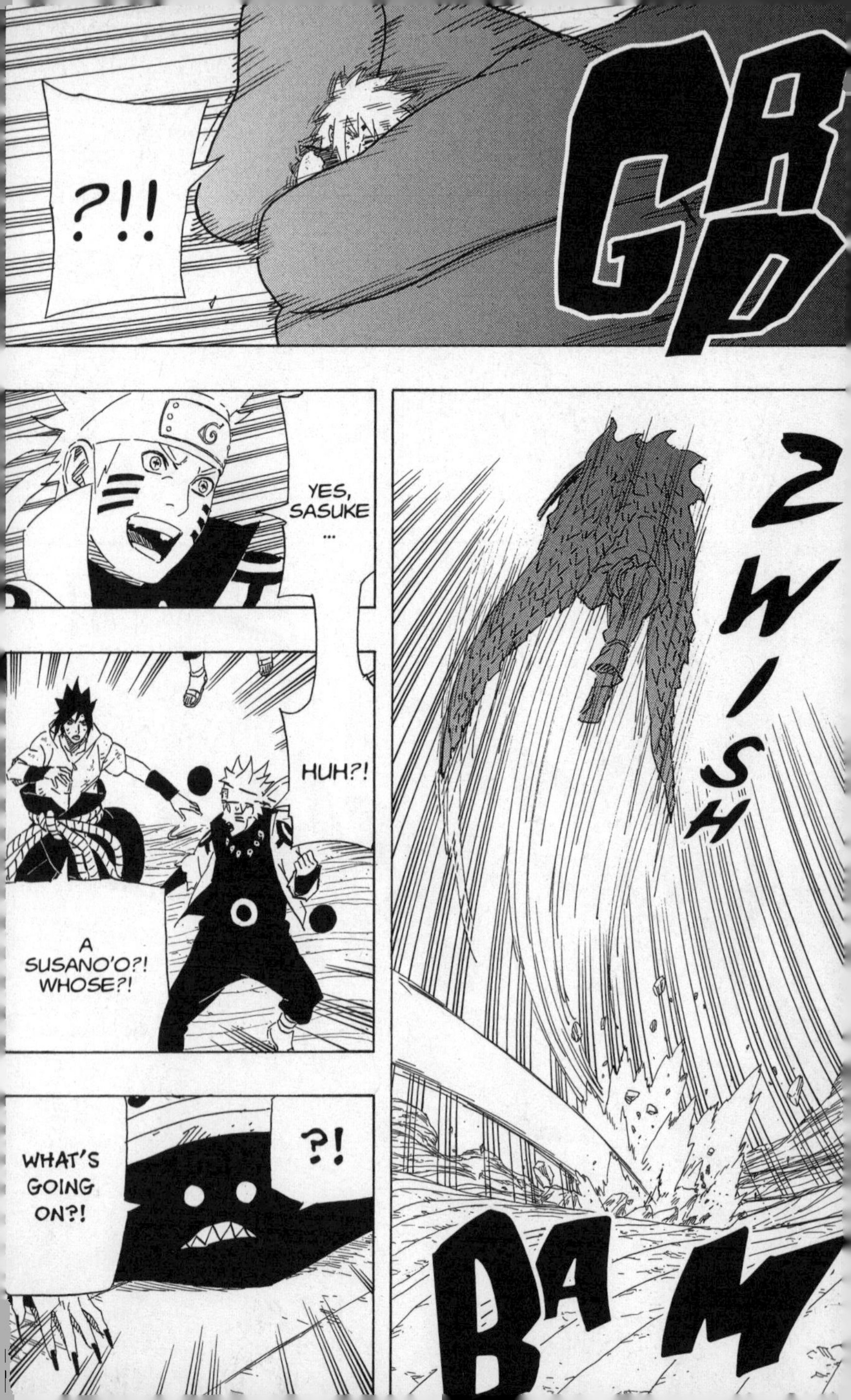
GRP
?!!
ZWISH
BAM
YES, SASUKE ...
HUH?!
A SUSANO'O?! WHOSE?!
?!
WHAT'S GOING ON?!

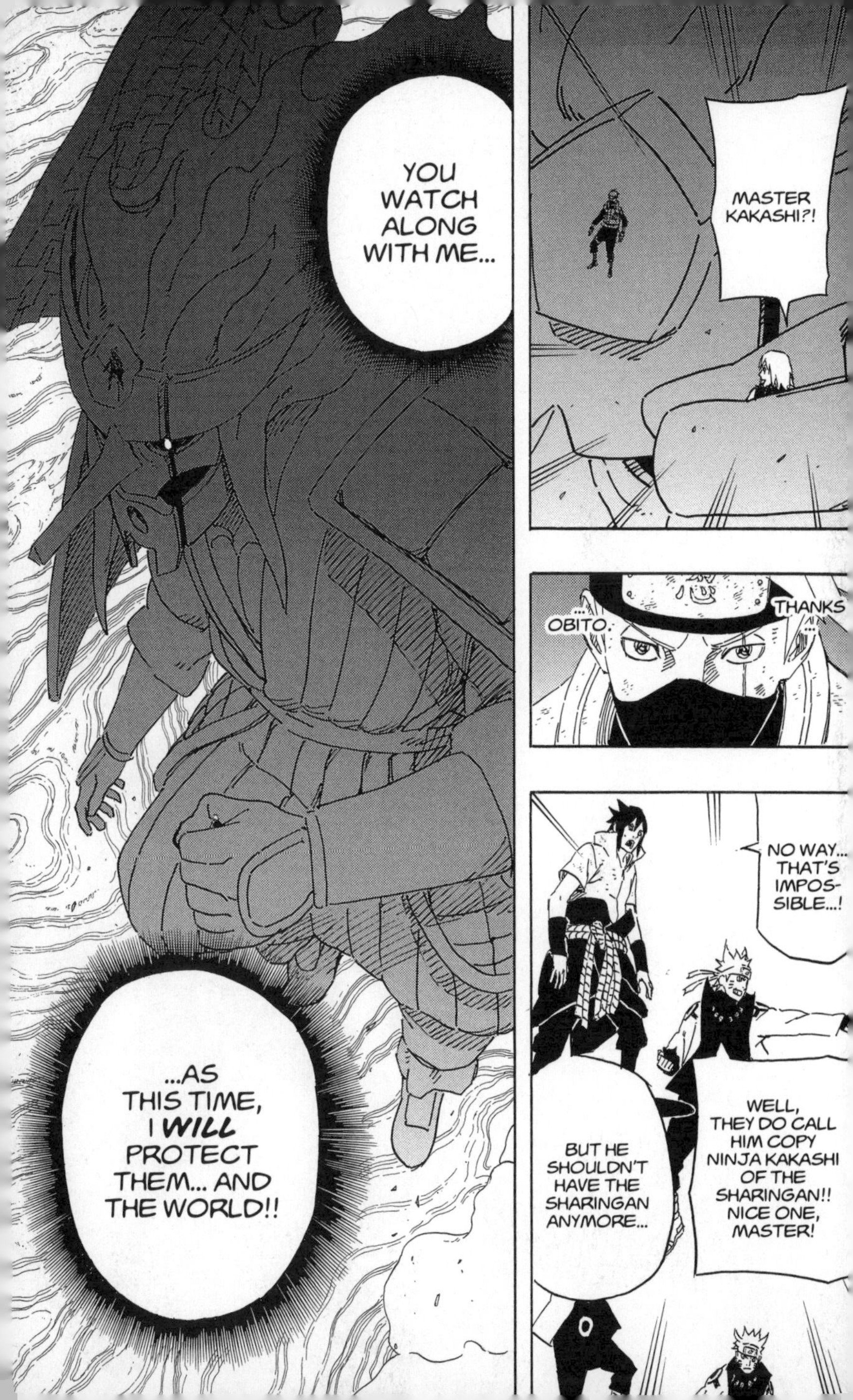
MASTER KAKASHI?!
THANKS...
...OBITO.
NO WAY... THAT'S IMPOSSIBLE...!
WELL, THEY DO CALL HIM COPY NINJA KAKASHI OF THE SHARINGAN!! NICE ONE, MASTER!
BUT HE SHOULDN'T HAVE THE SHARINGAN ANYMORE...
YOU WATCH ALONG WITH ME...
...AS THIS TIME, I ***WILL*** PROTECT THEM... AND THE WORLD!!

Number 689: I Love You Guys

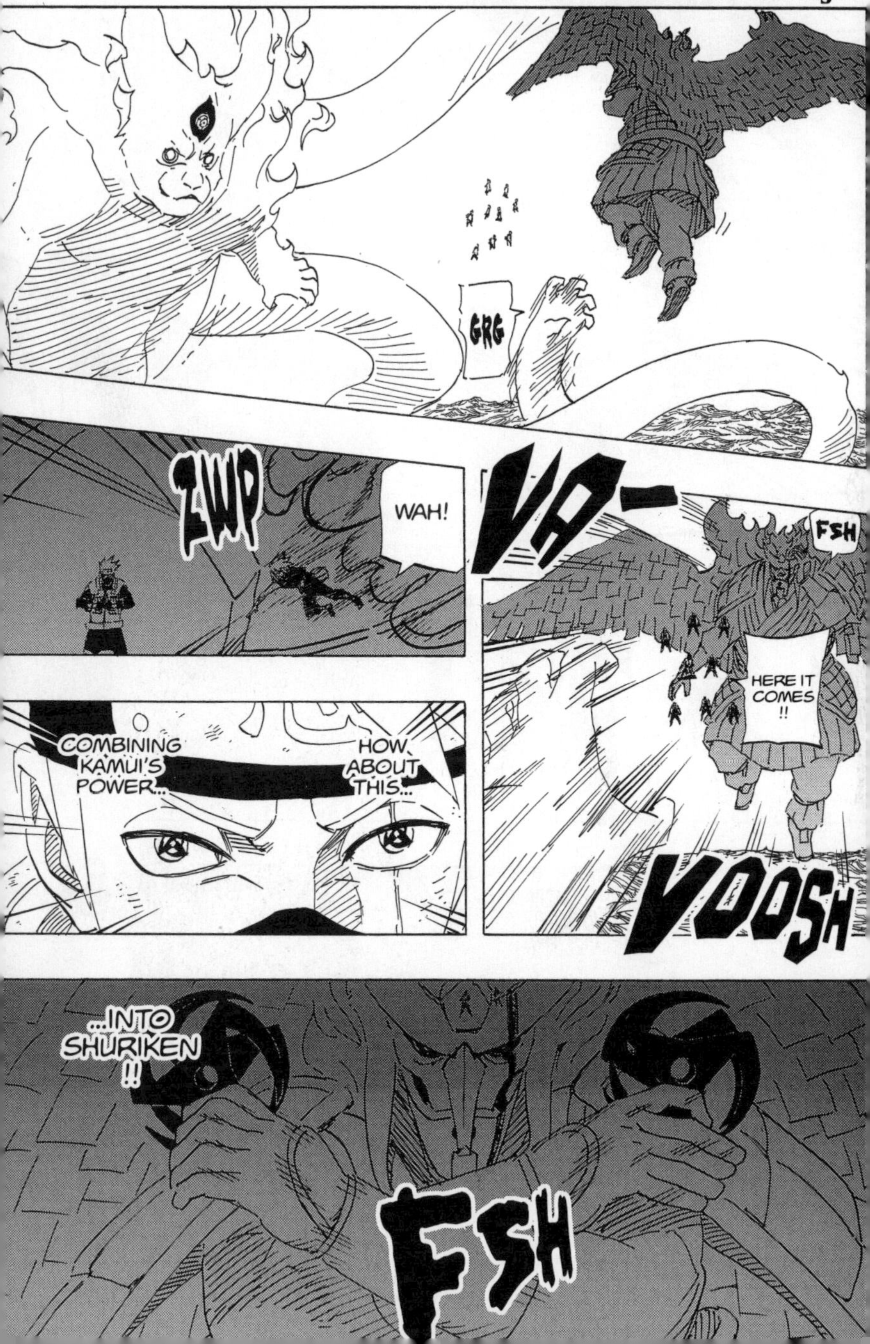
GRG
VA-
FSH
HERE IT COMES!!
VOOSH
WAH!
ZWP
HOW ABOUT THIS...
COMBINING KAMUI'S POWER...
...INTO SHURIKEN!!
FSH

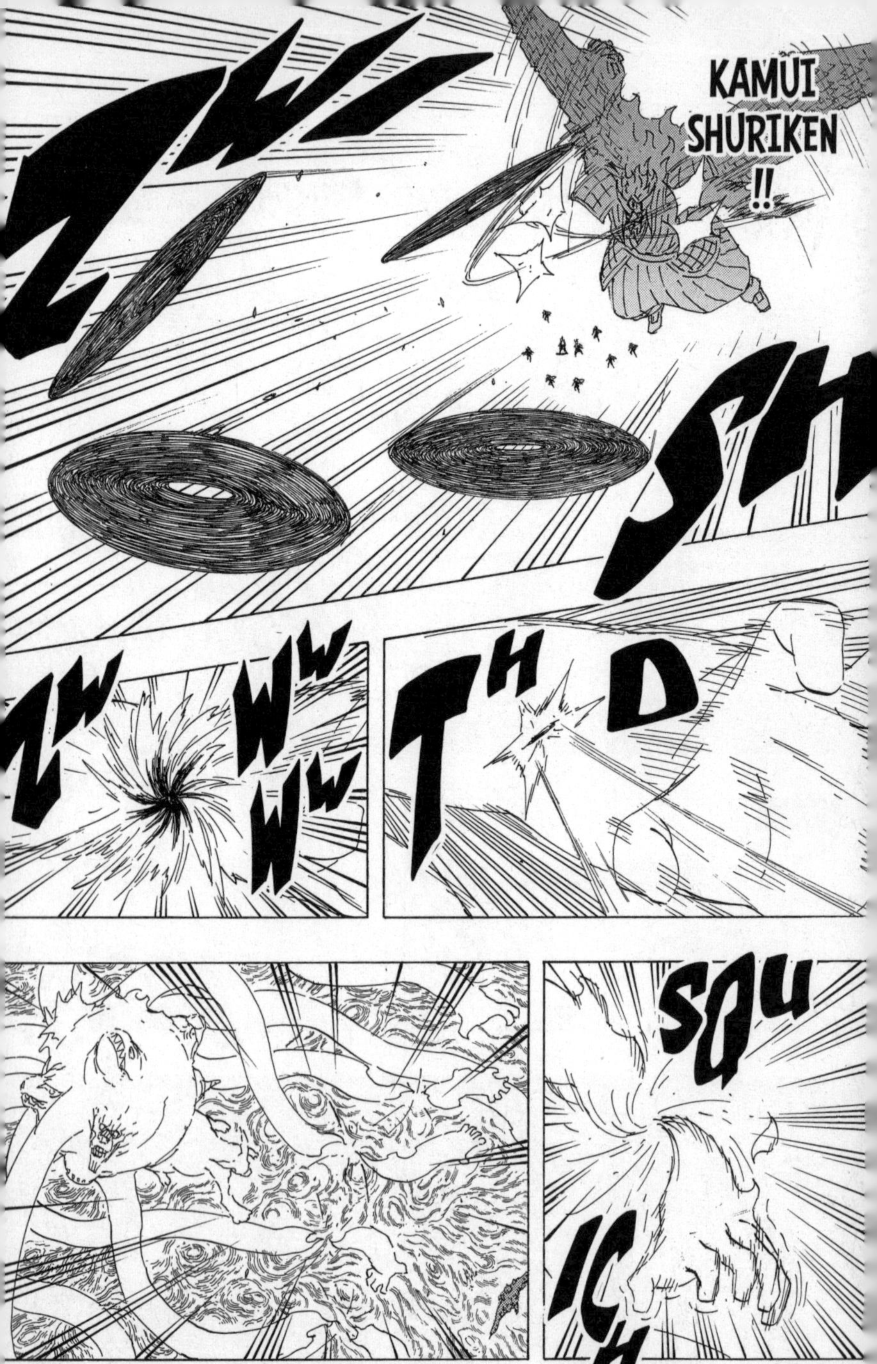
KAMUI SHURIKEN !!
THD
SQUICH

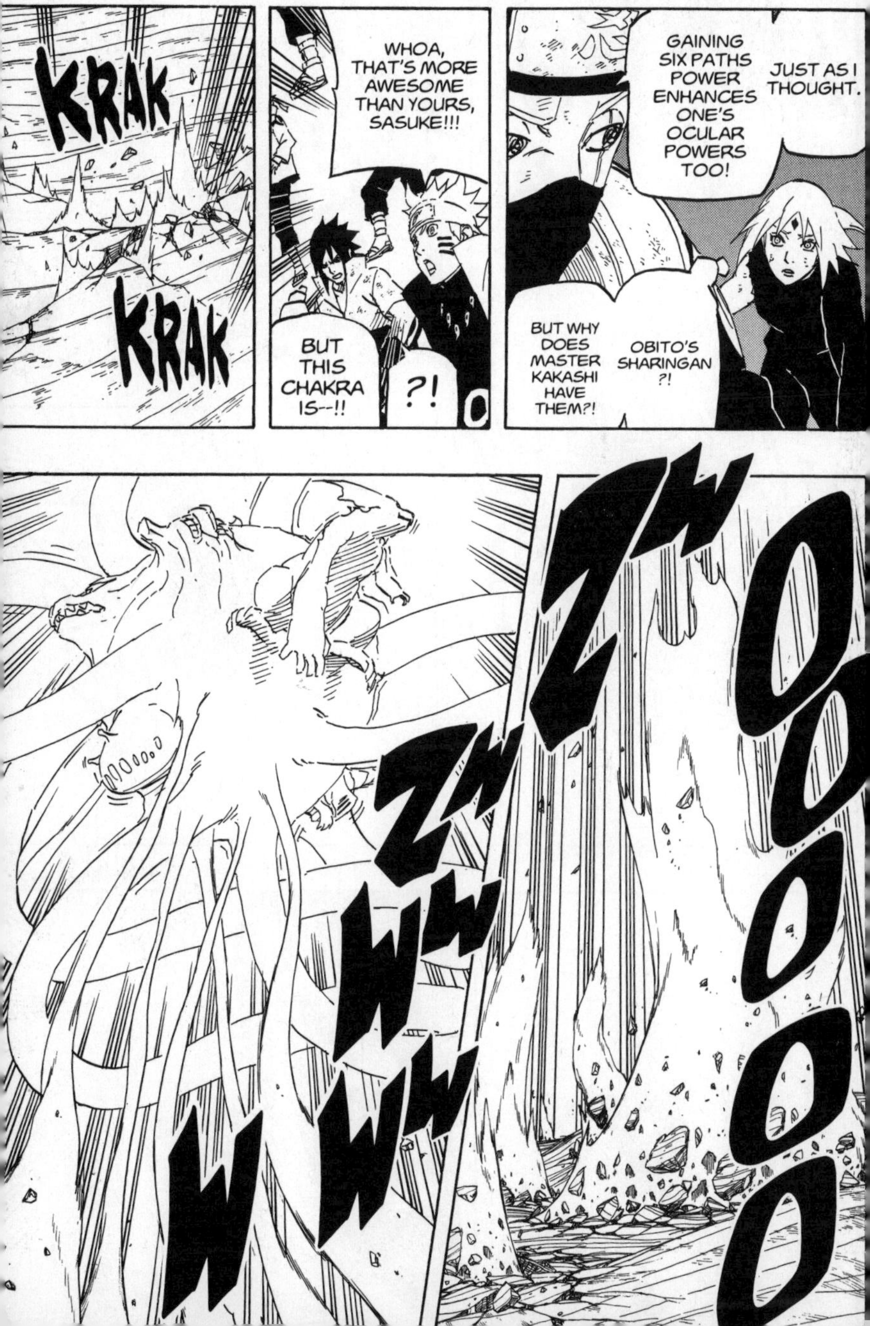
JUST AS I THOUGHT.
GAINING SIX PATHS POWER ENHANCES ONE'S OCULAR POWERS TOO!
OBITO'S SHARINGAN?!
BUT WHY DOES MASTER KAKASHI HAVE THEM?!
WHOA, THAT'S MORE AWESOME THAN YOURS, SASUKE!!!
?!
BUT THIS CHAKRA IS--!!
KRAK
KRAK
ZWOOOOOOO
ZWWWW
W

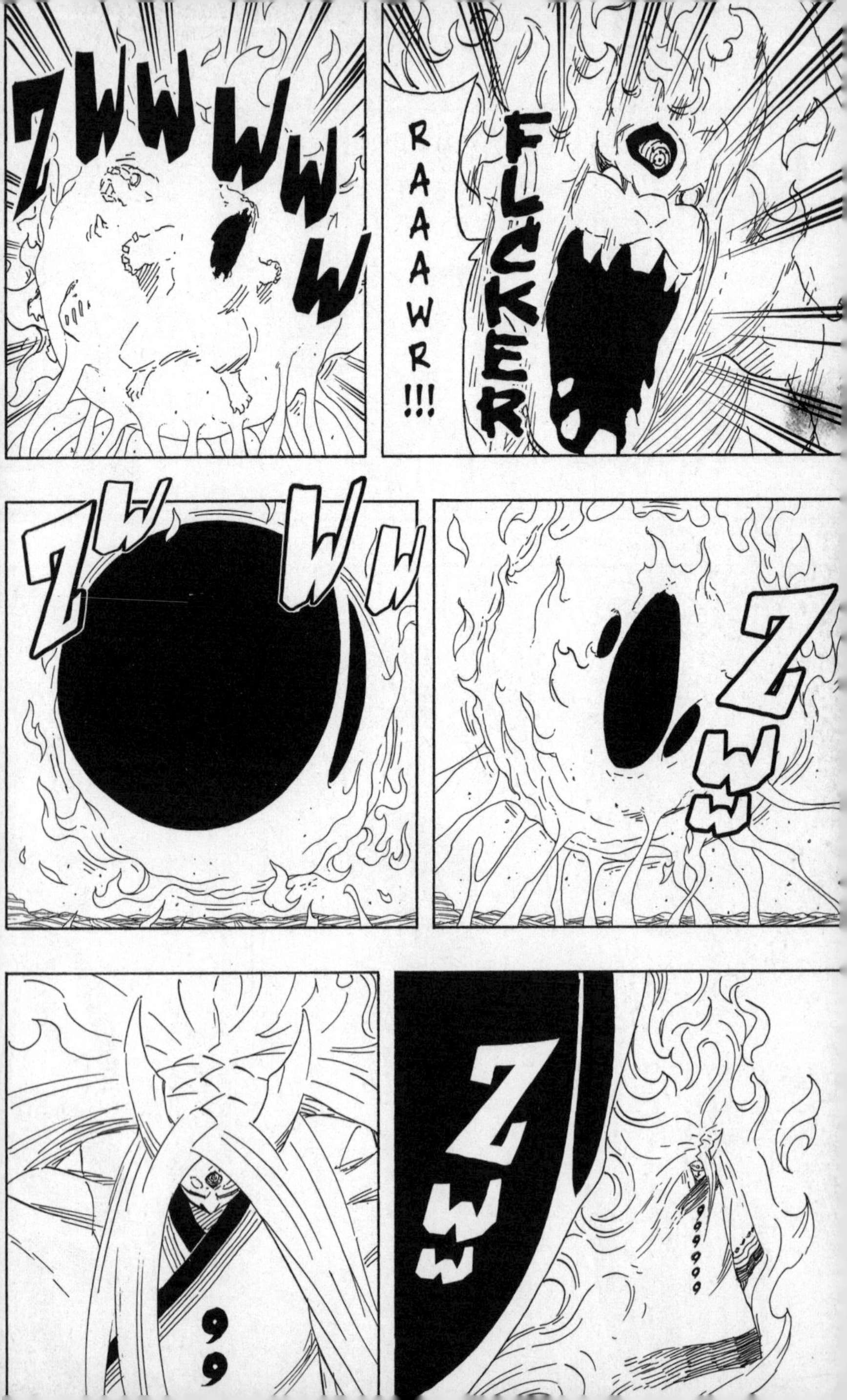
RAAAWR!!!
FLICKER
ZWWWWWW
ZWW
ZWWW
ZWWW

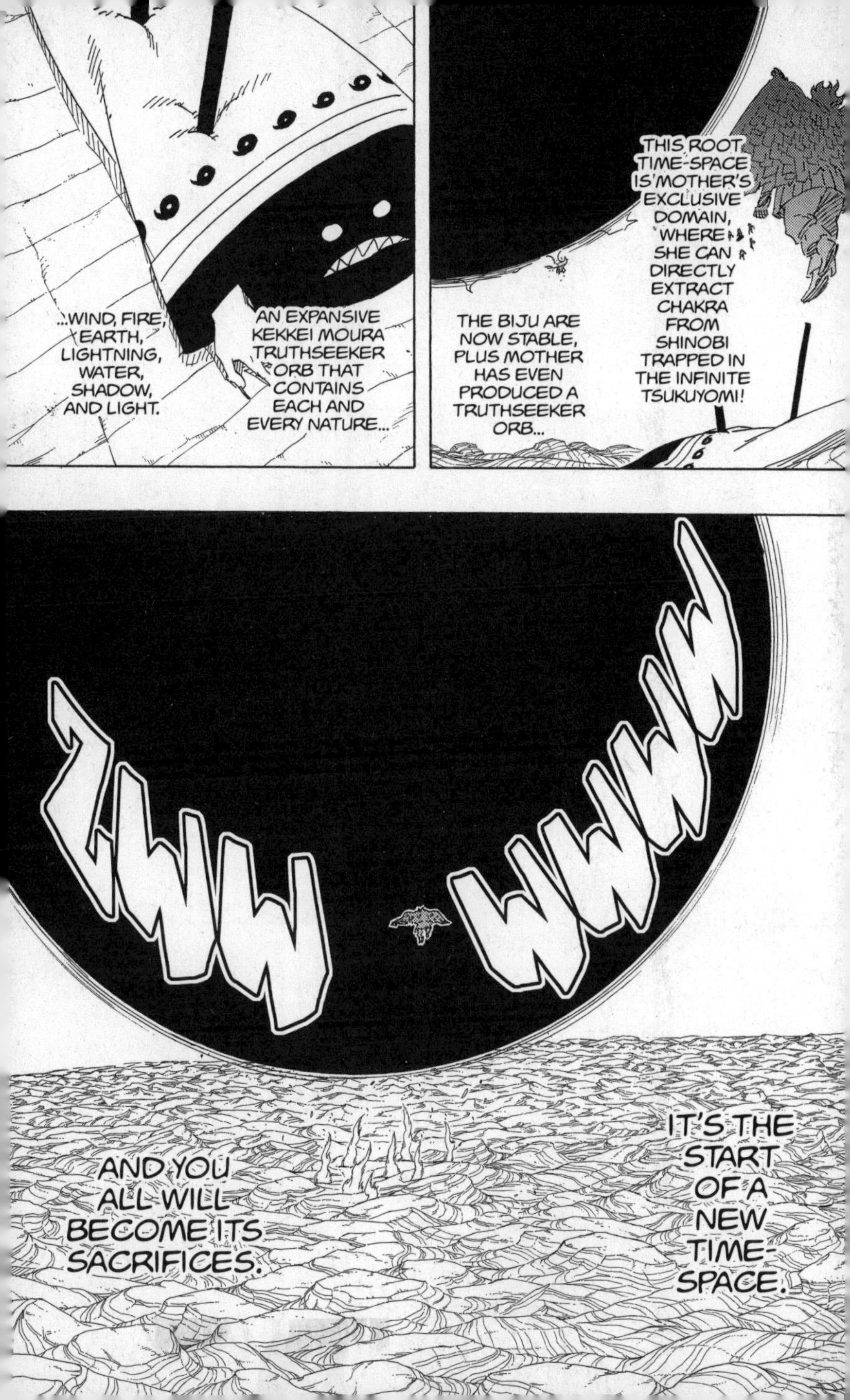
THIS ROOT TIME-SPACE IS MOTHER'S EXCLUSIVE DOMAIN, WHERE SHE CAN DIRECTLY EXTRACT CHAKRA FROM SHINOBI TRAPPED IN THE INFINITE TSUKUYOMI!
THE BIJU ARE NOW STABLE, PLUS MOTHER HAS EVEN PRODUCED A TRUTHSEEKER ORB...
AN EXPANSIVE KEKKEI MOURA TRUTHSEEKER ORB THAT CONTAINS EACH AND EVERY NATURE...
...WIND, FIRE, EARTH, LIGHTNING, WATER, SHADOW, AND LIGHT.
IT'S THE START OF A NEW TIME-SPACE.
ZWW WWWW
AND YOU ALL WILL BECOME ITS SACRIFICES.

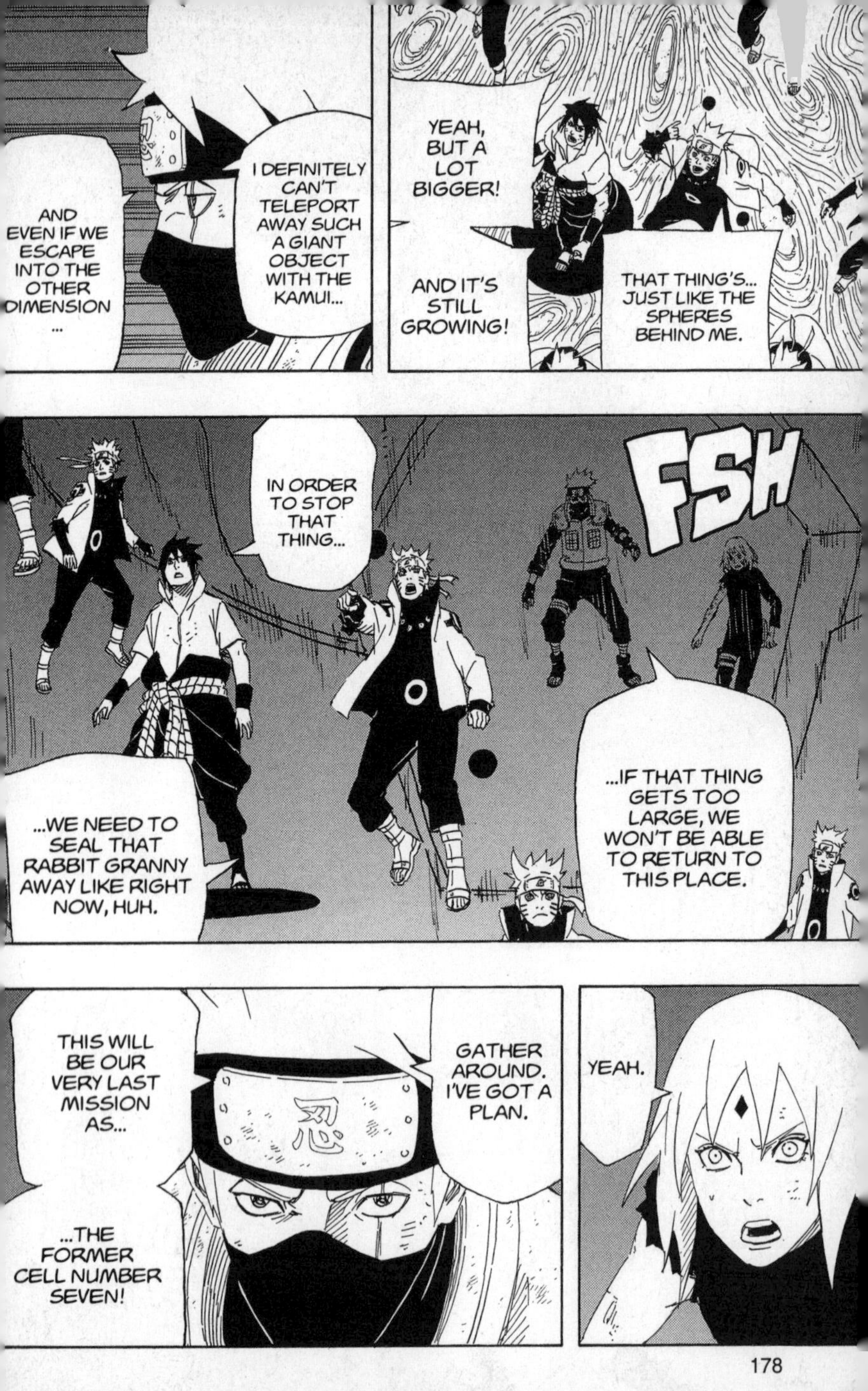
THAT THING'S... JUST LIKE THE SPHERES BEHIND ME.
YEAH, BUT A LOT BIGGER!
AND IT'S STILL GROWING!
I DEFINITELY CAN'T TELEPORT AWAY SUCH A GIANT OBJECT WITH THE KAMUI...
AND EVEN IF WE ESCAPE INTO THE OTHER DIMENSION ...
FSH
...IF THAT THING GETS TOO LARGE, WE WON'T BE ABLE TO RETURN TO THIS PLACE.
IN ORDER TO STOP THAT THING...
...WE NEED TO SEAL THAT RABBIT GRANNY AWAY LIKE RIGHT NOW, HUH.
YEAH.
GATHER AROUND. I'VE GOT A PLAN.
THIS WILL BE OUR VERY LAST MISSION AS...
...THE FORMER CELL NUMBER SEVEN!

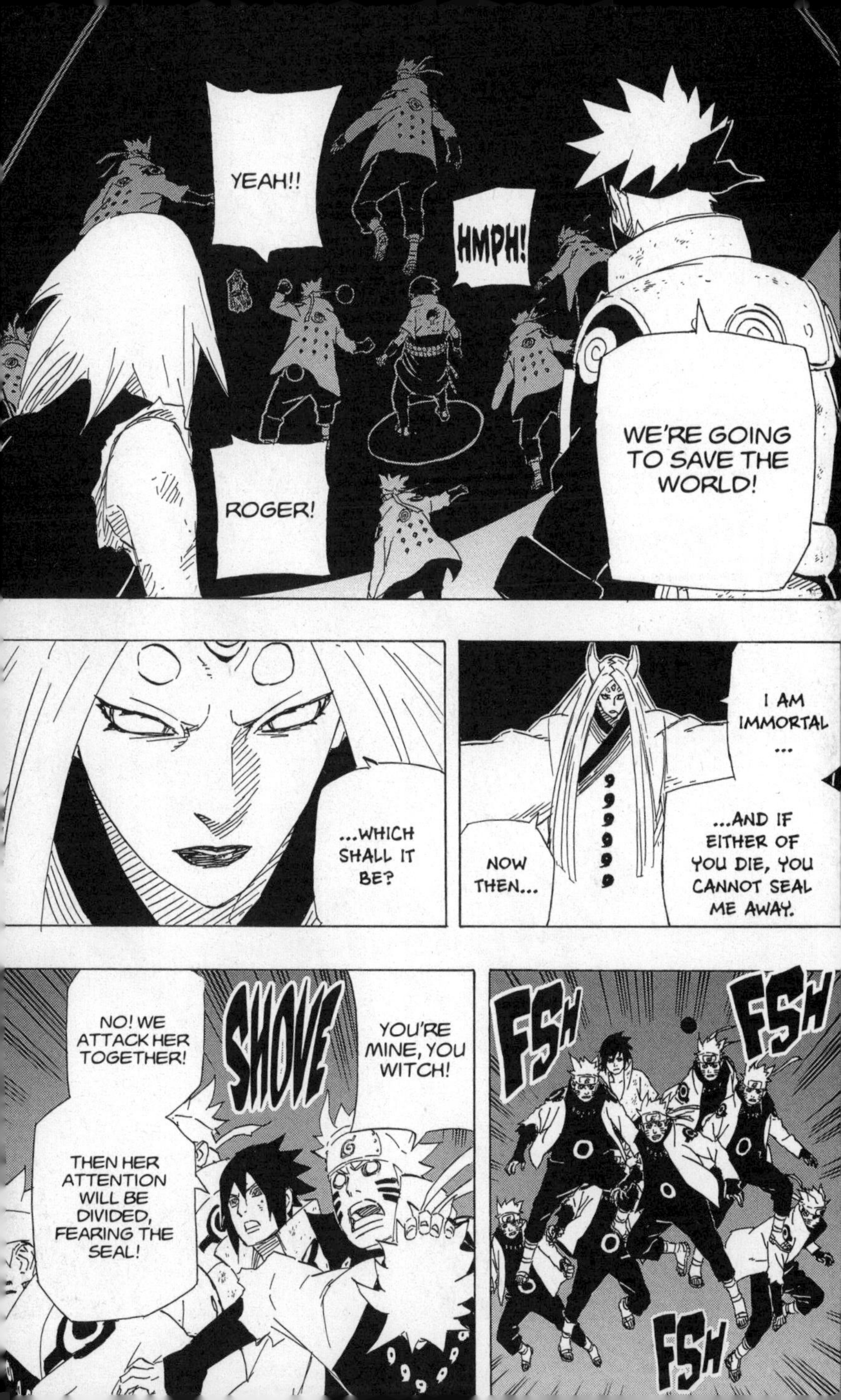
WE'RE GOING TO SAVE THE WORLD!
HMPH!
YEAH!!
ROGER!
I AM IMMORTAL ...
...AND IF EITHER OF YOU DIE, YOU CANNOT SEAL ME AWAY.
NOW THEN...
...WHICH SHALL IT BE?
FSH
FSH
FSH
YOU'RE MINE, YOU WITCH!
SHOVE
NO! WE ATTACK HER TOGETHER!
THEN HER ATTENTION WILL BE DIVIDED, FEARING THE SEAL!

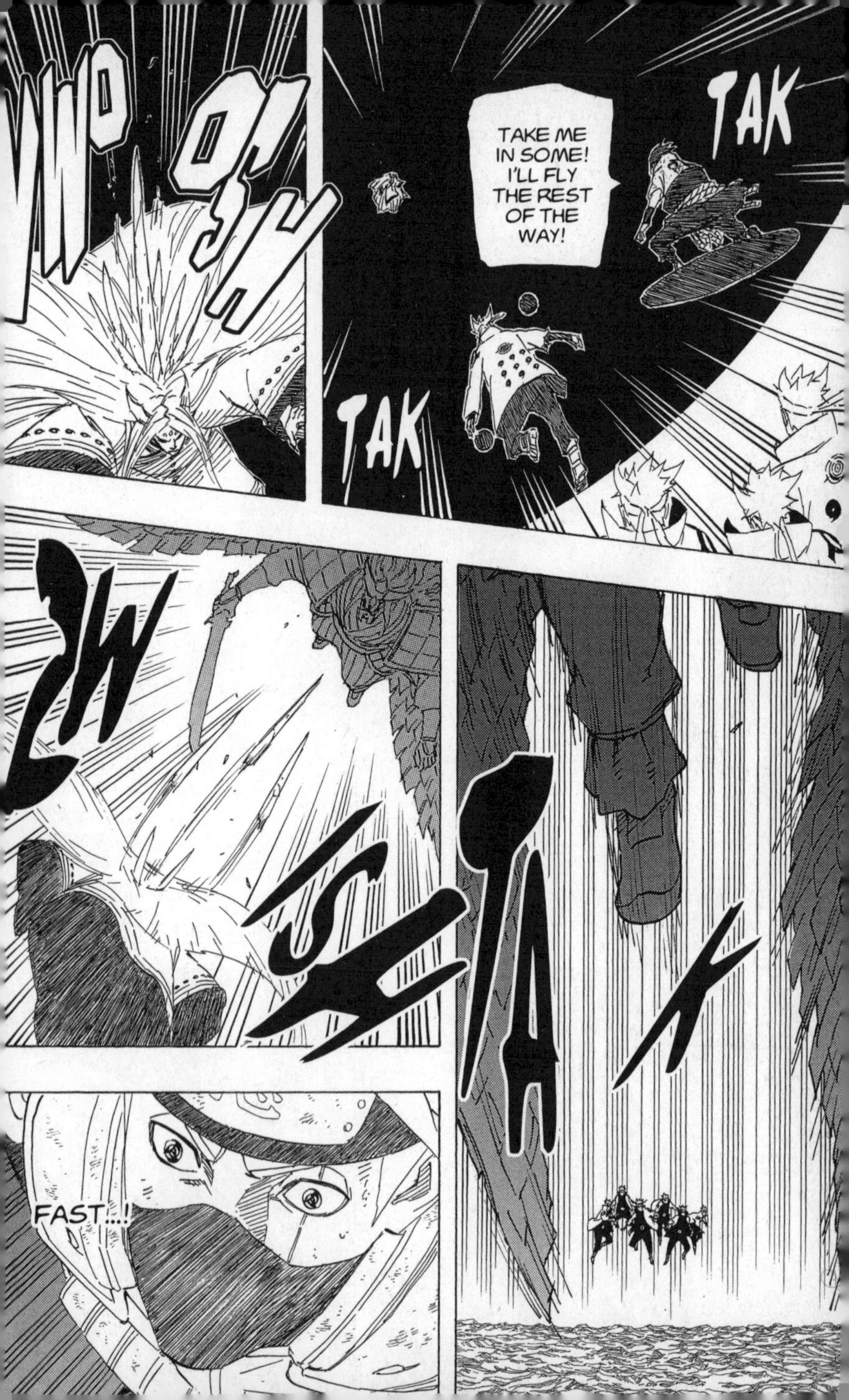
TAK
TAKE ME IN SOME! I'LL FLY THE REST OF THE WAY!
TAK
FAST...!

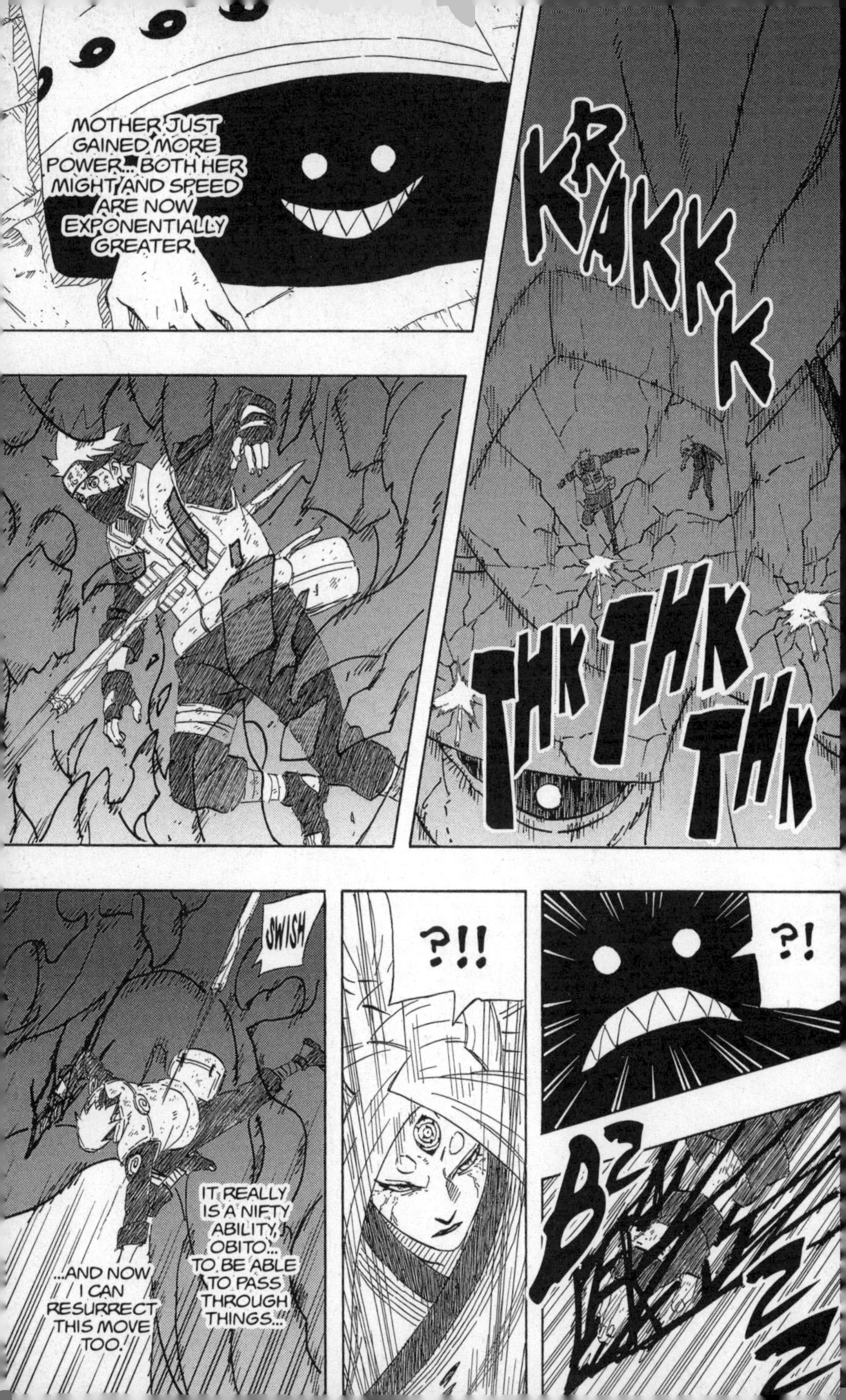
KRAKKK
THK THK THK THK
MOTHER JUST GAINED MORE POWER... BOTH HER MIGHT AND SPEED ARE NOW EXPONENTIALLY GREATER.
?!
?!!
IT REALLY IS A NIFTY ABILITY, OBITO... TO BE ABLE TO PASS THROUGH THINGS...
SWISH
...AND NOW I CAN RESURRECT THIS MOVE TOO.

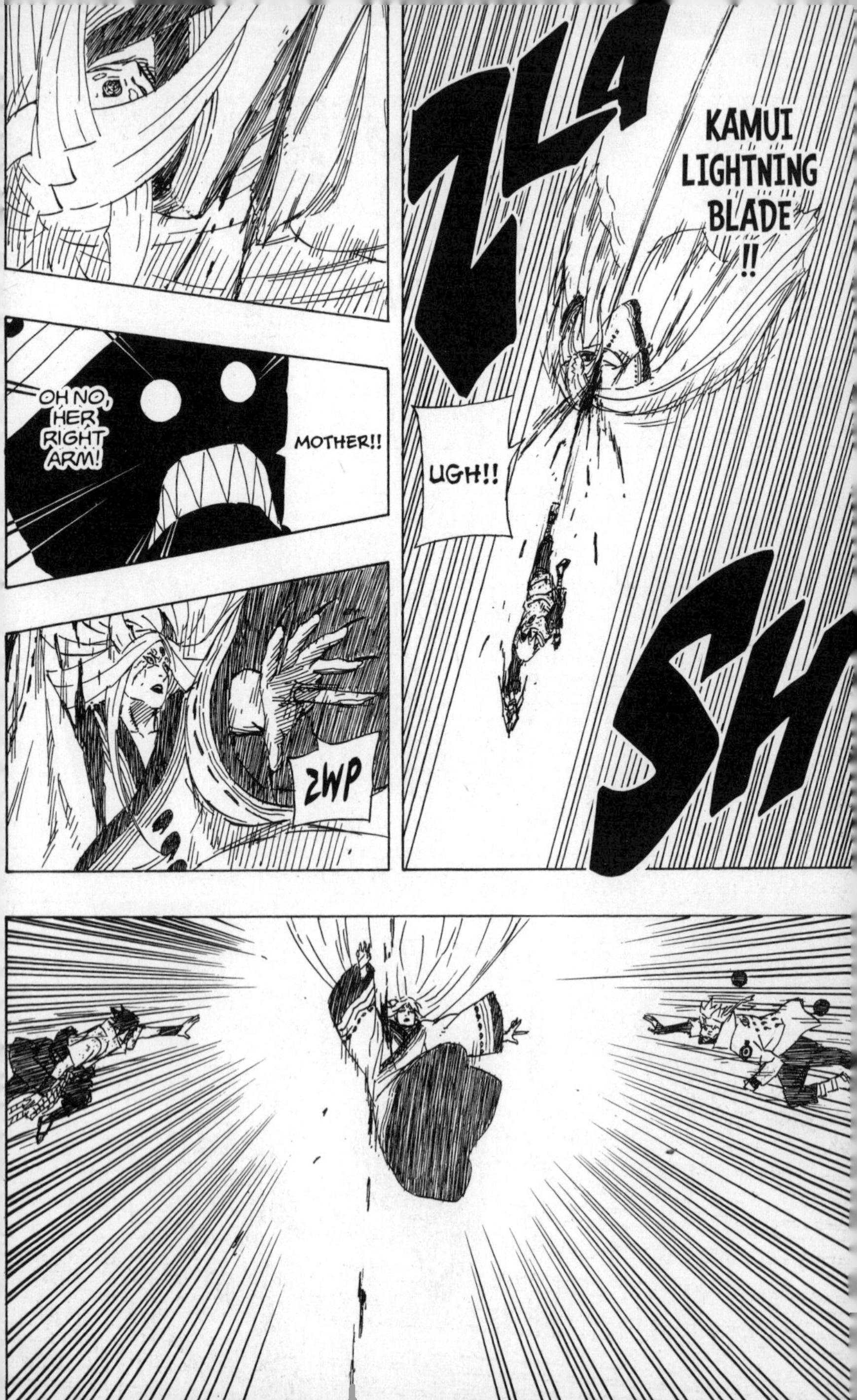
KAMUI LIGHTNING BLADE!!
ZZA
UGH!!
SH
MOTHER!!
OH NO, HER RIGHT ARM!
ZWP

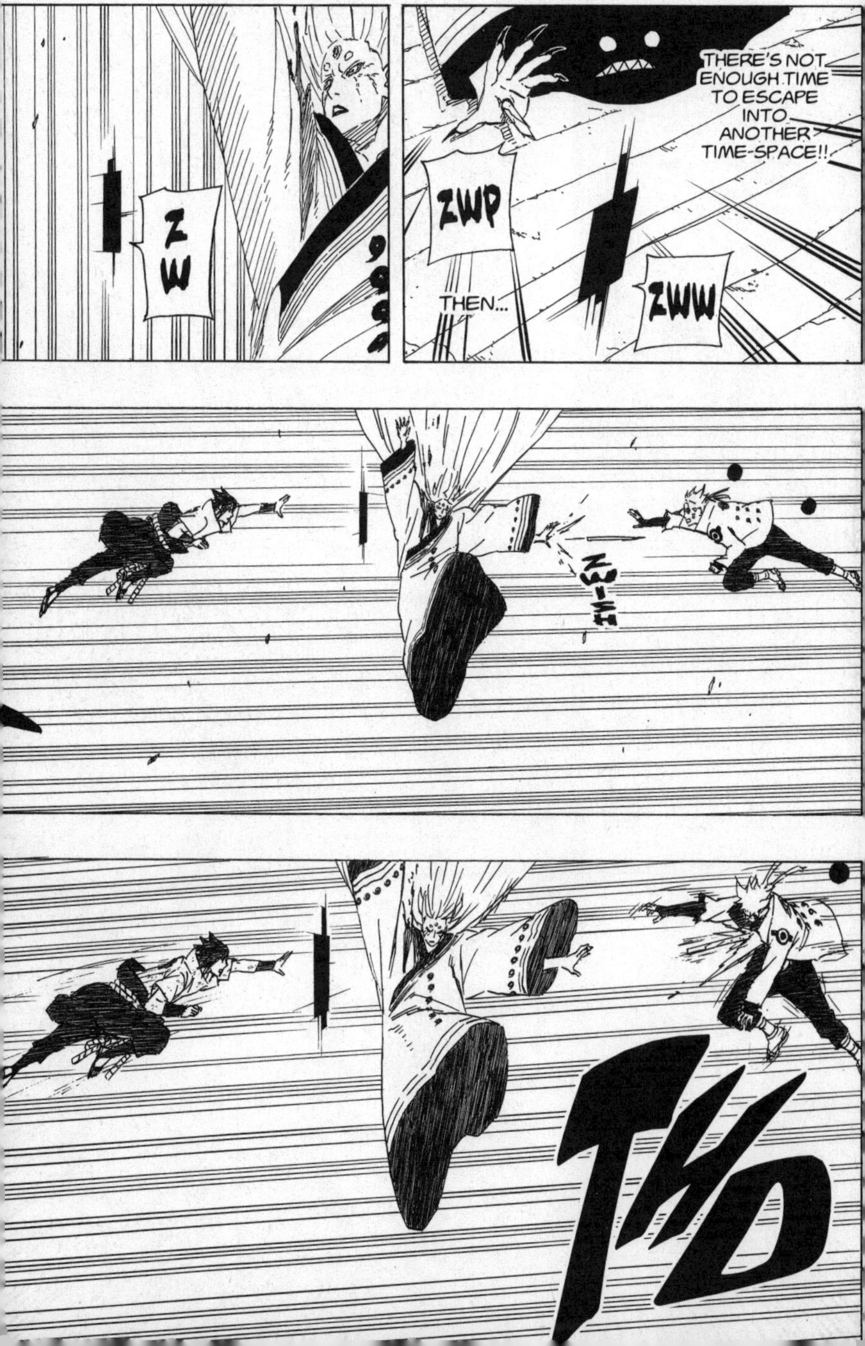
THERE'S NOT ENOUGH TIME TO ESCAPE INTO ANOTHER TIME-SPACE!!
ZWP
THEN...
ZWW
ZW
ZWISH
THD

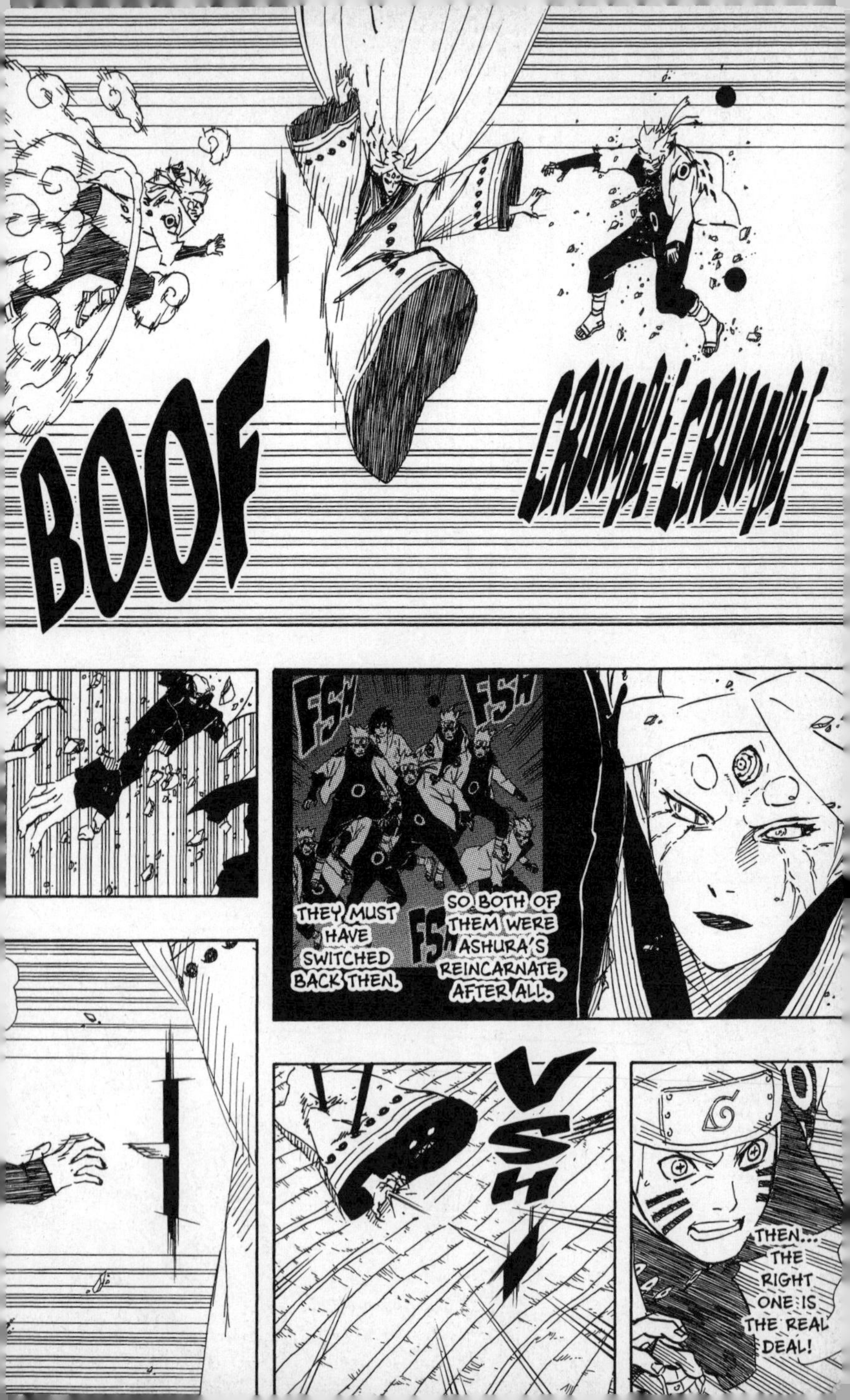
CRUMBLE CRUMBLE
BOOF
FSH
FSH
FSH
SO BOTH OF THEM WERE ASHURA'S REINCARNATE, AFTER ALL.
THEY MUST HAVE SWITCHED BACK THEN.
THEN... THE RIGHT ONE IS THE REAL DEAL!
VSH

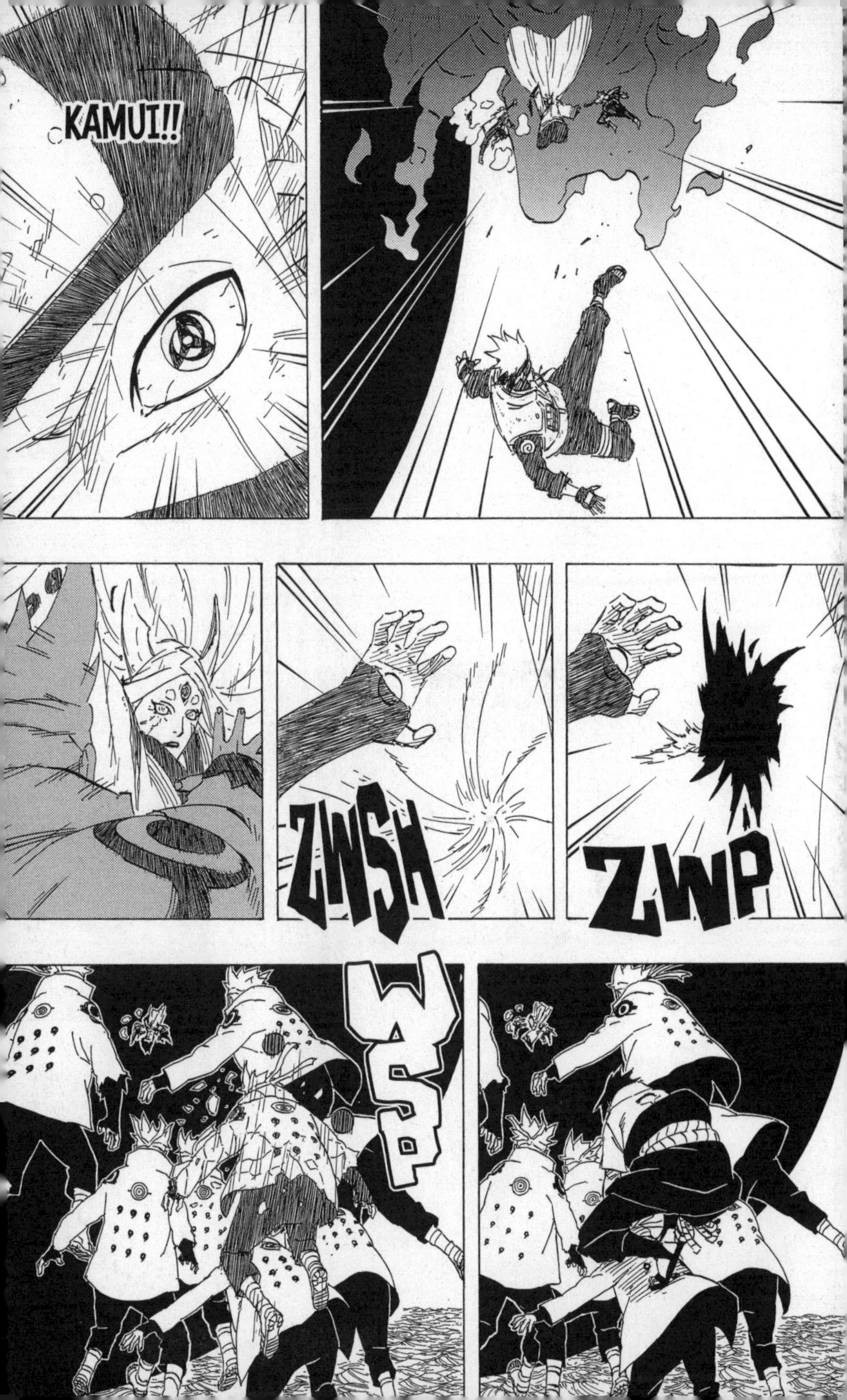
KAMUI!!
ZWP
ZWSH
WSP

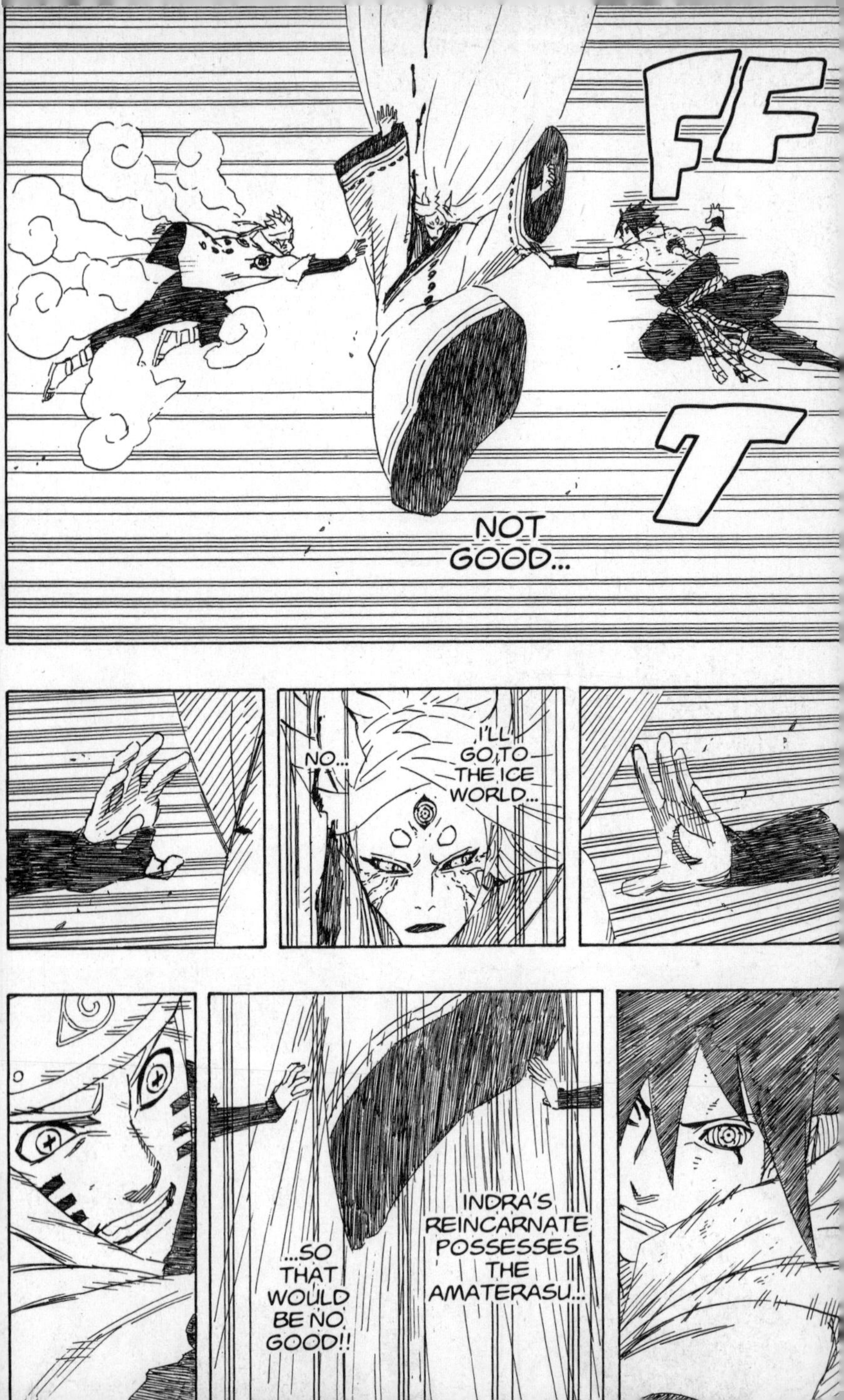
FF
T
NOT GOOD...
I'LL GO TO THE ICE WORLD...
NO...
INDRA'S REINCARNATE POSSESSES THE AMATERASU...
...SO THAT WOULD BE NO GOOD!!

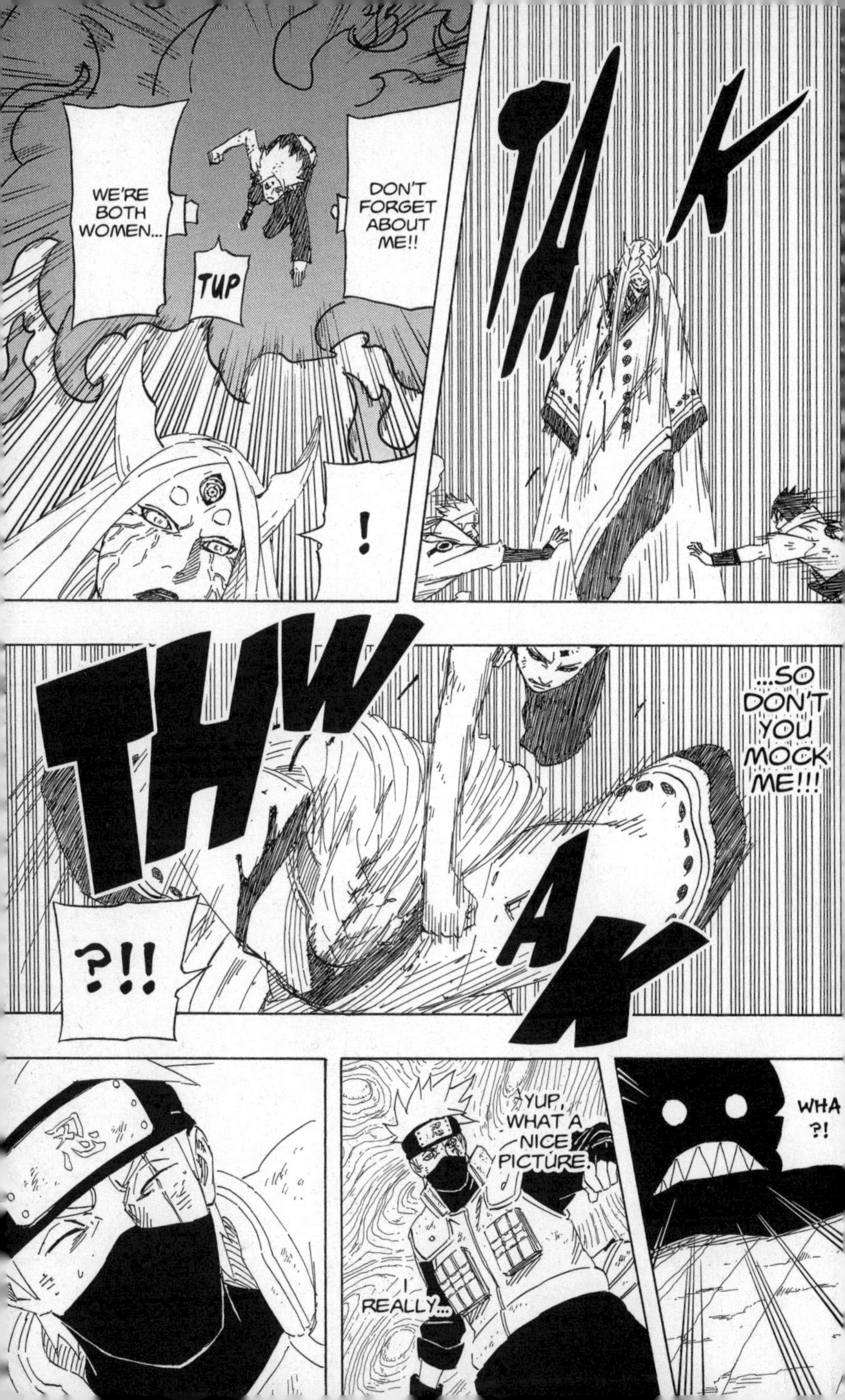
TAK
DON'T FORGET ABOUT ME!!
TUP
WE'RE BOTH WOMEN...
!
...SO DON'T YOU MOCK ME!!!
THWAK
?!!
WHA ?!
YUP, WHAT A NICE PICTURE.
I REALLY...

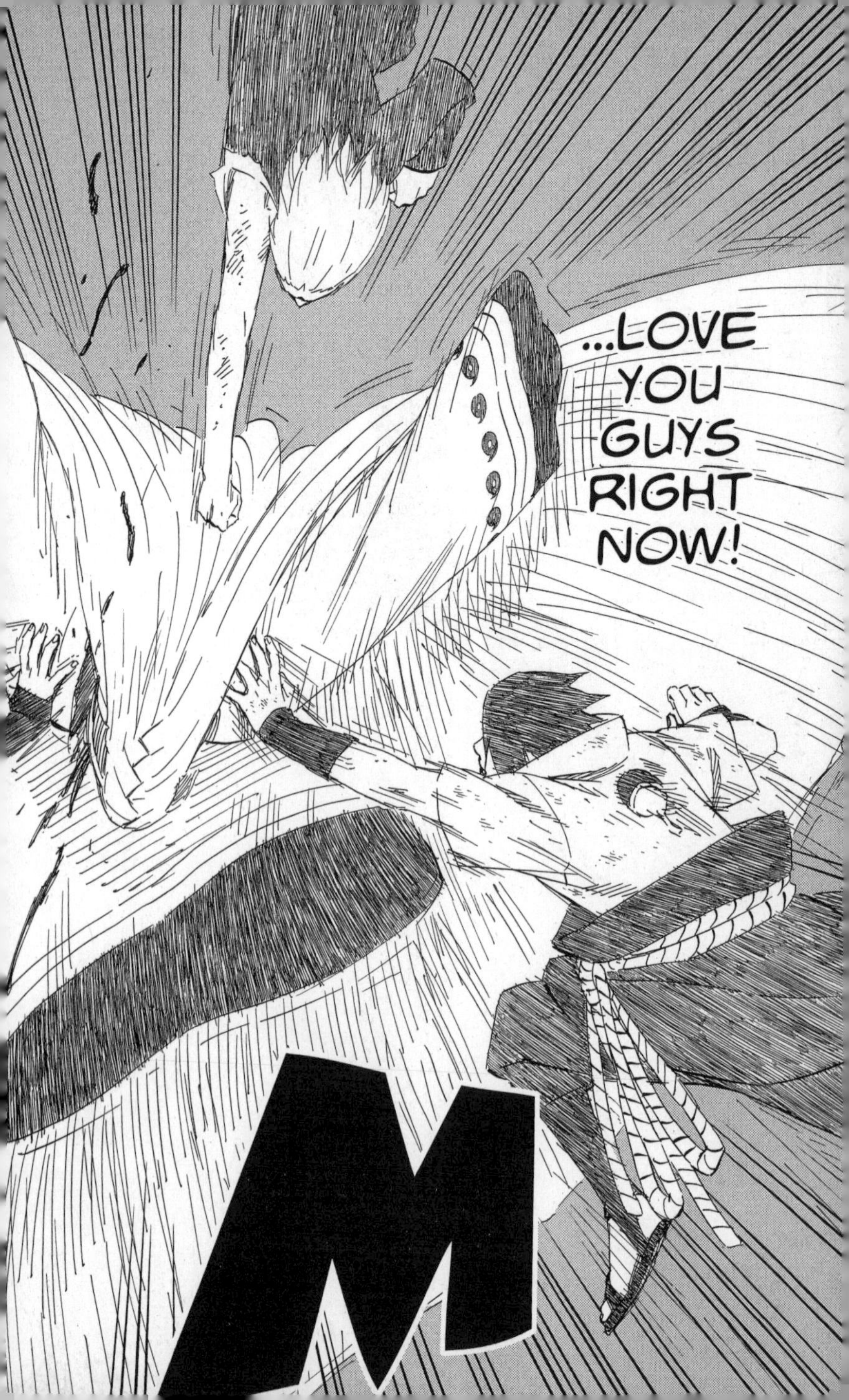
...LOVE YOU GUYS RIGHT NOW!
M

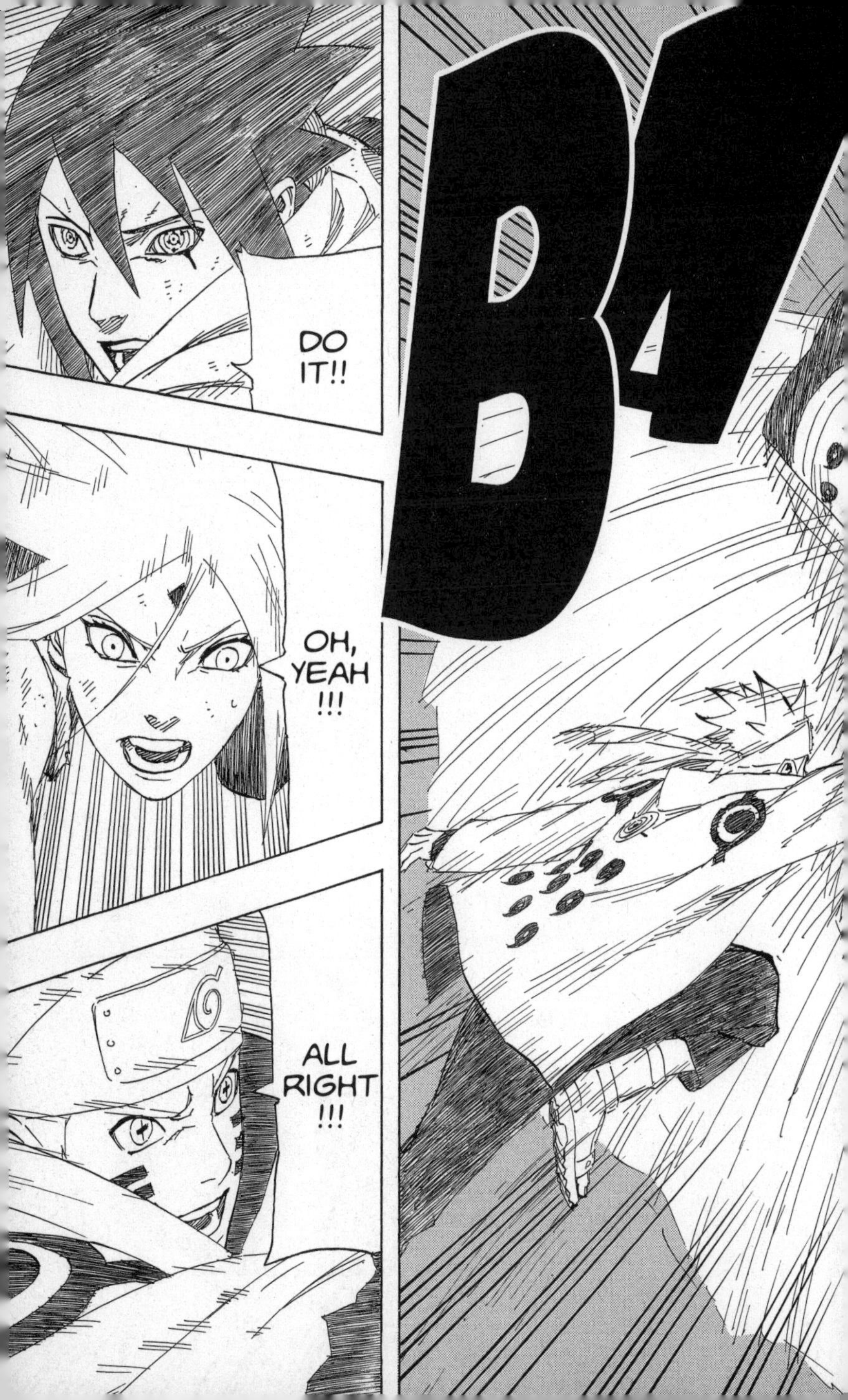
BA
DO IT!!
OH, YEAH!!!
ALL RIGHT!!!

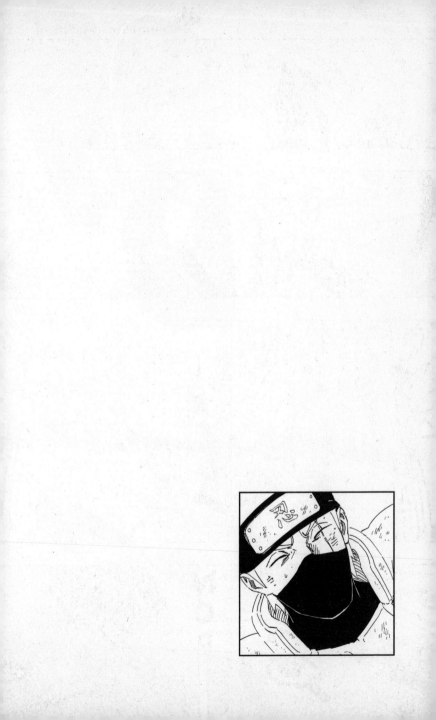

Number 690: Ninja History

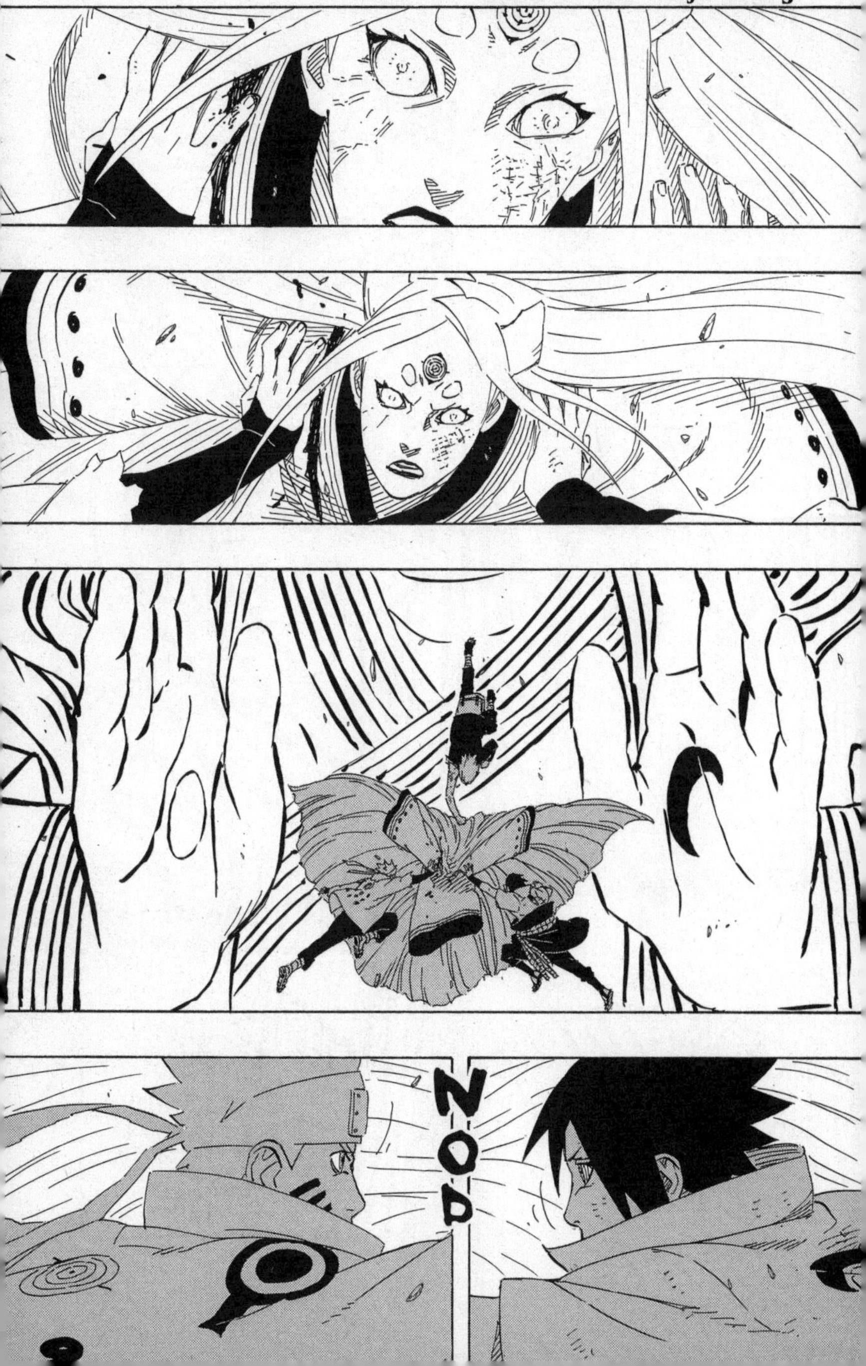
NOD

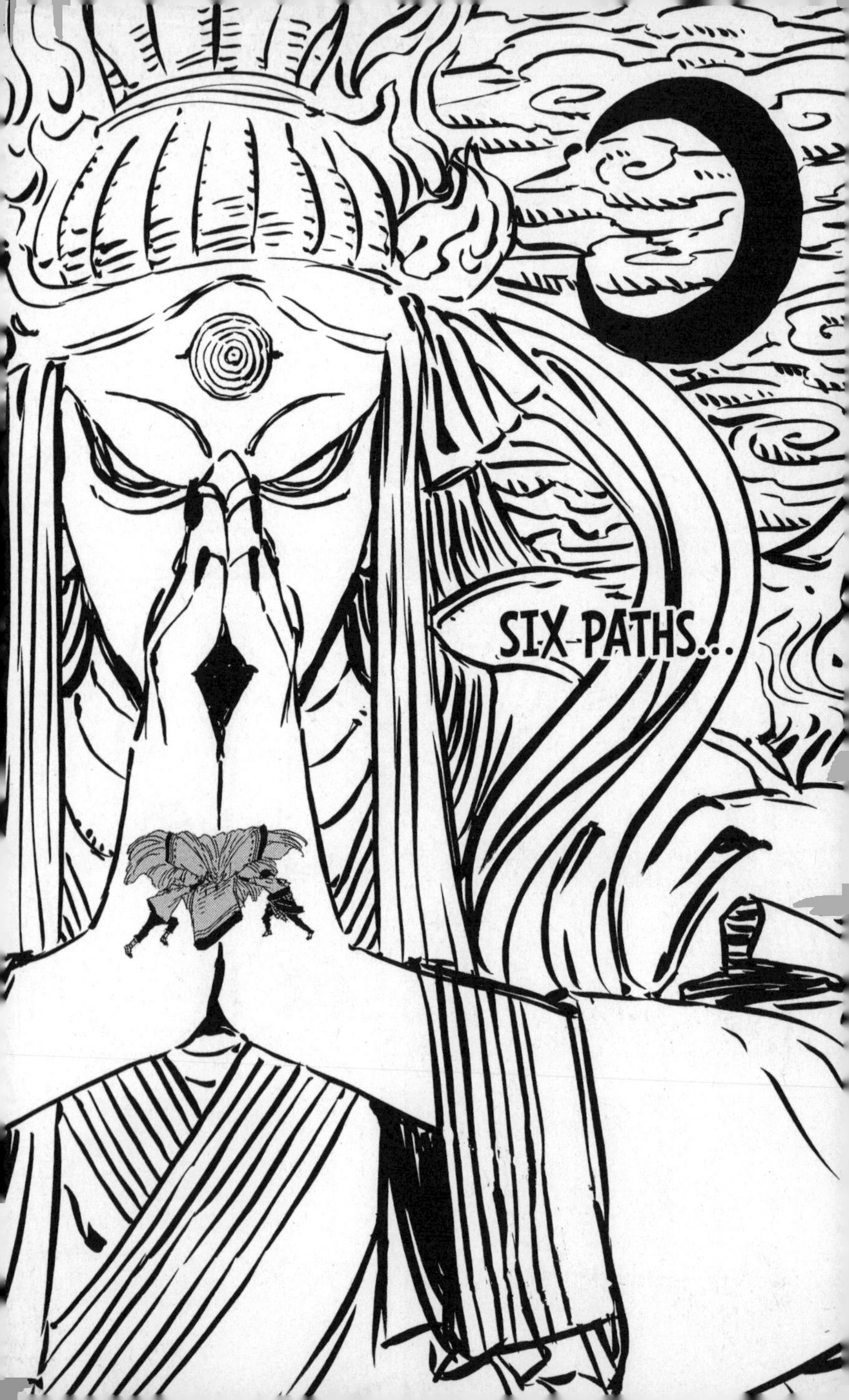
SIX-PATHS...

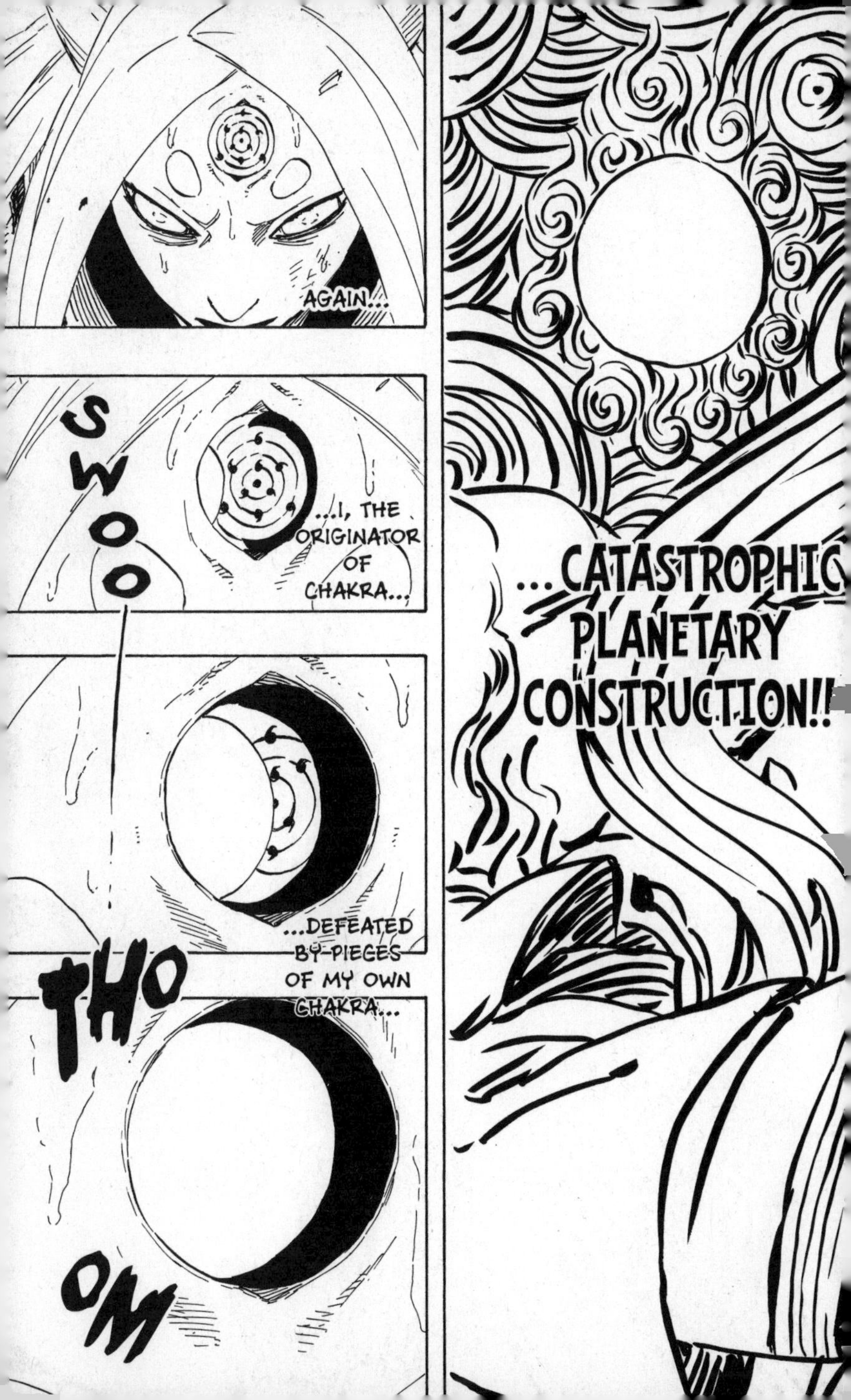
AGAIN...
SWOO
...I, THE ORIGINATOR OF CHAKRA...
...DEFEATED BY PIECES OF MY OWN CHAKRA...
THOOM
...CATASTROPHIC PLANETARY CONSTRUCTION!!

WHY
...?!!

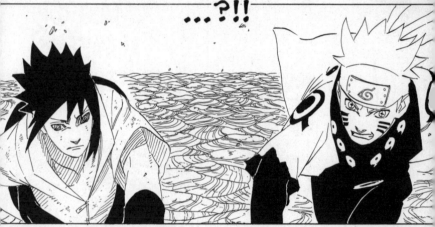

FW SH

FW SH

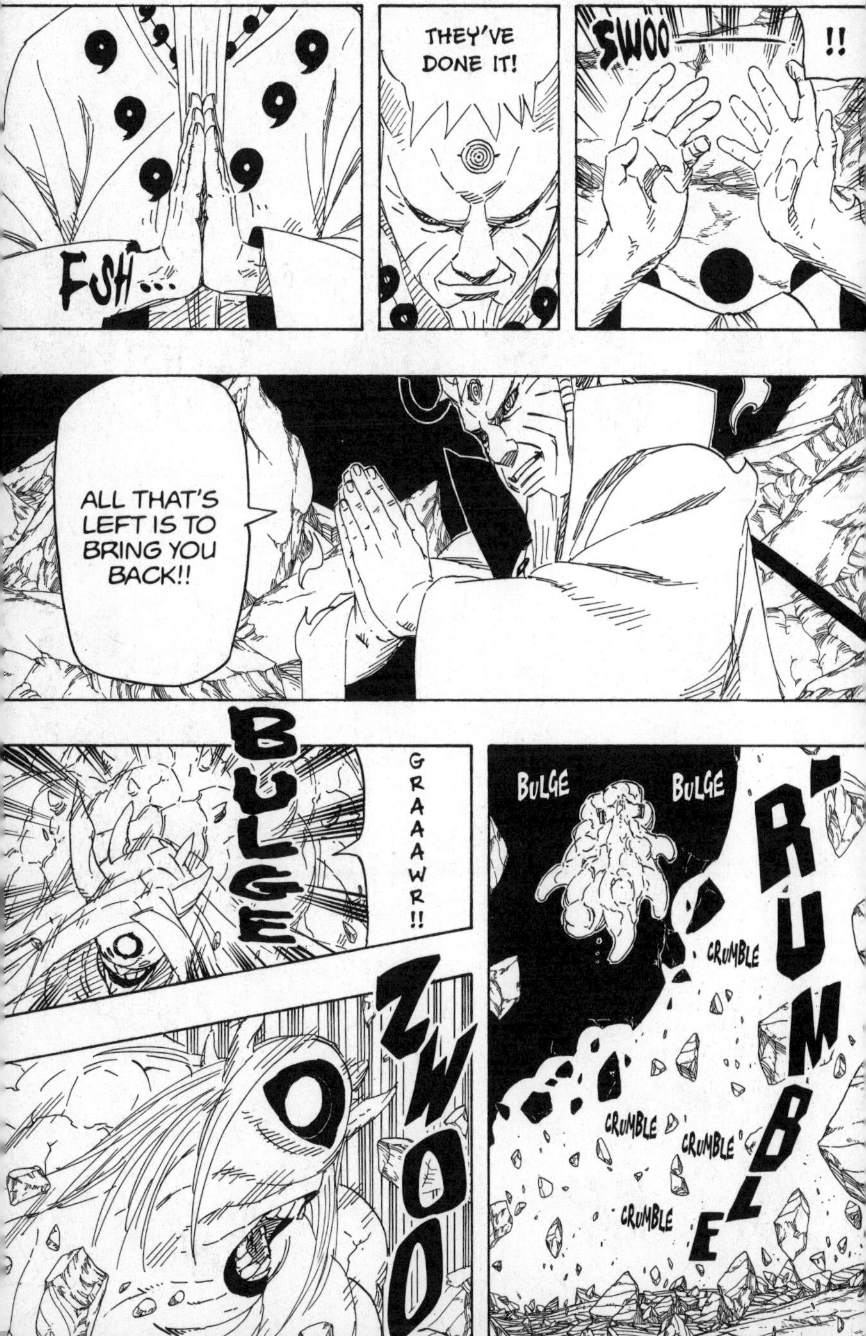
SWOO—
!!
THEY'VE DONE IT!
FSH...
ALL THAT'S LEFT IS TO BRING YOU BACK!!
BULGE
BULGE
RUMBLE
CRUMBLE
CRUMBLE
CRUMBLE
CRUMBLE
BULGE
GRAAAAWR!!
ZWOO

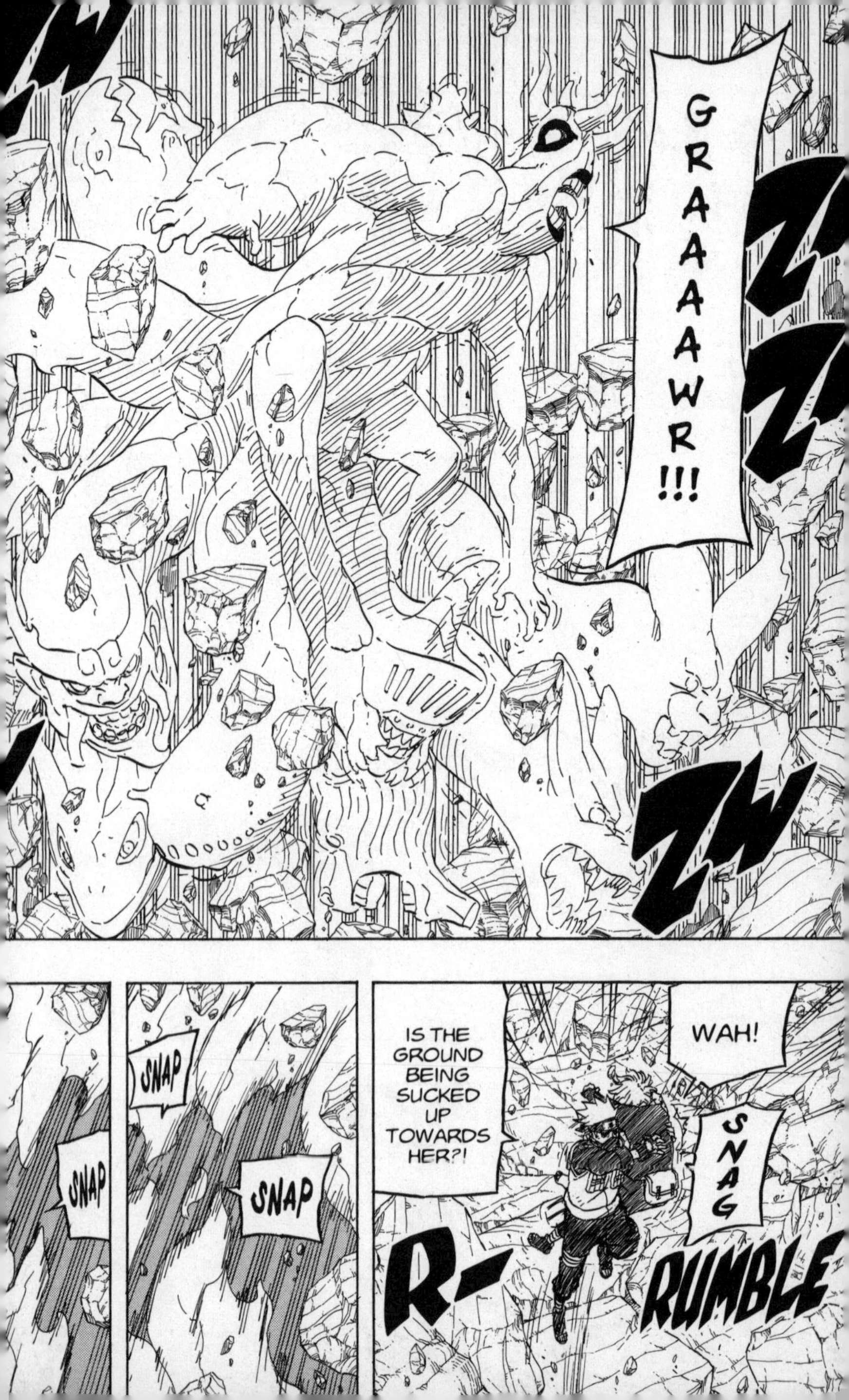
GRAAAAWR!!!
WAH!
IS THE GROUND BEING SUCKED UP TOWARDS HER?!
SNAG
R- RUMBLE
SNAP
SNAP
SNAP

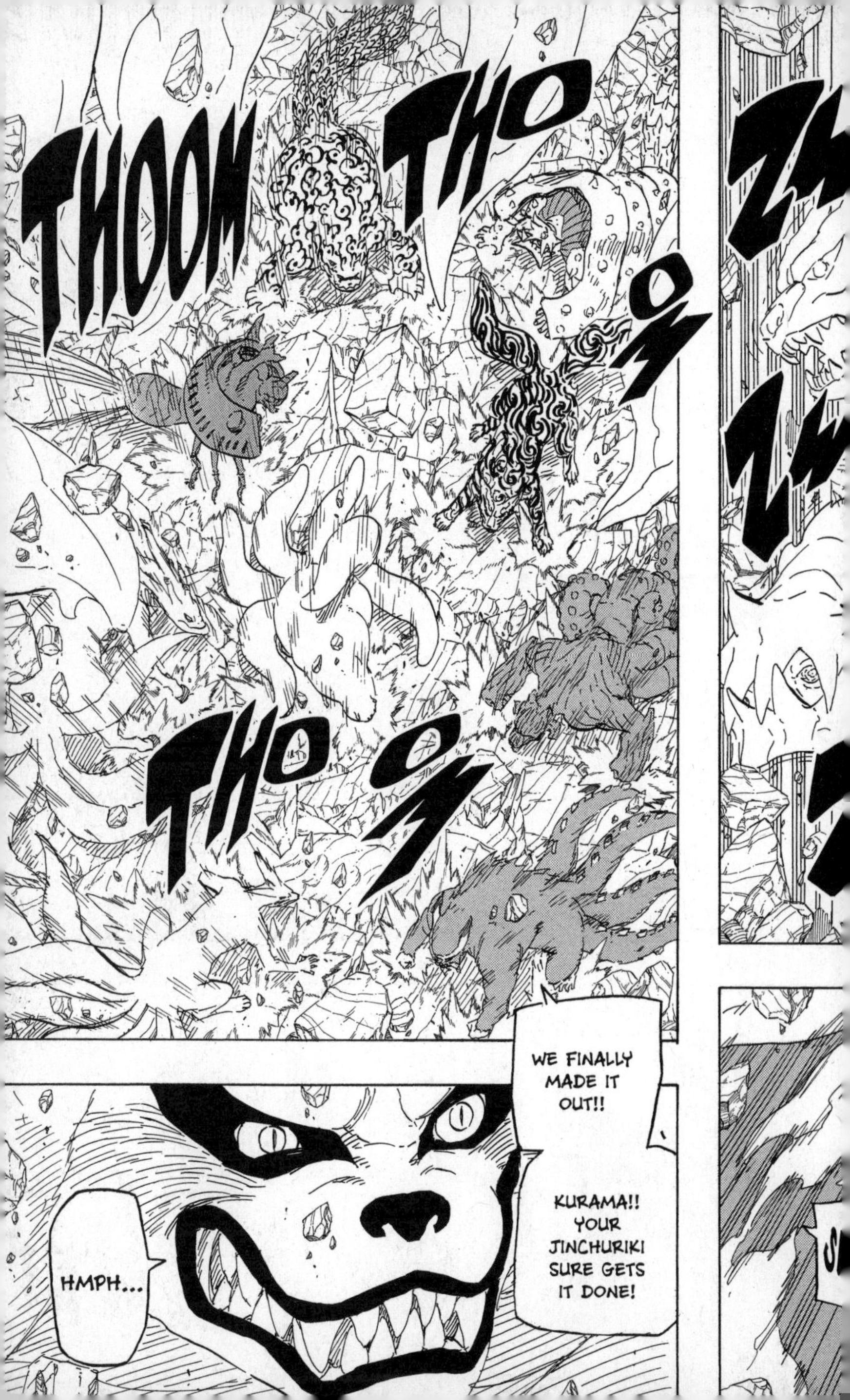
THOOM
THOOM
THOOM
WE FINALLY MADE IT OUT!!
KURAMA!! YOUR JINCHURIKI SURE GETS IT DONE!
HMPH...

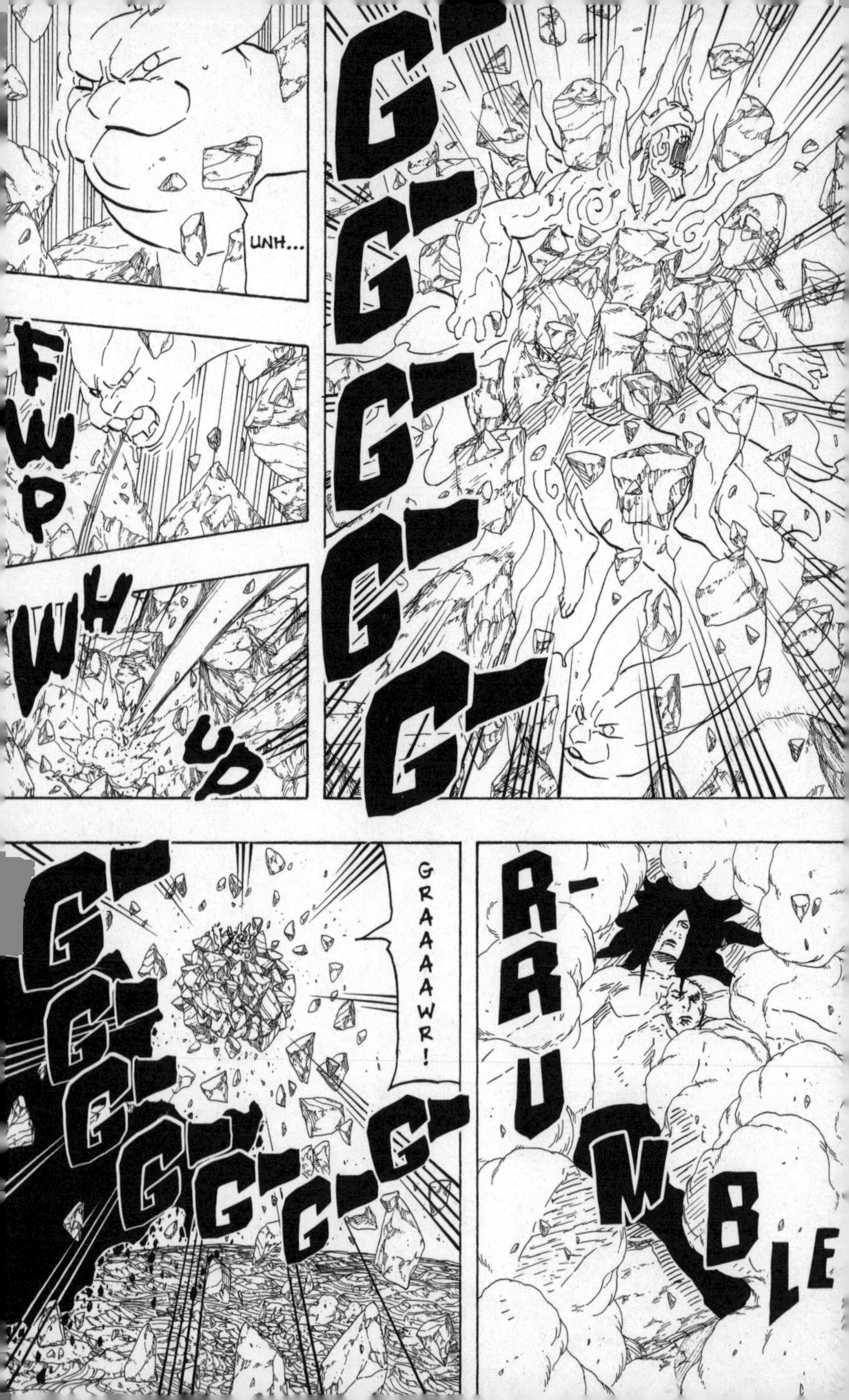
G-G-G-G-G-
UNH...
FWP
WHUD
R-RUMBLE
GRAAAAWR!
G-G-G-G-G-G-G-

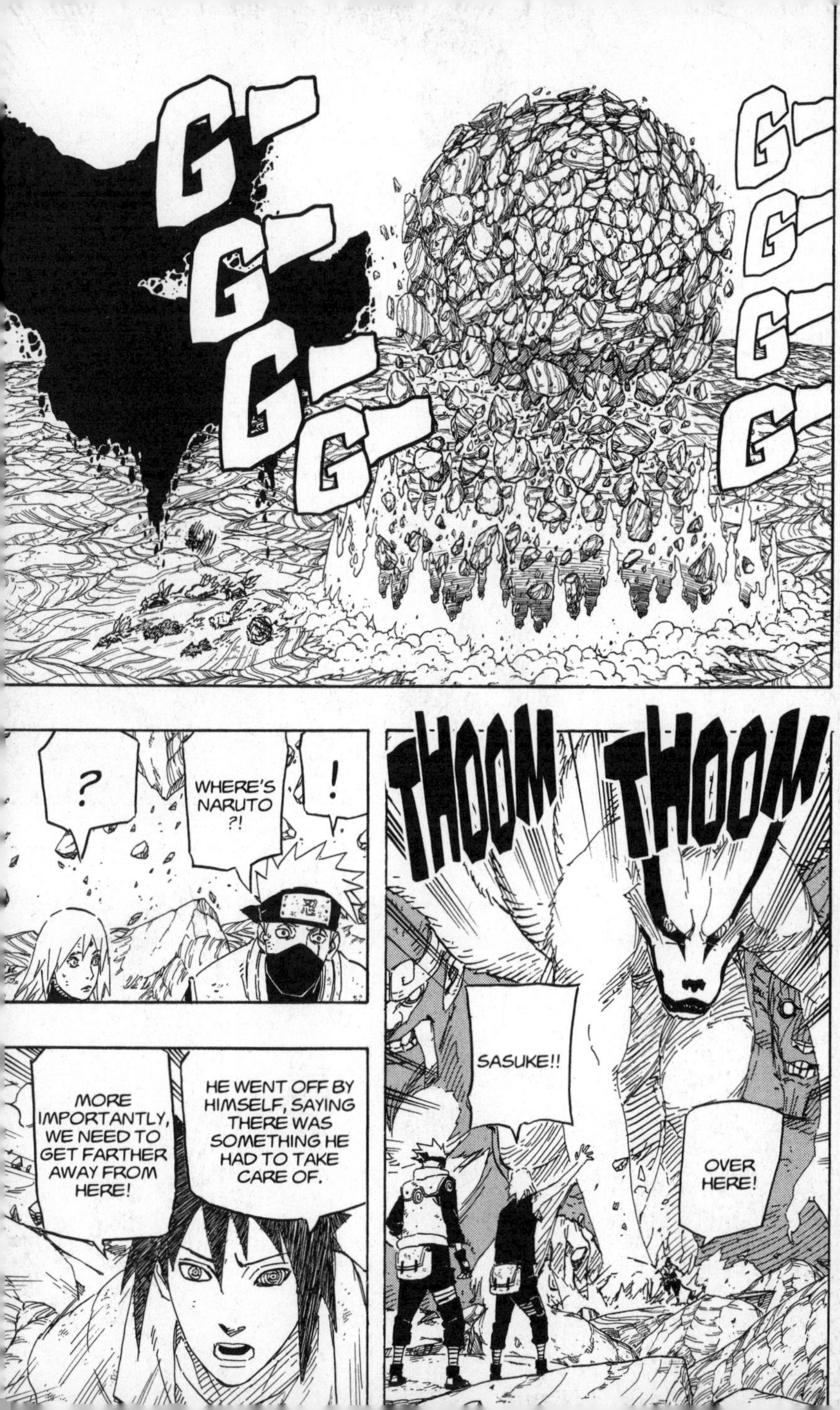
G G G G
G G G G
THOOM
THOOM
SASUKE!!
OVER HERE!
!
WHERE'S NARUTO?!
?
HE WENT OFF BY HIMSELF, SAYING THERE WAS SOMETHING HE HAD TO TAKE CARE OF.
MORE IMPORTANTLY, WE NEED TO GET FARTHER AWAY FROM HERE!

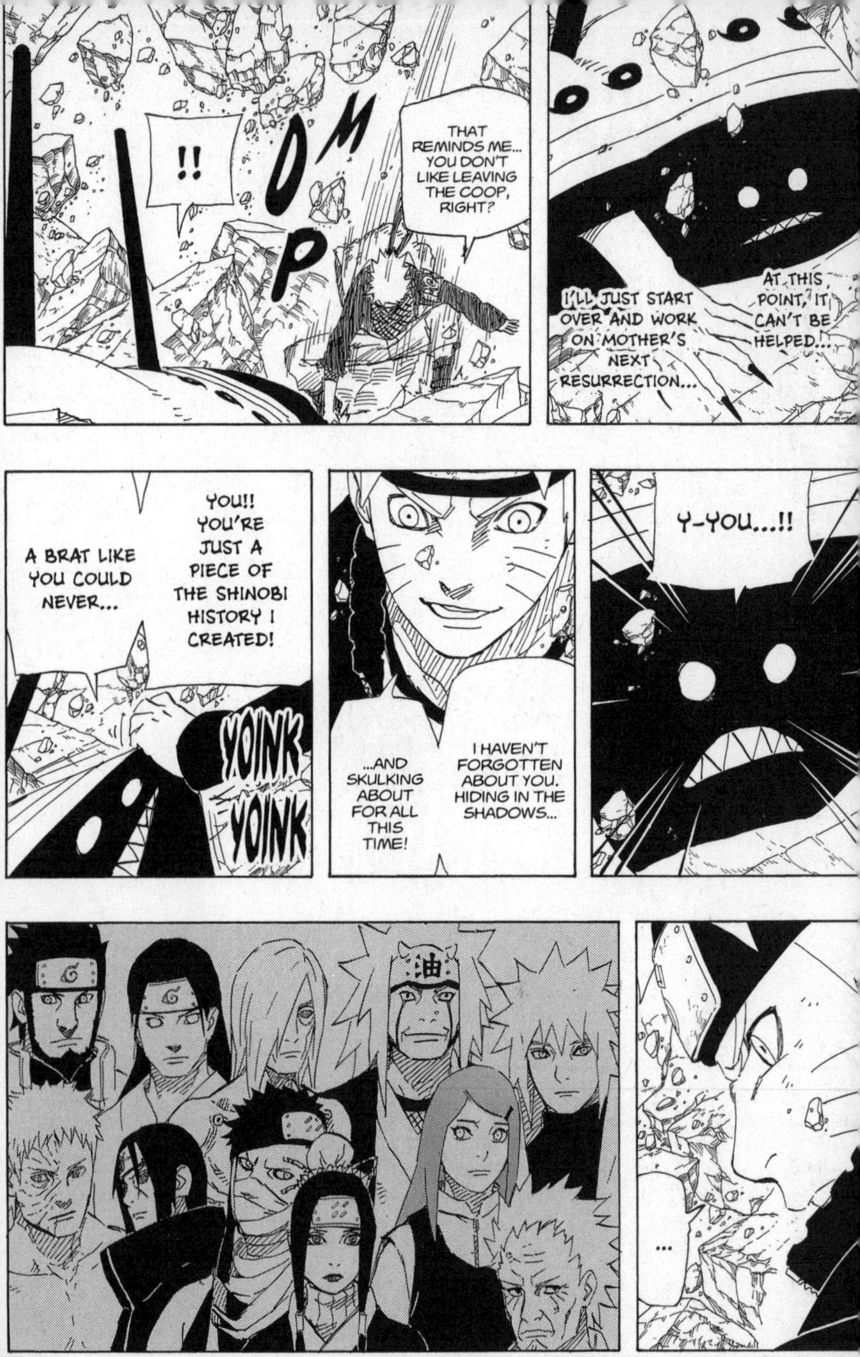
AT THIS POINT, IT CAN'T BE HELPED...
I'LL JUST START OVER AND WORK ON MOTHER'S NEXT RESURRECTION...
THAT REMINDS ME... YOU DON'T LIKE LEAVING THE COOP, RIGHT?
DOMP
!!
Y-YOU...!!
I HAVEN'T FORGOTTEN ABOUT YOU. HIDING IN THE SHADOWS...
...AND SKULKING ABOUT FOR ALL THIS TIME!
YOU!! YOU'RE JUST A PIECE OF THE SHINOBI HISTORY I CREATED!
A BRAT LIKE YOU COULD NEVER...
YOINK YOINK
...
油

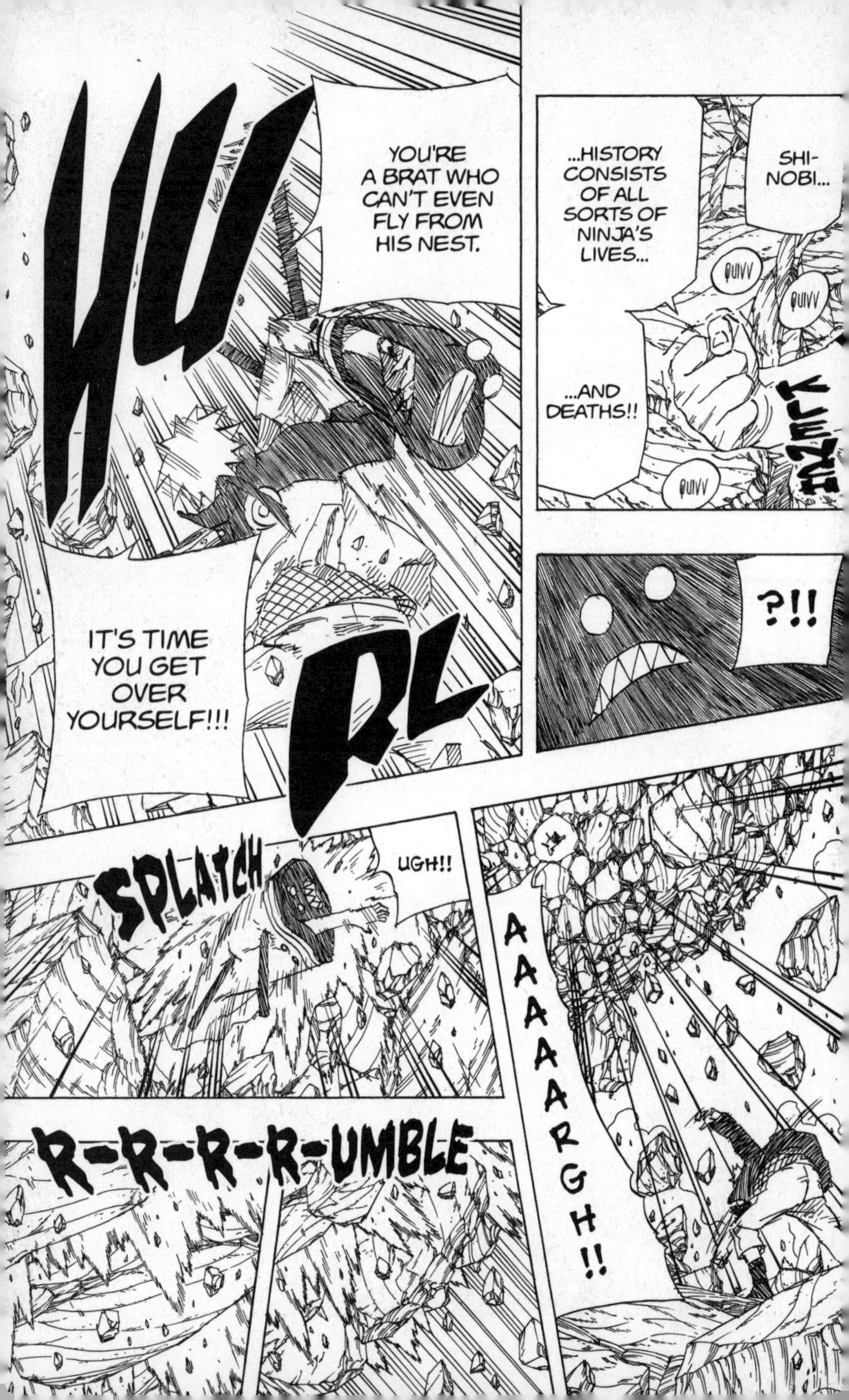

SHI-NOBI...
...HISTORY CONSISTS OF ALL SORTS OF NINJA'S LIVES...
...AND DEATHS!!
QUIVV
QUIVV
QUIVV
KLENCH
?!!
YOU'RE A BRAT WHO CAN'T EVEN FLY FROM HIS NEST.
IT'S TIME YOU GET OVER YOURSELF!!!
AAAAAARGH!!
UGH!!
SPLATCH
R-R-R-R-UMBLE

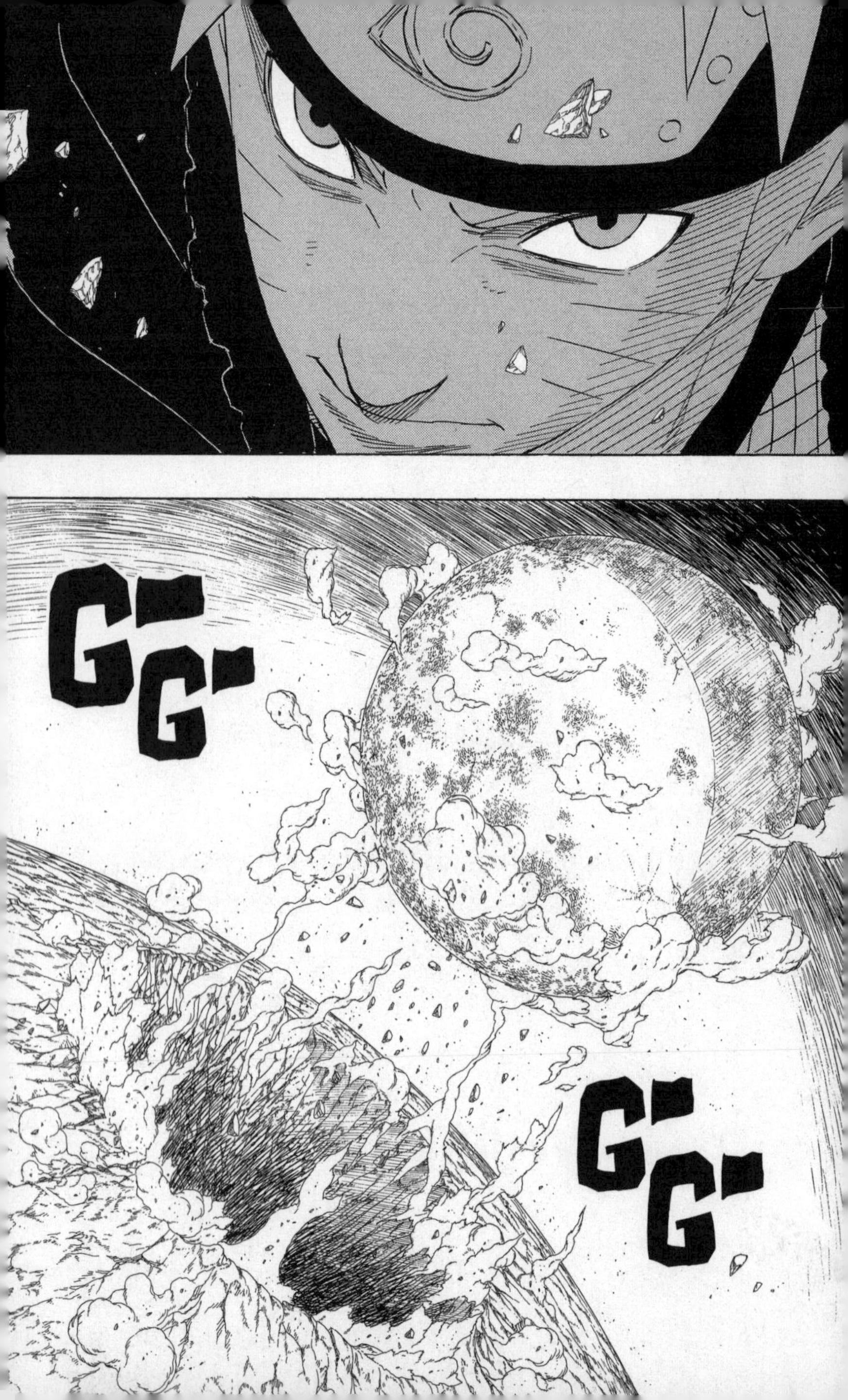
GGG
GGG

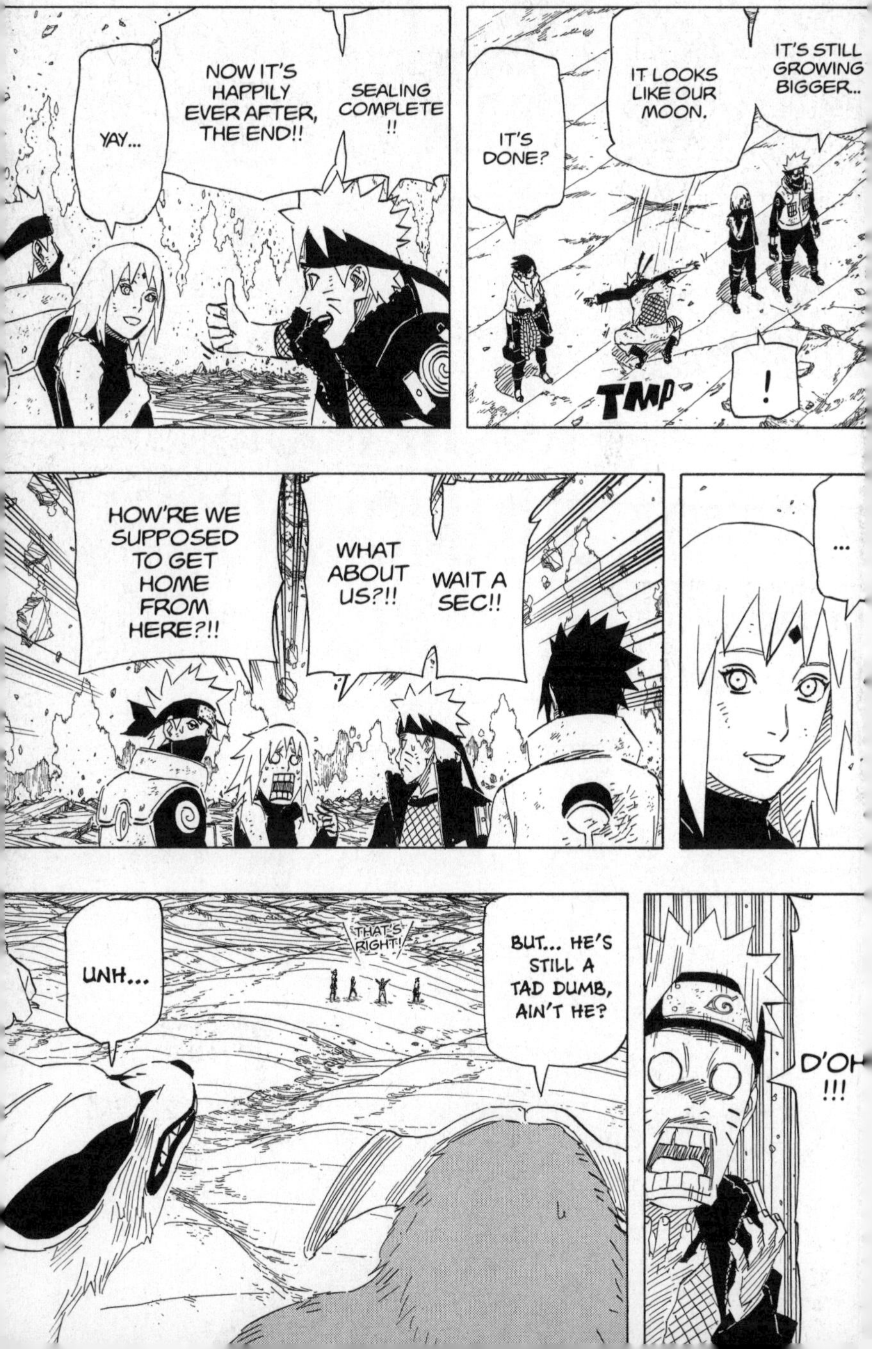
IT'S STILL GROWING BIGGER...
IT LOOKS LIKE OUR MOON.
IT'S DONE?
TMP
!
SEALING COMPLETE !!
NOW IT'S HAPPILY EVER AFTER, THE END!!
YAY...
...
WAIT A SEC!!
WHAT ABOUT US?!!
HOW'RE WE SUPPOSED TO GET HOME FROM HERE?!!
D'OH !!!
BUT... HE'S STILL A TAD DUMB, AIN'T HE?
THAT'S RIGHT!
UNH...

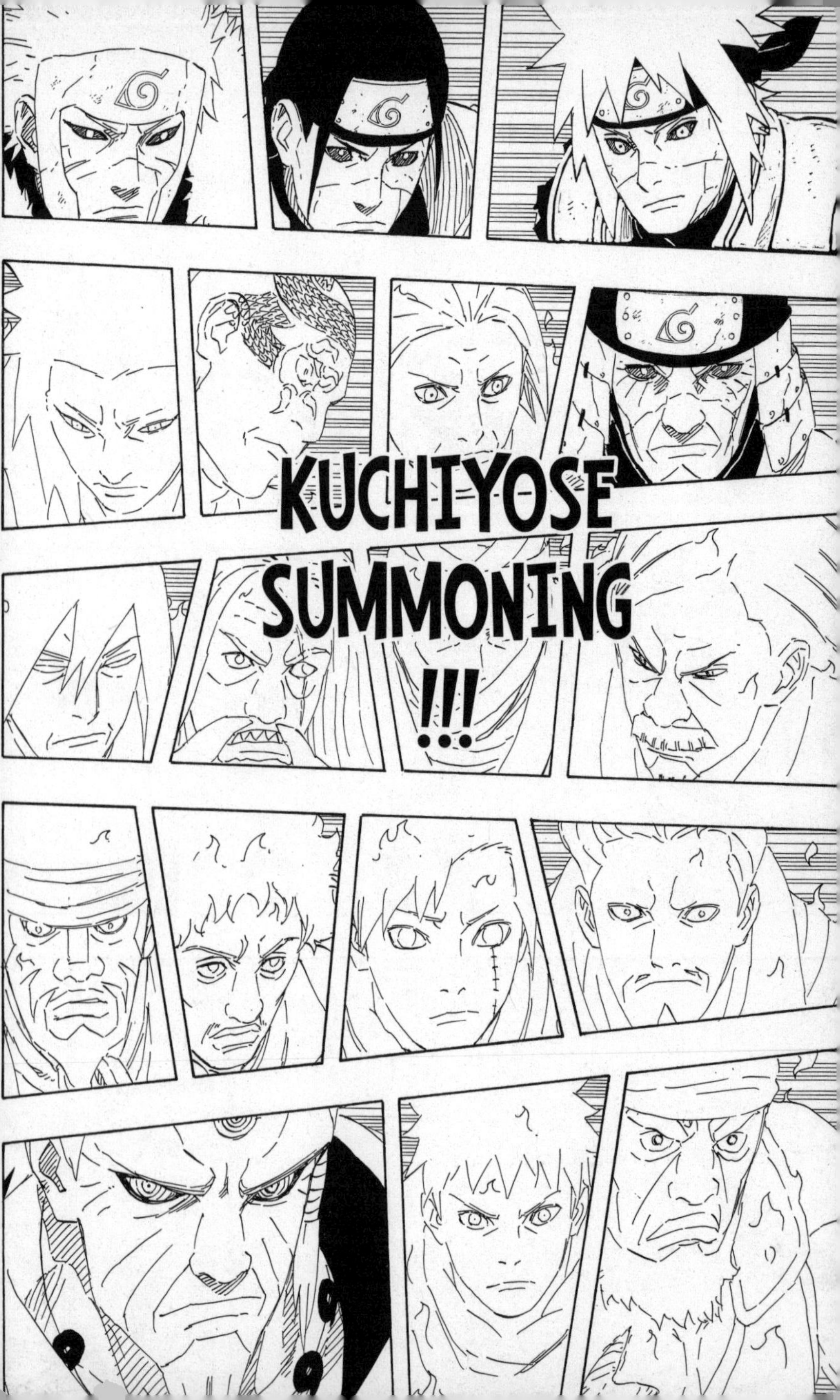
KUCHIYOSE
SUMMONING
!!!

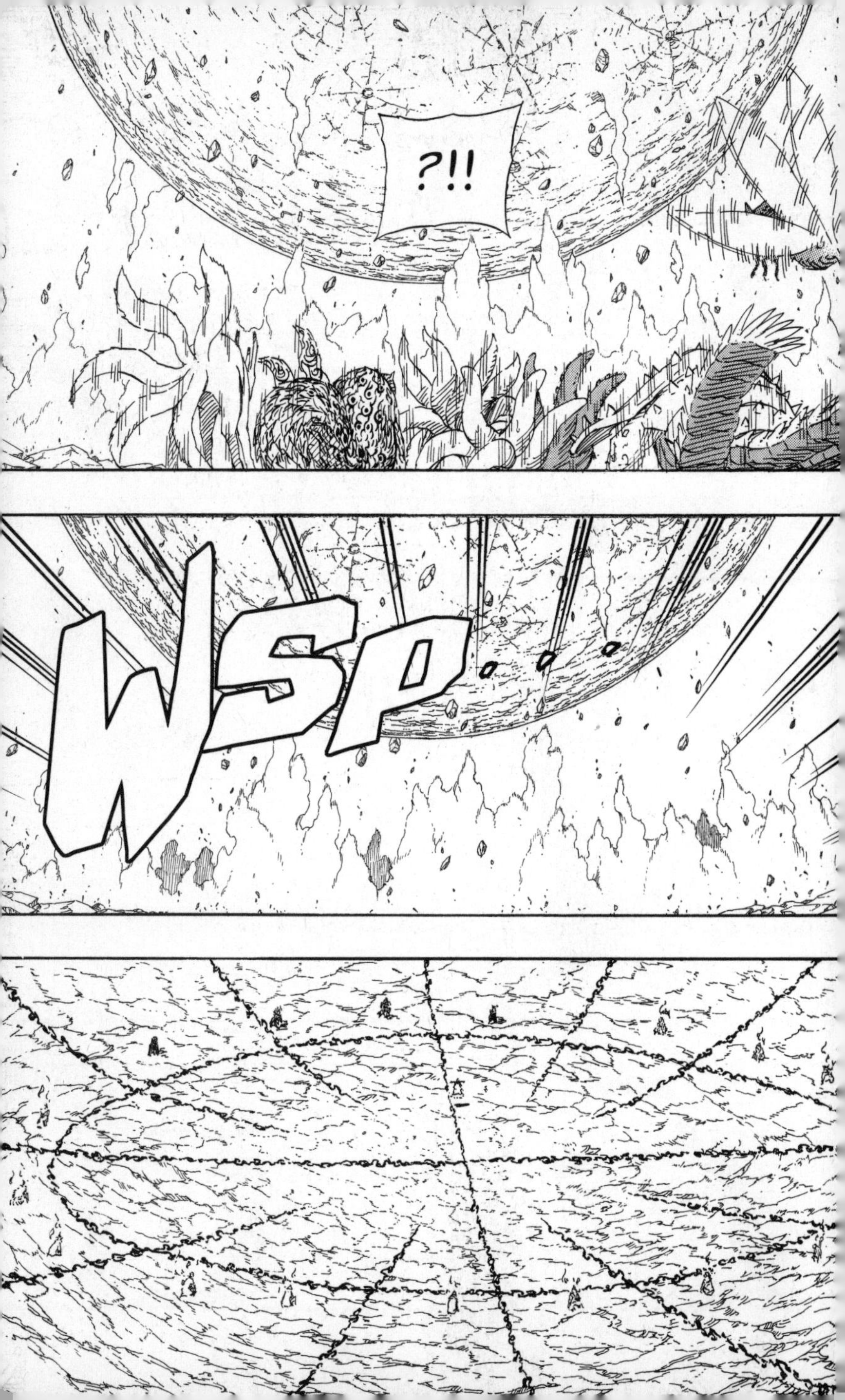
?!!
WSP...

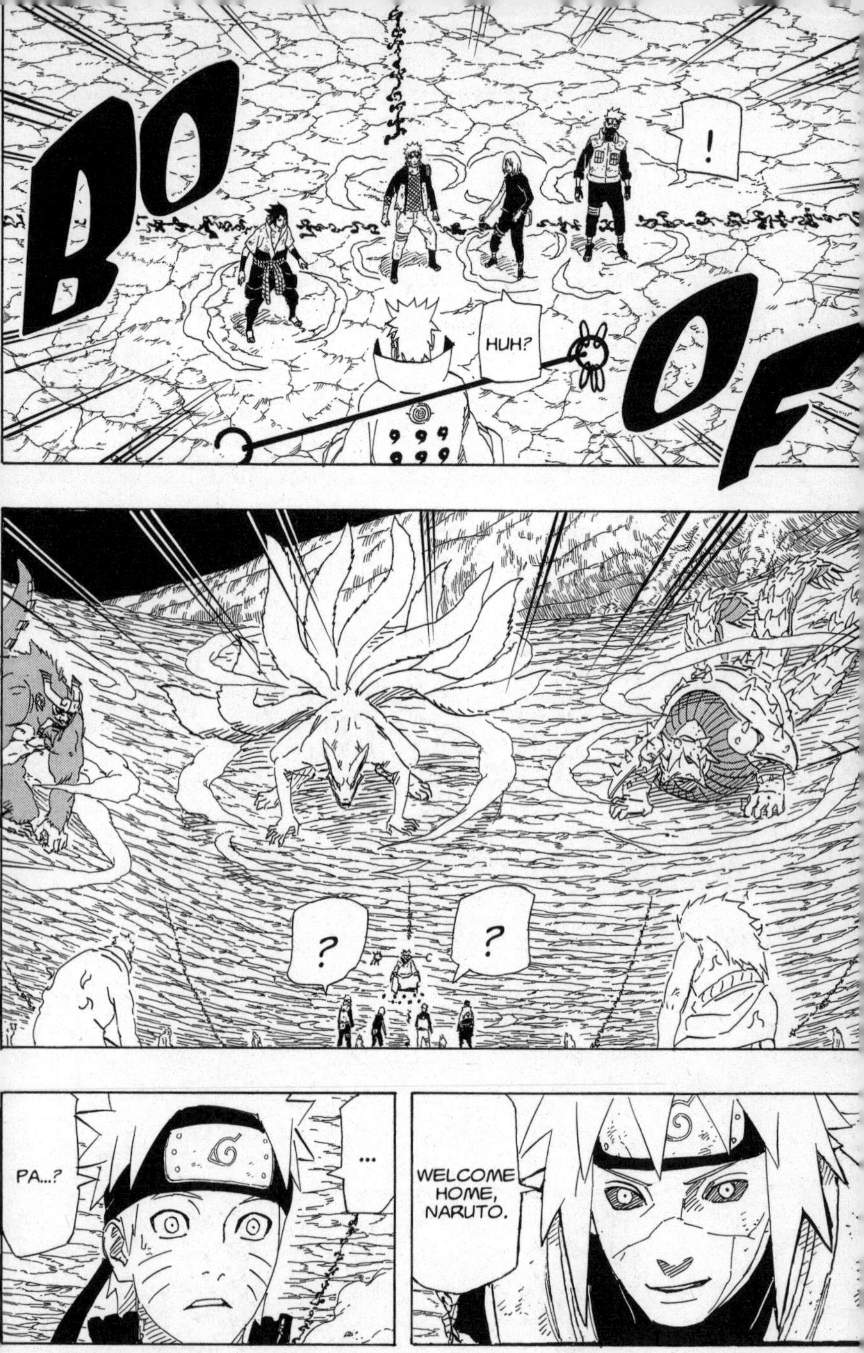
!
BOOF
HUH?
?
?
WELCOME HOME, NARUTO.
...
PA...?

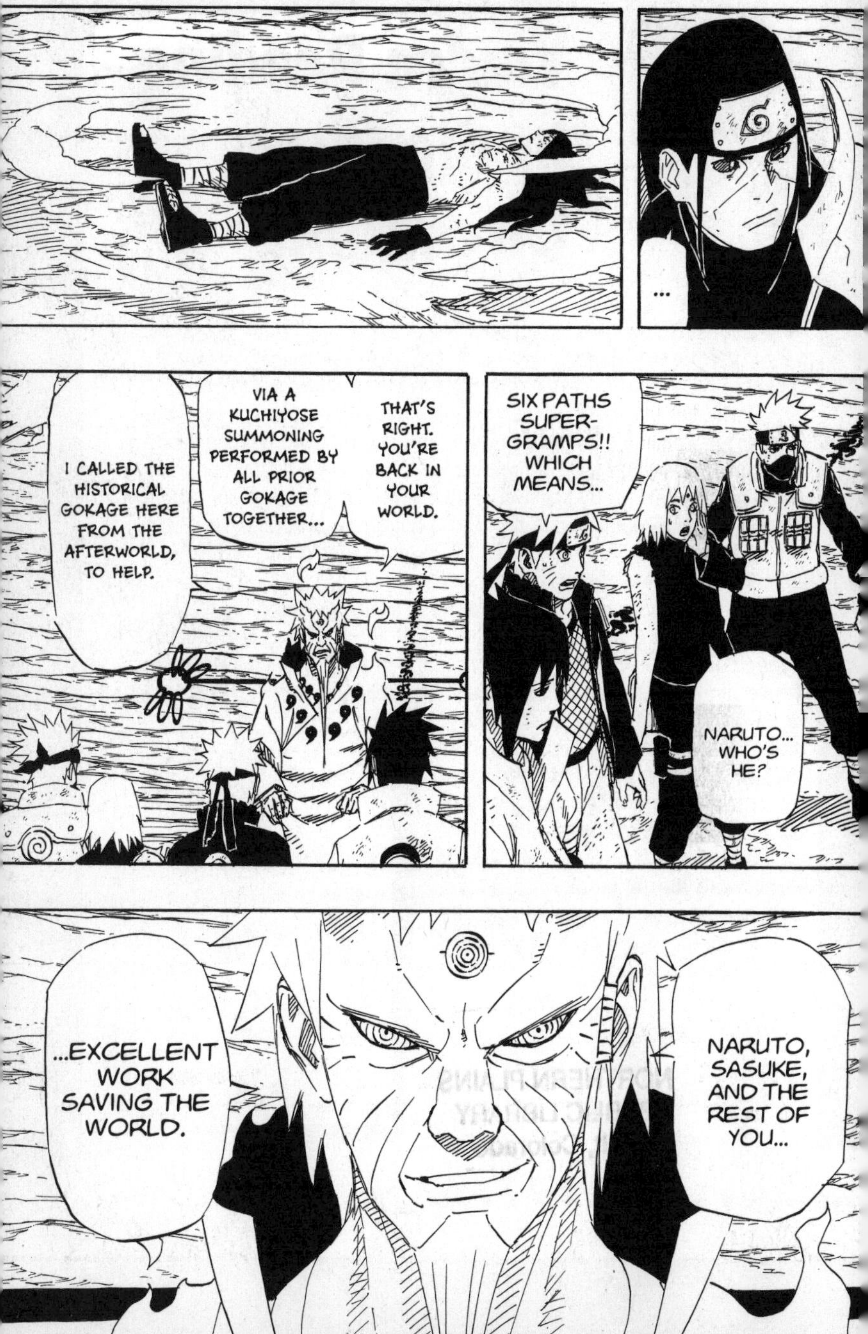
...
SIX PATHS SUPER-GRAMPS!! WHICH MEANS...
NARUTO... WHO'S HE?
THAT'S RIGHT. YOU'RE BACK IN YOUR WORLD.
VIA A KUCHIYOSE SUMMONING PERFORMED BY ALL PRIOR GOKAGE TOGETHER...
I CALLED THE HISTORICAL GOKAGE HERE FROM THE AFTERWORLD, TO HELP.
NARUTO, SASUKE, AND THE REST OF YOU...
...EXCELLENT WORK SAVING THE WORLD.

You're Reading in the Wrong Direction!!

Whoops! Guess what? You're starting at the wrong end of the comic!

...It's true! In keeping with the original Japanese format, **Naruto** is meant to be read from right to left, starting in the upper-right corner.

Unlike English, which is read from left to right, Japanese is read from right to left, meaning that action, sound effects and word-balloon order are completely reversed... something which can make readers unfamiliar with Japanese feel pretty backwards themselves. For this reason, manga or Japanese comics published in the U.S. in English have sometimes been published "flopped"—that is, printed in exact reverse order, as though seen from the other side of a mirror.

By flopping pages, U.S. publishers can avoid confusing readers, but the compromise is not without its downside. For one thing, a character in a flopped manga series who once wore in the original Japanese version a T-shirt emblazoned with "M A Y" (as in "the merry month of") now wears one which reads "Y A M"! Additionally, many manga creators in Japan are themselves unhappy with the process, as some feel the mirror-imaging of their art alters their original intentions.

We are proud to bring you Masashi Kishimoto's **Naruto** in the original unflopped format. For now, though, turn to the other side of the book and let the ninjutsu begin...!

—Editor

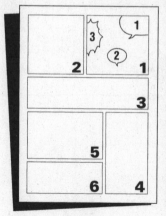